Maintaining International Relations Through Digital Public Diplomacy Policies and Discourses

Türker Elitaş
Hatay Mustafa Kemal University, Turkey

IGI Global
PUBLISHER of TIMELY KNOWLEDGE

A volume in the Advances in Public Policy and Administration (APPA) Book Series

Published in the United States of America by
IGI Global
Information Science Reference (an imprint of IGI Global)
701 E. Chocolate Avenue
Hershey PA, USA 17033
Tel: 717-533-8845
Fax: 717-533-8661
E-mail: cust@igi-global.com
Web site: http://www.igi-global.com

Library of Congress Cataloging-in-Publication Data

Names: Elitas, Turker, 1983- editor.
Title: Maintaining international relations through digital public diplomacy policies and discourses / Turker Elitas, editor.
Description: Hershey, PA : Information Science Reference, [2023] | Includes bibliographical references and index. | Summary: "This book reveals the tendencies of countries, institutions and their representatives to use communication technologies as a diplomatic tool in international relations practices especially highlighting the difference between the discourses built on digital media and classical diplomacy"-- Provided by publisher.
Identifiers: LCCN 2022033925 (print) | LCCN 2022033926 (ebook) | ISBN 9781668458228 (hardcover) | ISBN 9781668458235 (paperback) | ISBN 9781668458242 (ebook)
Subjects: LCSH: Digital media--Political aspects--Turkey. | Turkey--Foreign relations.
Classification: LCC DR477 .M295 2023 (print) | LCC DR477 (ebook) | DDC 327.561--dc23/eng/20220915
LC record available at https://lccn.loc.gov/2022033925
LC ebook record available at https://lccn.loc.gov/2022033926

This book is published in the IGI Global book series Advances in Public Policy and Administration (APPA) (ISSN: 2475-6644; eISSN: 2475-6652)

British Cataloguing in Publication Data
A Cataloguing in Publication record for this book is available from the British Library.

All work contributed to this book is new, previously-unpublished material. The views expressed in this book are those of the authors, but not necessarily of the publisher.

For electronic access to this publication, please contact: eresources@igi-global.com.

Advances in Public Policy and Administration (APPA) Book Series

ISSN:2475-6644
EISSN:2475-6652

Mission

Proper management of the public sphere is necessary in order to maintain order in modern society. Research developments in the field of public policy and administration can assist in uncovering the latest tools, practices, and methodologies for governing societies around the world.

The **Advances in Public Policy and Administration (APPA) Book Series** aims to publish scholarly publications focused on topics pertaining to the governance of the public domain. APPA's focus on timely topics relating to government, public funding, politics, public safety, policy, and law enforcement is particularly relevant to academicians, government officials, and upper-level students seeking the most up-to-date research in their field.

Coverage

- Government
- Law Enforcement
- Political Economy
- Politics
- Public Administration
- Public Funding
- Public Policy
- Resource Allocation
- Urban Planning

IGI Global is currently accepting manuscripts for publication within this series. To submit a proposal for a volume in this series, please contact our Acquisition Editors at Acquisitions@igi-global.com or visit: http://www.igi-global.com/publish/.

The Advances in Public Policy and Administration (APPA) Book Series (ISSN 2475-6644) is published by IGI Global, 701 E. Chocolate Avenue, Hershey, PA 17033-1240, USA, www.igi-global.com. This series is composed of titles available for purchase individually; each title is edited to be contextually exclusive from any other title within the series. For pricing and ordering information please visit http://www.igi-global.com/book-series/advances-public-policy-administration/97862. Postmaster: Send all address changes to above address.

Titles in this Series

For a list of additional titles in this series, please visit: www.igi-global.com/book-series/advances-public-policy-administration/97862

Handbook of Research on Transforming Government, Nonprofits, and Healthcare in a Post-Pandemic Era
Joanne E. Howard (Illinois Institute of Technology, USA)
Information Science Reference • © 2023 • 400pp • H/C (ISBN: 9781668423141) • US $270.00

Minding the Gap Between Restorative Justice, Therapeutic Jurisprudence, and Global Indigenous Wisdom
Marta Vides Saade (Ramapo College of New Jersey, USA) and Debarati Halder (Parul Institute of Law, Parul University, India)
Information Science Reference • © 2023 • 260pp • H/C (ISBN: 9781668441121) • US $215.00

Societal Transformations and Resilience in Times of Crisis
Ghazala Shoukat (University of Sindh, Jamshoro, Pakistan) and Muhammad Nawaz Tunio (Mohammad Ali Jinnah University, Karachi, Pakistan)
Information Science Reference • © 2023 • 252pp • H/C (ISBN: 9781668453261) • US $215.00

African Policy Innovation and the Political Economy of Public-Private Policy Partnerships
Fred Olayele (Sprott School of Business, Carleton University, Canada)
Information Science Reference • © 2022 • 297pp • H/C (ISBN: 9781799873839) • US $215.00

Interdisciplinary Approaches to the Future of Africa and Policy Development
Icarbord Tshabangu (Leeds Trinity University, UK)
Information Science Reference • © 2022 • 375pp • H/C (ISBN: 9781799887713) • US $215.00

Direct Democracy Practices at the Local Level
Christophe Emmanuel Premat (Stockholm University, Sweden)
Information Science Reference • © 2022 • 325pp • H/C (ISBN: 9781799873044) • US $215.00

Handbook of Research on Interdisciplinary Studies on Healthcare, Culture, and the Environment
Mika Markus Merviö (Kibi International University, Japan)
Information Science Reference • © 2022 • 365pp • H/C (ISBN: 9781799889960) • US $270.00

Challenges and Barriers to the European Union Expansion to the Balkan Region
Bruno Ferreira Costa (University of Beira Interior, Portugal)
Information Science Reference • © 2022 • 372pp • H/C (ISBN: 9781799890553) • US $215.00

IGI Global
PUBLISHER of TIMELY KNOWLEDGE

701 East Chocolate Avenue, Hershey, PA 17033, USA
Tel: 717-533-8845 x100 • Fax: 717-533-8661
E-Mail: cust@igi-global.com • www.igi-global.com

EDITORIAL ADVISORY BOARD

Table of Contents

Detailed Table of Contents

Virtually everything in the modern society we currently live in has become digitalized. The digitalization in communication technologies, especially in the last 30 years, has digitized the field of public diplomacy as in every field, and the concept of digital public diplomacy has emerged. Individuals and institutions are evaluated according to their image, and those with a good image are appreciated, admired, and followed. Those who do not have a good image fall into the opposite situation. For this reason, in digital public diplomacy, states are now pursuing to present their own images according to the conditions of the day. Today, with the rapidly developing new media tools, the value of image in the digital environment has increased, and public diplomacy has frequently used this field. At this level, public diplomacy nowadays utilizes opportunities in popular areas and converts the digital space into an image creation area. In this study, the image-building processes of public diplomacy in the digital field were examined.

Propaganda, which aims to influence the society to believe and act in a certain way in line with predetermined objectives, has been a form of practice that has been used extensively in the social and political field throughout history. Many ideologies have gained prevalence as a result of effective propaganda activities and have been able to walk to power. From Caesar to Napoleon, from Lenin to Hitler, many leaders went down in history as master propagandists, and they dragged the masses after them with their powerful and effective propaganda. Certain aspects of propaganda practices, which have been the most effective way to influence societies in long historical processes, have been a source of inspiration in many areas such as public diplomacy, political campaigns, advertising, public relations, and marketing in modern times.

With the end of the Cold War, the military-based structure, which was the only relatively single actor in the international system that went through a serious transformation, was replaced by a deepened structure with new actors such as individuals, companies, and international organizations alongside the state. This transformation of the system requires actors, especially states, to revise themselves through new security perceptions, and instead of military interventions, which are described as hard power, soft power resources such as education, science, sports, culture, art, and economy come to the forefront. In a world that has become interdependent in many respects, countries need to both protect and defend their national interests and maintain relations with other countries in the face of the risks of biased, false news and incitement to societies caused by increasing information resources. In this study, soft power and hard power concepts will be discussed, and their place in diplomacy will be examined.

With the digitalization of television broadcasting, an audience-oriented, modular, interactive, thematic, and mobilized broadcasting approach has become established. This new broadcasting approach attracts the attention of consumers with its advantages such as low subscription fees, language and subtitle support, ease of access and use, downloading and recording. Naturally, the number of platforms operating in the field of digital broadcasting is increasing and the content on these platforms is diversifying. On the other hand, these platforms serve as a kind of bridge for public diplomacy practices, and in this respect, they attract the attention of public diplomacy actors. Because these platforms—even if the user/viewer is not aware of it—are the means and mediators of the universal circulation of (national) culture, they are a component of public diplomacy.

Though the role of media in national security matters has been generally understood in academic and public spheres, limited studies have been conducted and published, especially in the context of Nepal. Most studies have been confined to the civil-military relations, post-conflict transformation and media advocacy, international diplomacy, among others. The discourses carried through and by the media has been given limited attention in both academic and professional circles. Conducting critical discourse analysis of the media coverage and documenting perspectives of the national security and international relations scholars as well as media researchers and practitioners, this chapter attempts to understand the inter-relationship between the media and security sector in Nepal through the securitization theory. Examining the patterns of the Lipulekh border dispute, the chapter explores the process of securitization through the 'speech act' and how it is shaping and has shaped public perceptions regarding national security and nationalism.

The importance of digital diplomacy, which we encounter as public diplomacy activities on digital platforms, has been recognized more and more, and it has been actively used by many countries through applications such as social media accounts and websites. In the light of this information, the aim of the study is to reveal the ways in which the ministry of sports, which is responsible for sports and athletes, which increases the awareness and prestige of countries in national and international platforms, uses websites as a digital diplomacy tool. The official websites of the Ministries of Sports of Turkey and Kyrgyzstan, which were determined as the sample of the study, were analyzed with the categorical content analysis method, and the similarities and differences between the use of the websites of the ministries were determined.

The aim of this study is to investigate whether the Embassy of the Republic of Turkey in Bishkek uses social media effectively in the context of digital public diplomacy activities. The posts and contents of the official Facebook account of the Embassy of the Republic of Turkey in Bishkek between January 1, 2019 and February 21, 2020 were collected and analyzed in the context of digital public diplomacy. Accordingly, the posts made on the official Facebook account of the Embassy of the Republic of Turkey in Bishkek were analyzed by content analysis method in categories such as daily, monthly, posts by subject (bilateral relations, economy, trade, culture, education, health, activities, etc.), likes, comments, number of shares, etc. As a result of the research, it was observed that the Embassy of the Republic of Turkey in Bishkek does not use Facebook effectively.

Chapter 10
Understanding Digital Diplomacy Through Ukraine-Russia Events: The Truth Behind Events in Ukraine and Donbass 121
Tolkun Bekturgan kyzy, Kyrgyz-Turkish Manas University, Kyrgyzstan
Niyazi Ayhan, Kyrgyz-Turkish Manas University, Kyrgyzstan

Digital diplomacy is a form of new public diplomacy that uses the internet, new information and communication technologies, and social media as a means to strengthen diplomatic relations. The main differences from classical public diplomacy are greater access to information, more interaction between people and organizations, and greater transparency. Diplomacy is radically transforming in front of our eyes. In the face of new challenges, its structure and methods are changing, and new directions are emerging. The chapter analyzes new opportunities and technologies for use by the diplomatic departments of the Russian Federation and Ukraine in the course of current activities in the field of international relations. The authors also presented a descriptive analysis of the document entitled "The Truth behind Events in Ukraine and Donbass (2014-2022)" published on the official website of the Ministry of Foreign Affairs of the Russian Federation.

Chapter 11
Reading Turkey's EU Accession Process Through Progress Reports in the Context of Public Diplomacy 136
Elifnur Terzioğlu, Ataturk University, Turkey

Public diplomacy, which is defined as an effort to influence the attitude and perception of the public in order to shape and implement the foreign policy in the desired direction, can also be evaluated as an effort to shape the public opinion of different countries in a positive and desired way. One of Turkey's most important goals in the international arena has been determined as membership to the European Union, and many governments have carried out activities in various dimensions in line with this policy for many years. The activities carried out by Turkey in the EU membership process are closely monitored by the EU and regularly reported since 1998. While evaluating the breakthroughs Turkey has made in terms of foreign policy in these reports, it is also possible to determine how the international community and the public perceive these efforts. Based on this foresight, in this chapter, Turkey's progress reports in the EU membership process will be evaluated in the context of public diplomacy, and a descriptive and analytical framework will be created in this context.

In addition to what the studies on the discourse and character modeling of the Valley of the Wolves series say, this chapter argues that there has been a Neo-Ottomanization and religiosity evolution in terms of the discourse and the hero's semiosis. The thesis of this section is that Valley of the Wolves series has evolved in terms of narrative and character since it began to appeal to international target audiences. It is the main assumption of the section that there is a parallel transformation with the public diplomacy practices of the Republic of Türkiye in the process following the fact that the audience groups, especially in Arab geography, Afghanistan and Pakistan, where Islamic influence is dominant, become fans of the Valley of the Wolves. In this section, it is aimed to explain the velvet evolution, which exemplifies the transition from the Republican ideology to the Neo-Ottoman ideology in diplomatic media narratives, through the historical rupture of the Valley of the Wolves.

Governments want to create foreign public opinion by spreading credible information to achieve their national goals, objectives, and interests. In the global balance of political power, it is important for a country to use the tools of public diplomacy. In the 21st century, Turkey intensively uses cultural values as a tool of public diplomacy. In this context, Turkey actively uses social media as a digital medium while promoting its cultural heritage as a soft power. Turkey, which has analyzed the impact of digital diplomacy well in the historical process, is using this field more and more widely. In this study, examples of the Republic of Turkey's public diplomacy practices on social media are presented and how it uses public diplomacy as soft power is investigated. In this context, four Twitter pages where public diplomacy is most widely used (The Republic of Türkiye Directorate of Communications, Turkish Maarif Foundation, TIKA, and Yunus Emre Institute) were analyzed through content analysis technique.

Public diplomacy practices carried out by states and non-state actors are instantly presented to the public of other countries thanks to the new media. This makes it easy to determine the level of influence of a public diplomacy practice on the public opinion of countries and helps states to produce new public diplomacy policies and to improve existing policies. In addition, new media allows one state to spy on public diplomacy practices conducted by another state and provides tips for taking action against it. This study aims to answer the question of how the practices of public diplomacy are shaped in new media environments. For this purpose, the Twitter account of the Turkish Cooperation and Coordination Agency (TIKA) was chosen as a case study and a netnographic study was conducted.

In 2011, Syrians fleeing the civil war in Syria tried to migrate to neighboring countries. While some countries did not accept Syrian refugees, others opened their doors to immigrants. Currently, Turkey is known as the country with the highest number of Syrians. These citizens, who left their countries and homes and migrated to other countries to protect their lives and children, faced different problems in the countries where they settled. Turkish authorities are taking steps to solve these problems. The aid and problem-solving steps taken for Syrian refugees are exhibited to the citizens of other countries through digitalized public diplomacy. In this study, firstly, information about the concept of migration is given and the migration from Syria to Turkey is discussed. Then, two different news published on the website of TRT World news channel were examined through critical discourse analysis to demonstrate how Turkey's attitude and benevolence towards Syrians is reflected to the world through digitalized public diplomacy.

Developments experienced in communication technologies have caused digitalization by changing and transforming all areas of life. Especially thanks to the opportunities and possibilities provided by new communication technologies, the authorities of different countries can convey their political and ideological thoughts to the citizens of other countries quickly and effectively. Social media is one of the most important digital communication networks with the power to influence the international agenda. Countries that take their place in digital diplomacy can more easily manage public perceptions with social media environments, which have an important place in international relations. In this study, by emphasizing the importance of social media channels in the digitalization of public diplomacy, the authors have shown the Turkish image displayed based on the posts made on TRT World's Twitter account. For this, the shares and comments selected by the purposeful sampling method will be analyzed with discourse analysis and the reflected Turkish image will be revealed.

The process of diplomacy and public diplomacy activities is known as ensuring communication from state to state or from state to public. However, with the global world formed with the increase in technological developments, diplomatic relations have started to be carried out between cities as well as states. The organization of activities to ensure the interests of cities in the international arena and to increase the recognition of their countries is explained as city diplomacy. It carries out activities through local governments and municipal organizations to establish and develop permanent relations between cities and other countries. In this study, the activities carried out by Eskişehir Metropolitan Municipality are examined in the context of public diplomacy and city diplomacy.

Preface

The advances in communication technologies in the 21st century have not only manifested themselves in the social sphere, but have also enhanced the capacity of states to create technology-oriented discourses in both domestic and foreign policies. The technological revolutions have redesigned the passive relationship between the state and the people, allowing both the state and the people to become active participants. Communication technologies have given autonomy to the public or, more narrowly, to the individual in this equation where both sides are involved in a mutual communication process, while states have had to be more transparent and careful in the face of this autonomy gained by the individual. However, it did not take long for states that wanted to benefit from the effective and impressive power of communication technologies to discover the necessity of adapting to digitalized life both in domestic politics and foreign policy, and to pattern their diplomatic actions with digital codes. While the integration of communication technologies into physical lives has given us McLuhan's interpretation of the global village, states in this village have started to implement a discourse and propaganda-based policy approach in their relationship practices with each other. For many years, a name was sought for this discourse and propaganda-based policy, but finally, in 1972, this policy was called public diplomacy.

The public diplomacy, which expresses multiple interactions, became especially prominent during the period of nuclear threats in a bipolar world that emerged during the Cold War years. When the world was divided into two, with a particular focus on Russia and the United States, the propagandistic discourses that both countries applied to other countries in order to justify themselves are considered as the first example of public diplomacy manifesting itself openly and clearly and being effective in a wide geography.

Public diplomacy, which is defined in many different ways, is generally considered to be the relationship established with other nations by pursuing national interests. At this point, the basic principle of public diplomacy is dialog. The most important arguments used for this purpose are communication tools and cultural exchange programs. Nakamura and Weed (2009) have added breadth and clarity to the concept by describing the public diplomacy as "providing information to the people of foreign countries through press, broadcast and internet media or other outreach activities; cultural diplomacy practices including art exhibitions and music performances, and organizing international education and exchange programs".

There are various methods of diplomacy used by states both in matters concerning humanity and in resolving disputes among themselves. From this perspective:

Cultural Diplomacy is seen as long-term campaigns aimed at getting to know the public opinion of foreign countries, gaining their sympathies and developing emotional ties with them. Exchange programs, foreign exhibitions, international cultural activities are examples of cultural diplomacy (L'Etang, 2009).

Shuttle Diplomacy is a type of diplomacy that is widespread today. In shuttle diplomacy, also known as mediation, a mediator state or an international organization is involved in negotiations with two states to solve problems between countries and to find a solution to the problem. It is a method frequently used especially in the Arab-Israeli Wars.

Coercive Diplomacy is a diplomacy method used when the balance and current situation between states is disrupted by creating de facto situations. This method of diplomacy, which aims to get an opponent to stop or back down from an action it has initiated/taken, is a crisis management strategy. In 1998, the position taken by the Turkish state for the removal of separatist organization leader Abdullah Öcalan from Syria is an example of coercive diplomacy (Şenel, 2012).

Environmental Diplomacy is a diplomacy method that focuses on environmental problems and aims to increase cooperation between countries to find solutions to these problems (Broadhurst & Ledgerwood, 1998).

Tourism Diplomacy is the presentation of a country's diplomacy messages to the public opinion of foreign countries by integrating them with tourism strategies (Sancar, 2017).

Although it is possible to multiply all these examples, modern diplomacy types and different methods used in modern diplomacy are shaped around public diplomacy.

Public diplomacy is a communication process. This process is one-way if it is carried out in the form of propaganda and two-way if it is carried out through dialog. Elected or appointed public officials are responsible for managing this process on behalf of states. Public diplomacy, which is a multi-faceted and multi-purpose concept, also refers to the whole of the perceptions to be created in order to form a wide environment against the other state and to put pressure on the other state. In this way, besides being a dynamic concept, it is possible to evaluate all kinds of actions, activities and initiatives that have communication at their center and aim to influence or form opinions under the umbrella of public diplomacy.

Public diplomacy is a highly effective and fast foreign policy strategy in determining the areas of power in the current era. However, in order to create and successfully execute this strategy, it is necessary to analyze the language, culture, history and, more importantly, the national interests of the target country. Thus, implementing an effective and comprehensive diplomacy requires a well-rounded knowledge, in-depth research, and competent officials.

Mass media is undoubtedly the most important tool of public diplomacy. Traditional communication tools as television, newspapers, and radio, which started to manifest itself effectively especially after the Cold War, have an important function in public diplomacy. Innovation processes in communication technologies have positioned traditional communication tools as old tools, whereas internet-based developments, which are defined as new, are called new communication technologies. This process of transition has not excluded the traditional one, on the contrary, it has given the user temporal and spatial independence with new features added to it. While the phenomenon of digitalization with new communication technologies has made itself felt in every field, public diplomacy has also been affected by this change, making it necessary to switch to a new digital-oriented model.

State and non-state actors to manage processes of international change define digital diplomacy, which has its intellectual background in Manuel Castells' "informationalism" proposition, as the use of internet and information technologies. Digital diplomacy has enriched the ways in which a message and/or image interacts with external public opinion and facilitated the way actors structure and organize their information resources. Digital diplomacy also provides diplomatic actors with the necessary data to analyze the changes and shifting trends in the field of international relations.

Concepts as digital diplomacy, Diplomacy 2.0, digital public diplomacy, and e-diplomacy have become frequently used concepts in the field of international relations with the increase in digitalization. In parallel with the transformation of the social structure in this new order, individuals have become actors in international relations and the understanding of international relations has become more complex and participatory.

The field of implementation of digital diplomacy activities is predominantly social media platforms. The reason is that social networks, with their digital, interactive, textual, virtual, networked and simulated features, create new experiences of texts and enable texts to reach their targets instantly and with a strong impact. It has also produced new models of organization and production by organizing new forms of relationships between users/consumers and media technologies, thereby adding new dimensions to the relationship between identity(s) and society (Lister et al., 2009). This has also been reflected in public diplomacy, and traditional public diplomacy, which emphasized a one-way, ideological process, has been replaced by political communication processes where performances are measured not in the corridors of foreign affairs, but on computer monitors and cell phone screens. On the one hand, digital diplomacy has diversified the target audience of states, and on the other hand, it has paved the way for users to easily convey their opinions to the diplomatic channels of the state (Seib, 2012).

Unable to be reduced to a mere technical skill of using technology, communication technologies have become an important means of individual and collective instantaneous impact and reaction. The most important result of communication technologies, the digitalization of traditional discourses by transferring them through tools, has heralded a new digital understanding in individual and social networks. Communication technologies, where discourses are constructed through digital codes, promise an instant, comprehensive, and widespread relationship practice unlike traditional ones. In this context, the tendency to use these features offered by communication technologies in international relations instead of only individual use has emerged as a result of building on the digital in diplomacy discourses.

The fact that digital public diplomacy is used more effectively with new communication tools does not mean that traditional public diplomacy is no longer used. On the contrary, although the tools have changed, the traditional concept of public diplomacy is still an important argument in the effectiveness and inclusiveness of digital.

Digital public diplomacy is a digital restructuring of classical diplomacy. However, the concepts of transparency and public disclosure, which are absent in classical democracy, are clearly evident in digital public diplomacy. Based on this fact, this book has tried to shed light on the subject with valuable authors in order to demonstrate how important the concept of digital public diplomacy is for countries and to highlight what leaders can do with just one click of a button, from perception formation to crisis management, and what kind of impact it will have on the public sphere and other countries.

ORGANIZATION OF THE BOOK

In Chapter 1, Serpil Kir Elitaş emphasized the importance of digital public diplomacy in the field of migration and migration management in Turkey, focuses on the diplomacy activities that Turkey and the international migration center develop with each other. Turkey is located at the center of Europe, Asia and the Middle East, thus being at an important and dangerous geographical point. Believing in the necessity of a more effective and solution-oriented digital public diplomacy in international platforms of Turkey, which is at the center of mass migration movements that emerged especially after the Syrian war, the author explains the activities that many countries dealing with the migration problem should implement in this process.

In Chapter 2, Sami Kiraz, one of our authors, made a conceptual examination of digital public diplomacy in crisis management and touched upon the new duties and responsibilities that states have undertaken and have to undertake in the digital public diplomacy process. In addition, the author, who describes the age we live in as the age of crises, shared his predictions for the future by seeking answers to questions such as how changing expectations and needs as a result of digitalization have altered the public diplomacy activities of states in the context of crisis management, whether the use of digital public diplomacy in crisis management has the same meaning for all states today, and whether the rapid transformation in diplomacy has caused a radical change in traditional diplomacy principles and practitioners.

In Chapter 3, Kadir Bendaş provides an overview of the concepts of popular culture and image in digital public diplomacy. The author argues that by utilizing the power of country leaders to address large audiences in digital environments or personal social media accounts, they achieve significant gains for their own and their country's image. The individual image of leaders is an element that develops in parallel with the image of the country. In this context, the author analyzed the image phenomenon, which is one of the important strategies of digital public diplomacy, through Donald Trump and shared the results of the study with us.

In Chapter 4, Fatih Değirmenci defends the thesis that propaganda is the starting point and inspiration of public diplomacy, has revealed the interaction and organic bond of propaganda and public diplomacy in depth. The researcher, who emphasized that many characteristic features of propaganda are similar to public diplomacy and that public diplomacy is a kind of propaganda, shed light on the subject with an interpretivist approach.

Chapter 5 is by Elifnur Terzioğlu. With the end of the Cold War, international systems have undergone a serious transformation, and military-based structures, which were relatively the only actors, have been replaced by a deepening structure with new actors such as individuals, companies and international organizations. Terzioğlu examines this transformation in the system by focusing on the concepts of hard power and soft power and focuses on their place in diplomacy.

In Chapter 6, Türker Elitaş focuses on digital content providers, which are at least as effective as social media in the culture of digitalization, and tries to explain through the example of Netflix that in addition to entertainment and enjoyment, traces of digital public diplomacy are also clearly manifested in content providers. In recent years, content provider platforms, which have been increasing day by day as an alternative to the traditional ones, are preferred due to the many conveniences and opportunities they offer to their users. The users who voluntarily access these platforms meet many of their needs such as having fun, spending time, and getting information, and also encounter diplomatic strategies.

In Chapter 7, Sudeep Urpety takes a critical approach to digital public diplomacy conducted by countries on social media through the case study of the India-Nepal border dispute. Focusing on the media portrayal of the Lipulekh border dispute, which is at the center of the study, the author analyzed in-depth the mainstream media and social media outputs of Nepal and India. The perceptions of the people of India and Nepal on the border dispute issue are noteworthy as another conclusion of the author.

Chapter 8 is by Atilla Çakar and Banu Erdoğan Çakar. One of the most important indicators of public diplomacy is sporting activities. While sporting activities consist of players who physically represent their countries in competitions abroad, this representation also constitutes an important pillar of public diplomacy. Sporting activities, which play an important role in public diplomacy with their physical presence, also constitute an important pillar of digital public diplomacy with their promotion, announcements, or achievements of their athletes through digital media. The authors, who designed their work with this awareness, examined the digital websites of the ministries of sports of Kyrgyzstan and Turkey and shared the results of their comparative analysis with their readers in this book.

Chapter 9 is by Erdoğan Akman and Zeki Okyay. One of the most important arguments of digital public diplomacy is undoubtedly the foreign representations of states. While these representations traditionally have the responsibility of representing their countries at a high level in the countries where they are located, they also have the responsibility of establishing diplomatic relations on behalf of their countries in the countries where they maintain their presence. As an important pillar of public diplomacy, the extent to which foreign missions can update themselves in the face of the concept of diplomacy that has evolved into digitalization is an important problem. Based on this fact, our authors, focusing on the Turkish Embassy in Kyrgyzstan, have tried to explain with the data they have obtained how the Turkish representation has taken an action plan and how much it has been able to update itself in the face of this problem.

Chapter 10 is by Tolkun Bekturgan kızı and Niyazi Ayhan. Focusing on the war between Russia and Ukraine, which has marked the last year of the world agenda and is one of the issues that the world is most interested in, our authors have examined the digital public diplomacy that Russia is trying to carry out as well as war diplomacy in this process. In this context, in this study, which constitutes an important example of the persuasion and propaganda of war through digital public diplomacy strategies, the social media accounts of the Russian foreign ministry were followed and data were collected. With the collected data, it was tried to understand the digital public diplomacy language and strategies used by Russia during the war.

In Chapter 11, Elifnur Terzioğlu analyzed Turkey's relationship and interaction with the European Union from the perspective of public diplomacy. The membership negotiations between Turkey and the European Union, which have been going on for many years, are still on Turkey's agenda as a process that has not yet concluded with a result. This process, which started with traditional public diplomacy, continues today both traditionally and digitally due to the compelling effect of technology. Based on this fact, the author has demonstrated how the long-standing traditional relationship between Turkey and the European Union has been maintained through digital media with the developing technology and how digital public diplomacy is used in the relationship between both sides.

In Chapter 12, Savaş Keskin analyzed the political discourses in Turkey through the *Valley of the Wolves* TV series, which broke the viewership record in Turkey for many years. He tries to verify the thesis that the series, which is especially important in terms of having consistent predictions about Turkey's domestic and foreign politics, legitimizes the dominant public discourse of nationalism and property structure, which is accepted as a soft power tool. In this context, focusing on the importance and effectiveness of the media in public diplomacy, the author also examines the relationship between the concepts of diplomacy and soft power.

Chapter 13 by Ömer Alanka and Ülhak Çimen examines the concepts of public diplomacy and digital public diplomacy in depth, identifying the commonalities and differences in these two concepts depending on the means of communication and revealing how the concept of soft power is affected by this change. Based on the thesis that Twitter is used effectively in conveying Turkey's cultural and historical heritage, the authors, who convey the data collected through social media, have also designed their work with the assumption that social media is an important soft power tool.

Chapter 14 is by Mehmet Ferhat Sönmez. Focusing on the social media usage practices of states, the author emphasizes the importance of the concept of soft power with the example of TIKA, a state institution in Turkey, and tries to explain its impact on foreign policy. The author, who examines the subject with a netrographic analysis method tried to reveal the limits of Turkey's soft power by seeking answers to the questions: 1) Which issues related to public diplomacy are discussed on the Tika Turkey account? 2) Which elements and methods of public diplomacy are emphasized in the Tika Turkey account?

Chapter 15, by Ömer Alanka and Selver Mertoğlu, focuses on how Turkey's attitude and benevolence towards Syrians is reflected to the world through digitalized public diplomacy, the authors contributed to the field by examining the content of the news published on the website of TRT World news channel through critical discourse analysis method.

Chapter 16 is by Selver Mertoğlu. TRT World channel, which is considered as the foundation of Turkey's public broadcasting approach, also undertakes an important task and mission in publicizing Turkey's foreign policy and creating an impact on the audience abroad. In this context, the author emphasizes the importance of TRT World channel and focuses on how the channel, which adopts both traditional and digital broadcasting approach, reflects Turkey's activities abroad and tries to determine the strategies used in the use of digital public diplomacy.

Chapter 17, by Yasemin Özçakıl, explains the activities of city diplomacy and examines how diplomacy is carried out through local governments. The author tries to explain how local governments in the global world try to come to the forefront in international politics through municipal activities, using the activities of Eskişehir Metropolitan Municipality as an example.

Türker Elitaş
Hatay Mustafa Kemal University, Turkey

REFERENCES

Broadhurst, A. I., & Ledgerwood, G. (1998). Environmental diplomacy of states, corporations and non-governmental organizations: The worldwide web of influence. *International Relations*, *14*(2), 1–19. doi:10.1177/004711789801400201

L'Etang, J. (2009). Public Relations and Diplomacy in a Globalized World: An Issue of Public Communication. *Sage*, *53*(4), 607–626. doi:10.1177/0002764209347633

Lister. (2009). *Jon Dovey, Seth Giddings, Iain Grant & Kieran Kelly, New Media: A Critical Introduction*. Routledge.

Nakamura, K. H., & Weed, W. C. (2009). US Public Diplomacy: Background and Current Issues. *Analyst in Foreign Policy Legislation*.

Sancar, A. G. (2017a). Turizm Diplomasisi Kapsamında Yer Markalama: Turkey Home Kampanya Analizi. *Selçuk İletişim*, *9*(4), 89–108.

Seib, P. (2012). *Real-time diplomacy: politics and power in the social media era*. Palgrave Macmillan. doi:10.1057/9781137010902

Şener, B. (2017). Savaş ile Barış Arasında Bir Kriz Yönetim Stratejisi Olarak Zorlayıcı Diplomasi ve Türk Dış Politikasındaki Örnekleri. *New Security Ecosystem and Multilateral Cost*. https://tasam. org/Files/Icerik/File/%C4%B0GK3_kit_(11)_(1)_pdf_77fa6849-12ac-42fe-8ea1-be5c4cdcb012.pdf

Acknowledgment

As an editor, I owe a great debt of gratitude to my dear academics who wrote chapters for this book.

This book will shed light on researchers, students, and academics interested in the field, thanks to the contributions of valuable authors. I would also like to express my gratitude to the academics of the editorial advisory board who provided full support in the constitution of the book, I would like to thank IGI Global Editors, who answered my questions in every detail about publishing the book and did not refrain to support.

I am grateful to my mother Nilgün Özdemir who have supported me throughout my education life and career. I am very grateful to my beloved my world Associate Professor Serpil KIR ELİTAŞ, who has given countenance to the development of the book.

Finally, I would like to thank the IGI Global publishing house for helping me to publish my book.

Chapter 1
An Assessment of the Relationship Between Turkey and the United Nations International Organization for Migration in the Context of Public Diplomacy

Serpil Kır Elitaş
https://orcid.org/0000-0002-6653-6102
Hatay Mustafa Kemal University, Turkey

ABSTRACT

Turkey is in a strategic position in terms of its geographical location. It is surrounded by seas on three sides, and there are only a few straits in the world that connect the two continents to each other to connect Asian countries to Europe. Combined with Turkey's strategic location, this makes Turkey an essential transit route in every activity in terms of both tourism and business resources. This strategic location of Turkey can be exploited by irresponsible and problematic elements from both inside and outside the country for both human trafficking and human smuggling activities. These groups of individuals or unions can openly collaborate with both internal and external parties due to the combination of many parties. Therefore, it is very crucial to continue the cooperation between the Turkish government and the International Organization for Migration (IOM) to overcome these problems. This study will examine the work done in cooperation between the Turkish Government and the International Organization for Migration (IOM) in dealing with these illegal activities.

INTRODUCTION

Every year, thousands of men, women and children are victimized by human traffickers in their own

DOI: 10.4018/978-1-6684-5822-8.ch001

countries or abroad. In this context, the fight against the crime of human trafficking and the protection of victims have an important place on the agenda of countries. The strategic geographical location of Turkey makes it a traffic lane for global trade. Turkey's location between two continents and two oceans makes it an international route with heavy traffic in terms of land, sea and air routes. It is a connecting route for various economic, social and cultural activities by countries around the world, particularly in Asia and Europe. Obviously, this creates a good economic potential which is very encouraging for developing countries such as Turkey. In addition, in terms of social and cultural aspects, having many interactions with the outside world, Turkey is better known in international relations and brings with it the possibility of acculturation, which can contribute to the existing cultural diversity between Turkish culture and surrounding countries. However, behind the current potential there are promising economic, social and even cultural benefits. This strategic location indirectly poses a challenge for Turkey.

Since the processes such as combating the crime of human trafficking, protecting those who have been subjected to this crime and providing support to victims of human trafficking fall under the jurisdiction of multiple institutions and organizations, the idea of establishing a common platform among all relevant institutions and organizations working in this field has made it necessary and in order to promote humanitarian and orderly migration, Turkey cooperates with the International Organization for Migration in order to help address the challenges related to the management of complex problems and to ensure that victims are less affected by the impacts of irregular and illegal migration through mutual trust and cooperation. In this context, the study will look at the cooperation between Turkey and the International Organization for Migration from a public diplomacy perspective.

BACKGROUND: THE UNITED NATIONS AND THE INTERNATIONAL ORGANIZATION FOR MIGRATION

The International Organization for Migration (IOM) is an international organization dealing with international migration issues, one of which includes the crime of Human Smuggling or Human Trafficking. It is an intergovernmental organization and it is independent. It currently has 173 member countries and 8 observer countries (IOM, 2022a). The International Organization for Migration presently has offices in more than 100 member countries. Today, Turkey has one of the largest country offices globally with over 820 staff in 15 different locations across the country. This is, naturally, in line with the United Nations, which aims to create world peace, and with the goals of the International Organization for Migration, which aims to create peace in terms of international migration. The International Organization for Migration is also one of the important actors and partners of the governments of the countries in order to create a humanitarian and orderly migration that can be beneficial for all its members, as well as to address cases and problems related to world migration and to help find solutions to each of its problems. In this context, it is also one of the important actors in the fight against human smuggling and human trafficking crimes in Turkey. The International Organization for Migration is an international and intergovernmental organization that aims to ensure the orderly and humane handling of migration, promote international cooperation on migration-related issues, provide humanitarian assistance and help find practical solutions to migration problems. It is committed to assisting migrants in need, both refugees, internally displaced persons and other residents forced to leave their homes (IOM, 2022b). From 1991 to date, the International Organization for Migration's anti-trafficking activities in Turkey have focused on awareness-raising activities and prevention of acts of trafficking, protection of victims of trafficking through direct assistance to victims and institutional capacity-building of governmental and non-governmental actors, training and capacity-building of law enforcement agencies, and partnering across sectors and governments with budget assistance in the development of anti-trafficking legislation, policies and procedures and infrastructure improvements by improving access to justice for victims of trafficking (IOM, 2022c).

In January 2017, the Director-General of the International Organization for Migration (IOM), Ambassador William Lacy Swing, signed the Agreement between the Government of the Republic of Turkey and the International Organization for Migration (IOM) on the Legal Status, Privileges and Immunities of the Organization and its Office in Turkey with the Ministry of Foreign Affairs of the Republic of Turkey. The agreement reflects the UN membership of the International Organization for Migration and strengthens the relationship of the IOM with the Government of the Republic of Turkey (IOM, 2018-2019). After this agreement, the partnership continued to grow stronger. IOM has a strong partnership with government agencies including the Ministry of Interior, Directorate General of Migration Management, Coast Guard Command, Ministry of Family and Social Policies, Ministry of Development, Ministry of Labor and Social Security, Ministry of National Education, Disaster and Emergency Management Presidency, Ministry of Food, Agriculture and Livestock, Ministry of Health, Ministry of Justice and various municipalities across Turkey (IOM, 2018-2019).

METHOD

The study will look at the cooperation between the Turkish Government and the International Organization for Migration from a public diplomacy perspective. In this context, the study will examine the relations from a normative perspective and social media materials or websites that provide secondary data will be included in the analysis. Narrative analysis techniques will be used to understand the cooperation between the Turkish Government and the International Organization for Migration.

DISCUSSION

The strategic geographical location of Turkey makes it a traffic lane for world trade. Being between two continents and two oceans makes Turkey an international route with heavy traffic in terms of land, sea and air routes. It is a connecting route for various economic, social and cultural activities by countries around the world, especially in Asia and Europe. Of course, this creates a good economic potential which is very promising for developing countries like Turkey. In addition, in terms of social and cultural aspects, with many interactions with the outside world, Turkey is better known in international relations and brings with it the possibility of acculturation, which can contribute to the existing cultural diversity between Turkish culture and the surrounding countries. However, behind the current potential there are promising economic, social and even cultural benefits. This strategic location indirectly poses a problem for Turkey.

Although the crime of human trafficking, which constitutes one of the most serious human rights violations in which human beings are turned into a commercial commodity, has its roots in the form of chattel slavery, it has gained a new momentum both in the world and in Turkey after it was defined as a crime in the Palermo Protocol, which was opened for signature in 2000. Turkey closely followed the developments in this field and became a party to the Palermo Protocol in 2003 and to another international convention, the Council of Europe Convention in 2009. The crime of human trafficking poses a serious threat to the freedoms of individuals, public order, public security and public health. Every year thousands of men, women and children are victimized by traffickers in their own countries or abroad. In this context, combating the crime of trafficking in persons and protecting victims have an important place on the agenda of countries.

According to the Turkish law on migration, human trafficking is "any act that aims, directly or indirectly, to make a profit for oneself or others". It can be broadly defined as bringing an organized or unorganized person or group of persons, who have no legal right to enter or leave and/or enter Turkish territory, or bringing an organized or unorganized person or group of persons to another person, where the person is in the territory of another country in which the person has no legal right to enter the country, whether legally, using a valid document or a forged document, or without using a travel document, with or without immigration controls. "Human trafficking in Persons ", which can be defined as "the abduction, forced detention and forced labor of women, children and men for the purpose of exploitation", is widespread all over the world due to reasons such as poverty and the desire for a better life, the destruction of social values, political and economic problems in the countries of origin, the demand for cheap labor and the entertainment industry, the high benefit obtained from the crime, and the fact that penalties are still far from deterrence in some countries.

The fact that the processes of combating the crime of trafficking in persons and protecting persons who have been subjected to this crime and providing support to victims of trafficking fall under the jurisdiction of more than one institution and organization, necessitated the idea of establishing a common platform among all relevant institutions and organizations working in this field and in order to promote humanitarian and orderly migration, Turkey cooperates with the International Organization for Migration in order to help address the challenges related to the management of complex problems and to ensure that victims are less affected by the impacts of irregular and illegal migration through mutual trust and cooperation. The first cooperation activity of the International Organization for Migration with the Government of the Republic of Turkey took place in 1991 following the Gulf War. The partnership of the International Organization for Migration with the Republic of Turkey was formalized in November 2004 when the International Organization for Migration was granted member status. The partnership between the International Organization for Migration and Turkey has continued to this day, including supporting the drafting of the Law on Foreigners and International Protection as well as the establishment of the Directorate General of Migration Management of the Ministry of Interior in 2013. The International Organization for Migration assists countries by providing accommodation, food, services, health care, counselling and voluntary repatriation options to migrants, in addition to providing financial support used for humanitarian assistance to illegal migrants apprehended/seized on Turkish territory.

With regard to the cooperation between the International Organization for Migration and the Turkish Government, which has positive objectives in addressing illegal migrants, the form of cooperation is not only targeted at migrants, but also addressed to the Turkish society as a whole in order to promote orderly and proper migration. The role of the Turkish people is also very important in supporting the cooperation between the International Organization for Migration and the Government of the Republic of Turkey. The cooperation carried out includes a strategy to combat trafficking in persons which, similar to other forms of transnational crime, cannot be stopped by one State alone and requires concrete international cooperation; (1) Facilitating regional cooperative efforts to combat trafficking in persons between countries of origin, transit and destination; (2) Providing comprehensive training designed to develop the skills necessary to combat trafficking in persons and refugee rights; (3) Temporary shelter assistance for asylum seekers; (4) Legal assistance to victims of trafficking/ smuggling; (5) Resettlement and voluntary repatriation to a third country; (6) Identification of the types of technical assistance needed by the Turkish Government to improve migration handling; (7) Labor migration; (8) Migration Health; (9) Immigration and Border Management; (10) Migration and Development (GIGM, 2022a).

1) Enhancing Regional Cooperation Efforts between the Turkish Government and the International Organization for Migration

The International Organization for Migration has been supporting the Turkish Coast Guard (TCG) since 2016 by providing food, water and non-food items (NFIs) including clothing, footwear and hygiene kits to migrants and refugees rescued in the Mediterranean and Aegean. International Organization for Migration experts also identify vulnerable migrants and refugees rescued at sea and refer them to the relevant authorities and institutions. In addition to Turkey, IOM also provides assistance in Greece, Serbia, Former Yugoslav Republic of Macedonia, Croatia, Slovenia, Italy, Libya and Niger (IOM, 2016).

2) Cooperation in Education between the Turkish Government and the International Organization for Migration

Cooperation in training is carried out from two different perspectives. The first group is differentiated from focusing only on incoming migrants or refugees and is related to training for Turkish security forces and legal units. The second group provides training for migrants on issues such as vocational training and information, repatriation and guidance.

a) *Training for the Community, Security Apparatus and Related Parties:* Security forces in Turkey are trained on the lack of understanding and other problems encountered with illegal migrants coming to Turkey. Through a strategic partnership with the Turkish Police, the General Directorate of Migration and the Ministry of Justice, the International Organization for Migration has agreed to provide training for police and migration officials from the Turkish side to improve their skills to combat human trafficking.

b) *Education for Migrants:* The aim of education for migrants is to help migrants to adapt to the place where they live and to support them to become more self-sufficient. In this way, migrants can adapt to the surrounding community so that they do not feel isolated or lonely, and they can be educated during their stay in Turkey so that they can be involved in certain occupational groups. The trainings provided include vocational courses such as carpentry, computer courses, communication courses such as English, Turkish and skills training, as well as programming, job placement, provision of in-kind and cash assistance, and entrepreneurship support training (IOM, 2018-2019). Trainings, which are mostly focused on the acquisition of skills and filling leisure time activities, also help migrants to have a profession (GIGM, 2022c). In addition to the trainings, which are very important in terms of the social integration process, Syrian refugees with work experience can contribute to the Turkish economy by sharing their expertise, commercial networks, Arabic language skills, and information on market opportunities in Syria and in identified locations in the region.

3) Temporary Shelter Cooperation between the Turkish Government and the International Organization for Migration

As the Syrian crisis has been ongoing for over a decade and more than 60 percent of shelter is still emergency-based, the International Organization for Migration supports medium-term shelter solutions by upgrading and repairing existing housing/shelters, taking into account Housing, Land and Property concerns. The influx of new arrivals into temporary reception centers in the south of the country continues to cause strain on existing humanitarian services, perpetuating the imperative need for reception centers. These reception centers play a vital role in receiving new arrivals and providing essential assistance such as food, protection, health and nutrition services (IOM, 2018-2019).

4) Cooperation between the Turkish Government and the International Organization for Migration on Legal Assistance to Victims of Human Trafficking/Smuggling

Supporting Turkey's Efforts to Combat Trafficking in Persons and Promoting Access to Justice for Trafficked People, by the International Organization for Migration Designed to ensure justice for victims of trafficking and to ensure effective criminal and judicial prosecution of trafficking crimes and criminals and to minimize trafficking through investigations and inquiries by law enforcement agencies. It is aimed to provide support to relevant NGOs in the field of combating trafficking in persons and to identify victims of trafficking in order to provide enhanced protection in line with the EU Acquis. Furthermore, as there is no single instrument or norm that covers all relevant rights and duties of migrants, it is important to gather information on international migration law and frame it in an accessible and understandable way. The International Organization for Migration aims to consolidate this information and make it more easily accessible through, inter alia, an online migration law database. In this context, the online migration law database has been created, which brings together migration-related instruments and relevant norms regulating migration at the international and regional levels. The following sources of information are included in the database: relevant international, regional and bilateral agreements, international and regional resolutions, declarations and other documents (OIM, 2022). In addition, support is also provided through the establishment of migration law offices in some locations within the country.

5) Resettlement and Voluntary Repatriation Cooperation between the Turkish Government and the International Organization for Migration

International Organization for Migration data and findings indicate that between January and November 2017, more than 800,000 displaced Syrians returned to their homes (IOM, 2018-2019). The vast majority of returnees (93%) are IDPs from Syria. Reasons for return include reunification with family members, protection of assets or property, an improved situation in the country of origin and/or a deteriorating situation in the place of displacement. Although returns of IDPs are spontaneous, this does not necessarily mean that returns are safe or sustainable or voluntary, considering the changing dynamics and ongoing conflicts in the country. There are a wide range of challenges associated with large-scale returns. These include limited economic opportunities, scarcity of essential items such as food, water, health and other critical services. In addition, the return of IDPs and refugees to their countries of origin can result in a high number of claims related to the use and occupation of land and property. Weak governance, limited infrastructure and public services can exacerbate the identified challenges. In the event of a significant deterioration of living conditions in neighboring countries or an increase in security in parts of Syria, a sudden mass movement of returnees to Syria is considered possible in the coming years. The International Organization for Migration (IOM) is responsible for advising on this issue and processing the return of migrants/refugees.

6) Technical Assistance Cooperation between the Turkish Government and the International Organization for Migration

The International Organization for Migration aims to build national ownership among key stakeholders by investing in the development of their organizational and technical capacities to provide quality humanitarian and long-term development assistance to countries of origin of migrants. This will enhance humanitarian and recovery assistance capacities and improve ownership of systems, processes and response mechanisms across Turkey. The support focuses on national and local organizations responsible for providing assistance to vulnerable households caught in crisis or in transition to recovery. In Turkey, this includes building the capacity of national and local government institutions as well as local partners to improve policy, legislation and migrant and refugee services.

7) Cooperation between the Turkish Government and the International Organization for Migration on Labor Migration

The International Organization for Migration works in almost all sectors and social spheres to create a safe environment for vulnerable households in crisis or in the transition to recovery. As the social sector includes the economic sphere, there are more forms of cooperation in this area than in others. The International Organization for Migration improves the quality of care for blocked and self-reported irregular migrants, for those asylum seekers referred to the International Organization for Migration by the Turkish Government and granted refugee status by the Directorate of Migration Management. In addition, the International Organization for Migration provides assistance for resettlement to a third country, but for migrants who wish to return home legally, if any, to their home country voluntarily, the International Organization for Migration covers all repatriation needs, including travel, documents and tickets.

8) Migration Health cooperation between the Turkish Government and the International Organization for Migration

Cooperation between the Turkish Government and the International Organization for Migration in the health sector is very important and cooperation with the health sector started in 2013. This cooperation is aimed at protecting the health of migrants, including stability and resilience so that they do not get sick and live a healthy life. Treatment is provided in the migrants' shelter, and Turkish Ministry of Health staff regularly visit the migrants' residences every month to check their health. This is not only limited to the physical health area, but also the psychological health of the migrants is checked and if any migrants are ill after the health checks, they are given the necessary medication (Republic of Turkey Ministry of Health, 2017).

9) Cooperation between the Turkish Government and the International Organization for Migration and Border Management

The influx of new arrivals into temporary reception centers in northern Syria continues to put a strain on existing humanitarian services, perpetuating the imperative need for reception centers. These reception centers play a vital role in receiving new arrivals and providing essential assistance such as food, protection, health and nutrition services. As displaced populations move out of reception centers, there is a need for continued emergency non-food assistance support. For those moving from reception centers to locations that offer some degree of stability but often lack basic infrastructure and services, there is a high level of shelter needs. Strong early recovery programming is needed to address needs related to equitable access to services, infrastructure rehabilitation and livelihoods to support the transition from humanitarian assistance to other opportunities and to acknowledge the mobility of displaced communities. In this regard, the Turkish government is stepping in and all supporting public institutions and organizations are moving towards cooperation with the International Organization for Migration and mutually supporting each other with different projects that are complementary, able to solve each other's problems and where the main objective is to address vulnerabilities. Collaboration is also important to encourage local institutions and NGOs to build strong internal systems, procedures and interventions to meet the needs of the affected community, including technical assistance and expertise.

10) Cooperation between the Turkish Government and the International Organization for Migration on Migration and Development

In 2002, the "Task Force on Combating Trafficking in Persons" was established under the coordination of the Ministry of Foreign Affairs with the participation of all relevant Ministries and other institutions and organizations. Until 2014, 20 national task force meetings were held with the participation of public institutions and organizations, international organizations and relevant non-governmental organizations involved in combating human trafficking. With the Law No. 6458 on Foreigners and International Protection in 2013, efforts in the field of combating trafficking in persons and protection of victims gained a new dimension with the cooperation with the International Organization for Migration. With this Law, the General Directorate of Migration Administration (transformed into the Directorate of Migration Management) under the Ministry of Interior was established and the Department for the Protection of Victims of Trafficking in Persons was established to carry out work and operations in the field of combating trafficking in persons and protecting victims (GIGM, 2022b).

In 2013, a book was published on the cooperation between the International Organization for Migration and the government in the field of information: (a) Guidelines for the Handling of Criminal Actions Related to Trafficking in Persons; (b) Code of Practice on the Handling of the Offense of Trafficking in Persons; (c) . (d) Trainer's Manual for Organizing Workshops; (e) Human Trafficking in Turkey; (f) A Trainer's Manual for Organizing a Workshop on Human Trafficking in Turkey International Organization for Migration supported the Turkish public, including refugees and asylum seekers in Turkey, through public service announcements, radio and print media information, as well as a large-scale campaign in 10 provinces. The International Organization for Migration has also been recognized by many institutions in Turkey as a source of information and practical experience on migration issues.

The International Organization for Migration is also conducting an Information Campaign with the Ministry of Family and Social Policies, the Directorate of Migration Management, Civil Society

Organizations and the Ministry of Family and Social Policies to promote a culture of safe migration as the main preventive strategy of the International Organization for Migration, which aims to promote a culture of safe migration in order to better understand the issue in relation to the problems faced by migrants both at home and abroad. In cooperation with the International Organization for Migration, within the framework of the project "Assistance to Victims of Trafficking in Persons in Turkey", the 157 Emergency Helpline for potential victims of trafficking was established with operators in Russian, Romanian, English and Turkish, 157 Emergency Helpline promotional material was distributed and information posters and boards were displayed (MFA, 2022).

CONCLUSION

Based on the description of the discussion of this research, it can be concluded that Turkey has a very good geographical position located on 2 (two) continents with trade routes and transportation routes from various countries. Turkey is a developing country and a gateway to Europe, which leads to a high level of human trafficking and other activities. It is a region where all aspects of the economy are not yet stable in every region, and also due to the fact that Turkey has many borders, because of its geographical location as a bridge connecting the continent of Europe with the continent of Asia, and not only because it has many unprotected roads around the borders, but also because of the developed transportation by sea, it is still a region where it is inevitable to experience lack of control from time to time. For this reason, the Government of the Republic of Turkey and all public institutions and organizations have moved towards cooperation with the International Organization for Migration and have supported each other with different projects that complement each other, solve the problems of each other and whose main goal is to eliminate victimization. At this point, Turkey has contributed positively in this sense as a facilitator, since Turkey trusts these activities carried out by the International Organization for Migration, which deals with groups of illegal migrants. In this cooperation, obstacles such as lack of shelter, ignorance of human resources, social problems among migrants, health problems that occur among migrants are possible, but they can be appropriately tackled and intervened. The success of Turkey's cooperation with the International Organization for Migration is inseparable, not only in these matters, but also in the training provided to migrants to give them specific skills. In this context, having initially focused its attention on the resettlement of Iraqi refugees in the 1990s, the IOM later expanded its work to include emergency intervention programs in response to the devastating earthquake in Van in 2011. Its mission emergency intervention programs have continued to grow rapidly with the onset of the Syrian crisis and the Mediterranean crisis in 2012 and since 2015 by building strong partnerships with Agencies/ Ministries. In addition to its role in meeting the needs of migrants during the crisis, the mission works closely with the Government of Turkey to address the longer-term impact of migration, including migrant assistance programmes, labour integration and migration management, border and migration management and research, and data collection on migration flows. In this context it is important to maintain and strengthen the good relations between Turkey and the International Organization for Migration and in the implementation of this cooperation, there are, obviously, significant implementation costs involved in each activity, so it is hoped that in the future there will be more effective, efficient, professional and systematic (excellence) procedures or agreements on costs.

REFERENCES

GIGM. (2022a). *Göç Hakkında Genel Bilgi*. Retrieved July, 22, 2022, from https://www.goc.gov.tr/genel-bilgi56420

GIGM. (2022b). *Göç İdaresi ve İnsan Ticareti*. Retrieved July, 22, 2022, from https://www.goc.gov.tr/insan-ticareti-sss

GIGM. (2022c). *Geçici Korumamız Altındaki Suriyeliler*. Retrieved July, 22, 2022, from https://www.goc.gov.tr/gecici-korumamiz-altindaki-suriyeliler

IOM. (2016). *Europe / Medıterranean Mıgratıon Response Internatıonal Organızatıon For Mıgratıon, Sıtuatıon Report*. Retrieved July, 22, 2022, from https://turkiye.iom.int/sites/g/files/tmzbdl1061/files/documents/20160829121909_3-2.pdf

IOM. (2018-2019). *MCOF: Göç Krizi Operasyonel Çerçevesi*. Retrieved July, 22, 2022, from https://turkiye.iom.int/sites/g/files/tmzbdl1061/files/documents/MCOF_TR.pdf

IOM. (2022a). *Members and Observers*. Retrieved July, 22, 2022, from https://www.iom.int/members-and-observers

IOM. (2022b). *Migration Management*. Retrieved July, 22, 2022, from https://www.iom.int/migration-management

IOM. (2022c). *İnsan Ticareti ile Mücadele*. Retrieved July, 22, 2022, from https://turkiye.iom.int/tr/node/108261

MFA. (2022). *Türkiye Cumhuriyeti Dışişleri Bakanlığı Türkiye'nin İnsan Ticaretiyle Mücadelesi*. Retrieved July, 22, 2022, from http:// www. mfa. gov. tr/ turkiye_nin- insan- ticaretiyle- mucadelesi-. tr.mfa

OIM. 2022. *Migration Law Database*. Retrieved July, 22, 2022, from https://imldb.iom.int/_layouts/15/IML.Portal/AppPages/Home.aspx

Sağlık Bakanlığı, T. C. (2017). *Suriyeli Sığınmacılar İçin 'SIHHAT' Projesi*. Retrieved July, 22, 2022, from https://sggm.saglik.gov.tr/TR,25460/suriyeli-siginmacilar-icin-sihhat-projesi.html

KEY TERMS AND DEFINITIONS

Asylum Seeker: A refugee is a person whose application for asylum has been accepted, while an asylum seeker is a person who has left his country claiming to be a refugee but whose application for refugee status has not been concluded.

Illegal Human Trafficking: Is an unlawful act against humanity on a global scale. The use of the modern slavery analogy for the crime of human trafficking also highlights the importance of criminalizing unlawful acts of trafficking. Human trafficking, which is the exploitation of individuals for various purposes; it is also closely related to human rights, employment policy, public health, and immigration policies. At the same time, human trafficking crime threatens the border security of countries.

Immigrant: A person who immigrates from one country to settle in another country. Legally, immigrants or immigrants concern at least two countries. One is the left country, the other is the settled country. Migration is an emigration for the country of departure, and an internal migration for the settled country. Those who migrate inwards are called immigrants, and those who migrate out are called emigrants.

International Organization for Migration (IOM): Is an international organization operating in areas such as emergency assistance, resettlement of refugees, assisting voluntary returns, migrant health, sending money and supporting legal immigration options.

Irregular Migration: It means entering a country illegally, staying in a country illegally, or entering legally and not leaving within the legal time limit. Irregular migration is an issue that needs to be evaluated separately in terms of destination, transit and source countries. Irregular migration; for destination countries, it covers people who come to their country illegally or who come legally and do not leave within the legal exit deadlines; It includes people who cross the country borders by not following the necessary procedures when leaving their country for the source country. For transit countries, they are people who enter the country legally or illegally from the source countries to reach the destination country, and use this country as a transit country and leave the country's border.

Migration: Is the geographical displacement movement of human communities by settling in another settlement unit to spend their whole or part of their lives due to religious, economic, political, social and other reasons.

Refugee: As defined by the UN, a refugee is "a person who has a well-founded fear of being persecuted because of his race, religion, nationality, membership of a particular social group or political opinion, and therefore leaves his country and does not or does not want to return because of his fear". Immigration is a legal status.

United Nations (UN): Was established on October 24, 1945. It is an international organization established to protect world peace and security and to establish an economic, social, and cultural cooperation among the international community.

Chapter 2
Digital Public Diplomacy in Crisis Management: A Conceptual Review

Sami Kiraz
https://orcid.org/0000-0002-6987-9856
Hitit University, Turkey

ABSTRACT

Internet technologies and digitalization have led to obvious changes in all areas of life. The main issues of international politics have started to transform around these concepts. Crisis management is one of them. In this study, it will be examined how crisis management actors keep up with new trends depending on the transformations in the crises and the expectations of the masses affected by the crisis due to international policy. In this context, the main claim of the study is that digital public diplomacy is included in the crisis management processes and this leads to differences in traditional methods. It has been tried to explain how the relationship between the motivations of the states and the expectations of the public, which are accepted as the basic characteristics of this process, is constructed. In this context, it is analyzed that social media has a transformative effect, and therefore, it is used in crisis management. In addition, the study will be completed with the determination that this transformation provides both advantages and disadvantages in crisis management.

INTRODUCTION AND BACKGROUND

The phenomenon of the age we live in is undoubtedly globalization, which has increased its impact with the development of internet technologies and digitalization in all areas of life. These new developments and transformations cause humanity to change its memorization in many areas from daily life routines to production relations, from scientific development to increased communication opportunities. In this context, international relations could not be exempt from this process. In particular, the unique positions of the states in foreign policy decision-making face a serious challenge, and public opinion increases

DOI: 10.4018/978-1-6684-5822-8.ch002

its influence every day in this process. Such a challenge requires adding digitalization to the decision-making processes, and this innovation requires the "traditional" to give way to the "new".

States are now responsible for taking into account the expectations of ordinary people and explaining their decisions to these people in their foreign policy decision-making processes, which they think are not in the public's interest. Such a responsibility necessitates the digitalization of "public diplomacy", which is a relatively new concept, in other words, keeping up with the requirements of the digital age. Public diplomacy is a tool that states use to communicate and mobilize these resources not only towards other states but also towards people. It is tried to draw attention to these potential resources by publishing various publications, engaging in cultural interaction, organizing exchange programs, and so on. "Digital" public diplomacy, in addition to these qualities of public diplomacy, has added the ability to produce policy and discourse instantly, especially with the inclusion of active use of social media networks and internet technologies. It should be noted that this transformation has both positive and negative aspects.

On the other hand, the digitalization of the age has not only necessitated a transformation in the relations of states with people, but also led to differences in the characteristics of international and national issues. Increasingly and at different levels, crises have begun to be observed in many regions of the world, and this period has even begun to be called the "age of crises". Therefore, the necessity for states and especially decision-makers to create policies for all these crises has emerged. Moreover, the differences between the crises of the 21st century and the previous ones have turned this responsibility into a difficult task. Accordingly, contemporary crises stem from the structure of the global information age. This structure gives crises transboundary qualities. In addition, increasing communication opportunities create a global society and interdependent relations. This situation makes critical security gaps for states and causes extremist organizations motivated to take advantage of these gaps. All these elements present new tasks for states and especially decision-makers to consider in crisis management processes. On the one hand, while foreign policy actions are being changed, on the other hand, these changes should be conveyed to the interlocutors and the whole public correctly. For this, digital public diplomacy activities organized in an appropriate format must be performed.

Starting from the crisis management and digitalized public diplomacy, this study is designed to answer the following research questions: How did the changing expectations and needs as a result of digitalization change the public diplomacy activities of states in the context of crisis management? Does the use of digital public diplomacy in crisis management mean the same for all states today? Does the rapid transformation in diplomacy lead to a radical change in traditional diplomacy principles and practitioners?

There are various studies in the literature to find answers to these questions or similar ones. In a study edited by Surowiec and Manor (2021), the authors drew attention to the role of public diplomacy in coping with uncertainties by examining public diplomacy practices for crises, which they call uncertainty policy, through crisis and country examples. Bjola and Holmes (2015) focused on the transformative effect of digital diplomacy on international politics, which they call a transformation that must be experienced already. Pamment (2016) examined the digital transformation of British public diplomacy in practice with the claim that it is a soft power instrument. Budak (2022), with the suggestion that public diplomacy should be digitalized, claimed that institutions should develop, especially with the use of social media, their digital public diplomacy capacities. In the study, which was prepared under the editorship of Karatzogianni, Nguyen, and Serafinelli (2016), with the presupposition that the public sphere has become digital, the authors discussed the reflections of this on crises. Boin (2009) discussed the change in crisis management in the new period and the transformation this created in decision-making mechanisms. Cassidy (2018) examined social media, which is the main tool used by today's diplomacy, that she called the age of real-time governance, in crisis communication. Bjola and Jiang (2015) compared the digital diplomacy strategies of the EU, USA, and Japan in the context of public diplomacy practices. Sevin (2018) examined Turkey's digital outreach after 15 July in his study, which deals with digital diplomacy as a crisis communication model. Payne, Sevin, and Bruya (2011) analyzed public diplomacy practices after digitalization, which they called the new generation, by comparing them through case studies. Westcott (2008) discussed the effects and transformative role of digital diplomacy on international relations, which was affected by the internet revolution. Manor (2021), who examines the use of social media in crisis management with a more critical view, argues that states use Twitter for framing other states, based on case studies.

This study consists of three main parts in order to find answers to the research questions of the study and to analyze how digital public diplomacy, which is not directly examined in the literature, is used in crisis management. In the first part, the transformations of conflicts and crises, especially in the 21st century, will be explained by making a literature revietoto analyze new expectations. In the second part, the basic principles, aims, and tools of crisis management will be examined and how these will be evaluated in the new generation of crisis management, and the importance of crisis communication will be emphasized. In the third part, the functions of digital public diplomacy in crisis management processes, especially in crisis communication, will be discussed and a conceptual infrastructure will be built in this regard. Digital public diplomacy practices of states in crisis management are not included in the study, since it is aimed to prepare a framework for subsequent studies.

There are two main outcomes of this study. First, it is revealed that states have the motivation to persuade the public and the international community by changing their traditional approaches in the management of the changing crises of our age. To achieve this, it is seen that especially foreign ministers and embassies have made institutional arrangements that are more inclined toward digital diplomacy. Second, states have to act with greater transparency in order to combat the spread of information that is out of the control of the state in today's world where the source of information is unclear and ordinary people are also a source of data.

CHANGING DYNAMICS OF CONFLICTS AND CRISIS

When the literature is examined, the idea that the concept of international security has changed and transformed to a great extent with the post-Cold War period comes to the fore (Baldwin, 1997; Williams, 2008; Buzan et al, 1998; Baylis and Smith, 2006; Buzan, 1991; Krause and Williams, 1996). Although this change and transformation have different dynamics, it is accepted as a common point that the state-centered approach is replaced by an individual-oriented perspective (Walt, 1991). The threats of the new era emerged in a much more incalculable nature, and these transformations, which led to the new era being called the era of uncertainty, led to the emergence of new concepts and concepts (Surowiec and Manor, 2021).

The most widely used of these was the term "new war". According to the definition made by Mary Kaldor, new wars are a new form of struggle in which state and non-state actors are on the field, identity-based policies and ethnic conflicts increase, and the perception of the war economy ceases to be state-centered (Kaldor, 2012, 71-94). According to the definition, the change in the nature of conflicts is emphasized as the main subject of international politics (Çıtak, 2019a, 53). Elements such as actors (state and non-state actors), motivations of actors (ideology, gain), scope of conflict (interstate, domestic, regional, global), economic and social structures, technological developments, and tools of war have been the main topics of changing qualities (Newman, 2004, 174).

On the other hand, these transformations have also led to a change in the perception of basic conflict concepts such as the definition of the enemy, the extent of violence, methods, and the beginning or end of the conflict (Vasquez, 2009). In addition, the change of the battlefield and the definition of war with new concepts such as psychological, cyber, economic, controlled, and asymmetrical have added new dimensions to all these uncertainties (Çıtak, 2019a, 53).

In summary, insight into the new war or conflict refers to the change that all concepts used for traditional definitions are exposed to. In the new period, concepts such as "struggle", "target", "violence", "parties", "organized conflict", "power", "enemy" have both different dimensions and they have become ambiguous. In this context, to understand the new concepts of conflict, it is necessary to express the transformation in many topics from the methods of struggle to the defense mechanisms, from the warring parties to the duration of the war, from the weapons and tools used to the alliance relations, from the battlefield to the victims of the war, from the sources of threat to the types of threats, from the legal dimension to the relevant economic order. Names such as hybrid wars, low-intensity wars, limited (small) wars, post-modern wars, and new generation wars can also be given to new kinds of wars (Çıtak, 2019b, 200).

In addition to wars and conflicts, one of the most considered phenomena in international politics is crises. A crisis is defined as "a difficult period, depression in a country or between countries, in the life of a society or an organization". However, there are various definitions of crises in the literature. J. Richardson (1994, 12) defines it as "an acute conflict between two or more states on a particular issue and involving the perception of a serious risk of war by decision-makers". On the other hand, Snyder and Diesing (1977, 6) define a crisis as "sequences of interactions between the governments involving a dangerously high probability of war".

There is a wide spectrum of causes of crises. Different types of crises such as economic crises, security crises, political crises, systemic crises, and humanitarian crises are on the agenda of international politics. In addition to this, it is seen that each crisis has different processes, and the measures taken accordingly change. While some crises explode as a result of the escalation and accumulation of problems over time, unexpected events in some crises lead to the emergence of crises. In some cases, it is observed that crises are experienced intentionally as a result of the provocation of one or more of the parties to the crisis. In indirect crises, on the other hand, it is possible for third parties affected by the actions of the parties to the crisis to be involved in the crisis. In addition to all these types, in some cases, crises can also occur as a result of incidental accidents, even if the parties do not provoke it or do not want it. According to the process of the crises, it is seen that they occur in four different stages in general. These are the initial phase of the crisis that characterizes the emergence of the crisis, the escalation phase of the crisis in the ongoing process, the peak where the crisis is now at its peak and where there is no possibility of further escalation, and the termination phase where it starts to fade by descending (Karadağ, 2019, 2).

Considering the 21st century crises, it is seen that all these types are also effective in various crises. Many crises arise from different reasons and motivations such as terrorist attacks, historical conflicts between countries, various accidents or disasters, epidemics, regional crises that started as a result of social movements, mass migration movements from conflict zones, food crises that started due to drought or similar reasons, production crises due to problems observed in industrial production appear as a phenomenon of our age.

While all these crises pose serious threats to both state sovereignty and individual security, their management by states is of great importance. Considering the Cold War period, it is generally accepted that crises were experienced with more traditional motivations and of a limited nature, so crisis management remained within a limited framework in this context. However, current crises require more than this because of their nature and the unpredictability of their consequences. Therefore, to understand this process and new methods, it is necessary to look at the crisis management processes from a wider perspective.

BASIC CONCEPTS OF CRISIS MANAGEMENT

There are various explanations in the literature to define the concept of crisis management. Snyder (1977) defines international crisis management as "the parties to the crisis trying to apply pressure flexibly and wisely according to the requirements of the situation or to coexist and reconcile states without incurring high costs or losses". Buck (1993) stated that crisis management means "resolving a dangerous conflict without the outbreak of war and at the same time protecting the vital interests of the parties involved". According to another definition, crisis management is "to reach an acceptable solution for the parties in the crisis without resorting to war." (Suleiman, 2012, 10) Crisis management is defined as "winning a victory in a crisis while keeping a crisis within acceptable risk limits for both sides". Phil Williams defines crisis management as controlling and regulating measures to prevent the crisis from getting out of control and causing war, and the resolution of the crisis on a basis that satisfies the parties and this protects their vital interests (Williams, 1976, 28-29).

There are also various explanations about how crisis management should be carried out and the requirements for effective crisis management. Accordingly, a comprehensive strategy should be determined for effective crisis management, and a crisis management organization should be established. A communication plan, press and public relations strategy plan, and a strong infrastructure should be prepared for this organization (Houben, 2005, 4-5). To manage crises successfully and ensure peace, there must be two basic features: The ability of crisis desk personnel and the strong deterrents in the hands of crisis management actors.

For peace to be permanent, the interests of the parties involved in the crisis must be reasonable and in line with international law and rules. Otherwise, the coming governments may start a new crisis with reasons or excuses such as their countries are deceived and their national interests are not taken care of. The crisis should not create a permanent benefit, harm, humiliation, or damage to national pride for one or more of the countries concerned. On the contrary case, there is a possibility that a new crisis will arise when these countries deem it appropriate for their national interests (Houben, 2005, 21-23).

Considering all these factors, it is of vital importance that an accurate communication plan is made and that the actors have effective infrastructures for this plan. However, the inclusion of ordinary citizens in the process due to the above-mentioned nature of today's crises and the changing international policy conditions makes these communication strategies and practices even more valuable. Transparency and instantaneous information transfer in order to make quick decisions and gain the trust of individuals affected by crises are essential elements for crisis management actors. In this context, the need for public diplomacy tools is increasing day by day, and an even more important role falls on the changing and digitalizing of public diplomacy in this context.

COMMUNICATION IN CRISIS MANAGEMENT AND DIGITAL PUBLIC DIPLOMACY

In times of crisis, the fear, stress, pressure, and confusion that arise due to the crisis affect the communication carried out in these periods in a way that often leads to bad results, far from the intended mutual understanding and dialogue environment. This situation necessitates that the communication to be carried out in times of crisis should be carried out very carefully and, if necessary, by planning (Aydemir, 2005, 212). In addition, it is also necessary to deal with questions to be asked by those who want to learn why, when, and how the crisis emerged, what the authority did, and what plans to do to deal with the crisis. Organizations that delay in answering questions that may be posed by the public incur unnecessary material and moral losses (Aydemir, 2005, 212). Today, in a crisis, communicating with the public effectively and quickly has become a necessity in the management of crises (Marra, 1998, 461).

All these obligations and the responsibility of the states increase even more when the nature of the crisis is international. As mentioned above, especially with the effect of the communication revolution in the 21st century, the nature of the crises has changed, and this change has created a structure in which ordinary people are also included in the process, together with the diversity of actors and the understanding of security based on individual security. Therefore, international politics is no longer just interactions between states and has turned into an area in which non-governmental actors, individuals, and groups actively participate. As a requirement of this new situation, there has been a significant increase in the actors of international political communication.

Although states continue to maintain their position as the main actors in policy-making and crisis management, both local and international public opinion has become a phenomenon that must be taken into account. This process is two-way. While the states have to adopt a communication strategy that will respond to the expectations of the public, on the other hand, they try to benefit from the public to protect their interests and to maximize these interests by emphasizing their rightness. In both cases, getting the support of the public is the main goal (Hobolt and Wratil, 2015, 239-240).

Providing this support only depends on convincing the international public opinion during the crisis, which requires a different communication process and application than in normal periods, namely crisis communication. What makes crisis communication possible in international crises is that the mass media has made states and societies open to the influence and information of other states and societies.

In this sense, for states, crisis communication means conveying certain messages to the international community and the public in case of a crisis. With the messages they will convey, the states aim to create public support in their favor in the international community and to prevent the threats directed to this support during an international crisis, and thus to continue the support that has been formed in their favor. These threats could be information, news, or events by other states or different powers that are party to the crisis that is directed to basic components of crisis management, or general crisis policies of the state in case of crisis, and that reduce the international community support, and damage the reputation and positive image of the state (Aydemir, 2005, 217).

A new type of diplomacy has emerged among the actors of international political communication, with the participation of non-governmental national groups and individuals outside the sphere of influence of traditional diplomacy in the international political communication process. The basic idea of this new type of diplomacy, called "Public Diplomacy", is to communicate with foreign people aimed at influencing their thoughts. During public diplomacy, governments can use several different channels and techniques such as mass communication and international broadcasts in particular (Gilboa, 2000, 275).

In this sense, crisis communication to be applied in case of an international crisis finds its application area within the framework of this diplomacy understanding.

Based on the general acceptance that public diplomacy is an area that serves the purposes of states such as justifying, finding support, and reaching their interests through new types of diplomacy (Gilboa, 2000, 290-292), the effects of this area in the crisis management process are also undeniable. In order to understand how public diplomacy is used in crisis management and what purposes it serves, it is necessary to mention the general aims and objectives of public diplomacy.

The basic idea of public diplomacy is “direct communication with foreign peoples to influence their thoughts and ultimately the thinking of their governments” (Malone, 1985, 199). In public diplomacy, mass communication channels are used to directly influence the masses (Gilboa, 2000, 291). The actors tried to be influenced by public diplomacy carried out in three different types are foreign state citizens, non-state actors, and local people. The tools (TV, radio, etc.) used by the public diplomacy carried out at each level may also differ according to its interlocutors. However, the public diplomacy activities carried out to find a response both at the level of the authorities and the public, and the success of the process can be measured by changing the positions of the interlocutors or forcing them to be changed in line with the interests of the actor carrying out public diplomacy (Gilboa, 2000, 291-294).

Today, public diplomacy serves the purpose of ensuring the interests of countries and strengthening the country’s positions in the eyes of local and foreign peoples with similar tools. However, the changing technological conditions and the nature of international politics also show themselves in public diplomacy, and especially the effects of the process called digitalization are observed. In state practices where the obvious effect of digitalization is seen, this process is called “digital diplomacy”. Digital diplomacy enables countries to engage and network with target audiences as well as disseminating messages. This dual function is similarly discussed in public diplomacy studies, which refer to various activities, such as international broadcasting and student exchanges, carried out to communicate with the foreign public (Sevin, 2017, 188).

Digitization in diplomacy forces states to act faster, reach wider audiences and make strategic communication plans. In this regard, to keep up with new developments, all relevant institutions, especially the Ministry of Foreign Affairs, strive to fulfill the requirements of digital diplomacy. At this point, it can be argued that the new diplomacy has developed the old one and facilitated the process thanks to the opportunities it covers instead of replacing it. Especially social media has been rapidly adopted by Foreign Ministers, as it allows them to follow public diplomacy and crisis communication strategies more effectively than their previous versions (Bjola and Manor, 2022, 478) Digital strategic communication, on the other hand, has completed the efforts of embassies to object or refute negative news in the print media (Manor and Bjola, 2021).

Although social media is one of the important tools of the new digital public diplomacy, it can help convey a powerful message extremely effectively, but it cannot replace good strategy planning, relationship building, and crisis management, which are well-established signs of professional diplomatic behavior (Bjola and Jiang, 2015, 87). Therefore, it would be more accurate to consider this tool as a complementary element.

When the process of social media becoming a part of diplomacy and digital diplomacy applications are examined, it will be more understandable what purposes this relationship was established for. Although it is claimed in the literature that this process started with the Arab Spring (Ghannam, 2011; Shirky and Gladwell, 2011), it is seen that such a transformation has been started before, especially by the US. Digital public diplomacy, whose main purpose is to strengthen the relationship between foreign publics and diplomats, has been directly related to the belief in maximizing interaction and shifting from one-way information flow to dialogue and interaction (Melissen, 2005).

The diplomatic transformation, which was initiated to combat the anti-Americanism created by the US policy in the first decade of the 21st century, forms the basis of digital public diplomacy in this sense. US decision-makers, who wanted to go beyond the traditional government-public relationship, changed public diplomacy with tools that were developed and adapted to new needs and tried to restore US influence on a global scale (Bjola and Jiang, 2015, 73). In this context, the active use of social media accounts and the design of the language used in a way that will contact the people have been the main components of this new transformation.

Although there are various approaches to the effectiveness of social media in public diplomacy, Bjola and Jiang (2015) draw a three-dimensional framework. Accordingly, the first dimension is *agenda-setting*. Public diplomacy, through social media, contributes to the creation of a positive image of the country by directing the attention of foreign followers to certain issues. Diplomats can therefore provide relevant information over and over again, creating a compelling and attention-grabbing topic for their audience. The second dimension is *presence-expansion*. The advent of social media extends the scope of diplomatic presence across time and space. In the digital age, presence-expansion becomes an even more critical condition for diplomats to have their voices heard. Diplomats' credibility and authority will likely suffer if they cannot keep up with ever-changing digital technologies. Not only would their messages be heard, but they would also lose their competing information campaigns. The third and final dimension is *conversation-generating*. Good public diplomacy can no longer be monologue-based, it must be dialogue-based. It should facilitate two-way or multi-way communication between the parties and encourage cooperation initiatives. With its interactive feature, social media has a lot to offer in this regard as it can create a semi-permanent dialogue between diplomats and the foreign public. Two-way talks allow diplomats to refocus their agendas, reduce misinformation, and improve mutual understanding. It is this special feature that enables social media to realize the purpose of public diplomacy differently from traditional methods (Bjola and Jiang, 2015, 74-75).

The use of digital public diplomacy in crisis management processes serves the same purposes. On the one hand, the changing nature of the crises, on the other hand, the increase in the rate of being affected by the crisis, and the differentiated responsibilities imposed on the states increased the importance of public diplomacy in this process. Therefore, it assigns important missions to public diplomacy, especially the use of social media at every stage of the crisis. It is not surprising that diplomats and decision-makers, in particular, need diplomatic mobility to keep up with this transformation.

Coombs and Holladay (2008) solidify these arguments by noting that the fact that social media evolves rapidly puts it at the forefront of research when a crisis begins. This is so because when a crisis occurs, it gives an opportunity to any organization, with all the participation of the community, to see what is being talked about and how they can solve the problem by bringing it up with the public (Apuke and Tunca, 2018, 202).

When the traditional crisis management literature is examined, five important tasks fall on the leadership in times of crisis: sense-making (in which participants try to grasp the nature, severity, and likely consequences of the unfolding crisis), decision-making (whereby the who, what, and when concerning the reaction to the crisis have to be agreed upon), meaning-making (during which public expectations are weighed and managed), terminating (which covers political and operational responses to the crisis) and learning (the crisis experience which offers a reservoir of potential lessons for contingency planning and training for future crises) (Boin et. al., 2005, 10-15). This framework also provides a valid infrastructure for the management of the transforming current international crises with digital public diplomacy tools.

In the first stage of the crisis, social media becomes a platform where the position of the relevant state regarding the nature, seriousness, and possible effects of the event is explained. At this point, making various "hashtag" studies are frequently used methods. After the preliminary consideration, making quick decisions and managing the process are also done through social media. Possible aid organizations, and directing the masses to policies with clear information are among the practices of this stage. On the other hand, unlike traditional diplomacy, opening channels of dialogue and producing answers that will satisfy people's curiosity or concerns are among the priorities of digital public diplomacy. At this stage, the skills of diplomats, who can be considered as field personnel, gain importance (Cassidy, 2018, 8). When the crisis is over or about to come to an end, explaining the approaches to the state in which the crisis is experienced and at the same time demonstrating solidarity with people is another application of digital public diplomacy and crisis management.

As a result, it is observed that digital platforms, especially social media, inevitably become one of the tools of public diplomacy in the digital age. With this new tool, it is seen that traditional crisis management plays an important role in eliminating the issues that are insufficient to intervene in the transforming crises. In this regard, other institutions and persons authorized to carry out public diplomacy, especially the Ministry of Foreign Affairs and embassies, are equipped with the tools and qualifications to keep up with the digital age. However, it should not be forgotten that the process in question no longer means that crises can be easily managed and that it is an important condition to realize it only with the right methods and motivation.

CONCLUSION AND RECOMMENDATIONS

The 21st century is witnessing major transformations and changes as a result of the spread of globalization in all areas of life. All actors on the globe are more or less affected by all these changes and transformations. These effects also transform behavior patterns, perceptions, expectations, and needs of actors. International politics cannot be expected to be exempt from such a process. Therefore, the traditional policy universe could not escape the effects of globalization and radical transformations were experienced, especially in the behavior of the state. Diplomacy, which can be accepted as the behavior of states, has been adorned with different notions and tools and has been revised to keep up with the new world.

Digital public diplomacy, which is the main subject of this section, has also been brought to the literature as a reflection of the revision in question. The expansion created by globalization for communication opportunities necessitated the digitalization of communication. With this digitalization, it has overcome the diplomacy patterns that remain in a relatively more closed box and in the privacy of the states. It has now become a part of global communication in which ordinary people are directly or indirectly involved wherever they are in the world.

In addition, the rise of the individual-centered security understanding both in the literature and in implementations and the new security understanding, where security is no longer the subject of only the military and the state, coincided with the digitalization period. The understanding that the expectations of individuals from states differ, that the transparency of state authority is demanded and that the state has to increase the happiness and welfare of the individual also necessitated the transformation of state behaviors. The pressure from the public has pushed governments to act in an individual-centered manner, and since the increasing communication opportunities have provided the states with the opportunity to be accessible to foreign citizens, it has led to the necessity of explaining their positions to both local and international publics. Of course, this necessity is also accepted as a peaceful way for the state to maximize its interests.

Such needs and motivations necessitated the regulation of public diplomacy, which has just started to be implemented during the Cold War, with new tools and the implementation of new concepts to increase its impact capacity. The digital or digitizing public diplomacy approach has emerged as a result of these expectations. Although the implementation areas of this new type (such as exchange programs, aid programs, and joint activities) and the motivation (interests) have not changed, but the tools (such as social media, and internet technologies) have diversified.

The current application area of digital public diplomacy is crisis management, as examined in this study. Crisis management, which can be briefly defined as the activities carried out for the parties in crisis to resolve their disagreements without turning them into war, is one of the main issues of international politics. Crisis management, which has vital importance in ensuring international peace and security, had to be revised in a way that would respond to the changes in the characteristics of the crises caused by the transformations and changes mentioned above. It has emerged as a new trend to manage a process in a way that will serve the motivation of crisis management actors to find support from the foreign public, on the other hand, to the new security understanding that emphasizes individual security.

While traditional crisis management processes are generally carried out at the level of diplomats and decision-makers and the public is not included much, the application of digital public diplomacy in this field has changed both the action styles and motivations. The use of public diplomacy in crisis management with new tools and motivations, whose goal is to directly respond to the local and foreign public opinion, requires both to act quickly and announce their position, and to implement a comprehensive strategic communication plan. This requirement has brought work both at the institutional level and at the level of qualifications of the actors. States transform their public diplomacy practices primarily through social media accounts and on the basis of dialogue; It also carries out crisis management by activating these tools.

Using digital public diplomacy in crisis management has various advantages and disadvantages. The most important advantage is the involvement of individuals in the process. In this way, accountability will be carried, transparency will be adopted in practices, and thus, a process will be carried out that protects not only the state's interest but also the individual's interest. Besides, thanks to the possibilities of social media and internet technologies, the processes will accelerate and the involvement of the international community in the crisis will be possible without permanent damage. Considering the Balkans region-centered crises of the 1990s, it becomes clear how important this factor is. Another important advantage of this new trend is that the process is based on dialogue rather than a monologue. While traditional diplomacy is a one-way transfer of information from the center to the periphery, digital public diplomacy communicates with individuals, especially through the use of social media, and enables decision-making mechanisms to act more prudently.

Despite all these advantages, there are various drawbacks and disadvantages of using digital public diplomacy in crisis management. First of all, states and related institutions should always be prepared for a new crisis and make various strategic plans. In such an interactive process, the state's unpreparedness can cause it to make obvious mistakes and cause the crisis to spread further or get out of control. In addition, healthy coordination should be established between state representatives, especially diplomats, and policy centers (capitals). If this communication cannot be established properly, there is a risk of transferring unconfirmed information to the public. Again, this possibility will reflect negatively on the crisis. Another drawback is the possibility of populist rhetoric and actions in order to protect and glorify the interests of states in these processes in which individuals are involved. Acting for various purposes such as blaming, suppressing, or putting other parties in a difficult situation will cause crises to get out of control.

In conclusion, the issue of the use of digital public diplomacy, which is accepted as the new trend of crisis management, has a place in the literature as it is also examined in this study. While these processes and practices are evaluated as an inevitable result of the new era, the main factor that should not be forgotten is that the use of social media or integrating other digital tools into public diplomacy cannot replace crisis management on its own. Studies and examinations show that it would be more appropriate to consider these new tools as complementary elements. In this context, in this study, an effort was made to introduce the new crisis management trend and it was aimed to prepare a conceptual infrastructure for new studies on this subject. In the next period, examining the state practices towards crises will enrich this literature and enable the analysis of incomplete or wrong perspectives.

REFERENCES

Apuke, O. D., & Tunca, E. A. (2018). Social media and crisis management: A review and analysis of existing studies. *EUL Journal of Social Sciences*, *9*(2), 199–215.

Aydemir, E. (2005). Uluslararası krizlerde kriz iletişimi ve uygulaması. *Sosyal Ekonomik Araştırmalar Dergisi*, *5*(10), 204–231.

Baldwin, D. A. (1997). The concept of security. *Review of International Studies*, *23*(1), 5–26. doi:10.1017/S0260210597000053 PMID:10164688

Baylis, J., & Smith, S. (Eds.). (2006). *The globalization of world politics*. Oxford University Press.

Bjola, C., & Holmes, M. (Eds.). (2015). *Digital diplomacy theory and practice*. Routledge. doi:10.4324/9781315730844

Bjola, C., & Jiang, L. (2015). Social media and public diplomacy: a comparative analysis of the digital diplomatic strategies of the EU, US, and Japan in China. In C. Bjola & M. Holmes (Eds.), *Digital diplomacy theory and practice*. Routledge. doi:10.4324/9781315730844

Bjola, C., & Manor, I. (2022). The rise of hybrid diplomacy: From digital adaptation to digital adoption. *International Affairs*, *98*(2), 471–491. doi:10.1093/ia/iiac005

Boin, A. (2009). The new world of crises and crisis management: Implications for policymaking and research. *The Review of Policy Research*, *26*(4), 367–377. doi:10.1111/j.1541-1338.2009.00389.x

Boin, A., Hart, P., Stern, E., & Sundelius, B. (2005). *The politics of crisis management: public leadership under pressure*. Cambridge University Press. doi:10.1017/CBO9780511490880

Buck, R. C. (1993). *International crisis and conflict*. Martin's Press.

Budak, M. M. (2022). Kamu diplomasisi ve dijital iletişim. *Erciyes İletişim Dergisi*, *9*(1), 317–335. doi:10.17680/erciyesiletisim.997103

Buzan, B. (1991). New patterns of global security in the twenty-first century. *International Affairs*, *67*(3), 439–451. doi:10.2307/2621945

Buzan, B., Weaver, O., & De Wilde, J. (1998). *Security: a framework analysis*. Lynne Rienner Publishers.

Cassidy, J. (2018). *Digital diplomatic crisis communication: reconceptualising diplomatic signalling in an age of real time governance*. Working Paper No 3. Oxford Digital Diplomacy Research Group. Retrieved June 15, 2022, from https://www.qeh.ox.ac.uk/sites/www.odid.ox.ac.uk/files/DigDiploROxWP3.pdf

Çıtak, E. (2019a). Değişen güvenlik anlayışında savaş ve barış. In E. Çıtak & S. Kiraz (Eds.), *Uluslararası İlişkiler Kuramlarında Savaş ve Barış* (pp. 39–62). Orion.

Çıtak, E. (2019b). Silahsız savaş sahası: Yeni savaş anlayışında istihbaratın yeri. *Güvenlik Bilimleri Dergisi*, *8*(2), 191–213. doi:10.28956/gbd.646263

Coombs, W. T., & Holladay, S. J. (2008). Comparing apology to equivalent crisis response strategies: Clarifying apology's role and value in crisis communication. *Public Relations Review*, *34*(3), 252–257. doi:10.1016/j.pubrev.2008.04.001

Ghannam, J. (2011). *Social media in the arab world: leading up to the uprisings of 2011*. Center for International Media Assistance. Retrieved June 15, 2022, from https://www.cima.ned.org/wp-content/uploads/2015/02/CIMA-Arab_Social_Media-Report-10-25-11.pdf

Gilboa, E. (2000). Mass communication and diplomacy: A theoretical frame work. *Communication Theory*, *10*(3), 275–309. doi:10.1111/j.1468-2885.2000.tb00193.x

Hobolt, S. B., & Wratil, C. (2015). Public opinion and the crisis: The dynamics of support for the euro. *Journal of European Public Policy*, *22*(2), 238–256. doi:10.1080/13501763.2014.994022

Houben, M. (2005). *International crisis management: the approach of european states*. Routledge.

Kaldor, M. (2012). *New&Old wars: organized violence in a global era*. Polity Press.

Karadağ, H. (2019). Kriz yönetimi ve uluslararası ilişkiler. *Güvenlik Yazıları Serisi*, 34. Retrieved June 15, 2022, from https://trguvenlikportali.com/wp-content/uploads/2019/11/KrizYonetimi_HalukKaradag_v.1.pdf

Karatzogianni, A., Nguyen, D., & Serafinelli, E. (Eds.). (2016). *The digital transformation of the public sphere: conflict, migration, crisis and culture in digital networks*. Palgrave Macmillan. doi:10.1057/978-1-137-50456-2

Krause, K., & Williams, M. C. (1996). Broadening the agenda of security studies: Politics and methods. *Mershon International Studies Review*, *40*(2), 229–254. doi:10.2307/222776

Malone, G. D. (1985). Managing public diplomacy. *The Washington Quarterly*, *8*(3), 199–213. doi:10.1080/01636608509450301

Manor, I. (2021). When diplomats go MAD: How the crisis framing of ministries of foreign affairs results in mutually assured delegitimization. *Journal of Public Diplomacy*, *1*(2), 75–116.

Manor, I., & Bjola, C. (2021). Public diplomacy in the age of "post-reality. In P. Surowiec & I. Manor (Eds.), *Public diplomacy and the politics of uncertainty* (pp. 111–143). Palgrave Macmillan. doi:10.1007/978-3-030-54552-9_5

Marra, F. J. (1998). Crisis communication plans: Poor predictors of excellent crisis public relations. *Public Relations Review, 24*(4), 461–474. doi:10.1016/S0363-8111(99)80111-8

Melissen, J. (2005). *The new public diplomacy: soft power in international relations*. Palgrave Macmillan. doi:10.1057/9780230554931

Newman, E. (2004). The 'new wars' debate: A historical perspective is needed. *Security Dialogue, 35*(2), 173–189. doi:10.1177/0967010604044975

Pamment, J. (2016). *British public diplomacy and soft power: diplomatic influence and the digital revolution*. Palgrave. doi:10.1007/978-3-319-43240-3

Richardson, J. L. (1994). *Crisis diplomacy: the great powers since the mid-nineteenth century*. Cambridge University Press. doi:10.1017/CBO9780511559112

Sevin, E. (2017). Digital diplomacy as crisis communication: Turkish digital outreach after July 15. *Mexican Journal of Foreign Policy, 113*, 185–207.

Shirky, C., & Gladwell, M. (2011). From innovation to revolution: do social media make protests possible? *Foreign Affairs*. Retrieved June 15, 2022, from https://www.foreignaffairs.com/articles/2011-01-19/innovation-revolution

Snyder, G., & Diesing, P. (1977). *Conflict among nations: bargaining, decision-making and system structure in international crises*. Princeton University Press.

Suleiman, K. A. (2012). *The international crisis and the international system: a study on the interplay between the management of international strategic crises and the structure of the international system.* Arab Center for Research & Policy Studies (Research Paper). Retrieved June 15, 2022, from https://www.jstor.org/stable/resrep12667?seq=1

Surowiec, P., & Manor, I. (Eds.). (2021). *Public diplomacy and the politics of uncertainty*. Palgrave. doi:10.1007/978-3-030-54552-9

Vasquez, J. A. (2009). *The war puzzle revisited*. Cambridge University Press. doi:10.1017/CBO9780511627224

Walt, S. (1991). Renaissance of security studies. *International Studies Quarterly, 35*(2), 211–239. doi:10.2307/2600471

Westcott, N. (2008). Digital diplomacy: The impact of the internet on international relations. Oxford Internet Institute, Research Report.

Williams, P. (1976). *Crisis management: confrontation and diplomacy in the nuclear age*. John Wiley.

Williams, P. D. (Ed.). (2008). *Security studies: An introduction*. Routledge. doi:10.4324/9780203926604

KEY TERMS AND DEFINITIONS

Crisis Management: Resolving a dangerous conflict without the outbreak of war and at the same time protecting the vital interests of the parties involved.

Digital Diplomacy: The use of the Internet and new information communication technologies to help achieve diplomatic objectives.

Digitalization: The process of changing data into a digital form that can be easily read and processed by a computer.

Globalization: The fact that different cultures and economic systems around the world are becoming connected and similar to each other because of the influence of large multinational companies and of improved communication.

Public Diplomacy: It is a tool that states use to communicate and mobilize these resources not only towards other states but also towards people. It is tried to draw attention to these potential resources by publishing various publications, engaging in cultural interaction, organizing exchange programs, and so on.

Social Media: Websites and software programs used for social networking.

Chapter 3
Image and Popular Culture in Digital Public Diplomacy

Kadir Bendaş
https://orcid.org/0000-0003-3145-8703
Sivas Cumhuriyet University, Turkey

ABSTRACT

Virtually everything in the modern society we currently live in has become digitalized. The digitalization in communication technologies, especially in the last 30 years, has digitized the field of public diplomacy as in every field, and the concept of digital public diplomacy has emerged. Individuals and institutions are evaluated according to their image, and those with a good image are appreciated, admired, and followed. Those who do not have a good image fall into the opposite situation. For this reason, in digital public diplomacy, states are now pursuing to present their own images according to the conditions of the day. Today, with the rapidly developing new media tools, the value of image in the digital environment has increased, and public diplomacy has frequently used this field. At this level, public diplomacy nowadays utilizes opportunities in popular areas and converts the digital space into an image creation area. In this study, the image-building processes of public diplomacy in the digital field were examined.

INTRODUCTION AND BACKGROUND

Since the first periods when human beings started to live collectively, they have not been satisfied with what they have and have constantly wanted more. This situation arising from human nature has been a feature that affects social life as the urge to continually pursue more and more. The human being who desires more and more has created an order for himself in which he is in competition with other people and in which he is dependent on competition. In this order, there is no place to stand still, and people and institutions are constantly seeking to get ahead of their competitors. With the emergence of social life, attempts by state governments and societies to influence other states and societies in line with their own ideology and values have also begun. In the early days, this was done through wars, invasions and other military options, but over time it became clear that this could be done more effectively and with fewer or no casualties than wars.

DOI: 10.4018/978-1-6684-5822-8.ch003

People and societies have realized that they can influence other societies through diplomacy by talking and explaining themselves to them. In this context, societies have started to prioritize public diplomacy in the light of such an opportunity. Through public diplomacy, states have started to influence both their own domestic public opinion and different states and publics by spreading their own ideology and values. In this way, image is one of the main reasons for individuals and institutions that carry out diplomacy against different societies or their own society. Because in fact, trying to influence different societies can also be seen as an effort to create an image in their eyes. Since every effort to influence is fundamentally concerned with leaving an impression, this can also be considered as an image work.

Mass media is one of the most important elements of public diplomacy. What is important for public diplomacy is the dissemination of information to as many people as possible, and this is best accomplished by mass media such as radio and television. However, in recent years, rapid developments and innovations in communication technologies and increasing digitalization have affected public diplomacy as in every field. A new media environment in which public diplomacy can operate has emerged with digitalization. Developments in communication technologies and the ability to circulate information much more quickly have led to the emergence of a new media environment. With this digitalization, which has led to the formation of a global network society, and the spread of this digitalization all over the world has created networks that connect people and a new global media ecology that allows information to flow continuously within these networks (Budak, 2022: 321). In this new field, the flow of information cannot be restricted by time, space or national borders. These developments have obliged public diplomacy to undergo a digital transformation. Individual or public figures of public diplomacy have started to interact directly with other people within the multiple structure of the digital environment, and individuals or institutions have started to create their image through new digital channels. By doing this through popular culture, they have gained the power to influence the segments they can reach more easily. One of the extreme examples of the recent period is the former President of the United States of America Donald Trump, who not only introduced his image to the whole world by using popular culture through numerous posts on Twitter, a social media platform, but also conducted his public diplomacy through digital media by making numerous posts about different countries and politicians as an American President. As can be understood from this example, with digital public diplomacy, country leaders have started to share decisions about other countries and influence them in this way. In addition, they have also started to engage in image-building efforts by making use of popular culture.

PUBLIC DIPLOMACY AND IMAGE

Although public diplomacy is generally seen as a process in which a society tries to influence other societies in the international arena in line with its own political and ideological ideas, it is seen in the literature that public diplomacy is defined in different ways by different researchers. For example, according to Joseph Nye, one of the first researchers to use the concept of public diplomacy, public diplomacy is the ability of states to penetrate and influence other actors with instruments beyond their military instruments (Nye, 2005: 14). According to Gregory, public diplomacy has a broader definition. States use public diplomacy to understand the cultures, attitudes and behaviors of other states, non-state actors and state entities, to build and manage relationships, and to advance their interests and values by influencing opinions (Gregory, 2011: 353).

The basis of public diplomacy is a communication process based on influence. In this context, communication has been the most emphasized issue since the first time the concept of public diplomacy was used. From a global perspective, especially during the Cold War period when the world was divided into two different poles, it was easier to deliver messages with a defined framework to their recipients than in other periods. In this competitive environment, the most important tools used by both sides to deliver their messages were mass media such as television and radio, which could be easily monitored and kept under control. The aim of public diplomacy using these tools has been to produce and disseminate information as much as possible. Because information and its dissemination are of vital importance in public diplomacy. In this way, institutions or individuals try to strengthen their own image positively against their own societies and different societies by spreading information that is right for them. In this context, although the main purpose of public diplomacy is impact and communication, the most valid reason behind it is image. Public diplomacy, which disseminates information in an impressive way through mass media, actually creates its own image against the society.

POPULAR CULTURE AND MASS MEDIA

Particularly in the last 30 years, great developments and advances in the field of technology have directly affected people's lives and in this direction, there have been significant changes in people's daily lives. In this respect, mass media, which were not in people's lives before, have now become an integral part of individuals and society. Mass media, which people devote most of their days to, include television, radio, newspapers, magazines, cell phones, tablets and the internet. People receive most of their daily information from these mass media. In this context, mass media have a great influence in determining the economy, politics, sports, culture, attitudes and behaviors of people (Giddens, 2000: 388). The widespread use of mass media and the easy accessibility of these tools have caused people to be open to the influences of these tools and the information coming from these tools, especially on consumption and culture, has started to be effective in people's attitudes and behaviors. Knowing the effects of mass media on people's attitudes and behaviors, the dominant groups spread their own desires and ideologies, especially through popular culture, by using mass media used by millions of people every day in order to increase their influence on society and to direct people towards certain behaviors. In short, people are actually turned into a mass through popular culture.

Popular culture first emerged in the West with industrialization and modernization, the period when mass production began, and then spread to other regions en masse. Popular culture, which emerged as urban culture, has been accepted as the "culture of everyday life" because it makes people who work and get tired all day long forget their tiredness and have fun (Güllüoğlu, 2012: 65). The disseminator of this new order that emerged after industrialization has been the mass media, and today, the mass media are the most important tools that contribute to the formation of popular culture and spread it to society. Popular culture spread through mass media, including social and political events, is made to be perceived in a way other than its real value by the viewers who consume them. Under the influence of popular culture, people are transformed into mass people by entering a way of life according to the needs and realities spread as popular culture, rather than according to the reality and needs they need or adopt themselves. The tabloidization of events to make them interesting and the reconstruction of reality offers a kind of escape to people who are bored with the realities of daily life and are looking for an escape (Güllüoğlu, 2012: 65-66). According to Rowe (1996: 22), popular culture is a set of meanings and texts as well as changing social and cultural relations. According to this definition, the popularization of culture predicts that another culture replaces the existing culture.

John Fiske (1999) states that the factors that create popular culture are basically built on the economy. According to him, cultural products that reveal popular culture operate simultaneously through both financial and cultural economy. According to this definition, while financial economy is about exchange values, cultural economy is focused on meanings, uses such as pleasure and social identity. Since these two seemingly separate economies are interconnected, there is a constant communication between them. In this way, the dominant powers that spread the mass culture try to distract the majority of the people, who make up the majority of the society, from their real problems and injustices by dragging them into empty dreams. There is no need for people with a high level of appreciation for the formation of popular culture. Because this culture appeals to a very low level of appreciation. In this direction, this situation causes the intellectual abilities and aesthetic understanding of the majority of the people to not develop (Güngör, 2011: 243). The provider of the functioning in this process is the mass media that make up the media such as newspapers, magazines, TV channels, social media tools, cinema.

IMAGE AND MASS MEDIA

In today's world, where communication technologies are rapidly developing and people can talk almost face to face thanks to technological devices regardless of time and space, the characteristics and values that people have gain great importance. In this context, people and organizations that want to put themselves at the forefront of society take steps in this direction. This starts with their own image. In the age of communication we live in, one of the most common concepts we encounter in daily life is image. The concept of image comes from the Latin word "imago", i.e. picture, and from an epistemological point of view, it refers to a cognitive and psychological image developed in the human mind about a person, institution, product or event etc. (Dinçer, 1998: 7). According to another definition, image is defined as "a manufacturing or public impression created to appeal to the target audience instead of representing reality" (Mutlu, 1998: 184). Based on the definitions, it would not be wrong to say in general terms that image is the picture that a person or organization portrays in other people's minds.

Image can also be seen as an accurate reflection of people's knowledge, skills and abilities, but image is also seen as manipulation, fraud and a skillful make-up on appearances (Türkkahraman, 2004: 5). According to Robins, images that can guide and seduce people in terms of influence can also arouse suspicion (Robins, 1999: 28). According to Bennett, image is a product shaped by the suggestive symbolism of political messages (Bennett, 2020: 165). From this point of view, it can be said that image serves a purpose such as hiding the truth or making what does not exist appear to exist.

In today's globalized world and information-intensive environment, the importance of the concept of image is increasing day by day. The reason for this is that people have become more conscious about image as in every subject. People are becoming more knowledgeable about what image can change and what it can express. In today's competitive environment, individuals and organizations no longer have the luxury of missing opportunities that come their way. Because every missed opportunity causes a step back in the competition, which can lead to image loss and cause the person or organization to deviate from its goals. From this perspective, a well-managed image can attract opportunities like a magnet, while a poorly managed image can repel opportunities like a magnet (Baykasoğlu et al., 2004: 4). Today, image finds a production area in every aspect of life. Social events, concerts, festivals or rallies held in public spaces are turned into image production areas. Apart from this, the most effective medium for image creation is the mass media. Through mass media, millions of people can be reached at the same time and the desired image can be marketed. Lifestyles that are deemed worthy of being demonstrated through mass media and that can be watched by a large segment of the society are ready to be imitated and taken into consideration (Bauman, 1999: 43). In other words, people are influenced by what they see in mass media. This situation increases the chances of success of the image created and disseminated.

Nowadays, mass media plays the most important role in image creation and the development and dissemination of the created image. The media, which is seen as the fourth estate and even increases this power in some periods, has a vital importance in terms of both personal and corporate image today. Because in the age of communication we live in, what individuals or institutions do or fail to do is followed and evaluated by the vast majority of the public through communication tools (Türkkahraman, 2004: 8). In this respect, it is seen that mass media is a very important factor in the perception of the images created by individuals or institutions in a positive or negative way by the society. Since society often receives information from the mass media in a one-sided manner, it generally accepts the one-sided information it receives and even information that has been reconstructed and filtered by the media is perceived as true by the society.

The mass media often present news and information not as it is, but after passing it through certain filters. These filters, which are related to political economy concerns, cause the information to be reproduced and detached from its real context. This is usually due to the ownership structure of the mass media. However, mass media also have the function of making information that has no meaning on its own meaningful and understandable (Hall, 1999: 100). This situation stems from the informative feature of mass media. At this level, Baker also draws attention to both informing and shaping features of mass media. In other words, he states that mass media, like schools and teachers, both inform and shape (Baker, 2006: 101). Baker also draws attention to the fact that due to the functional position of the mass media, that is, the power they possess, the position between them and the governments is important and decisive.

DIGITAL PUBLIC DIPLOMACY

In an era of intensive communication, where we cannot go out without a mobile phone or internet connection, the media has begun to determine not only what the society will think about, but also how and in what way it will think, and what kind of attitude and behavior it will exhibit in the face of what it watches. When viewed in this way, "the media brings certain political issues or problems to the agenda, selects a certain political issue or problem among others, brings it to the forefront or prioritizes it on the media agenda; talks, presents and discusses political events, facts, issues and problems through the audience" (Çalışır, 2014: 229). When we add multimedia tools such as Youtube, Facebook, Twitter, Instagram, which have emerged especially in the last 20 years to these features of the media that we can call traditional, it can be said that the audience has started to take a more critical approach against the one-sided broadcasting approach of the media. Because in today's digitalized world, events and information that are not covered and shown in the mainstream media can be shared and circulated among millions of people with a single click.

Rapid developments in digital technologies, especially in recent years, have brought social/public structures, lifestyles and communication processes between individuals to a different point. Social structures and social communication networks established through digital communication networks have created new elements in terms of creating a common public opinion and sharing this common opinion. Especially with the digitalization of mass communication structures in accordance with the process and the opportunity to create a personalized communication structure through internet addresses such as Facebook, Twitter, Youtube, which are called social networking sites, people have the opportunity to influence other individuals who make up the society with the ideas they share here, to convey their ideas to them, and to discuss these ideas they convey. Digital technologies and digital platforms, which have developed rapidly especially in recent years, have not only changed the speed and form of information dissemination, but have also brought social discussion areas to the digital environment. Political communication methods have also been one of the biggest areas affected by these new digital technologies and platforms (Ceyhan, 2020: 86).

The developments in information technologies and their rapid incorporation into our lives have led to a transformation in most political, economic and military relations, including the methods and structures of international relations. Although the old understanding of power and order has been maintained, new ones have been added to them. Information and digital technical skills are now included among the old power and order. From this perspective, digital communication skills are now seen as an element of power that can provide more advantages.

With the increase in digitalization, concepts such as digital diplomacy, diplomacy 2.0, digital public diplomacy and e-diplomacy have become frequently used concepts in the field of international relations. In parallel with the transformation of the social structure in this new order, individuals have also become actors in international relations and the understanding of international relations has become more complex and more participatory (Gürdal, 2021: 419). Developments in communication technologies and the increase in digitalization have led to changes in public diplomacy as everywhere else. With digitalization, leaders, states, politicians and institutions that want to protect their image in public diplomacy have sought the fastest way to benefit from digital opportunities. With digitalization, global virtual embassies have started to be established, the peoples of countries have gained the opportunity to interact with the peoples of other countries and limitations have begun to disappear. In this respect, digitalization has created an environment in which a large number of actors compete in social media in order to attract the public's attention and support, and has also led to the formation of an online public opinion that wants to listen to and adopt its own views (Yücel, 2016: 759). The public sphere, which is a communication area where all ideas and thoughts within the society can be discussed and the results of this discussion environment target the political power or political institutions in the decision-making position, can also determine the structure of the global society with the interests and interests of the general society in line with today's global structure (Ceyhan, 2020: 93). It is useful to look at the concept of public diplomacy within the framework of the elements mentioned above. The primary goal of public diplomacy is to increase political effectiveness and gain influence, and to use the gained influence for its own purposes. However, in order to remain in power, a political power or institution must not only increase its international influence but also gain the support and consent of domestic public opinion. As a result of these obligations, in addition to gaining the trust of other peoples, which constitutes the primary goal of public diplomacy, it also has to gain the trust of people within the national structure (Ceyhan, 2020: 94). Today, as communication has become extremely fast, comprehensive and widespread with digitalization, it has become possible for international actors to ensure that different public opinion groups have a certain mindset by making use of digital communication tools and opportunities. To put it differently, a young field has emerged where public diplomacy, which includes the soft power policies implemented by each state towards foreign public opinion outside its own public opinion, can be carried out through digital platforms and tools (Gürdal, 2021: 419).

In the 21st century, both technological and social innovations have caused traditional public diplomacy to undergo a number of changes and this has enabled traditional public diplomacy to adapt to the conditions of the day. These new developments and digitalized public diplomacy are shaped on the ideal of building relationships. In this new digital era, efforts to establish cooperation and dialogue have come to the fore in accordance with the structure of digitalization. This situation appears as an order applied with a large number of actors in many channels. In this structuring, the role of non-state actors and cultural elements is especially important. Digital public diplomacy utilizes almost all communication technologies. It is not only limited to digital technologies or social networks, but also continues to utilize traditional means of communication. At this level, the advanced mass media of the 21st century are used intensively (Ceyhan, 2000: 95).

As the name suggests, digital public diplomacy makes effective use of digital communication technologies of the digital era. The use of digital technologies in digital public diplomacy is not limited to the internet and social media, and strategies are developed by blending internet and social media structures with traditional media elements. Therefore, it acts in an interconnected and horizontal operational structure. In order to ensure cooperation, a message exchange is at the forefront for this cooperation. In this respect, mutual understanding, dialog and policy making through these come to the fore (Ceyhan, 2020: 97).

Today, almost every aspect of life is now digitized. Transactions that people used to perform in government institutions by waiting in line for hours in the past can now be performed by the person himself/herself within seconds in the digital environment. The majority of the active population on earth now has access to the internet and this active population is a user of digital technologies. This situation has also made it necessary for states to make differences. For example, with digitalization, the state can no longer act in a single-centered management approach. The fact that even the borders, which the state holds as an element of power, have become more transient in some places and free in some places shows that rules and norms need to be stretched or eliminated when necessary. In digital public diplomacy, institutions such as the Ministry of Foreign Affairs, which are important in traditional public diplomacy, are still important. However, these political institutions are not the primary actors in digital public diplomacy as they used to be. It can be said that both the internal structure of the state and the actors outside the state in the international arena are in cooperation. More than one state, sub-state or supra-state institutions and civil society act together by creating an understanding of cooperation. In this new structure, creating intercultural relations and adopting multicultural structures are at the forefront.

Digital public diplomacy is a strategic communication process. The aim is to persuade the masses with their own consent. In this context, it is important that information is important in the process of establishing dialogue and that it can be used effectively at the most appropriate time. Therefore, it is important to obtain data. Data should also be based on facts. Because digital public diplomacy is based on transparent, open and real information, not processes such as lies, misinformation and slanders based on false information (Rugh, 2014: 77-78).

In digital public diplomacy, the metanarrative format used in traditional diplomacy has been transformed into a multiple narrative format and designed to include the society within the idea of how it can include the individual the most. These designed multiple narrative elements are circulated with traditional media tools and digital communication technologies within the logic of maximization (Ceyhan, 2020: 98). The purpose of doing so is to ensure that partner institutions, independent actors and public actors are part of domestic and foreign policy. In addition, the shaping of political behavior according to the political agenda is also ensured by this structure.

CONLUSION AND RECOMMENDATIONS

Communication is one of the most determining elements of social life. Human beings have been in communication with each other from the first moment of their existence and have ensured the continuation of their existence by living collectively. This has also been one of the most important features of survival. In the following processes, the growth and development of different societies and the formation of states also started competition between people and societies, and societies have now entered into a struggle to get ahead of each other. At first, these struggles were fought with knives, swords and wars in general. However, with the impact of the developments in communication technologies in the historical process, people and societies have discovered that there are many different ways to influence and dominate each other. With this situation, which gained importance especially after the industrial revolution, societies have gained the opportunity to influence different societies through diplomacy and to present themselves to them in certain image frames. Through diplomacy, the public sector has not only had the chance to show its own image to the public opinion of different societies in the way it has shaped itself, but also to have mass media, which is one of the most important elements to realize this. While public diplomacy could only be carried out in certain areas and among certain people without mass media, after mass media became a part of social life, it has become one of the most important tools through which public diplomacy can convey information both to its own public and to the public opinion of different states.

Public diplomacy, which has continued in this way until today, has undergone a transformation, especially with the digitalization of communication technologies in the last 30 years. Digital transformation has caused transformations in the field of public diplomacy as in all fields. In this context, digitalized public diplomacy has started to use digital opportunities along with classical methods. In this direction, by using popular culture, it has started to present its image as a personal or institution in the digital environment.

In this study, the processes of creating an image with the help of popular culture and mass media in digital public diplomacy are examined in general terms. In this direction, first of all, public diplomacy and the process of image building in public diplomacy were examined. In the examination, it was understood that one of the main supporting elements behind public diplomacy, which is based on influencing different publics, is the effort to create an image. Afterwards, the place of mass media in social life and the relationship between popular culture and mass media were examined and it was understood that popular culture is a consumption culture that spreads rapidly to all segments of society through mass media. In the continuation of the study, the way the image is presented to the society through mass media is analyzed. Finally, it was examined how public diplomacy has undergone a digital transformation in the digitalized world as a result of developing communication technologies, and it was seen that digital public diplomacy has now transformed the metanarrative form of digital public diplomacy into a multiple narrative form and has entered into the idea of how to include the individual the most.

In digital diplomacy, the monotonous structure of the past, which was only used to convey messages, has been replaced by a space that is more intertwined with individuals and interacts with them on social media platforms such as Facebook, Twitter and Instagram. The fact that there is mutual interaction in this digital environment has made it somewhat difficult to create an image in these channels. However, in digital public diplomacy, this path has been made easily overcome by using popular culture that appeals to the majority of the public.

REFERENCES

Baker, C. (2006). *Zorunlu Eğitime Hayır* (A. G. Sönmezoğlu, Trans.). Ayrıntı Publishing.

Bauman, Z. (1999). *Sosyolojik Düşünmek* (A. Yılmaz, Trans.). Ayrıntı Publishing.

Baykasoğlu, A., Dereli, T., Sönmez, A. İ., & Yağcı, E. (2004). İmaj Yönetimi. *Journal of the Social Sciences*, *1*(1), 3–18.

Bennett, W. L. (2000). *Politik İlüzyon ve Medya* (S. Say, Trans.). Nehir Publishing.

Çalışır, G. (2014). *Siyaset ve İletişim Bağlamında Kitle İletişim Araçları Üzerine Bir Değerlendirme* (M. Tosun & N. Yılmaz, Eds.). Değişim Publishing.

Ceyhan, A. İ. (2020). Dijitalleşen Kamu Diplomasisi Üzerine Kısa Bir Analiz. *International Journal of Economics Administrative and Social Sciences*, *3*(2), 85–100.

Dinçer, M. K. (1998). *Kişisel İmaj*. Alfa Publishing.

Fiske, J. (1999). Popüler Kültürü Anlamak. Ark Publishing.

Giddens, A. (2000). *Sosyoloji*. Ayraç Publishing.

Gregory, B. (2011). American Public Diplomacy: Enduring Characteristics. Elusive Transformation. *The Hauge of Diplomacy*, *6*(3-4), 351–372. doi:10.1163/187119111X583941

Güllüoğlu, Ö. (2021). Bir Kitle İletişim Aracı Olarak Televizyonun Popüler Kültür Ürünlerini Benimsetme ve Yayma İşlevi Üzerine Bir Değerlendirme. *Global Media Journal*, *2*(4), 64–86.

Gürdal, E. (2021). Dijital Kamu Diplomasisi mi Dijital Gözetim mi? *Mecmua Uluslararası Sosyal Bilimler Dergisi*, *6*(11), 417–434.

Hall, S. (1999). "Kültür, Medya ve İdeolojik Etki" Medya, İktidar, İdeoloji (M. Küçük, Comp. and Trans.). Ark Publishing.

Nye, J. S. (2005). *Yumuşak Güç: Dünya Siyasetinde Başarının Yolu*. Elips Publishing.

Robins, K. (1999). *İmaj* (N. Türkoğlu, Trans.). Ayrıntı Publishing.

Rowe, D. (1996). *Popüler Kültürler Rock ve Sporda Haz Politikası* (M. Küçük, Trans.). Ayrıntı Publishing.

Rugh, W. A. (2014). *Front Line Public Diplomacy: How Us Embassies Communicate with Foreign Publics*. Palgrave MacMillan. doi:10.1057/9781137444158

Türkkahraman, D. D. M. (2011). Günümüzün Büyüsü İmaj Ve Gerçek Hayat. *Istanbul Journal of Sociological Studies*, *0*(30), 1–14.

Yücel, G. (2016). Dijital Diplomasi. *TRT Akademi*, *1*(2), 747–760.

KEY TERMS AND DEFINITIONS

Digital Image: Image of the individual in the virtual environment.

Digital Public Diplomacy: Digital public diplomacy, also referred to as Digiplomacy and eDiplomacy, has been defined as the use of the Internet and new information communication technologies to help achieve diplomatic objectives.

Image: The general impression that a person, organization, or product presents to the public.

Mass Media: Mass media refers to a diverse array of media technologies that reach a large audience via mass communication. The technologies through which this communication takes place include a variety of outlets.

Popular Culture: Popular culture is generally recognized by members of a society as a set of the practices, beliefs, and objects that are dominant or prevalent in a society at a given point in time. Popular culture also encompasses the activities and feelings produced as a result of interaction with these dominant objects.

Chapter 4
Public Diplomacy as a Tool of Propaganda

Fatih Değirmenci
Ataturk University, Turkey

ABSTRACT

Propaganda, which aims to influence the society to believe and act in a certain way in line with predetermined objectives, has been a form of practice that has been used extensively in the social and political field throughout history. Many ideologies have gained prevalence as a result of effective propaganda activities and have been able to walk to power. From Caesar to Napoleon, from Lenin to Hitler, many leaders went down in history as master propagandists, and they dragged the masses after them with their powerful and effective propaganda. Certain aspects of propaganda practices, which have been the most effective way to influence societies in long historical processes, have been a source of inspiration in many areas such as public diplomacy, political campaigns, advertising, public relations, and marketing in modern times.

INTRODUCTION

It would not be wrong to say that the history of the efforts made to influence and determine the thoughts of people and to shape them in the desired direction by guiding their movements in this way is as old as the history of humanity. Efforts in this direction have changed over time in parallel with the development of language and writing, and have gained new dimensions with the development of communication techniques and technologies. The activities based on motivation, manipulation and persuasion, which have been implemented with the aim of mass directing the society and channeling it towards the determined direction, have revealed the whole activity called propaganda.

Propaganda, which aims to influence the society to believe and act in a certain way in line with predetermined objectives, has been a form of practice that has been used extensively in the social and political field throughout history. Many ideologies have gained prevalence as a result of effective propaganda activities and have been able to walk to power. From Caesar to Napoleon, from Lenin to Hitler, many

DOI: 10.4018/978-1-6684-5822-8.ch004

leaders went down in history as master propagandists, and they dragged the masses after them with their powerful and effective propaganda.

The power of propaganda to influence the masses and to direct them to the desired thought and action has become possible with various methods and techniques applied within this scope. These methods and techniques, the majority of which are based on mass psychology, can also include unethical practices such as exaggeration, lies, and distortions when necessary. In order for the propaganda to have the expected effect on society, all kinds of tools could be used within the conditions and possibilities of the period. All kinds of communication media and media can be mobilized for propaganda, from an effective language and oratory to written and printed means, from audio and visual communication tools to new communication technologies.

Certain aspects of propaganda practices, which have been the most effective way to influence societies in long historical processes, have been a source of inspiration in many areas such as public diplomacy, political campaigns, advertising, public relations and marketing in modern times.

Public Diplomacy as a Concept

International relations, which is one of the results of interstate interaction, tries to resolve interstate conflicts and disputes with different methods, and this is achieved through diplomacy, which has become increasingly important after the Cold War period. The decrease in the threats of war and the increase in the effectiveness of international law at the global level also highlight some foreign policy activities among states. Many different concepts are used to express these foreign policy activities of states today. Public diplomacy, which is described as propaganda and new diplomacy, which has been frequently used in the last century, are some of these concepts. A state's expectation from the international system is its foreign policy goals; The tools and methods used to achieve these goals also mean diplomacy (Sander, 2008: 13). Therefore, the main purpose of diplomacy is to solve the problems that arise in foreign policy issues through peaceful methods and negotiations (Giddens, 1985: 116). With the developments in the communication age, it has started to be seen that traditional diplomacy is insufficient in influencing foreign public opinion in the international arena, and the orientation to public diplomacy, which is now called new diplomacy, has been realized. Public diplomacy, with its current meaning, was used for the first time in 1965 by Edmund Gullion, Dean of the Fletcher School of Law and Diplomacy at Tufts University in the USA (Cull, 2009: 19).

Public diplomacy, which is called conveying the national interests and policy of a country to the foreign public through soft power elements such as culture, art, education and sports (Tuch, 1990: 3), beyond the classical diplomacy of governments against other governments, the activities of influencing the public opinion of the countries include the interaction of foreign students, academia, media representatives, businessmen and NGOs (Cull, 2006). While classical diplomacy is the execution of interstate relations by government representatives, public diplomacy includes a country's policy of communicating with citizens of other countries (Fisher, 2011: 273) and aims to explain a nation's thoughts, goals, ideals, current policies, institutions and culture to foreign public opinion. Kalin (2011:11) states that public diplomacy is carried out in two main frameworks, from state to public and public to public. According to him, activities from state to public, state policies through official means; public-to-public activities are conveyed to the target public via NGOs, research centers, opinion leaders, media, universities, associations and foundations. Public diplomacy activities are examined in three categories as informing, influencing and including (Kelley, 2009: 73). In the information phase, information management and dissemination are involved for short-term activities, while in the influencing phase, long-term campaigns aiming to change the attitude towards the target public are seen. In the category of inclusion, there are objectives such as building relations between organizations in the international arena and developing long-term trust and mutual understanding (Parmar, 2007: 249). Stating that there are four basic concepts explaining public diplomacy, Gregory (2011:355) lists these as understanding, planning, connection and advocacy. According to him, experts and practitioners may have different approaches to the meaning and use of each. Understanding is that public diplomacy actors know their own cultural, political and communicative templates and their differences from other cultures. Planning is an effort to guide leaders in policy setting and implementation, develop strategies, offer strategic direction, coordinate public diplomacy actors, and orchestrate change. Connection, on the other hand, includes the dialogue that emerges in the process of communicating with the target audience, being open to the ideas of others, and learning activities by asking questions. On the other hand, advocacy refers to an effort to attract attention, gain trust, and try to persuade for someone's benefit through certain activities, speeches, and images that appeal to the mind and emotions (Gregory, 2011: 357). Public diplomacy activities are carried out through tools such as printed publications, traditional and new media and cultural interaction (Gienow-Hecht & Donfried, 2013:14).

Propaganda as a Concept

In order to fully understand the concept of propaganda, it will be useful to look at the origin of the concept first. The term propaganda, which is of Latin origin, is a concept derived from the word 'propagare'. The Latin equivalent of the word propagare means planting the plant shoots in the ground and making them grow and producing new shoots. As the origin of the word propaganda shows, the concept evokes meanings such as the establishment, strengthening and dissemination of new ideas in society.

It is extremely difficult to give a single and inclusive definition of the concept of propaganda. Because this concept has been dealt with and put into practice at different levels and dimensions throughout history, both in theory and in practice. The concept of propaganda, which is the subject of many scientific disciplines from sociology to communication, from psychology to political science, has been defined many times by these disciplines and different approaches, in a way that emphasizes different dimensions. As each definition illuminates a different dimension of propaganda, the main ones of these definitions will be cited and explanations will be made about them.

H. Lasswell was one of the first researchers to examine the issue of propaganda in a scientific sense with its modern dimensions. Lasswell's work in which he analyzes the propaganda issue in detail is his work called 'Propaganda Technique in the World War' published in 1927. In this study, Lasswell stated that propaganda means the control of thoughts through various symbols or other forms of social communication. Lasswell, in his later studies on the subject of propaganda, defined this concept as a technique of influencing human action by directing presentations (oral, written, visual, auditory) (Bektaş, 2002). Jean-Marie Domenach, another researcher known for her work on propaganda, defined this concept as "an attempt to influence people to adopt a certain view or a certain behavior in order to change the view and behavior of society" (Domenach, 1995). In this statement of Domenach, it is emphasized that the masses are tried to be mobilized in a direction that they do not really like or know exactly, by being hypnotized and put to sleep, leaving them to lose their power of understanding and evaluation in a fully conditioned way. These definitions emphasize that propaganda, in the most general sense, influences the views and opinions of individuals and society on a certain issue and shapes them in the direction they aim.

As stated above, the subject of propaganda falls within the scope of many fields such as sociology, politics, psychology and communication. One of the definitions highlighting the psychological dimension of the concept was made by J. Ellul. The concept of propaganda has been defined by Ellul as "the whole of the methods used to enable a psychologically integrated and organized mass to act in a desired way, either actively or passively, by using psychological tools" (Barlas, 1975). Although Ellul has made this definition, he reveals that because of the widespread practice of propaganda, it may become almost impossible for people to understand what is propaganda and what is not, after a point, and that propaganda keeps the social structure, lifestyle and people as a whole under control. This statement; It reveals that propaganda in political, economic and cultural sense penetrates into the social structure and can be found in a structure that is very difficult to notice by affecting many areas in human life. The blurring of its borders in this way brings with it many discussions such as whether every act of persuasion is propaganda, where does propaganda begin and where it ends.

Another definition that emphasizes the psychological aspect of propaganda is by L. W. Doob. Doob defines propaganda as "an attempt at a particular time in a society to influence personalities and to control the behavior of individuals for purposes that are considered unscientific or questionable" and he described the efforts within this scope as the systematic activities of the relevant person (or persons) to control the attitudes of their groups and ultimately the movements of these groups by means of suggestion (Bektaş, 2002).

The statement made by T. H. Qualter can be shown as an example of its comprehensive definitions, which also emphasizes the communicative aspect of propaganda. According to Qualter, propaganda is to determine and shape the attitudes of an individual or group of other individuals or groups, and to control them. It can be defined as a conscious activity undertaken by these individuals or groups, using the means of communication to change, and hoping that their response in a particular situation or situation will be in accordance with their own ends (Qualter, 1980).

When the phenomenon of propaganda is evaluated in a communicative sense, it can be stated that this concept has a direct link with communication, in that it contains communicative actions such as giving information and persuading. Although propaganda uses many techniques of communication, it basically relies on a one-way message transmission from the source to the target audience, whose goals and results are predetermined. In this way, it is a matter of instilling the selected messages in propaganda activities rather than adopting them. In this process, at the point of determining the message, rather than designing the message that will attract the attention of the target audience, it is essential to transmit the messages selected and prepared for the predetermined targets. While all these processes are being carried out, many unethical methods such as exaggeration, concealment, distortion, lies and similar methods may be used to realize the ideological purpose determined to increase efficiency.

Features and Distinguishing Characteristics of Propaganda

It is possible to determine the main features and distinctive aspects of this concept, based on the definitions made about propaganda.

The first striking feature of the activities described as propaganda is the conscious and purposeful implementation of these initiatives. In order for any action or initiative to be considered as propaganda, actions that will affect the thoughts, attitudes and behaviors of the community must be consciously and purposefully formed. In propaganda activities, the purpose is determined before the activity, and this purpose is shaped entirely within the framework determined by the propagandist.

Propaganda activities, like all other professional influence efforts, are carried out in accordance with a systematically designed planning. In order to mobilize the society, which is the main target of propaganda activities, in the desired direction, the activities to be carried out in this direction must be carefully planned in a predetermined order. Success in propaganda activities largely depends on acting in line with the plan determined at the beginning. In the said plan, propaganda activities are determined and put into practice from the beginning to the end. Some elements need to be included in the propaganda plan. These are; The purpose of propaganda, the timing of propaganda, the stages of propaganda, the message and slogans to be conveyed and the mass media to be used can be listed as.

Propaganda activity is carried out systematically in line with the plan that includes the above-mentioned elements, and preparations are always made for unexpected situations.

By nature, propaganda activities target large groups rather than individuals. In other words, individuals are not narrowly considered as the target audience in propaganda activities, and the general or the majority of society is seen as the addressee of propaganda activities. The reason for addressing the widest possible audience is that the propaganda activities have a political aim to a large extent. It is thought that it will be possible to achieve the political aim determined at the beginning by directing the widest possible segments of the society in the determined direction in propaganda activities.

Propaganda activities are centrally coordinated from a single source during the implementation phase, just as they are in the planning phase. The fact that all activities are managed from a single center is due to the non-debatable nature of propaganda. In other words, in propaganda activities, there is no mutual interaction with the society at any level. Instead, there is a direct transmission of messages whose accuracy is in no way considered indisputable. This feature of propaganda is also an indication that it does not include any level of discussion. There are fixed truths in propaganda and all activities are directed and managed by a narrow staff who firmly believes in them.

As a natural consequence of the above-mentioned features of propaganda, it can also be mentioned that it is sustained in a one-way communication axis. The main reason for adopting such an understanding of communication is the fact that propaganda is a form of activity largely practiced by totalitarian systems throughout the history. These administrations, which are based on monopoly and absolute obedience in the political sense, inevitably present a structure that is closed to dialogue and interaction. Therefore, it is not possible to establish mutual and two-way communication with the society in propaganda activities, which is one of the main instruments of such understandings. Messages prepared from the center within the scope of propaganda activities are only transmitted and a number of methods and techniques, which will be mentioned below, are used to increase the effectiveness of these messages. Feedback, which means the reaction of the target audience to the message sent, is not seen as a determining factor for the propagandist in directing his activities.

Mass media are used extensively in propaganda activities in order to carry out the above-mentioned communication activities. Since propaganda activities are designed for the masses, communication tools are preferred to reach the maximum number of people possible. Radio, television, open-air meetings, written and printed materials are used effectively in propaganda activities according to the conditions of the period in which they are applied.

Development of Propaganda in the Historical Process

It would not be wrong to state that the history of propaganda is parallel to the history of mankind. Since the earliest periods of history, people's need to establish social orders has emerged, and within this framework, organized systems and structures have begun to be formed. The most prominent aspect of the mentioned structures and systems was the establishment of mechanisms based on the distinction between the ruler and the ruled. At this point, those who have been in a position or aim to manage the society since the earliest ages of history have engaged in a number of efforts and activities to ensure that the people adhere to themselves, the orders they have established or certain goals. All of the practices carried out in this direction can be considered as propaganda in essence.

Since the earliest periods of history, administrators or those who want to direct the society have made various attempts in order to shape the thoughts, feelings and beliefs of the masses in the direction they want. Since the earliest times, the rulers have been in an intense effort to demonstrate their power and magnificence and thus to consolidate their legitimacy by establishing their dominance over the subjects. For example, the monumental architectural works that they have built as symbols of their power can be considered as a sign of power by the rulers towards friendly and enemy communities. The magnificent palaces, statues, monuments and similar works that were built without any expense were intended to be shown as symbols of power and therefore government. In addition to this, managers generally adopted a style and style emphasizing their differences from others (managed) in terms of their lifestyles. The effort to be different from the public in almost every area that can come to mind, from their clothing to eating and drinking, from their education to their aesthetic understanding, has been a general characteristic of the ruling groups. All this pomp and differentiation effort can be considered as propaganda mechanisms implying that they are not ordinary but are 'superior' and capable of governing. However, heroic stories, legends, mythologies, and various teachings, examples of which have been seen since the earliest periods of history, can also be seen as propaganda elements that shape the people, strengthen the social structure and riveting loyalty to the order.

It is known that powerful rulers throughout history were also strong orators. Encouraging the people and the military with effective speeches in times of war, and keeping the faith and support of the masses alive with strong speeches in times of victory and peace have been seen as one of the most important skills that rulers should have throughout history. The fact that the rulers would not be able to maintain their power only by brute force caused them to feel the need to clinch their dominance over the masses by using the aforementioned methods and techniques. The fact that the maintenance of power requires the element of 'consent' as well as the element of 'power' has made the attempts of systematic influence, in other words, propaganda, an inevitable necessity throughout history, in order to make the domination of rulers over the people permanent.

Propaganda activities, which have been used in the strengthening and spread of civilizations and in channeling the people for certain purposes since ancient times, have had an effective effect in the religious field as well. Missionary activities, which started from the first periods of Christianity, gained momentum especially in the Middle Ages, and it was seen that different practices that could be evaluated within the scope of religious propaganda were made within the scope of the Crusades and later, Protestantism and similar new faith forms.

In the social structure of the Middle Ages, 'reality' remained largely within the framework of what the current authorities imposed. Undoubtedly, propaganda is one of the most important tools used by the ruling class to establish its authority. All kinds of thoughts that were incompatible with the interests of the class in question were met with the reaction of the state power and the church and were exposed to censorship to a large extent. In this sense, censorship has been an important tool that has been used in propaganda activities throughout history.

In the middle of the 15th century, the use of the printing press in Europe was the trigger for revolutionary developments. With the intensive use of the printing press, different ideas and information began to spread rapidly to large segments of society, and as a result, it became easier for new opinions and ideologies to become widespread. In this way, established beliefs and ideologies became questionable, and the Renaissance and Reform movements gained momentum. In this process, new forms of belief, such as Protestantism, had the opportunity to find a response in large segments of the society, thanks to an effective propaganda activity, especially by using the means of printing and publication.

The fact that the concept of propaganda came to the fore for the first time is a development that has been experienced as a result of religious persuasion efforts. Reform movements that started to gain strength in Europe since the 16th century, and the Catholic Church took a series of measures and activities in order to stand up to this new trend, which it found dangerous, during the formation and expansion of the Protestant sect. One of these initiatives was to establish an organization in order to defend, protect and spread Catholicism against the Reform movements and Protestantism. The name of this organization, which was founded in 1622, was determined as 'Congregatio De Propaganda Fide' (Organization for the Propagation of Faith), and thus the word 'propaganda' came into general use for the first time. The term 'propaganda', which was used in the sense of spreading a religious belief in its first use, has gained a wider content over time and has become a concept used in political, social and similar fields in the sense of spreading any thought or ideology.

The French Revolution, which took place in 1789, was a decisive turning point in the use of propaganda in the political field and gaining a modern appearance over time, while it was a form of activity used by the Church for religious purposes. Intense propaganda activities were carried out before and after the revolution led by the bourgeois class, in the dissemination of principles such as 'justice', 'freedom' and 'fraternity' and in making the Liberal ideology adopted. Since this period, both the printing press and the developments in transportation and communication techniques had a great impact on the intensification of propaganda activities and gaining a modern look.

Along with the industrialization that accelerated in the approaching 20th century, new techniques and technologies in the field of communication began to become widespread, as well as the diversification of political ideologies and increasing their effectiveness, and a rapid increase and intensity in propaganda activities began to be experienced.

During the 20th century, propaganda has become an indispensable form of practice for different ideologies and especially states. Particularly in the great wars, propaganda has been used as an effective weapon. During the First World War, almost every state engaged in propaganda activities on the widest possible scale, and carried out effective propaganda activities to influence both their own public opinion and the public opinion in enemy countries. The states, which tried to convince the public opinion of their own countries that their entry into the war was legitimate and justified, also carried out intensive propaganda work to influence the international public opinion on how unfair, murderous and unsuccessful their enemies were. In this way, the states, which tried to ensure that the peoples of their own countries would support them until the end in this struggle, on the other hand, carried out propaganda activities aimed at breaking the morale and motivation of the peoples and soldiers of the enemy countries and thus ensuring that they were defeated. In this way, propaganda wars were carried on with great intensity as much as the hot conflicts on the front. In this context, a fierce propaganda struggle was undertaken to the extent possible, from posters to motion pictures, from radio speeches to warplanes to flyers thrown at soldiers and the public.

Realizing how effective propaganda activities were in manipulating public opinion during the First World War, the states accelerated their efforts in this direction in the following periods. In the following years, they started to establish official institutions and organizations such as intelligence services, press offices and even the Ministry of Propaganda in order to handle the issue in a more professional way.

It is noteworthy that in the period between the First World War and the Second World War, propaganda activities were highly intensified, developed, and given a corporate and professional appearance. In the mentioned period, with the October Revolution (Bolshevik Revolution) that took place in 1917, the tsarist administration, which had been ruling in Russia for centuries, was overthrown by the socialist forces led by Vladimir Ilyich Lenin and a socialist administration was established in its place. The Union of Soviet Socialist Republics (USSR), which was founded afterwards, has been one of the important actors in world history until its dissolution in 1991. In the process leading up to the formation of the Soviet Union, propaganda undoubtedly has an important place in the way a socialist ideology can gain power through a revolution in a geography where a traditional management approach, like Russia, is dominant. Lenin gave great importance to propaganda in order to reach the level of revolution by adopting socialist and communist ideology to large sections of the people and to ensure its continuity with a solid institutionalization after establishing the state. In this model, which is one of the most important propaganda examples of the 20th century and can be described as Lenin-type propaganda, a wide-ranging activity is envisaged in order to instill the ideology to the whole people after the state has been seized. In such a propaganda approach, it was aimed to create an ideal Soviet person by realizing institutional breakthroughs in all fields from education to art, from science to sports. The ideal Soviet society, which was developed in every field and consisted of these people who were devoted to the revolution and ideology, was seen as the guarantee of the state's establishment and continuity. Therefore, all the aforementioned areas were handled in parallel with the propaganda, and the state's facilities were mobilized for this purpose.

Another important example of the propaganda practices that left their mark on the 20th century is undoubtedly the one carried out by Adolf Hitler. Hitler became one of the leaders who used propaganda most effectively in the process that led him to take over all the powers as the 'Führer' in 1933, and in his entire life until his suicide in 1945. The propaganda carried out by Hitler differs from the Lenin-type propaganda mentioned above in certain points. In Lenin's practice, propaganda is an important tool to be used to seize the state and, most importantly, to establish the state on solid foundations. In Hitler's understanding, on the other hand, it looks like a goal in itself, and it is aimed to drag the mass unconditionally to every target that will be displayed, thanks to activities in this direction. Hitler's view of propaganda as a weapon can also be understood from his attempts in this direction. The understanding of mobilizing all the means of the state for propaganda during the period he was in power became concrete with the 'Ministry of Propaganda' he established. Hitler brought Joseph Goebbels, one of his most trusted names, to the head of this ministry, and thus carried out an institutional, continuous and systematic propaganda practice.

The propaganda methods and techniques of Goebbels, who is famous for his skill in propaganda, were accepted as the most effective tactics and strategies on this subject, and these principles were not only limited to propaganda, but also made usable to a certain extent for all kinds of attempts to influence people. For example, the 'Big Lie Theory' used by Goebbels is based on the fact that the bigger and more importantly, the more often something is false and false, the more likely people will believe it. This 'repetition' rule, which will be discussed in the section on the application and rules of propaganda below, has become an important principle applied in advertising and similar fields as it is in propaganda.

Within the scope of the propaganda activities carried out by Hitler, the communication opportunities of the period were utilized to the fullest. For example, the state provided the radio to enter almost every household at a very low cost and it was made possible for the public to listen to Hitler's propaganda speeches frequently. In addition to this, flyers, posters, posters, movies and every imaginable communication medium were used effectively for propaganda. In Hitler-type propaganda, a professional study was carried out to make the masses obey without question in a completely conditioned manner by subjecting them to psychologically intense motivation. As a result of these efforts, it was possible to drag a significant part of the German people after Hitler, as if they were hypnotized.

The understanding of the use of propaganda as a weapon during the wars also showed itself in the Second World War, as it did in the 1st World War. The World War II, in which the world system was shaped and new balances were created, brought along the ideological divisions, as well as military struggles. All the countries participating in the war engaged in an intense propaganda struggle in order to prove their power and justification on the one hand, and to attract other countries to the ideological blocs they were in, on the other hand. For example, propaganda played an important role in the entrance of United States into the Second World War and its subsequent becoming a determinant in the world system. The USA, which was out of the war in the initial stages of the war, needed an effective justification to convince the American people who were reluctant to join the war in the following periods. This justification is the event that took place in 1941 in the second year of the war and is known as the Pearl Harbor attack. This event, of which a series of Hollywood films were shot, mostly with propaganda content, until recently, took place in the form of the bombing of the American navy by the Japanese and as a result, serious military and financial losses to the United States. The fact that the issues such as why the Japanese made such a move and, moreover, why America suffered such a great loss by condoning this raid, are still not clarified; It has brought up the debates that America's entry into the war, what it did in the war and its position in the new order after the war, were designed as a deliberate propaganda event for both its own public and the international public.

The Second World War resulted in the defeat of the Nazi and Fascist governments by the allied powers, which described themselves as 'democrats', and a bipolar world led by the USA and the USSR was created in the new world order that was established afterwards. This process passed with the struggles described as the 'cold war' between the liberal bloc led by the USA and the socialist bloc led by the USSR, and the USA became the dominant country with the dissolution of the USSR in 1991. Intense propaganda activities were carried out in the ideological struggles of the Cold War period and in events such as the Vietnam and Korean Wars that took place in this process. The conflict situation that started with the Gulf War that broke out in the early 1990s and has continued until today as the operation to shape the Middle East has also witnessed intense propaganda processes. The efforts of the Western powers to constantly present their attacks against the Middle East as 'bringing democracy to the region' show that they follow the principle of the propaganda master Goebbels, "The bigger and more often the lie is repeated, the more convincing it is". All means of communication are used effectively both in wars and in modern propaganda activities for the purpose of spreading certain ideologies or world views. Numerous tools and media, from movies to computer games, from entertainment programs to the internet, today, albeit under different names, actually function as propaganda mechanisms that aim to manipulate the society to think and act in the determined direction.

RULES OF PROPAGANDA

Although propaganda activities have been carried out in different ways throughout history, the main target, the understanding of prompting the audience to think and act in the determined way, has always been valid and in the efforts for this, certain rules, methods and techniques have come to the fore.

It is possible to list the rules that make propaganda practices successful as follows (Domenach, 1995): (i) Simplicity and one enemy rule, (ii) Magnification and disruption rule, (iii) Regulation rule, (iv) Vaccination rule, (v) Unity and Contagion rule.

It is expressed as the rule of simplicity that the messages to be given in the propaganda should be easy and in a way that can be understood by everybody. Since propaganda, by its very nature, appeals to an extremely wide audience, which includes the general public, it has to appeal to the lowest level of understanding of the segments it is dealing with. At this point, slogans and similar expressions and various symbols are used, which can be highly memorable due to their simplicity and brevity. Symbols, signs, anthems, flags, pennants that reinforce the message to be delivered and support the memorability function as materials that strengthen the effectiveness and retention of the propaganda.

In addition to the use of plain and understandable language in propaganda, the target must be clearly and clearly defined. It is thought that a propaganda application that concentrates on the target and directs all the energy to a single point has a high chance of success. The clear identification of the enemy in a clear and focused manner as possible is considered essential for the concentration criterion in propaganda.

The rule of amplification and distortion refers to the design of the messages and information given in the propaganda in line with the purposes of the propagandist. In propaganda activities, it is impossible to talk about an ethical principle such as conveying the news correctly. Applying to exaggeration, lies or deforming information when necessary are events that are considered normal for propaganda.

The regulation (repetition) rule is used to mean the systematic repetition of certain thoughts in propaganda activities. According to this principle, there is a basic message to be conveyed in propaganda, and this message must be repeated as often as possible. However, messages are sent in support of this message from different channels, and as a result, the main arrangement in propaganda is to repeat a single message as often as possible, albeit from different channels, to create a belief and motivation in this direction in the audience.

The rule of grafting refers to the development of a strategy that can be accepted by the society at the point of making the masses adopt an idea. For an idea to be accepted by the society, the messages to be conveyed must not conflict with existing values and acceptances. A message that is designed to relate to values that have already been adopted or will be accepted by the majority will be more likely to have the expected impact on the target audience. For example, in order to make the masses adopt their ideology, Liberalism, and to mobilize the masses in this direction, the bourgeois class chanted the generally accepted principles such as 'equality', 'freedom' and 'fraternity' in line with their own approach, and in this way, they were able to make large sections of the public support themselves.

In social life, people tend to think and act within the framework of general acceptance. Being different from the majority is often perceived as an undesirable and risky situation. In order not to be excluded from society, individuals may feel the need to think and act, or at least to appear that way, in accordance with the generally accepted beliefs. This situation, which is also known as the 'spiral of silence' in communication science; It is the situation where the opinions that are expressed more intensely and strongly are perceived as the dominant opinion of the society at the time, due to the fact that the holders of different and contrary views feel obliged to remain silent. The rule of unity and contagion also means that the propagandist first creates a sense of unity in the society in the direction he wants, and in this way, individuals are directed to this artificial unity axis, which has been created due to the motive of not contradicting the community. It is tried to create the impression that this sense of unity that the propagandist will create in the society will infect everyone in the society over time, and that what is actually the purpose of the propagandist is the general idea of the society.

In propaganda activities, large and crowded events are frequently used in order to ensure a certain level of unity over the general public and thus to affect those who have this different opinion (contamination) from this unity. Mass meetings, parades, public demonstrations with large participation and similar events are among the means of creating a mass spirit and making it dominant in the general public.

METHODS AND TECHNIQUES OF PROPAGANDA

The above-mentioned propaganda rules are taken into account to some extent in most applications. However, some methods and techniques are put into practice in line with the strategy determined in propaganda activities. Although the methods and techniques applied in propaganda practices may change and develop from time to time, seven application forms determined by the Institute of Propaganda Analysis have been evaluated as the methods and techniques frequently used in propaganda activities. In this context, the methods and techniques of propaganda can be listed as follows (Bektaş, 1996): Name calling, Flamboyant generalization, Transfer, Testimonial, Plain folks, Card stacking, Band wagon.

Name calling method, which is frequently used in propaganda activities, is to describe the person or persons determined as enemies or opponents with an unwelcome and unpopular adjective/name. For example, attributions such as 'criminal', 'murderer', 'terrorist' or nicknames with negative connotations can have devastating effects on the image of the opposing side.

The flamboyant generalization, which has the opposite function of name-calling, refers to the propagandist's use of adjectives that are generally accepted and welcomed by the society for himself or for his purposes. For example, qualifying the propagandist as a 'genius leader' and a 'recipe for salvation' for his activities may have a positive effect in terms of image and reputation.

The transfer technique can be described as an effort to gain the support of the majority by giving the impression that the society is on the side of the values that are adopted and respected. For example, the propagandist's owning a work, belief, and value that is respected by the majority in society provides the possibility of transferring the positive impression of it to himself.

The method of testimonial is that the propagandist takes people who are valued and cared for by the society in his activities and takes advantage of their dignity. For example, the fact that the propagandist has respected and famous people with him at rallies or public meetings can become a positive image element, as it may create the impression that he also witnesses what he has done.

In the plain folks method, which expresses the impression that the propagandist is a part of the society he is addressing and that he is not different from them, it is tried to make the public see the propagandist as one of their own close and sympathize with them.

The card stacking method refers to the use of only the most functional aspects for the propagandist by separating the positive or negative aspects of an event to be used within the scope of propaganda activities.

The band wagon method refers to creating the impression that the direction that the propagandist wants to drag the audience to is adopted by everyone. When the propagandist believes that he is making a claim that is accepted by the general public, he will be able to guide the majority more easily thanks to the habit of individuals to conform to the community.

It cannot be said that the methods and techniques used within the scope of propaganda activities consist of the above mentioned. In addition to these most commonly used and generally accepted techniques, factors such as the conditions of the period, the aims and approach of the propagandist can differentiate and enrich the methods to be used. Most methods and techniques used in propaganda activities target mass psychology to a large extent and include elements such as manipulation, consciousness management and mind manipulation.

Relationship Between Propaganda and Public Diplomacy

It is called public diplomacy when a country tries to communicate with foreign public opinion so that it can manage its foreign policy and protect its national interests (Paul, 2011: 35). According to Gienow-Hecht and Donfried (2013:14), public diplomacy includes programs funded by the government and aimed at influencing public opinion in other countries by informing. In this way, the perception of foreign public opinion can be changed in the desired direction, and negative perceptions are tried to be removed. For this reason, many activities such as image creation, propaganda and nation branding are described as public diplomacy practices, and public diplomacy highlights the issues of image, national interest and common interest (Zhang, & Swartz, 2009: 382). Walter (2007:331) emphasizes that public diplomacy is a form of propaganda because public diplomacy has the feature of determining the perceptions, attitudes and behaviors of the target audience and is a form of communication aimed at persuading. According to him, propaganda is a word that created a negative perception due to the First and Second World Wars (Walter, 2007: 332). As there is propaganda in the past of public diplomacy activities, the concept of propaganda, which has an important place in international relations, forms the basis of today's public diplomacy. One of the common points of public diplomacy and propaganda is that it is a planned and purposeful activity (Pamment, 2013: 3). Public diplomacy is called the process of a state influencing the people of another country culturally, educationally, politically and expresses two-way communication; Propaganda, on the other hand, is seen as a unilaterally organized communication activity to influence people's thoughts and activities. However, many scholars argue that the concept of public diplomacy is used to disguise propaganda that has become discredited and has negative connotations over time (Laswell, 1973: 9). It is stated that many countries are now carrying out activities that were previously considered as propaganda, now under the name of public diplomacy (Snow, 2010:78). It is seen that propaganda generally aims to direct the subconscious of the target audience towards the determined purpose, while public diplomacy aims to persuade the target audience through soft power and effective communication. Despite being fed from the same root, the propaganda and public diplomacy activities in question differ from each other in terms of scope and content, but they can also meet on a common ground at some points (Laswell, 1973: 12).

CONCLUSION

Since the middle of the 20th century, public diplomacy has become a modern method and one of the main components of international relations and classical diplomacy, whose importance and effectiveness have increased gradually. While the world system was being reshaped after the Second World War, the understanding of international relations was also seriously transformed. The international system, which was closely tied to the understanding of nation-state and sovereignty in the past, has now begun to take shape on the basis of interdependence and international associations and cooperation. In this process, in which different actors began to act legitimately in international relations, the interactions between states and societies intensified and a holistic framework called the 'international community' and 'international public opinion' was formed. Diplomacy, which has the mission of ensuring that states establish healthy relations with their target audiences, as well as all kinds of institutions and organizations, has become one of the most important instruments used at the international level and in relations.

Classical diplomacy has developed as a concept used to express official links between states. Diplomacy, which characterizes the process of peaceful communication of a state's opinion and approach on a particular issue to other states and interacting in this way, is carried out through the institutions and authorized representatives of the states authorized in this regard. Diplomatic relations can be carried out by the heads of state themselves, or they can be carried out by foreign affairs specialists. Diplomats who express official views and approaches on behalf of a state in the international arena are in the position of carriers of official messages rather than personal opinions.

Public diplomacy, which constitutes the most up-to-date dimension of classical diplomacy, is based on the activities of states aimed at influencing the public opinion of different countries and the international community, apart from official organs. In this context, a series of methods and techniques can be applied to strengthen the reputation and positive image of a state in the eyes of other countries and the international public. The purpose of these activities, which are carried out with different methods and techniques, from lobbying to sponsorship, from artistic and cultural collaborations to educational aid, is to create a positive image and reputation in the eyes of different countries.

Public diplomacy activities, in essence, constitute an important dimension of propaganda in the most general sense in terms of forming a dimension of motivational communication. All of the planned communication efforts aimed at directing people's thoughts and behaviors in an expected way can be considered within the scope of propaganda. Therefore, public diplomacy is an important dimension of this understanding.

Public diplomacy has the qualities that can make you forget the negative connotations of propaganda in the 20th century. Public diplomacy on the basis of persuasive communication activities has been largely transferred to digital platforms today. As a result of the rapid spread of digital technologies throughout the world, propaganda and public diplomacy activities seem to have been largely moved to digital media.

REFERENCES

Bektaş, A. (1996). *Public opinion, communication and democracy*. Bağlam Publishing.

Bektaş, A. (2002). *Political propaganda*. Bağlam Publishing.

Conserva, H. (2009). *Propaganda: a question and answer approach*. AuthorHouse.

Cull, N. J. (2003). Public diplomacy. In N. J. Cull, D. H. Culbert, & D. Welch (Eds.), *Propaganda and mass persuasion: a historical encyclopedia. 1500 to the present* (p. 327). ABC-CLIO, Inc.

Cull, N. J. (2006), *Public diplomacy before gullion: the evolution of a phrase*. Retrieved July 26, 2022, from https://www.uscpublicdiplomacy.org/blog/public-diplomacy-gullion-evolution-phrase

Cull, N. J. (2009). Public diplomacy before gullion: the evolution of a phrase. In N. Snow & P. M. Taylor (Eds.), *Routledge handbook of public diplomacy* (pp. 19–23). Routledge.

Domenach, J. (1995). *Politics and Propaganda*. Varlık Publishing.

Fisher, A. (2011). Looking at the man in the mirror: understanding of power and influence in public diplomacy. In A. Fisher & S. Lucas (Eds.), *Trials of engagement: the future of us public diplomacy* (p. 273). Martinus Nijhoff Publishers. doi:10.1163/ej.9789004179400.i-309.72

Giddens, A. (1985). *The Nation-State and Violence*. Polity Press.

Gregory, B. (2011). American public diplomacy: Enduring characteristics, elusive transformation. *The Hague Journal of Diplomacy*, *6*(3-4), 351–372. doi:10.1163/187119111X583941

Jessica, C. E., Gienow-Hecht, J. C. E., & Donfried, M. C. (2013). The model of cultural diplomacy: power, distance, and the promise of civil society. In Searching for a cultural diplomacy (pp. 13-30). Berghahn Books.

Kalın, I. (2011). Soft Power and Public Diplomacy in Turkey. *Perceptions Journal of International Affairs*, *16*(3), 5–23.

Kelley, J. R. (2009). Between "take-offs" and "crash landings"- situational aspects of public diplomacy. In N. Snow & P. M. Taylor (Eds.), *Handbook of public diplomacy* (pp. 72–86). Routledge.

Laswell, H. D. (1973). *Propaganda technique in world war*. The MIT Press.

Pamment, J. (2013). *New public diplomacy in the 21st century*. Routledge.

Parmar, I. (2007). Responding to anti-americanism: the politics of public diplomacy. In B. O'Connor & M. Griffiths (Eds.), *Anti-Americanism: in the 21st century* (pp. 239–263). Greenwood World Publishing.

Paul, C. (2011). *Strategic communication: origins, concepts, and current debates*. Praeger.

Qualter, T. H. (1980). Propaganda theory and development of propaganda. *Journal of Ankara University Faculty of Political Sciences*, *35*(1), 255–307.

Rugh, W. A. (2014). *Front line public diplomacy: how us embassies communicate with foreign publics*. Palgrave MacMillan. doi:10.1057/9781137444158

Sander, O. (2008). *The rise and fall of phoenix: an essay on the history of ottoman diplomacy*. İmge Publishing.

Snow, N. (2010). *Propaganda. inc.: selling america's culture to the world*. Seven Stories Press.

Tolan, B. (1975). *Introduction to sociology*. Kitle Publishing.

Tuch, H. N. (1990). Communicating with the world: U.S. public diplomacy overseas. New York: St. Martin's Press.

Waller, J. M. (2007). *The public diplomacy reader*. Institute of World Politics Press.

Zhang, J., & Swartz, B. C. (2009). Public diplomacy to promote global public goods (GPG): Conceptual expansion, ethical grounds, and rhetoric. *Public Relations Review*, *35*(4), 382–387. doi:10.1016/j.pubrev.2009.08.001

KEY TERMS AND DEFINITIONS

Communication: The imparting or interchange of thoughts, opinions, or information by speech, writing, or signs.

Digitalization: The increasing adoption of digital technologies, digital transformation.

Method: The prescribed process for completing a task.

Politics: Politics is the set of activities that are associated with making decisions in groups, or other forms of power relations among individuals, such as the distribution of resources or status.

Propaganda: Propaganda is communication that is primarily used to influence or persuade an audience to further an agenda, which may not be objective and may be selectively presenting facts to encourage a particular synthesis or perception, or using loaded language to produce an emotional rather than a rational response to the information that is being presented.

Public Diplomacy: Public diplomacy broadly speaking, is any of the various government-sponsored efforts aimed at communicating directly with foreign publics to establish a dialogue designed to inform and influence with the aim that this foreign public supports or tolerates a government's strategic objectives. These also include propaganda.

Technic: The way of doing something by using special knowledge or skill.

Tool: The object that can extend an individual's ability to modify features of the surrounding environment.

Chapter 5
Soft or Hard Power in Diplomacy

Elifnur Terzioğlu
Ataturk University, Turkey

ABSTRACT

With the end of the Cold War, the military-based structure, which was the only relatively single actor in the international system that went through a serious transformation, was replaced by a deepened structure with new actors such as individuals, companies, and international organizations alongside the state. This transformation of the system requires actors, especially states, to revise themselves through new security perceptions, and instead of military interventions, which are described as hard power, soft power resources such as education, science, sports, culture, art, and economy come to the forefront. In a world that has become interdependent in many respects, countries need to both protect and defend their national interests and maintain relations with other countries in the face of the risks of biased, false news and incitement to societies caused by increasing information resources. In this study, soft power and hard power concepts will be discussed, and their place in diplomacy will be examined.

INTRODUCTION

With the end of the Cold War, the military-based structure, which was the only relatively single actor in the international system that went through a serious transformation, was replaced by a deepened structure with new actors such as individuals, companies, and international organizations alongside the state. This transformation of the system requires actors, especially states, to revise themselves through new security perceptions, and instead of military interventions, which are described as hard power, soft power resources such as education, science, sports, culture, art and economy come to the forefront. In a world that has become interdependent in many respects, countries need to both protect and defend their national interests and maintain relations with other countries in the face of the risks of biased, false news and incitement to societies caused by increasing information resources. For these reasons, states have started to focus on public diplomacy, a concept related to diplomacy, in order to create attraction and support in foreign policy by explaining their own culture, world views, interests and goals in the opposite

DOI: 10.4018/978-1-6684-5822-8.ch005

society, and to protect the image they create by avoiding negative judgments. With the development of technology in the new international system, public diplomacy activities, which have roots in ancient times and have the capacity to produce soft power instead of hard power, have become an important foreign policy tool preferred by international actors today. Now, while developing their military capabilities on the one hand, the states have started to try to realize their international policies with soft power activities on the other hand. This has led to the increasing importance of public diplomacy activities. McLuhan's Global Village has caused political, economic, cultural, social and technological changes, and this has significantly affected and changed not only the course of international relations, but also the public diplomacy and practices that have developed in the discipline of international relations. Despite the difference between domestic and foreign policy in the postmodern period after modernization, when the analyzes made on the relationship between foreign policy and public opinion are examined, it is seen that ignorance and indifference about foreign policy issues are dominant in the public, and the main reason for this is expressed as that foreign policy cannot affect people as much as domestic policy decisions. Globalization has caused the difference between domestic and foreign policy to disappear, the borders between states to lose their importance, the interdependence of states to increase, and therefore the need to create a positive image in the international arena before the peoples of other countries. Especially after the 1945s, the idea of states to be the only actor in international relations began to be questioned, and governments that could not carry out public diplomacy alone, non-governmental organizations, foundations, associations, academia and the economy, the environment, sports, health, art, technology, education, youth, women's rights and humanitarian aid have started to operate in areas. These organizations, which also play a role in public diplomacy, influence the decisions and activities of the state and governments, carry out lobbying activities to change their policies, and can change public opinions in the desired direction. Because a successful public diplomacy activity is possible with the joint action of all these social actors for a certain purpose. In the globalized world, the expanding concept of public relations and public diplomacy intersect in many ways. Therefore, if we consider that two-way symmetrical and perfect public relations are considered as the models of the 21st century and are built on consensus, mutual understanding, participation, and two-way strategic communication, public diplomacy, which we can consider as the art of communicating with different societies, is discussed together in this study. The tool that states resort to in order to protect their country's policy, prestige and cultural integrity is generally referred to as diplomacy and public diplomacy. In this study, soft power and hard power concepts will be discussed and their place in diplomacy will be examined.

BACKGROUND

The nature and scope of the concept of power in international relations have also changed with the new actors emerging in the globalizing world. After the relations were carried out at the level of states until World War II, it became discussed with new actors on different platforms after the war, and even these new actors and new technology forced the production and dissemination of information, the distribution of communication, and the functioning of democracy and administration processes. This change has caused countries to carry their trump cards that they can no longer share on war platforms to the international arena with factors such as economy, technology and nuclear power (Nye, 2004: 262). It would not be wrong to say that countries have begun to take different measures for their security in the face of developing war technology, and that hard power, that is, the areas where weapons are at the forefront, are gradually leaving the soft power. According to Nye (2008: 102), like many concepts in social sciences, the concept of power is a concept that has different definitions and is used in different contexts. According to some, power is influence, according to some it is the purpose of policy, while for others it is a tool used to achieve the goal. Morgenthau stated that power consists of the factors that make a state invincible against other states, and it consists of qualitative and quantitative elements. Quantitative elements: Geography, degree of military preparedness, industrial capacity, population and natural resources, while the quality of diplomacy and government, national morale and national character also constitute qualitative elements. Many authors, such as K.J Holsti and Frankel, have defined power as the capacity to influence the behavior of others. When power is mentioned, the first thing that comes to mind is that something is revealed through violence as a sign of power. If the military power is not supported by technological, economic and political power or the interests in these areas are not protected by military power, no power alone makes sense (Cooper, 2004: 173). With the change in the concept of power and the differentiation of the determinants over time, the nations holding the power tried to influence other countries and nations. While the number of soldiers, their abilities, and their combativeness were power factors in the period until the Industrial Revolution, industrial production capacity and the capacity to produce new technologies became more important as military capabilities alone were insufficient to define the national power with industrial production. Throughout the Cold War, the concept of power in international politics was expressed as military, political authority and owned resources (Leonard and Small, 2003: 19). Some thinkers consider the 19th century as the age of parliaments, the 20th century as the age of masses, and the 21st century as the age of public opinion. From this point of view, it would not be wrong to say that the most effective power in today's information age is public opinion. So much so that even in international policies, governments may have to act with the power and views of the public. Especially in countries governed by democracy, it has become much more important to get the support of the public. The most effective way of influencing public opinion is about the correct use of soft power (Cull, 2009: 18). We can say that making more moderate studies to persuade people to cooperate rather than hard power elements such as military and economic explains soft power.

According to Joseph Nye (2008: 94), the first name that comes to mind when it comes to soft power, power is the ability to direct your opponent to the results you want, and this is achieved in three ways: Pressure and threats (hard power), incentives and investments, and finally getting someone to want what you want (soft power). According to him, if a state wants to achieve the desired results in world politics, other states should follow it and envy its values, and thus ensure that the other side can be drawn in the direction they want. Although it is possible to do this with threats or bribery, it is an undeniable fact that the solidarity between the actors has increased through soft power and that states have started to want what each other wants. Nye states that the crux of soft power lies in shaping the preferences of other countries, and that this can be achieved through culture, political values and institutions (Melissen, 2005:9). In this direction, it can be said that the effect can also be created with the elements of hard power, but the magic underlying soft power is to attract people to the desired point. It is possible to say that Public Diplomacy and soft power show parallelism in terms of implementation. In international relations, while the concept of power in the traditional sense is handled on military and security-related issues, in addition to these, in the modern sense, directing the public and communication based on persuasion and bargaining rather than brute force come to the fore (Wilson, 2008a: 116). Although soft power is a concept that includes the element of power, it is carried out by influencing methods without pressure and coercion. Gilboa also says that the combination and coordinated implementation of communication, persuasion and training have become key elements of foreign relations because of the costs of military power. According to

Gilboa (2008: 61), who states that communication is a more precise factor among these, power is used in the process of directing the behavior of others in the desired direction, but the actor uses soft and hard power together to reach the result. Some authors do not accept soft power as a power element and emphasize that hard power can be soft (moderate) when used appropriately. Soft power increases when people begin to act in cooperation without forcing and when the policies of states or their image in the international arena are respected. Public diplomacy is also expressed as official policies that transform these soft power resources into action (Gilboa, 2008: 62). Although both are elements of power, there are differences between hard power and soft power. While hard power involves changing the other side's attitude with force and encouragement, soft power is about changing these attitudes through influence. While military and economic power are the forces of hard power, cultural power is expressed as the element of soft power. Soft power is unpredictable and intangible, while hard power is tangible and predictable to some extent. While hard power has an immediate effect, soft power shows its effect later.

SOFT POWER AND HARD POWER APPROACHES

When looking at the difference between hard power and soft power, while hard power shows these: Ability to change the attitudes of others with force or encouragement, military or economic strength, Oppression, force, Concrete, Easy to measure, predictable to some extent, controlled by government or organizations, direct, short time, immediate effect. Soft power shows these: Ability to change the attitude of others through influence, cultural strength, Abstract, hard to measure, unpredictable, Indirect, long time, effect seen later, It has the feature of communicating with nation branding (Gallarotti, 2011: 28). In the last century, under the domination of information, development, change and sharing also affect economy, politics, technology and social structures and force them to change. In particular, countries with knowledge and economy are in the position of dominant power today. Computer networks, which remove international borders, increase individual and social interactions gradually. According to Nye, in the midst of such a mass of information, civil actors will play a greater role, and many of these organizations will have their own soft power as they pull people across international borders. Thus, sharing information and reliability will become an important source of strength. Countries that are communication channels in the global information age, have a dominant culture, whose opinions are valued, whose credibility reaches both local and international dimensions, will most likely be more interesting and as a result, they will gain soft power (Nye, 2005a: 38). However, it should not be forgotten that soft power will not always be through the state, and that different actors in the international arena can act in line with the interests of the country, and it is about effective cooperation and correct guidance. In this information age, target audiences have become more "smart". With the increasing prevalence and use of the media, the populations of Asian, African and Latin American countries have become more conscious, have begun to learn more about other countries and societies, and have had less chance to be affected by hard or soft power activities from other nations. Therefore, this educated new public in the information age expects to be treated differently from the past. For this reason, it is necessary to determine strategies by considering each of the hard and soft power separately and to analyze these two power elements correctly (Wilson, 2008b: 113-114). In today's world, the chance of nations to exist in the universal arena with a single policy, method or strategy is decreasing. Multiple actors, differentiating relations necessitate multifaceted international instruments. Public diplomacy is one of the multidimensional tools that can be used by nations to influence each other, to direct, to create a communication environment and to build a reputation with the soft power factor.

Cowan and Arsenault (2008: 6) state that wars bring new concepts to our lives. Camouflage from the 1st World War, kamikaze and surprise attack from the 2nd World War, and containment and intimidation (policy) from the Cold War years have been included in our lives. Although it is possible to come across the first public diplomacy practices in the seventeenth century, the concrete traces of the practices in this field can only be seen in the Cold War years. As an example, persuasion efforts to spread western values and rules can be given to Eastern European countries called "Iron Curtain" (Bostancı, 2012: 40). Another example can be given from the work done for the image. After its defeat in the Prussian War, the French government established the Alliance Française in 1883 in order to improve its image, which was negatively affected, and through this institution, people began to be sent under the name of cultural ambassadors in order to spread and teach their language both to the French colonies and to other countries. Thus, the Alliance Française, which was the first official initiative made for foreign peoples, increased the prestige of France among foreign communities and provided great convenience for France to achieve its later goals. Moreover, Italy, Germany and other countries followed it closely, and many of the countries, including the USA, established such offices in order to spread their propaganda during the First World War (Nye, 2008: 96). After the French cultural centers taught their own language before 1965, explaining their culture and adopting their values, the effective use of British Culture by establishing it in 1934, the launch of the BBC in 1938, and the establishment of the US Information Office in 1953 can be given as examples of public diplomacy (Hackbarth, 2008: 13). After 1965, practices related to public diplomacy were interrupted in the 80s-90s, and countries tried to engage in public diplomacy activities in line with their own beliefs, especially in the period until the collapse of the Berlin Wall and the dissolution of the Soviet Union (Nye, 2004: 261). In the public conflict between the USA and the Soviet Union during the Cold War, both states used their own proxies in order to reach the target audiences. In this process, the superpowers maintained their hegemony in the field of information as well as their global influence (Seib, 2009: 778). After the Cold War, a second superpower has emerged in the field of international relations, and they consist of a joint movement of millions of people who are social development and human rights, environmentalism and health. With globalization, non-governmental organizations started to take a role in world diplomacy, the development of communication technologies and thus the establishment of relations between the organizations formed by political action groups in different countries and the increasing influence in the field of international relations (Smith-Windsor, 2000: 54) have led to the development of public diplomacy and taking its current form. The fight against terrorism, which started with the events of September 11, has also brought the concept of public diplomacy, which has been practiced for years, but has not seen the necessary importance in the world public opinion, to the international platform. According to Cull, who has the same opinion (2009: 23), the need for public diplomacy was felt even more with the end of the Cold War. The reason for this is the freedom and democracy gained by the defeat of the enemy in the war of ideas. It can be said that the concepts of soft power and public diplomacy were rediscovered in the events of September 11, because when it was understood that the use of hard power in the fight against terrorism did not bring a solution, it was understood that this struggle went through mutual understanding and public diplomacy activities started to revive. For example, five weeks after the attack, news began to be published in many American newspapers, and the Washington Post newspaper gave its headline that public diplomacy was urgently needed. In summary, public diplomacy has begun to be expressed universally (Roberts, 2007: 36). In the years when public diplomacy emerged, it was used only by the state actor, but with the development of communication technologies, it is seen that the area of use has changed and shaped. Institutions such as non-governmental organizations, pressure groups and organizations that make up the structure of a state and are responsible for communicating with foreign governments within this structure are accepted as public diplomacy actors. These actors of public diplomacy begin to establish a relationship with the state over time and indirectly participate in public diplomacy. This shows that the source of public diplomacy does not consist only of the state (Sancar, 2012: 89). According to Szondi (2008: 17-18), actors of public diplomacy are: State and non-state actors, cultural organizations, government and its organizations, embassies, Ministry of Culture, Ministry of Foreign Affairs, non-governmental organizations and diasporas. According to Sancar (2012: 89); civil society organizations, internal target audience, supra-state organizations, private sector and global businesses, opinion leaders, media and news agencies, pressure groups, universities and schools are among the public diplomacy actors and social stakeholders. Supra-state institutions: In public diplomacy, the verification of the strategies of governments and the legitimacy of their activities are realized by the supra-state institutions, which are social stakeholders. Supra-state organizations such as the International Monetary Fund (IMF), the United Nations (UN), the Organization for Economic Development and Cooperation (OECD) and the North Atlantic Treaty Organization (NATO) make some arrangements within the political, commercial and legal scope and persuade states to comply with these regulations. In short, it is clear that supra-state organizations are determinants on political, economic and social strategies to increase their role. Private sector and multinational global businesses: Multinational companies, which are as effective as governments, can show themselves on a global scale in terms of their capital, operating power and equity. These global businesses, which operate in many countries and can contact with decision makers in the international arena, are as powerful as a state and are actors that can influence decisions. With globalization, material and moral values and accumulations of economic, political, social and cultural nature are spreading across the world by exceeding international borders and enabling businesses to reach universal dimensions (Wagner, 2005: 78). For this reason, global businesses and universal brands have a greater impact on the lives of societies than the government and its members (Goodman, 2006: 7). In particular, the USA, which has famous brands such as Microsoft, Coca Cola, Apple and Sony, contributes to the image of the country and provides the public diplomacy purposes of the state by using the advantage of having global companies (Nye, 2008: 105). Non-Governmental Organizations: Today, with the development of the understanding of civil society and its increasing importance in international politics, governments begin to mobilize the masses with Non-Governmental Organizations (NGO) to increase the effectiveness of public diplomacy. After the second half of the 20th century, NGOs began to gain strength and make their voices heard, and thanks to the information revolution, they greatly strengthened soft power by staying beyond the scope of activity of individual states (Cull, 2009: 26). NGOs are organisms that do not have any ties to a state within the framework of public diplomacy and they try to explain the country, culture and experiences they are in, accurately and as it should be. In addition, they carry out activities and lobby activities in favor of their own countries (Yalçıntaş, 2013: 212-224). According to a study, Amnesty International, Greenpeace and Oxfam, the World Wildlife Fund, were chosen as the most trusted non-governmental organizations in England, France and Germany (Tench and Yeomans, 2006: p.116). Universities and schools: Educational institutions on public diplomacy activities are another social stakeholder that takes responsibility for informing and raising awareness of the society due to their aspects that provide research and culture flow (Steinberg, 2008:3). With their highly effective networks, universities and academic actors can be effective public diplomacy executives, and they can also easily involve foreign societies in their activities during academic periods. Although the main purpose of many universities and schools in the world is education, they have been established by governments to spread culture and influence societies (Riordan, 2007: 188-191). For this reason, it is possible to say that students participating in international exchange programs of universities and academicians participating in events such as international conferences and congresses convey their cultural values to people from other countries. Opinion Leaders: Within the scope of impact studies conducted at Columbia University under the leadership of Katz, Berelson, and Lazersfeld until the mid-1950s, it was concluded that interpersonal relationships played a large role in transferring information and changing attitudes (Wilson, 2008a:113). Thus, it has emerged that communication takes place in a two-stage flow process, and the concept of an opinion leader, who has an impact on a group or society, can manage perceptions, is easily adopted and listened to in society, has emerged (Goodman, 2006: 9). Opinion leaders are people whose opinions are valued and who are likely to contact decision-makers on topics such as politics, sports, economy, science and civil society. These are individuals such as artists, NGO leaders, businessmen, athletes, politicians, academics and scientists. Pressure groups: In the most general way, they are expressed as groups trying to put pressure on politicians for their common interests (Melissen, 2005: 13). Pressure groups, like other actors of public diplomacy, convey the messages they want to convey to the target audience using digital communication methods. The effects of pressure groups in public diplomacy vary according to the role of political power, and bureaucrats, who negotiate processes together with pressure groups, try to establish a balance in many areas, especially in economy (Becker, 1983: 396). Chambers of commerce, large companies, employers' unions, holdings and various associations constitute pressure groups and function based on ideological, political and economic classes (Nye, 2008:113). Media and international news agencies: It is possible to say that the media is the most effective actor in influencing public opinion by shaping the images of countries and disseminating information about countries to international audiences through mass media such as newspapers, television, radio and internet (Kunczik, 1997: 7). Foreign governments are tried to be influenced by establishing various agendas through public diplomacy. Foreign media organizations play an important role in the creation of national image. Before reaching the target, the messages sent can be changed by the media practitioners and affect the target audience, and with this role, it acts as a social stakeholder in public diplomacy. Moreover, the role of the media in forming public opinion has been revealed in many theories. In the agenda setting theory, it is stated that mass media is one of the possible ways to be effective on the public (Nye, 2008: 101). Internal target group: In public diplomacy, the internal target group, which is an important actor in the realization of tasks such as ensuring internal integrity and transferring it to the world, is stated as a social stakeholder rather than external success. The internal target audience, which is also called the target audience in addition to its social stakeholder position, is in the position of receiving the message when states explain their policies, while it is in the position of giving the message in the transmission of these policies to others (Sancar, 2012: 96-99). It has been mentioned that public diplomacy is a state trying to influence the people and policies of another nation in order to turn it to its advantage. For this reason, governments are communicating with different societies in various fields of application of public diplomacy in line with these purposes. The diversity of the application areas has increased with the globalization and the states that practice effectively have become more and more successful (Potter, 2002: 3). Activities and long-term projects carried out in the fields of practice such as culture, education, art, health, faith and sports in order to achieve international political goals are used in the field of public diplomacy, thus ensuring communication from transnational, civil society and other institutions and organizations to the public.

The concept we call culture is the common beliefs, values, behavior and behavior styles learned by individuals in a society and including language, songs, dances, clothing, education styles and social rules between these individuals. Culture changes from society to society, is shared by individuals and is built on needs, so it consists of parts that fit together or complement each other (Bilgin & Elis, 2008: 16). Looking at the cultural process of modern societies, it is seen that the economic system is integrated with the consciousness industry, cultural production and information. Thus, both the social and economic system creates the culture that it needs and does this in accordance with its own conditions and functioning. The mass media, which dominates the mental and emotional processes of the age (Girgin, 2008: 31), also transfers this cultural process, which is included in public diplomacy activities, to its target audience. Cultural diplomacy, which is seen as a sub-title of public diplomacy, is a communication strategy that a state establishes both to achieve its diplomacy or foreign policy goals and to spread its culture to foreign target audiences and to affect them positively (Mark, 2009: 1). According to Nye (2002: 10), the appeal of a country's culture and ideology encourages others to follow it. Cultural diplomacy is the first example of influencing social values and ideologies through culture with soft power rather than hard power (Schnider, 2007: 147-148). According to another definition of cultural diplomacy, it is to introduce a cultural benefit by influencing the perception of the target audience in the desired direction and to include it in the perceived ideas (Fisher, 2009: 253). In this way, the messages conveyed by cultural diplomacy to the target audience arouse curiosity and interest in that culture, and enable them to approach the political messages that will come from it in the next periods. Cultural relations are the best way to create deep impacts between countries, create positive reputation and change misconceptions (Szondi, 2009:302). In this context, cultural interaction methods implemented in art, sports, literature and different fields help to achieve the political goals that are desired to be achieved in the international arena. Activities carried out in areas such as theatre, cinema, exhibition, sports, music, dance, literature, painting and fashion can be used in the public diplomacy process by taking into account different target audiences (Erzen, 2012: 134-135). Thanks to international exchange programs and cultural associations of foreign countries, cultural diplomacy is seen to be used in public diplomacy. Exchange programs such as Fulbright, Erasmus+, organizations in different countries such as the French Cultural Center, Alliance Française, and British Council can be given as examples that come to mind first (Cull, 2009: 25). The power to manage the masses without resorting to force and to persuade them on certain issues derives from the language (Brown, 200: 7). Education and language are the two main factors that are important for governments using cultural diplomacy. The concept of language is of great importance in terms of cultural diplomacy, especially because a state spreads its own language over the other state and is more effective. On the other hand, education that supports language aims to teach the art and culture of that state (Sönmezoğlu, 2000: 362). France's placement of French and French culture under the name of "Francophony" is a good example in this sense (Cull, 2009: 33). Educational programs are seen as a cultural diplomacy activity and a form of strategic communication because of their ability to bring students from different cultures together. In the field of education, not only sending students to foreign countries, but also accepting students from different countries is among the objectives of public diplomacy. That's why student exchange programs are important for cultural exchange. In addition to universities and schools, non-governmental organizations are also actively used in public diplomacy in order to win minds and hearts (Sancar, 2012: 79). It is assumed that the participants of these training programs will have a positive view of the country they are studying in. While these student exchange programs provide mutual benefits to the countries, they also allow the public diplomacy activities to be recognized by different cultures (Kalın, 2011: 11). States use education as a tool to enable young people to define their country's cultures in the desired direction and to spread them to other masses. Thanks to the cultural exchange programs, it is tried to be influenced by the peoples of other countries within the scope of public diplomacy activities. In this context, with the funds provided by the states, thousands of students and academics go to various countries every year, take part in international studies and contribute to the building of bridges between countries. Therefore, it is stated that education, which is seen as a field work area in public diplomacy activities, has a great importance in the creation of common values and the development of dialogue by introducing cultures (Wagner, 2005: 63). Religion is a factor that also affects foreign policy, due to interstate relations. For this reason, it can be the cause of international conflicts, and it is also used for the political interests of the countries. In the history of humanity, it is stated that religion has a dominant role in the lives of individuals and in political communities in general. In this direction, it is necessary for people to have a clear understanding of the role of faith in order for public diplomacy to be carried out properly (Seib, 2011: 9). Public diplomacy practitioners need to develop their strategies by taking into account the role of religion, which is at the center of politics and domination over other nations. Strategies created in this direction also create faith diplomacy, actors such as religious leaders, communities and organizations can act on the basis of religious violence, as well as resolve conflicts and provide international humanitarian aid (Zaharna, 2010: 118). China's Buddhist diplomacy can be given as an example of faith diplomacy. The World Forum of Buddhism, organized by the Chinese Government in 2006, brought together a thousand Buddhists with academics from thirty-seven countries with the theme of "A harmonious world begins in the mind". As can be understood from the example, this Buddhist diplomacy of China appears as an example of cultural diplomacy and provides the spread of Buddhism culture. As a result, public diplomacy cannot ignore faith diplomacy because of the impact of religion on societies and its important role in international politics. Lobbying, which is expressed as the initiatives applied by individuals or special interest groups in order to influence the political decision-making processes, is based on the lobbying activities carried out to ensure that the legislators are supported by voting in the desired direction in the parliaments and is an area that supports public diplomacy activities (Sancar, 2012: 82). Lobbying, which is an important application area for public diplomacy, is an indispensable method especially in contemporary democracies, and it is informative activities that support government policies in order to manage the perceptions of the public. Its purpose is to manage problems, to strengthen its reputation, to increase recognition, and it achieves these goals through its effective work on the legislative assembly. Lobbying activities, which cannot be considered separately from the public diplomacy strategies of countries, are successful if they are supported by international public works (Cull, 2009: 17). Advocacy refers to the relationship work carried out with different social stakeholders while communicating the perceptions formed in the minds to other nations (Patterson and Wilkins, 2008: 124). Advocacy is used to promote an ideology, policy or general interest in foreign nations in order to develop mutual understanding, create consent and persuade by attracting the attention of foreign people (Sancar, 2012: 183). Advocacy, which is seen in all areas of public diplomacy today, takes place within the information studies and press relations generally found in embassies. The tendency to place the closest bureaucratic elements in a public diplomacy study has caused a bias in all areas of public diplomacy since the past (Cull, 2009: 19). The benefit of advocacy is short-lived and its role is self-fulfillment by providing one-sided information. Therefore, advocacy cannot be said to comply with the principles of mutual understanding and dialogue of public diplomacy. States see advocacy as a means by which they can express themselves as they want to be perceived and correct misunderstandings. The lack of advocacy, which has a one-way feature, is not so important because of the existence of other tools and the fact that these tools carry out dialogue (Sancar, 2012: 184-185).

CONCLUSION

After the Cold War, countries started to play an active role in the political sense, especially in regions with strong historical and cultural ties, and this role led the countries to soft power generation from classical diplomacy understanding over time. After the war in foreign policy and the struggle in the field of diplomacy, the concept of independence, which was determined as the first target, left its place to the phenomenon of "peace". It can be said that the participation of the Western countries in the Kellog-Briand Pact, which entered into force in 1929 and which promised that all disputes would always be resolved by peaceful means, contributed to the widespread adoption of the understanding of public diplomacy. The power generation activities, which have intensified especially in the last period, have made public diplomacy studies gain importance in the world. Hard power based on military and economic sanctions has now evolved into soft power because of the increasing inter-communal interdependence as a result of globalization and the increasingly costly hard intervention. As access to information became easier with advanced communication technologies, societies began to intertwine, and for this reason, countries tried to get the support of the public, who had become the subject of foreign policy production and implementation processes. The concept of diplomacy defines the relations between states and emerges as the efforts of states to create an impact outside their sphere of influence in the international arena. Public diplomacy, on the other hand, is a state communication technique that emerged in the Cold War environment and, unlike classical diplomacy, tries to create a positive perception by influencing the minds of foreign societies in a positive way, and by this means, it is a directly established state communication technique to influence the behaviors of their governments. Although the phenomenon of "state" is at the heart of both concepts, it is no longer sufficient to define the new international system only through states. Since public diplomacy continues its activities in these fields where diplomatic methods are limited, it appears to be a more complex and important system than diplomacy. Aiming to conquer the minds and hearts of foreign peoples, public diplomacy also aims to establish the image, reputation and brand of the country represented in different geographies. Although public diplomacy seems to be within the discipline of international relations, when viewed from the perspective of public relations, it is seen that public diplomacy fulfills its public relations functions in the way of building a country brand, and continues its activities in this direction by performing public relations applications, since it includes public relations practices in its own process. Public diplomacy, as a new political communication strategy implemented by countries, has gained as much importance as classical diplomacy. In particular, the value given by developed countries and the requirements of the information age increase the popularity of public diplomacy and also become an indispensable element of foreign policy. With the increasing importance given by the states to the public, it has become inevitable to consider the non-governmental organizations operating abroad as an opportunity in the field of public diplomacy. In this way, the capacity of conducting public diplomacy through both official and civil means increases. Although many activities, such as social responsibility projects, cultural and social events, become indexed to the foreign policies of the countries in the communication age, this situation causes inefficiency in the long run and a decrease in the dynamism of strategy development in terms of institutions. In addition, it can lead to overlooked elements such as sustainability and image renewal, which are the top priority issues in the field of public diplomacy. In order to avoid this situation, public relations campaigns play an important role in the analysis of the field and the target audience. However, the measurability of the results of the activities in the field of public diplomacy is another important issue. For this reason, it can be said that public relations campaigns are in an essential position for new policies in which the target audience is addressed and the soft power elements are highlighted and implemented from the point of view of public diplomacy. The world order, which started to dissolve in a single pot with globalization, makes itself felt in all environments with the dynamics revealed by the communication discipline. In this cycle, it is unavoidable to change the application areas, target audience and strategies of multidisciplinary public relations. Parallel to the growth and expansion of the structures in the world order, public relations practitioners have also started to raise their communication fields to the international public level. When the basic functions of public relations are carried to the global and international dimensions, public diplomacy, which meets with international public relations, has begun to come together on common points both theoretically and practically due to their approaches from the same perspective. Public diplomacy, which aims to provide a common understanding such as obtaining the consent of the target audiences, maintaining the mutual dialogue process, and creating environments for negotiation and reconciliation, is similar to the two-way symmetric public relations model, which is the public relations model of the 21st century, with its features such as consensus, mutual understanding and two-way communication. In today's world political arena, which is the age of technology, states, various institutions and organizations, including the European Union, carry out public diplomacy in different forms and styles on an international scale. These international actors convey their views, policies and forms of communication to the national and international public in different ways, with the practices of public diplomacy, which has started to be used as a new method not only in the field of international relations but also in the discipline of public relations. The language, tools and methods used in public diplomacy show serious differences according to each international actor, as they are closely related to the history and cultural knowledge owned as well as the policies followed. The definition of public diplomacy is expressed in the simplest terms as international actors trying to transform the policies of these nations to their own advantage by injecting their own policies into the people of other nations. In this respect, it is stated that the aim of the countries is to use concepts such as democracy, freedom and human rights as soft power elements and to try to explain themselves to the foreign public more accurately and without prejudice. With the changing world dynamics and globalization becoming an element that makes it necessary to live in harmony with the world, it is no longer surprising that some concepts have changed and transformed. Public diplomacy, unlike the classical understanding of diplomacy, which is described as from state to state, has been transformed from state to public and from public to public, and in this sense, it has become a method of promotion and persuasion that will benefit the countries. This method means creating a positive perception about a country, creating sympathy and creating mutual cooperation through cultural, social and educational activities created by opinion leaders from the state and outside of the state in different societies. In this context, nations trying to get to know and promote each other resort to public relations campaigns in order to establish a communication link between them, to gain the sympathy of the people in the places they operate and to manage their perceptions in a positive way. As can be understood, public diplomacy and public relations campaigns are concepts with common values with their tools, functions and methods.

REFERENCES

Becker, G. S. (1983). A Theory of Competition Among Pressure Groups for Political Influence. *The Quarterly Journal of Economics*, *98*(3), 371–400. doi:10.2307/1886017

Bilgin, P., & Elis, B. (2008). Hard Power, Soft Power: Toward a More Realistic Power Analysis. *Insight Turkey*, *10*(2), 5–20.

Brown, J. A. C. (2000). Beyin Yıkama. İstanbul: Boğaziçi Yayınları.

Cooper, R. (2004). Hard Power, Soft Power and the Goals of Diplomacy. In D. Held & M. Koenig-Archibugi (Eds.), *American Power in the 21st Century* (pp. 167–180). Polity Press.

Cowan, G., & Arsenault, A. (2008). Moving From Monologue to Dialogue to Collaboration: The Three Layers of Public Diplomacy. *The Annals of the American Academy of Political and Social Science*, *616*(10), 6–10. doi:10.1177/0002716207312143

Cull, N. (2009). *Public Diplomacy: Lessons From the Past*. Figueroa Press.

Fan, Y. (2008). Soft Power: Power of Attractıon or Confusion? *Place Branding and Public Diplomacy*, *4*(2), 7–9. doi:10.1057/pb.2008.4

Fisher, A. (2009). Four Seasons in One Day. In Handbook of Public Diplomacy. Routledge.

Gallarotti, G. (2011). Soft Power: What it is, it's importance, and the conditions for its effective use. *Journal of Political Power*, *4*(1), 25–47. doi:10.1080/2158379X.2011.557886

Gilboa, E. (2008). Searching for a Theory of Public Diplomacy. *The Annals of the American Academy of Political and Social Science*, *616*(1), 55–77. doi:10.1177/0002716207312142

Goodman, M. B. (2006). The Role of Business in Public Diplomacy. *Journal of Business Strategy*. *27*(3).

Hackbarth, J. R. (2008). *Soft Power and Smart Power in Africa*. Strategic Insights.

Kalin, I. (2011, Autumn). Soft Power and Public Diplomacy in Turkey. *Perceptions*, *16*(3), 5–23.

Kunczik, M. (1997). *Images Of Nations and International Public Relations*. Lawrence Earlbaum.

Leonard, M., & Small, A. (2003). *Norwegian Public Diplomacy*. The Foreign Center.

Lukes, S. (1974). *Power: A Radical View*. MacMillan Press. doi:10.1007/978-1-349-02248-9

Mark, S. (2009). A Greater Role For Cultural Diplomacy. Discussion Papers in Diplomacy, Netherlands Institute of International Relations 'Clingendael', 1.

Melissen, J. (2005). *The New Public Diplomacy: Soft Power in International Relations*. Palgrave Macmillan. doi:10.1057/9780230554931

Nye, J. S. (2002). *The Paradox of American Power*. Oxford University Press.

Nye, J. S. Jr. (2004). Soft Power and American Foreign Policy. *Political Science Quarterly*, *119*(2), 255–270. doi:10.2307/20202345

Nye, J. S. Jr. (2008). Public Diplomacy and Soft Power. *The Annals of the American Academy of Political and Social Science, 616*(1), 94–109. doi:10.1177/0002716207311699

Potter, E. H. (2002). Canada and the New Public Diplomacy. Discussion Papers in Diplomacy, Netherlands Institute of International Relations. doi:10.2307/40203812

Riordan, S. (2007). Dialogue-based Public Diplomacy. A New Foreign Policy Paradigm? In The New Public Diplomacy Soft Power in International Relations. Palgrave Macmillan.

Roberts, W. R. (2007). What Is Public Diplomacy? Past Practices, Present Conduct, Possible Future. *Mediterranean Quarterly, 18*(4).

Sancar, G. A. (2012). *Kamu Diplomasisi ve Uluslararası Halkla İlişkiler*. Beta Yayınları.

Schneider, C. P. (2007). Culture Communicates: US Diplomacy That Works. In The New Public Diplomacy: Soft Power in International Relations. Palgrave Macmillan.

Seib, P. (2011). Preface. In Essays on Faith Diplomacy. Figuroa Press.

Smith-Windsor, B. A. (2000). Hard Power, Soft Power reconsidered. *Canadian Military Journal, 1*(3), 51–56.

Steinberg, J. B. (2008). Real Leaders do Soft Power: Learning Lessons of Iraq. *The Washington Quarterly, 31*(2), 155–164. doi:10.1162/wash.2008.31.2.155

Szondi, G. (2008). *Public Diplomacy and Nation Branding: Conceptual Similarities and Diffirences*. Netherlands Institute of International Relations Clingendael.

Tench, R., & Yeomans, L. (2006). Exploring Public Relations. Prentice Hall.

Wagner, C., (2005). From Hard Power to Soft Power? *Heidelberg Papers in South Asian and Comparative Politics, 26*.

Wilson, E. J. III. (2008a). Hard Power, Soft Power, Smart Power. *The Annals of the American Academy of Political and Social Science, 616*(1), 110–125. doi:10.1177/0002716207312618

Wilson, E. J. (2008b). Public Diplomacy in a Changing World. *The Annals of the American Academy of Political and Social Science, 616*, 110–124. doi:10.1177/0002716207312618

Zaharna, R. S. (2010). *Battles to Bridges*. Palgrave Macmillan. doi:10.1057/9780230277922

Zhang, J. (2011). China's Faith Diplomacy: Inıtıatives and Vulnerabilities. In Essays on Faith Diplomacy. Figuroa Press.

KEY TERMS AND DEFINITIONS

Diplomacy: Diplomacy is the art and science of maintaining peaceful relationships between nations, groups, or individuals. Often, diplomacy refers to representatives of different groups discussing such issues as conflict, trade, the environment, technology, or security.

Hard Power: In politics, hard power is the use of military and economic means to influence the behavior or interests of other political bodies. This form of political power is often aggressive (coercion), and is most immediately effective when imposed by one political body upon another of lesser military and/or economic power. Hard power contrasts with soft power, which comes from diplomacy, culture, and history.

Military Strength: Capability in terms of personnel and materiel that affect the capacity to fight a war. A military, also known collectively as armed forces, is a heavily armed, highly organized force primarily intended for warfare. It is typically authorized and maintained by a sovereign state, with its members identifiable by their distinct military uniform. It may consist of one or more military branches such as an army, navy, air force, space force, marines, or coast guard. The main task of the military is usually defined as defence of the state and its interests against external armed threats.

Public Diplomacy: In international relations, public diplomacy, or people's diplomacy, broadly speaking, is any of the various government-sponsored efforts aimed at communicating directly with foreign publics to establish a dialogue designed to inform and influence with the aim that this foreign public supports or tolerates a government's strategic objectives.

Public Perception: A belief or opinion, often held by many people and based on how things seem. Public perception is simply the type of information obtained from a public opinion survey. That is, "publicopinion" is merely the aggregate views of a group of people (usually a randomly selected sample) who are asked directly what they think about particular issues or events.

Soft Power: In politics (and particularly in international politics), soft power is the ability to co-opt rather than coerce (contrast hard power). In other words, soft power involves shaping the preferences of others through appeal and attraction. A defining feature of soft power is that it is non-coercive; the currency of soft power includes culture, political values, and foreign policies.

Chapter 6
The Role of Digital Platforms in Public Diplomacy and Netflix

Türker Elitaş
https://orcid.org/0000-0001-8018-1208
Hatay Mustafa Kemal University, Turkey

ABSTRACT

With the digitalization of television broadcasting, an audience-oriented, modular, interactive, thematic, and mobilized broadcasting approach has become established. This new broadcasting approach attracts the attention of consumers with its advantages such as low subscription fees, language and subtitle support, ease of access and use, downloading and recording. Naturally, the number of platforms operating in the field of digital broadcasting is increasing and the content on these platforms is diversifying. On the other hand, these platforms serve as a kind of bridge for public diplomacy practices, and in this respect, they attract the attention of public diplomacy actors. Because these platforms—even if the user/viewer is not aware of it—are the means and mediators of the universal circulation of (national) culture, they are a component of public diplomacy.

INTRODUCTION

The emergence of public diplomacy due to the inadequacy of traditional diplomacy methods in international relations is being redefined in parallel with the development of information and communication technologies. In the digital age, a number of social media platforms such as Facebook, YouTube and Twitter have opened new doors for individuals/audiences to align with agendas beyond their borders. It has also enabled states and nonstate actors to present their diplomacy activities to large audiences and develop new public diplomacy strategies (Connoly-Ahern & Ma, 2015). This has paved the way for the emergence of the concept of digital diplomacy, which is defined as any diplomatic activity conducted by states and non-state actors on the internet and especially on social media. Digital diplomacy, which means the visibility and activity of foreign ministries and offices, foreign missions, non-governmental organizations operating on behalf of the state, national aid organizations, development and cooperation agencies in online environments, is predominantly carried out on Twitter, Facebook and Instagram.

DOI: 10.4018/978-1-6684-5822-8.ch006

Nevertheless, it should not be forgotten that the internet is a universe that opens up unlimited space for action and enables the establishment of unlimited platform(s) to meet different consumption preferences. It is possible to access a wide range of content in this universe such as various forms of e-commerce, e-books, e-encyclopedias, blogs, movies, music videos, thousands of different kinds of videos, social media networks, digital animations, 3D movie models (Çakır, 2014). Digital television broadcasting platforms are also an element of the internet universe and it should not be disregarded that they play a role in public diplomacy processes as well as media that fulfill the need for entertainment/consumption.

Diplomacy: Concepts, Transformations, Histories

The concept of 'diplomacy', which is used in conjunction with foreign policy practices, refers to the processes of negotiations between states and the instruments through which these processes are carried out. This concept, which means "the arrangement and management of international relations through negotiation", has a long history dating back to the written history as it refers to the process of orderly conduct of relations between a group of people and a group of foreign people (Nicolson, 1939). In institutional terms, it is defined as "the means by which the international community conducts its business through negotiation, communication and representation" (Clinton, 2016).

Although the history of diplomacy is rather old, the concept has been used in international relations since the 18th century. The Irish politician Edmund Burke was the first to use the concept of diplomacy and described it as the skills and tactics necessary for the conduct of interstate relations and negotiations etmiştir (Tuncer, 1995). The establishment of the idea of modern diplomacy (continuous diplomacy) in the field of international relations became possible with the emergence of the embassy institution in the 15th century. In the course of time, the method of continuous diplomacy became practiced throughout Europe (Tuncer, 2009). With the method of permanent diplomacy, which is defined as "the presence of diplomatic representatives in another country for a considerable period of time in order to carry out diplomatic activities on behalf of their country and to obtain information about the country and report back to their country" (Anderson, 1993), diplomatic relations became institutionalized and gained a continuous character. Thus, the ad hoc diplomacy was replaced by embassies free of time and subject matter restrictions, and diplomatic representation became more important than the diplomatic representative (Watson, 1982). In the 19th century, Britain, taking the advantages of the Industrial Revolution, became the new imperial power and dominated international relations with its naval power, economic size and commercial skills (Kennedy, 2001).

The World War I was the decisive event that separated the old and new diplomacy ideas with sharp boundaries. After the end of the war, the old diplomacy methods fell off the agenda and a new understanding of diplomacy was adopted under the leadership of the United States. As a result of the principles known as Wilson's Principles and announced by US President Woodrow Wilson, international politics was shaped around a brand new idea of diplomacy şekillenmiştir (Gönlübol, 1993). The Cold War, which started after World War II, led countries to prioritize structuring and operations over diplomacy and diplomatic action in their foreign policies. This situation resulted from the positioning of countries as one of the parties of the Cold War or the other and therefore diplomacy displayed a static outlook in this period (Huntington, 2004). States that wanted to consolidate their sovereignty in the Cold War, on the one hand, put diplomacy on the back stage, and on the other hand, brought international organizations and non-governmental organizations on the stage as new diplomatic actors. These new actors of diplomacy, together with the developing communication technologies, have played an active role in the production, distribution and classification of information. In this way, publics as well as states became both the subject and practitioner of diplomacy, and eventually the foundations of public diplomacy were laid (Akçadağ, 2022). As political, economic and cultural interaction between countries revitalized towards the end of the Cold War, the policies of escalation were abandoned and the views on the concept of public diplomacy changed accordingly. The one-way and propaganda-oriented communication approach of the Cold War was replaced by a symmetrical understanding of diplomacy focused on interaction and persuasion. Realizing that it is impossible to persuade societies through pressure and imposition, states have realized the importance of persuading public opinion and have introduced methods/tools/elements to the field of diplomacy that can influence the public opinion of countries/societies and thus ensure competitive advantage (Özkan, 2015).

Types and Methods in Modern Diplomacy

As the concept of modern diplomacy has become widespread among states, new types of diplomacy have emerged and the methods used in the diplomacy process have also diversified. This is because globalization has accelerated the interaction processes between countries/states/societies. Globalization has provided advantages for societies in terms of access to information, shared prosperity, world peace, democracy, and humanitarian crises. On the other hand, globalization has also opened the door to conflicts of priorities between states, and has led to the emergence of new crises and concerns in international politics. In order to prevent this situation, states have resorted to diplomacy and tried to use the opportunities of diplomacy as much as possible. There are many diplomacy methods used by states both in matters concerning humanity and in resolving disputes between them. From this point of view;

Cultural diplomacy is seen as long-term campaigns aimed at getting to know the public opinion of foreign countries, gaining their sympathies and developing emotional ties with them. Exchange programs, exhibitions abroad, international cultural activities are examples of cultural diplomacy (L'Etang, 2009).

The shuttle diplomacy is a type of diplomacy that is widespread today. In shuttle diplomacy, also known as mediation, a mediator state or an international organization is involved in negotiations with two states to solve problems between countries and tries to find a solution to the problem. It is a method frequently used especially in the Arab-Israeli Wars (Femic, 2021).

Coercive diplomacy is a diplomacy method used when the balance and the current situation between states are disrupted by creating actual situations. This diplomacy method, which aims to get the opponent to stop or step back from an action initiated/taken by the opponent, is a crisis management strategy. In 1998, the position taken by the Turkish state for the removal of separatist organization leader Abdullah Öcalan from Syria is an example of coercive diplomacy (Şenel, 2012).

Environmental Diplomacy is a diplomacy method that focuses on environmental problems and aims to increase cooperation between countries to find solutions to these problems (Broadhurst & Ledgerwood, 1998).

Tourism diplomacy is the presentation of a country's diplomacy messages to the public opinion of foreign countries by integrating them with tourism strategies (Sancar, 2017).

Although it is possible to multiply all these examples, modern diplomacy types and different methods used in modern diplomacy are shaped around public diplomacy. Therefore, it would be appropriate to examine the concept of public diplomacy.

Soft Power of Diplomacy: Public Diplomacy

While diplomatic communication processes in inter-state relations were in a two-way (state-state) compression until the 18th century, this situation has changed since the 19th and especially the 20th century, and diplomacy has gained a multidimensional character through international organizations and institutions. This transformation has increased the importance of the concept of 'public opinion' (Gönlübol, 1993). Eventually, the concept of "soft power" emerged in international politics, and coercion was replaced by behavior manipulation and persuasion (Nye, 2004). According to Nye, the crucial importance of soft power elements in diplomacy lies in the fact that the concept of force/power has many definitions, includes different components and has different connotations for individuals and (or) states. This is because 'power' is knowing "what actors/agents can do". Therefore, in behavioral terms, the concept of power is evaluated according to the results that occur "after the action". This is not the case in politics and policy practitioners need predictions to guide their actions. Therefore, in international relations, the power of the centers of interlocutors needs to be known "before action" (Nye, 2020)

According to Gilboa, public diplomacy has been shaped through three different periods. In the first period, the 'basic cold war model' of public diplomacy practices were in place in line with the cold war era, and public diplomacy activities were used by governments to achieve long-lasting results on foreign communities. In the second period, there was a shift to 'non-state transnational' public diplomacy practices. This involved the activities of groups, institutions, non-governmental organizations and individuals outside national borders. In the third period, the 'domestic public relations model' was used, in which governments worked with public relations companies and public lobbies to ensure the legitimacy of their policies (Gilboa, 2008). In other words, public diplomacy was used intensively between the countries that were parties to the Cold War, especially after World War II. Naturally, the understanding of public diplomacy of this period was tough, part of military power and propaganda-oriented. The target of the public diplomacy of this period was of the foreign publics, but the aim was purely political (Gilboa, 2008). With the developments in globalization and communication technologies, diplomacy has turned into a public relations activity and public diplomacy has started to be used together with concepts such as cultural diplomacy, public relations, political communication, public perception management, propaganda, dialogue of civilizations, crisis management, media management, media relations, strategic communication, strategic influence, psychological operations, information operations and media operations (De Gouveia & Plumridge, 2005).

The traditional understanding of diplomacy defined the roles and responsibilities of actors in international relations and limited their fields of activity. However, this reductionist understanding has been insufficient to meet the needs in the blurred world of post-modern transnational relations. Moreover, the interlocutors of foreign relations officers are no longer their counterparts, and a wide range of people engaged in diplomatic activities or on the receiving end of international politics have begun to have a voice in diplomacy. Consequently, the fields of activity, elements and actors of diplomacy have diversified and a model of diplomacy based on more cooperation and interaction has emerged. Public diplomacy is an indispensable component of such cooperation (Melissen, 2005) because it is a discipline that goes beyond diplomacy and diplomatic work, and has the potential to influence social change processes such as democratization, globalization and the communication revolution (Huijgh, 2016). From this perspective, the new public diplomacy (Fitzpatrick, 2011);

- Envisions a more collaborative approach to international relations.

Table 1. Differences between Old and New Public Diplomacy (Cull, 2009)

Characteristic	Former Public Diplomacy	New Public Diplomacy
Actor	State	State and non-state
Approach	Political propaganda	Corporate branding/network theory
Terminology	International image	Nation marking
Hierarchy	Vertical	Horizontal
Tendency	Targeted content	Relationship building content
Technology	Radio, TV, newspapers, landlines	Satellite, internet, mobile phones
Overall objective	International environmental management	International environmental management

- It contributes to mutual understanding between international actors and foreign publics.
- It helps to build and maintain relationships between nations/international actors and foreign publics.
- It facilitates networks of relationships between organizations and people in both the state and private sectors.
- It is based on the principles of dialogue and mutuality, and is of interest to both domestic and foreign publics.
- It prioritizes human-to-human interaction over mass messaging techniques.
- It aims to establish long-term relationships.

Considering all these features, it is possible to summarize the differences between the old diplomacy and the new public diplomacy in the table below:

The Technological State of Diplomacy: Digital Diplomacy

Digital diplomacy refers to the conduct of public diplomacy practices through information and communication technologies, also known as digital technologies. With the developing technology, states have not only become transparent within their own borders and for their own people, but have also become accessible on an international scale thanks to the internet. From this perspective, digital diplomacy corresponds to the efforts to explain the functioning and policies of the state within and outside the country, to promote national and international policies by connecting with individuals, groups and organizations on digital platforms, and thus to increase national prestige (Yağmurlu, 2019).

Digital diplomacy, whose intellectual background is based on Manuel Castells' "informationalism" proposition, is defined as the utilization of internet and information technologies by state and non-state actors to manage international exchange (Ekşi, 2016). Digital diplomacy has enriched the ways in which a message and/or image can interact with external public opinion and facilitated the way actors structure and organize their information resources. In addition, digital diplomacy provides diplomatic actors with the necessary data to analyze the changes and trends in the field of international relations (Bjola, 2015). In this respect, it is possible to say that information technologies and their transformative effects on politics have contributed to the establishment of digital diplomacy. The playground of digital diplomacy, also called cyber diplomacy, virtual diplomacy, network diplomacy, Twitter diplomacy, is internet platforms such as Twitter, Facebook, WhatsApp, Youtube, Periscope and Google+ (Ekşi, 2016).

The concept of digital diplomacy, based on the coexistence of social media and foreign policy on the same platform, gained traction in 1984 with an analysis by Allen C. Hansen entitled "'Public Diplomacy in the Computer Age'". In 1994, the first e-mail exchange took place between Swedish diplomat Carl Bildt and former US President Bill Clinton. Since the 2000s, digital diplomacy practices have diversified. The first virtual embassy was opened by the Maldives in 2007, followed by Sweden (diplomacy data, 2022). The scope of digital diplomacy practices initiated by the US government expanded over time, with the US State Department publishing its first blog post in 2007. Later, the US State Department officially started its own blog on public diplomacy, which is called "Dipnote". In the same year, the US government launched the America.gov portal for interactive media such as webcasts, blogs, videos, YouTube, Twitter, Facebook and even Second Life, where users can socialize through free voice and text chat (Zhang & Fahmy, 2015).

The field of implementation of digital diplomacy activities is predominantly social media platforms. Social networks, with their digital, interactive, textual, virtual, networked and simulated features, have created new experiences for texts. It has also produced new models of organization and production by organizing new forms of relationships between media technologies and users/consumers, thereby adding new dimensions to the relationship between individual(s) and society (Lister, Dovey, Giddings, Grant, & Kelly, 2009). This situation has also been reflected in public diplomacy, and traditional public diplomacy, which emphasized a one-way, ideological process, has been replaced by political communication processes in which performances are measured not in the corridors of foreign affairs, but on computer monitors and mobile phone screens. On the one hand, digital diplomacy has diversified the target audience of states, and on the other hand, it has paved the way for users to easily convey their opinions to the diplomatic channels of the state (Seib, 2012).

Digital Publishing and Netflix

Advances in communication technologies have had an impact on television broadcasting as in every field. The priorities of television broadcasting have changed with the convergence of the information and media sectors, and this change has been reflected in watching habits (Dönmez & Kırık, 2019). Digitalization in television broadcasting has transformed the technology, distribution, economics and media policies of television, enabling collaboration between television and other technologies that have come to define the contemporary media world (Mikos, 2016).

With the digitalization of television broadcasting, broadcaster-audience interaction has increased. The audience has been able to access the broadcast content they want anywhere and anytime on any device with an internet connection, as well as provide feedback on broadcasts on various websites, blogs and forums. In addition, they were able to access broadcast content on digital platforms wherever and whenever they wanted. Furthermore, the viewer/user has gained the freedom to follow the broadcasts on his/her own time rather than according to the broadcast time. In addition, disruptions such as image and sound distortion that occur in traditional broadcasts have been eliminated, and it has also become possible to transfer screens not only from televisions but also from smartphones and tablets (Karaduman & Aciyan, 2019). The advantages such as thematic content prepared according to the different interests and priorities of viewers, multiple language options and subtitle opportunities, low subscription fees, recording and downloading opportunities are among the factors that increase the attractiveness of digital platforms today.

An example of digital platforms that are very popular in the world and in Turkey as well is the US-based Netflix. Established in 1997, Netflix is a subscription-based streaming service that allows its members to watch TV series and movies on an internet-connected device without advertisements. The content on Netflix varies by region and may change over time. Content on the platform can be watched on any internet-connected device with the Netflix app, such as smart TVs, game consoles, media players, set-top boxes, smartphones and tablets (Netflix, 2022). As of 2022, the total number of subscribers worldwide exceeded 221 million and the platform's net profit in the same year was 1.6 billion (NTV, 2022).

RESEARCH OBJECTIVE

The objective of a research is a clear statement of why and for what purpose the research is being conducted. Every research has a specific purpose and this purpose may be to determine a situation in some cases or to determine the relationship between variables in some cases (Aziz, 2010). The purpose of this study is to investigate whether the Netflix platform, which provides digital broadcasting services on a universal scale, is also a digital diplomacy element that mediates public diplomacy. For this purpose, the following questions are sought to be answered:

Research Question 1: Do the digital contents on the Netflix platform overlap with the activities for public diplomacy practices?

Research Question 2: What kind of reactions do Netflix users give to the content on the platform?

RESEARCH METHOD

Determining the research method in a scientific research will help to identify the path to be followed in the research. The research method is the stage in which the research topic is transformed from abstract to concrete, the problem is explained with facts as well as how to analyze them, and it points to the process of operationalizing the research (Aziz, 2010).

This research was handled within the framework of descriptive research approach. Descriptive research is concerned with the characteristics of any phenomenon and aims to clarify and describe "what is" a situation, a condition, a relationship, an organized activity, and (or) a communication process (Erdoğan, 2012). As the first of the scientific research methods identified within the scope of the research, the non-participant observation technique was used. Observation is a widely used data collection technique and is used in any social and (or) institutional environment that the researcher deems appropriate for the research objective. Observation technique contributes to the researcher in collecting the necessary data for the research, determining the relationship between the facts, reaching the findings and concluding the research (Yıldırım & Şimşek, 2013; Aziz, 2010). In this respect, observation is not conducted to understand a single thing, but a unity (Erdoğan, 2012). Unattended observation is a type of observation in which the researcher has no intervention or control over the subject under investigation. Since the situation observed in unattended observation is not revealed by the researcher, there is no participation in the observed subject. Therefore, the phenomena, activities and interactions are handled in their natural context (Baker, 2006). In the unattended observation method, the researcher does not participate in the activities in the observed event, object or environment. However, this method guides the researcher in determining the characteristics of the observed event, object or environment and helps him/her to classify and judge the context and interaction as it is (Fraenkel, Wallen, & Hyun, 2012).

The second research method identified to increase the validity of the research was the standardized open-ended interview method. This method consists of a carefully crafted and organized set of questions with the aim of recruiting each participant in the same order and asking each participant the same questions in essentially the same words. Standardized open-ended interviewing is used when it is important to minimize variation in the questions asked to the interviewees (Patton, 1988) and asking the same questions in a systematic order minimizes subjective judgments and interviewer influence, which makes it easy to analyze the data (Yıldırım & Şimşek, 2013). Following the second research method determined for the research, the interview form was prepared and tested. Then, the necessary preparation was made to interview the participants and then the interviews were conducted. The principles of "writing easy-to-understand questions, preparing focused questions, asking open-ended questions, avoiding directing, avoiding multidimensional questions, preparing alternative questions, writing different types of questions, organizing questions logically, and developing questions" (Yıldırım & Şimşek, 2013) that should be taken into consideration in the preparation of the interview form were adhered to and research ethics were ensured.

Sample and Study Group

The sample of the study was determined through "maximum variation sampling". The aim of this sampling type is to create a relatively small sample and to reflect the diversity of the people who will be a part of the problem at the maximum level. Creating a sample based on maximum diversity does not mean generalizing. On the contrary, it is to determine whether there are any common or shared phenomena among diverse situations. In other words, maximum variation sampling is to describe in detail the unique dimensions of each situation/person/object/community included in the sample (Yıldırım & Şimşek, 2013); Patton, 1988). The universe of this study consists of foreign students studying at universities in Turkey. In accordance with the maximum variation sampling method; Kyrgyzstan, Nigerian and American students studying at university in Turkey were determined as the study group. While determining the study group, it was taken into account that the participants actively used Netflix.

FINDINGS AND DISCUSSION

The first research method identified for this study is unattended observation. In this method, the researcher is not in the observed subject/object/environment, but has the opportunity to observe the relationship context of the subject/object/environment and collect data (Erdoğan, 2012). The data obtained as a result of the observation on the Netflix platform, which was selected as the subject of the research, were analyzed using semantic content analysis. Semantic content analysis is used to examine and interpret representations related to the presented information. In semantic content analysis, data are collected according to the categories determined about the phenomena subject to the research and the words/concepts included in these categories, inferences are made about the categories and the concepts within them, and these selected words/concepts are analyzed in logical, predictive or causal contexts (Erdoğan, 2012). In this context, in order to understand the logic of the functioning of the Netflix platform and to make inferences, it is possible to say the following when we need to evaluate the data obtained as a result of the observation in the context of public diplomacy:

- The content on the platform is offered to users in different languages and with subtitle support. In this respect, Netflix contributes to foreign language learning activities and fulfills a function just like online language courses or exchange programs. This is a public diplomacy method that is equivalent to the dissemination of the national language, which is a public diplomacy method practiced by states and non-state actors. In this way, Netflix is not only an entertainment and leisure-themed digital platform, but also a digital diplomacy element that mediates public diplomacy practices.
- The content on the platform is categorized by country (Turkish Made, US Made, Indian Made, etc.). If a production published on the platform attracts attention, it is placed on the global agenda. The best example of this is the Korean series called Squid Game. This series, which is among the most watched productions on Netflix, has increased interest in Korean series (medyafaresi, 2021) and popularized Korean culture. Similarly, anime-themed content has paved the way for increased interest in Japanese anime art (Webrazzi, 2021). From this perspective, Netflix is not only an entertainment and leisure-themed digital platform, but also a platform that mediates public diplomacy practices.
- Although the content on the platform is predominantly movies and TV series, it also includes content that focuses on a culture, country and (or) nation. For example, Club, a Turkish TV series about Sephardic Jews, was both welcomed by the Turkish Jewish community and cited as an example of successful work in the Turkish film industry (BBC Türkçe, 2021). This is an act of cultural diplomacy for both Turkish and Jewish cultures, and Netflix has acted as a bridge for public diplomacy by mediating this situation.

The second research method determined to increase the validity of the research is the standardized open-ended interview method. In this context, "Netflix and Digital Diplomacy Interview Form" was developed by the researcher in order to obtain opinions on the digital public diplomacy function of Netflix. While preparing the interview questions, a literature review was conducted and questions were prepared. Expert opinions were taken before the interview form was finalized and the interview phase started after the necessary revisions were made. Participants were identified as KIR1, KIR2, NIJ1, NIJ2, USA1, USA2 according to their countries. The interviews were recorded by the researcher and the collected data were digitized and analyzed. The following questions were asked to the participants during the interview:

Question 1: What are the reasons for preferring Turkish productions on the Netflix platform?

Question 2: What information about Turkish culture did you learn from any Turkish production you watched on the Netflix platform?

Question 3: How is the Turkish image reflected in any Turkish production you have watched on the Netflix platform?

Question 4: How has any Turkish production you have watched on the Netflix platform contributed to your learning Turkish?

Answer 1: I follow Turkish productions to learn Turkish. The topics of the productions are not very important for me, I want to learn Turkish and consider the career option in Turkey. (KIR1)

Answer 2: In the productions I watch, the subjects are mostly set in metropolitan cities. Although I have not been to Istanbul, I learned many things about Istanbul from the productions. The most basic information I learned about Istanbul is that it is an important city between Asia and Europe and that many civilizations have left important artifacts. (KIR1)

Answer 3: There are many Turkish productions on Netflix. I focus more on the productions of Turkish actors that I like. These productions are usually action and emotional content, but even in these productions, I always see the Turkish flag as an image. (KIR1)

Answer 4: It contributed a lot. I can say that I learned Turkish from Turkish content. (KIR1)

Answer 1: We are actually countries with a common history. The most basic characteristic of Kyrgyz and Turks is the fact of kinship from history. I understand Turkish, but I cannot speak it, but I watch Turkish productions because I am curious about where and how our cognates live. (KIR2)

Answer 2: Turkish culture is similar to Kyrgyz culture in many ways. Respect for elders and family concepts are important dynamics for both countries. However, Turkey is bigger and stronger, so it has more opportunities to demonstrate these cultural values in the international arena. In addition to this, from the productions I have watched, one can immediately understand how sensitive they are in terms of religion with the size of the mosques. (KIR2)

Answer 3: Turkish productions actually describe exactly the Turkey I envision in my mind. Although the productions are scripts, I don't think they are disconnected from reality. The productions have taught me that Turkish people are a warrior society just like us and that they are the guardians of justice. (KIR2)

Answer 4: I cannot actively speak Turkish because I am not very successful in language learning. I do not believe that I can learn a new language from Netflix. (KIR2)

Answer 1: I don't consciously choose Turkish productions. I prefer content because I benefit from Netflix recommendations. Among these, Turkish productions can sometimes appear. (NİJ1)

Answer 2: There are many cultural elements that attract my attention in Turkish productions that I watch by chance. Especially in the content, it is possible to see many mosques and Turkish flags. In addition, I think that historically there have been many civilizations in Turkey and it is a cosmopolitan country. (NİJ1)

Answer 3: There are a lot of subliminal messages from the Turkish flag and mosques as an image of Turkey... If you are a careful viewer, you can understand that Turkey has a high level of love for homeland and religion. (NİJ1)

Answer 4: I see Netflix as a helpful element in language learning, but I am not planning to learn Turkish yet. (NİJ1)

Answer 1: I have a special interest in European cinema on Netflix, especially the French and the Turks are producing very successful productions. Almost every place in these two countries is like Hollywood studios prepared for cinema. Spatial diversity is one of the most important reasons why I especially prefer Turkish productions. (NİJ2)

Answer 2: I learned a lot of information especially about the food culture. I learned that there is a society that loves to eat and that eating is a socialization environment for Turks." (NİJ2)

Answer 3: Of course Turkish society is a very different culture compared to our society. What is important for us is sometimes not important for other countries. The same is true for Turkish content. In a way that I cannot understand, big buildings and bridges are always at the forefront of construction. (NİJ2)

Answer 4: I have never been to Turkey, but I think the promotion of Netflix Turkey is a good opportunity. Thanks to Netflix, maybe one day I can visit Turkey. However, I do not feel ready to learn the language at the moment. (NİJ2)

Answer 1: I have lived in Turkey for many years. I have accumulated many beautiful memories. Now I am in the US, but I support all kinds of activities to promote Turkey on international platforms. This applies to Turkish productions on Netflix. I have watched almost all Turkish productions. I follow Turkish productions because I feel emotionally close to them. (USA1)

Answer 2: Turkey is a big country and there are many different cultures in this big country. I have had many experiences about this diverse culture that differs regionally. However, Netflix was an important opportunity for me to get to know the cultures in different regions that I could not physically visit. For example, I learned about the life in touch with nature in northern Turkey and the wedding traditions in eastern Turkey from Turkish content. (USA1)

Answer 3: Turks are very fond of their country and history. Therefore, there are many images of their past in the content they create. (USA1)

Answer 4: I made a concerted effort to learn Turkish while living in Turkey, but it is a much more difficult language than English. Platforms like Netflix offer an important opportunity to revitalize the language I started to forget. (USA1)

Answer 1: I have no serious interest in Turkish productions. However, I enjoy using the opportunities offered by digital media to get to know different geographies. (USA2)

Answer 2: I didn't follow a lot of Turkish content, but I realized that the image of Turkey in the content I followed and the image of Turkey in my mind were not at all similar. I learned that Turkey, which I thought was a closed and conservative society, was actually no different from other European countries. (USA2)

Answer 3: As far as I understand, Turks are a very history-conscious society and they like to use cultural images and metaphors in their productions, especially from the Ottoman period. (USA2)

Answer 4: I have tried to learn Turkish from Netflix's original language options, but I don't think I can succeed. (USA2)

CONCLUSION

Developments in the Internet and information technology have brought about many fundamental changes in television broadcasting. This change was not limited to television channels broadcasting on internet-based platforms, but also paved the way for digital broadcasting platforms. These platforms, which offer modular, mobilized and thematic services to their viewers, have managed to attract the attention of viewers due to their advantages such as low subscription fees, advertisement-free content and ease of use.

The Internet and new media have not only brought innovations in the field of television broadcasting, but have also opened the door to transformations in many fields ranging from politics to economy. One of these fields is diplomacy. The concept of public diplomacy, which emerged when traditional diplomacy methods were insufficient, has evolved into digital diplomacy with the new media, and all kinds of new media applications and platforms have also become an element of public diplomacy.

This study is based on the problematic of how and in what way digital television broadcasting platforms mediate digital diplomacy. For this purpose, the digital broadcasting platform named Netflix was analyzed to answer the question of what kind of contributions this platform makes to public diplomacy practices. As a result of the findings, it has been observed that Netflix is not only an entertainment and leisure-themed digital publishing platform, but also a digital diplomacy element that mediates public diplomacy practices, and it has been concluded that it has some functional aspects especially in the field of cultural diplomacy. As a matter of fact, the interviews with the participants also revealed results that confirm this judgment. For example, participant USA1 stated that he learned about different cultures in Turkey by watching content on Netflix, and participant USA2 emphasized that the perception of prejudice against Turkey in his mind was broken thanks to the Turkish productions he watched on Netflix. Similarly, participant KIR1 said that the reason why he followed Turkish productions was to learn Turkish. He also stated that he learned a lot about Istanbul thanks to Netflix. Participant NİJ1, on the other hand, stated that he did not plan to learn Turkish, but Netflix was a helpful element to learn the language.

As can be seen, Netflix functions as an element of digital diplomacy and has functional features for viewers to get to know different cultures. This is due to both the way the Netflix platform operates and the characteristics of new media. The facilitating effect of Netfix in public diplomacy processes certainly attracts the attention of public diplomacy actors. Therefore, it is possible to say that these platforms similar to Netfix will become widespread over time with different concepts and modeling forms. The level of impact of these platforms, which are among the factors affecting public diplomacy, is the subject of another discussion.

REFERENCES

Akçadağ, E. (2022). *Dűnya'da Ve Tűrkiye'de Kamu Diplomasisi*. Retrieved from Kamu Diplomasisi Web Sitesi: http://www.kamudiplomasisi.org/pdf/emineakcadag.pdf

Aziz, A. (2010). Sosyal Bilimlerde Araştırma Yöntemleri ve Teknikleri (5. ed.). İstanbul: Nobel.

Baker, L. M. (2006, Summer). Observation: A Complex Research Method. *Library Trends*, *55*(1), 171–189. doi:10.1353/lib.2006.0045

BBC Türkçe. (2021). Retrieved from https://www.bbc.com/turkce/haberler-turkiye-59223909#:~:text=Netflix'te%206%20b%C3%B6l%C3%BCm%20olarak,kendi%20ifadeleriyle%20%22g%C3%B6r%C3%BCn%C3%BCr%22%20oldu

Bjola, C. (2015). Making sense of digital diplomacy (Introduction). In C. Bjola & M. Holmes (Eds.), *DIGITAL DIPLOMACY Theory and practice*. Taylor & Francis Group. doi:10.4324/9781315730844

Broadhurst, A. I., & Ledgerwood, G. (1998). Environmental Diplomacy of States, Corporations and Non-Governmental Organizations: The Worldwide Web of Influence. *International Relations*, *14*(2), 1–19. doi:10.1177/004711789801400201

Çakır, M. (2014). Küresel Şirketlerin Yeni MedyaOdaklı Tüketim ve Tüketici Tasarımları. In S. Çakır (Ed.), *Medya ve Tasarım* (pp. 163–196). Urzeni.

Clinton, D. (2016). Diplomacy and International Law. In C. M. Constantinou, P. Kerr, & P. Sharp (Eds.), The SAGE Handbook of Diplomacy (pp. 185-196). SAGE Publications. doi:10.4135/9781473957930.n16

Connoly-Ahern, C., & Ma, L. (2015). Taking It to the Streets: The Evolving Use of VNRs as a Public Diplomacy Tool in the Digital Age. In G. J. Golan (Ed.), *International Public Relations and Public Diplomacy* (pp. 229–244). Peter Lang Publishing.

Cull, N. J. (2009). *Public Diplomacy: Lessons from the Past*. Figueroa Press.

De Gouveia, P. F., & Plumridge, H. (2005). *European Infopolitik: Developing EU Public Diplomacy Strategy*. The Foreign Policy Centre.

Dönmez, E., & Kırık, A. M. (2019). Yeni Medya ile Değişen Televizyon Yayıncılığında İçerik Üretimi: Küresel ve Yerel Ölçekli Platformlar. In Ü. Üniversitesi (Ed.), 6. Uluslararası İletişim Günleri Dijital Dönüşüm Sempozyumu (pp. 182-206). Academic Press.

Ekşi, M. (2016). Türk Dış Politikasında Diplomasinin Yeni İletişimsel Boyutları ve Mekanizmaları: Dijital Diplomasi. In B. S. Cankurtaran (Ed.), *Uluslararası İlişkilere Disiplinlerarası Bir Yaklaşım: Uluslararası İletişim Perspektifi* (pp. 75–92). Röle Akademik Yayıncılık.

Erdoğan, İ. (2012). Pozitivis Metodoloji ve Ötesi (5. ed.). Ankara: Erk.

Femic. (2021). Irena. In M. Güneş (Ed.), *Diplomasi Kavramları Sözlüğü* (pp. 117-120). Ankara: Stratejik Düşünce Enstitüsü Yayinlari.

Fitzpatrick, K. R. (2011). U.S. Public Diplomacy. In *A Post-9/11 World: From Messaging To Mutuality*. Figueroa Press.

Fraenkel, J. R., Wallen, N. E., & Hyun, H. H. (2012). How to Design and Evaluate Research in Education (8. ed.). The McGraw-Hill.

Gilboa, E. (2008). Searching for a Theory of Public Diplomacy. *The Annals of the American Academy of Political and Social Science*, *616*(1), 55–77. doi:10.1177/0002716207312142

Gönlübol, M. (1993). *Uluslararası Politika: İlkeler, Kavramlar, Kuramlar*. Atilla Kitabevi.

Huijgh, E. (2016). Public Diplomacy. In C. M. Constantinou, P. Kerr, & P. Sharp (Eds.), *The SAGE Handbook of Diplomacy* (pp. 437–450). SAGE Publications. doi:10.4135/9781473957930.n36

Huntington, S. P. (2004). *Asker ve Devlet Sivil Asker îlişkilerinin Kuram ve Siyasası* (K. U. Kızılaslan, Trans.). Salyangoz Yayınları.

Karaduman, S., & Aciyan, E. (2019). Netflix'in İlk Türk Dizisi "hakan Muhafiz" Üzerine Bir Alımlama Analizi. *AKİL Akdeniz İletişim Dergisi*, (32), 669–687. doi:10.31123/akil.620457

Kennedy, P. (2001). *Büyük Güçlerin Yükseliş ve Çöküşleri* (B. Karanakçı, Trans.). Türkiye İş Bankası Yayınları.

L'Etang, J. (2009). Public Relations and Diplomacy in a Globalized World: An Issue of Public Communication. *The American Behavioral Scientist, 53*(4), 607–626. doi:10.1177/0002764209347633

Lister, M., Dovey, J., Giddings, S., Grant, I., & Kelly, K. (2009). New Media: A critical introduction (2. ed.). Taylor & Francis Group.

medyafaresi. (2021). Retrieved from https://www.medyafaresi.com/haber/squid-game-diger-kore-yapimlarina-da-ilgiyi-artirdi/975357

Melissen, J. (2005). The New Public Diplomacy: Between Theory and Practice. In J. Melissen (Ed.), *The New Public Diplomacy* (pp. 3–27). Palgrave Macmillan. doi:10.1057/9780230554931_1

Mikos, L. (2016). Digital Media Platforms and the Use of TV Content: Binge Watching and Video-on-Demand in Germany. *Media and Communication, 4*(3), 154–161. doi:10.17645/mac.v4i3.542

Netflix. (2022). Retrieved Nisan 20, 2022, from https://help.netflix.com/tr/node/412

Nicolson, H. (1939). *Diplomacy.* Oxford University Press.

NTV. (2022). Retrieved from https://www.ntv.com.tr/teknoloji/netflixin-abone-sayisi-dustu-hisseleri-cakildi,ruqaZq6qXk2OgbI4KlhDwg

Nye, J. (2020). Soft power: The evolution of a concept. *Journal of Political Power, 14*(1), 196–208. doi:10.1080/2158379X.2021.1879572

Nye, J. S. (2004). *Soft Power.* PublicAffairs.

Özkan, A. (2015). 21. Yüzyılın Stratejik Vizyonu Kamu Diplomasisi ve Türkiye'nin Kamu Diplomasisi İmkânları. Stratejik Rapor, TASAM.

Patton, M. Q. (1988). Qualitative Evacuation Methods (9. ed.). Sage Publications.

Sancar, G. A. (2017). Turizm Diplomasisi Kapsaminda Yer Markalama: Turkey Home Kampanya Analizi. *Selçuk İletişim Dergisi, 9*(4), 89–108.

Seib, P. (2012). *Real-Time Diplomacy, Politics and Power in the Social Media Era.* Palgrave Macmillan.

Şenel, B. (2012). Savaş İle Barış Arasında Bir Kriz Yönetim Stratejisi Olarak Zorlayıcı Diplomasi ve Türk Dış Politikasındaki Örnekleri. *Security Ecosystem and Multileteral Cost*, 157-190.

Tuncer, H. (1995). *Eski Ve Yeni Diplomasi.* Ümit Yayıncılık.

Tuncer, H. (2009). *Diplomasinin Evrimi*. Kaynak Yay.

Watson, A. (1982). *Diplomacy: The Dialogue Between States*. Routledge.

Webrazzi. (2021). Retrieved from https://webrazzi.com/2021/03/29/netflix-2021-de-40-yeni-anime-yayinlayacagini-acikladi/

Yağmurlu, A. (2019). Dijital Diplomasi: Kamu Diplomasisi Çerçevesinden Avrupa Birliği Üye Ülkeleri Ve Türkiye Dişişleri Bakanliklari İnternet Uygulamalari. *Gümüşhane Üniversitesi İletişim Fakültesi Elektronik Dergisi*, *7*(2), 1267–1295.

Yıldırım, A., & Şimşek, H. (2013). Sosyal Bilimlerde Nitel Araştırma Yöntemleri (9. ed.). Ankara: Seçkin Yay.

Zhang, J., & Fahmy, S. (2015). Live Tweeting at Work: TheUse of Social Media in Public Diplomacy. In G. J. Golan (Ed.), *International Public Relations And Public Diplomacy* (pp. 315–332). Peter Lang Publishing.

KEY TERMS AND DEFINITIONS

Digital Broadcasting: Is the practice of using digital signals rather than analogue signals for broadcasting over radio frequency bands. Digital television broadcasting (especially satellite television) is widespread. Digital audio broadcasting is being adopted more slowly for radio broadcasting where it is mainly used in Satellite radio.Digital links, thanks to the use of data compression, generally have greater spectral efficiency than analog links. Content providers can provide more services or a higher-quality signal than was previously available. It is estimated that the share of digital broadcasting increased from 7% of the total amount of broadcast information in 2000, to 25% in 2007. Some countries have completed a Digital television transition.

Digital Diplomacy: Also referred to as Digiplomacy and eDiplomacy (see below), has been defined as the use of the Internet and new information communication technologies to help achieve diplomatic objectives. However, other definitions have also been proposed. The definition focuses on the interplay between internet and diplomacy, ranging from Internet driven-changes in the environment in which diplomacy is conducted to the emergence of new topics on diplomatic agendas such as cybersecurity, privacy and more, along with the use of internet tools to practice diplomacy.

Digital Publishing: It means using online technology to digitize print material and disseminate it through electronic devices. Content developers, readers, and viewers alike are moving away from traditional publishing methods and relying more often on digital publishing because of print media's limitations. For businesses, this may be a longer publishing process, or, for readers, decreased ease of access to content or information. Compared to old-school publishing methods, digital publishing has immense benefits, such as: Attracting a Larger Audience, Fixing Mistakes Easily, Engaging Your Target Audience.

Diplomacy: Is the art and science of maintaining peaceful relationships between nations, groups, or individuals. Often, diplomacy refers to representatives of different groups discussing such issues as conflict, trade, the environment, technology, or security. People who practice diplomacy are called diplomats.

Modern Diplomacy: Does not fall into the traditional mold. Modern diplomacy has evolved into a modern mold with, in many re spects, changed norms of behavior. The traditional definition of diplomacy as the conduct of foreign affairs of a sovereign nation really no longer applies. Diplomacy is not simply the process by which nations deal with each other; the role of the diplomat is no longer simply to represent his sovereign in the court of another sovereign. Diplomacy has now become so related to foreign policy and to the process of foreign policymaking that the diplomat is as much involved in the foreign policy process as he is in the process of conducting foreign relations. And in the fullest sense, the foreign policy process that we follow today which is reflected in the practice of modern diplomacy - includes the formulation of policy decisions that affect the direction the country is going to take and the implementation of those aspects of the national interest that are involved with our relations with other nations.

Netflix: Is an American subscription streaming service and production company based in Los Gatos, California. Founded on August 29, 1997 by Reed Hastings and Marc Randolph in Scotts Valley, California, it offers a film and television series library through distribution deals as well as its own productions, known as Netflix Originals.

Public Diplomacy: In international relations, public diplomacy or people's diplomacy, broadly speaking, is any of the various government-sponsored efforts aimed at communicating directly with foreign publics to establish a dialogue designed to inform and influence with the aim that this foreign public supports or tolerates a government's strategic objectives.

Soft Power: In politics (and particularly in international politics), is the ability to co-opt rather than coerce (contrast hard power). In other words, soft power involves shaping the preferences of others through appeal and attraction. A defining feature of soft power is that it is non-coercive; the currency of soft power includes culture, political values, and foreign policies. In 2012, Joseph Nye of Harvard University explained that with soft power, "the best propaganda is not propaganda", further explaining that during the Information Age, "credibility is the scarcest resource".

Chapter 7
India–Nepal Border Dispute, Media and Securitization in Nepal:
A Critical Discourse Analysis

Sudeep Upretty
https://orcid.org/0000-0002-9650-8321
Nepal Institute of Research and Communications (NIRC), Nepal

ABSTRACT

Though the role of media in national security matters has been generally understood in academic and public spheres, limited studies have been conducted and published, especially in the context of Nepal. Most studies have been confined to the civil-military relations, post-conflict transformation and media advocacy, international diplomacy, among others. The discourses carried through and by the media has been given limited attention in both academic and professional circles. Conducting critical discourse analysis of the media coverage and documenting perspectives of the national security and international relations scholars as well as media researchers and practitioners, this chapter attempts to understand the inter-relationship between the media and security sector in Nepal through the securitization theory. Examining the patterns of the Lipulekh border dispute, the chapter explores the process of securitization through the 'speech act' and how it is shaping and has shaped public perceptions regarding national security and nationalism.

INTRODUCTION

Nepal has gone through a major political shift in the last two decades starting with the 'People's War', transition from monarchy to a republican state and current federalism unrest. National Security has thus remained a core topic of national debates and discourses. Particularly border disputes between Nepal and India have regularly drawn attention, triggering 'patriotic' sentiments. Media, particularly, has been instrumental in terms of being the 'agent' and even sometimes an 'actor' in carrying forward the discourse.

DOI: 10.4018/978-1-6684-5822-8.ch007

The role of media has increasingly been prominent how a national security matter is perceived. Syed Nasser Qadri (2019) views that media can be an active participant in the social (de)construction of security threats and the (de)legitimization of exceptional measures. He adds that since the primary form of exposure for general citizens to foreign policy issues is through the media (as public cannot experience security/foreign policy/diplomacy matters first-hand), they are susceptible to framing effects in the news.

Michael C. Williams (2003) talks about the relationship of security and the speech act, as a form of communication where he says that security is not just any kind of speech-act, not just any form of social construction but rather, through the process of securitization, an issue can be labeled as an "existential threat", thereby requiring extraordinary measures to address it. Elaborating on securitization, Balzacq (2005) talks about three assumptions for effective securitization viz. audience centered, context-dependent and power-laden. Particularly on media's role in securitization, Cristina Archetti (2010) talks about three different ways media is used as a tool for foreign policy and international exchange: public diplomacy (using media to influence public opinion), media diplomacy (for communicating with disputing parties and promoting conflict resolution) and media-broker diplomacy (journalists serving as temporary mediators in international negotiations).

Specific to Nepal, Deepak Adhikari, in his paper, *The Role of Media in Shaping Foreign Policy Discourse in Nepal* talks about the how the specialized reporting of foreign policy and national security issues in Nepal began as late as the 2000s through *Kantipur* and *The Kathmandu Post* dailies. Prior to that, the foreign policy reporting was limited to covering bilateral visits, parliamentary hearing of the ambassadors—designate and activities of the foreign missions. *The Kathmandu Post* also started set up a bureau in New Delhi in 2005 and continues to hold an office there. The other media houses also followed suit, but they have not been able to have a permanent presence (Adhikari, 2016).

The story of the latest border dispute between Nepal and India inaugurated construction of 'Link Road', passing through Lipulekh in 2020. The Lipulekh Pass is a disputed territory and claimed by both Nepal and India. India had released a revised political map in November 2019 which included the disputed territories of Lipulekh, Kalapani, and Limpiyadhura. This act was condemned by the Ministry of Foreign Affairs of the Government of Nepal through its Press Release, which called upon the Government of India to "refrain from carrying out any activity inside the territory of Nepal" (MoFA, 2020). Following this incident, the Nepali parliament was also quick to act on, with the amendment of the constitution to endorse the updated map with the disputed areas included (Ghimire, 2020).

This paper, thus concentrates on the media portrayal of Lipulekh border dispute issue and discusses the nature and extent of securitization in the Nepali and Indian mainstream and online media space, including social media.

METHODS

A qualitative research design using Critical Discourse Analysis (Fairclough, 1995) framework was adopted for this study. Conceptualized by Norman Fairclough, the Critical Discourse Analysis (CDA) consists of three dimensions: the object of analysis (including verbal, visual or verbal and visual texts); the processes by means of which the object is produced and received (writing/speaking/designing and reading/listening/viewing) by human subjects; and the socio-historical conditions which govern these processes.

Content analysis of media coverage during 2020 and 2021 by Nepali and Indian media and online media was conducted. To understand the nature and type of discourses happening in social media, two

Figure 1. Conceptual framework of the study

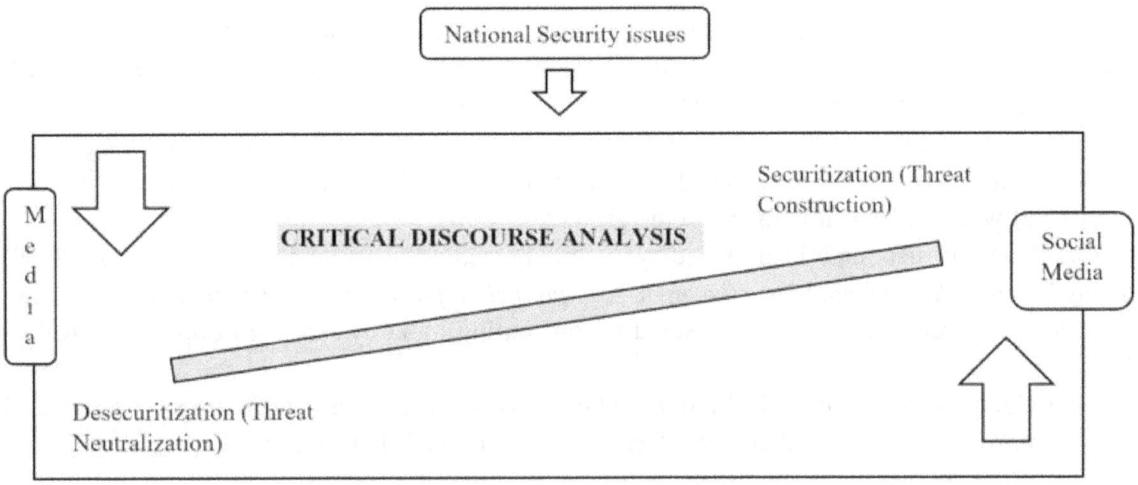

social media sites, Facebook and YouTube were selected, primarily as these two sites have been the dominant and popular social media platforms for public discussion and debates in Nepal.

To identify the relevant posts in the social media, the following words/phrases and their combination were used in the search bar of Facebook and YouTube: "Lipulekh", "Kalapani", "Indo-Nepal border conflict", "border conflict in Nepal", "Lipulekh and Kalapani", and "border encroachment".

Furthermore, ten key informant interviews (KIIs) were undertaken to understand the intention and practice of media reporting on border issues in Nepal, specifically on Indo-Nepal relations. The KII respondents were national security and international relations researchers and academicians, media researchers, media professionals, among others. The interviews were conducted virtually considering the COVID-19 pandemic situation. The interviews were transcribed directly into English and coded into themes and codes using Grounded Theory (Tie, Birks, & Francis, 2019). For ethical considerations, the identity of the respondents have been kept confidential.

Specific to this study, the CDA was modified to understand what sorts of language/texts were used in the media reports, the public perception on the coverage (based on comments, reactions) and the broader geopolitical context (if and how was there any agenda setting). The CDA framework has been further complemented by the theories of Securitization and Desecuritization (Waever, 2007) whereby the study particularly investigated whether the texts and the agenda setting has been driven by motives of threat construction (securitization or encouraging polarized opinions) or threat neutralization (desecuritization or discouraging any polarized opinions), which is the core component of the securitization theory. In a nutshell, the overall conceptual framework for this study is explained figuratively as shown in figure 1 below:

FINDINGS FROM CONTENT ANALYSIS

The sections below describe various observations made while doing the content analysis of the media reports and social media articles and videos on the Lipulekh/border "encroachment" issue.

Some of the titles of YouTube videos directly contributes to threat construction, leading towards securitization of the issue. As for instance, a video title says, *Bharat le Kalapani Lipulek nadiye je pani huna sakcha* (KhabarNepal, 2019) suggesting 'anything can happen' if India doesn't give back Kalapani and Lipulekh areas to Nepal. Likewise, another video title has provocative title, *Ekkasi Lipulek chiryo Nepali Sena, Nepali Senapani Actionma Utriyo* (EtvNepal, 2020) meaning, 'suddenly Nepal Army enters Lipulekh area and straightaway goes into action' indicating some sort of a war/battle ongoing. The language used in this title is very strong and provoking some sort of a violent response from the viewers, irrespective of what the real situation is on the ground.

This kind of securitization is also carried by the Indian media and social media channels. A YouTube title reads *Nepal dikharaha hai bharat ko ankh, Kalapani sima par bheje sainik* (The Hindustan Mirror, 2020) which in literal terms means that Nepal is confronting India by sending troops to the Kalapani border.

Another video article by Bisbo (2020) does not have such provocative title as compared to the earlier videos. The title reads, 'Nepal's Kalapani border dispute with India: What is the crux of the issue'. However, when we read the description of the video, there is an aggressive tone prevalent as these lines suggest:

Nepal and India have always been friends, the Gorkha Regiment has fought wars for India; but suddenly there has been a dramatic pro-China shift in KP Sharma Oli's stance and unnecessary aggressiveness towards India. What more is in store in the dispute of Kalapani, Liplulekh and Limpiyadhura.

The phrase 'unnecessary aggressiveness' does indicate the Indian stand on the issue as it suggests that Nepal is pushing this agenda on the backdrop with its good relations with China and China's persuasion to do so. From this view, the story has the element of securitization as it opens up the discourse of threat to Indian existence/sovereignty.

Zee News, which is another very popular and one of the mainstream news outlets in India have been often branded as 'ultra-nationalist' and 'pro-Modi'. The visit of its senior journalist, Sudhir Chaudhary to Nepal, interview with the then Prime Minister KP Sharma Oli and visit to the northern region in Nepal (bordering China) received quite a flak from the Nepali press and public for the tone and message of reporting Chaudhary conducted after his return. When KP Sharma Oli and then parliament passed the new geographical map of Nepal (including the disputed Lipulekh, Kalapani areas), it created a lot of buzz in the Indian media. One such reporting by Chaudhary in Zee News (2020) is provocative in its tone. The title itself suggests such as it reads, *Naye nakshe se akhir saabit kya karna chahta hai Nepal?* meaning 'By issuing new map, what does Nepal want to prove?'

In general, most right-wing media in India openly claimed that the actions by the Nepali government were mainly to "appease" China. Some of the reactions were also sexist and misogynist, speculating "honey-trap" involving the role of Ms. Hou Yanqui, the Chinese ambassador for Nepal. Nepal's cable and satellite television providers even stopped airing Indian news channels for some days as a protest against inappropriate broadcasting of a video clip of the then Prime Minister KP Sharma Oli honey trapped by Ambassador Yanqui (Shakya, 2020). However, most of the mainstream Indian media distanced itself from such misogynist attacks but treated this border dispute with outrage and anticipated a strong Indian backlash.

Times of India, another mainstream and prominent news outlet in India in one of its stories posted on Facebook (2020) has covered the issue of how the residents of Uttarakhand villages bordering Nepal have been exposed to anti-India songs captured through radio frequency from the Nepal side of the territory.

The story suggests that such songs have been very provocative and aired to instill aggression among the public. One statement, "Nepalese propaganda needs to be strongly countered". This statement qualifies the act of securitization as there seems a deliberate attempt to build the threat and send a message to the Nepali community that some 'counter action' would be taken.

Discussing more about reactions on Facebook, Routine of Nepal Banda, which is one of the most popular Nepali Facebook pages with 2.7 million likes, had published a post on its page regarding a high-level meeting among the Prime Minister and other key government officials, opposition party leaders and border experts to have a common consensus regarding Nepal's take on the Kalapani, Lipulekh border (Lipulekh Border Dispute Case, 2019). Given the sensitivity and the nationalist sentiment the story carries, it attracted wide sort of responses from the general public. One such public comment (translated in English) reads as such:

"We need to sacrifice our blood and sweat to retrieve back our lost territories, not just Lipulekh, Limpiyadhura areas but also all the territories of Greater Nepal region up to Tista and Kangada. These territories should return to Nepal at all costs. We are ready to defend and even die to protect our motherland."

The tonality of the public comment on the Facebook post from a Nepali citizen also qualifies the act of securitization and threat construction. There are some strong expressions used such as "ready to sacrifice blood", "even die to protect our motherland" which clearly establishes element of threat and creates antagonistic feelings towards the other party (India). The fact that such comments have been liked and appreciated by others too indicates the impressions public reactions on social media platforms can have.

In one of the columns published in The Kathmandu Post (Wagle, 2020), one of the premier English news outlets of Nepal, Achyut Wagle criticizes the national leaders and stands of authorities in power taking the escapist route and owing to provocative politics and ultra-nationalist jingoism. He opines, "When governments fail to address contemporary problems, they resort to provocative nationalistic demagogy."

On a positive note, there have also been some genuine efforts of securitization and threat neutralization. This has been done primarily to put facts and contexts as they are, without fabricating or distorting the reality. Dhruv Rathee is one of the popular YouTubers, who produces informative and context specific content, especially sociopolitical affairs surrounding India. In an informative video article, Rathee (2020) puts facts and history of Indo-Nepal border dispute in front and explains the current scenario. There is no dramatization in the presentation and therefore, neutralizes the excessive reactions that readers/viewers would otherwise derive from other types of sensationalist reporting. The Quint (2020), another emerging news and social media outlet, especially popular among the youth in India follows suit in their balanced reporting of the situation. In a similar vein, Gaurab Shumsher Thapa in an article for Asia Times (Thapa, 2020) opines that the border disputes are a matter of geopolitics and diplomatic affairs, that have been interpreted in various ways by respective countries based on their convenience. Henceforth, claiming a territory should not be looked upon as an antagonizing step. He shares:

Nepalese government should come out with a map that includes these disputed territories on its side. Historically, Nepal has been reluctant to produce such a map so as not to antagonize India. Both India and China publish maps based on their own interpretations of disputed boundaries and territories, including Kashmir and Arunachal Pradesh. Therefore, Nepal should not hesitate to publish a map that it deems to be correct.

IMPRESSIONS AND INDICATIONS FROM KEY INFORMATION INTERVIEWS

The opinions and perspectives of the KII respondents, categorized into four dominant themes are discussed below:

Nationalism Sells

The respondents came to a common conclusion that nationalism has remained a hot topic for debate and discussion in the media. News stories related to border encroachment have appeared in the banner news and triggered greater attention in the social media too. The national security and international relations experts also acknowledge that they are more "in action" whenever a news floats around some activity in the Indo-Nepal border.

"We become busy whenever there is some news about some border activity, especially encroachment related news. We are inquired by news agencies for some opinions or views. There have been instances where I have been interviewed by five news channels in a single day." – International Relations scholar, interviewed virtually in October 2021

The media fraternity also acknowledge this phenomenon of Indo-Nepal border issue creating a major buzz.

"I cannot hide the fact that our coverage related to national security/border encroachment triggers more attention compared to other news/incidents. I think this is primarily because of two reasons. On one hand, there is overwhelming response from the public. On the other hand, we, from journalistic lens, also want to put the responsible bodies and persons on the spotlight – for the public to know, what, how and why it happened." – Editor of an online news portal, interviewed virtually in September, 2021

In a similar vein, a media researcher also shares an interesting trend about how 'digital revolution' is intensifying public reactions:

"During the print era, the only source of garnering attention was to publish on the front page, as a banner news. Now, in the digital era, with the access to smart phones and internet by the public, it has been much easier for the media agencies to push the news (and subsequently their agendas) through different medium. Now you can shoot an interview and make "viral" content posting in various platforms such as Facebook, Instagram, Twitter and YouTube easily, which will provoke various reactions from the subscribers." – Media scholar, interviewed virtually in September, 2021

On the other hand, the media scholars have highlighted that while there is increased attention to the national security and border encroachment issues, the mushrooming effect of the often-unregulated online news portals and social media outlets have sensationalized to the extent of securitization and diluted the issue, which is discussed in the next section.

Nature of Media Coverage

The key informants acknowledge that the Nepali (and international) media can and have been influential in creating a 'buzz' and thereby creating discourses of national security, over the years. The respondents have been critical of some selected media, from both Nepal and India, who have been quite 'hostile' in their coverage towards the other country.

"Whenever there is news about border conflict between Nepal and India, there would be flurry of media reports, with anti-Nepal sentiments. We have witnessed Nepal being linked to favoring China and Pakistan and 'conspiring' for national insecurity of India. There would be several clickbait titles even in mainstream Indian print and online media as well as primetime television, often with lots of provocation." – Media scholar, interviewed virtually in October, 2021

Nepali media is also not free from this sort of behavior. Although mainstream Nepali media have often taken the 'softer tone', there have been instances in some of the online media and social media where there is largely 'anti-India' sentiment prevailing.

"We cannot deny the fact that sometimes we it is called 'playing to the gallery'. It is also sometimes necessary to catch the attention of the decision makers. Unfortunately, that has also been the norm here in Nepal, where sensitive issues need to be taken through that route of pressurization, in the form of protests, strikes, blockades and front-page coverage of confrontation with the police. The reluctance of the State, especially the Home and Defense ministries to handle the matter in a timely and smart manner is not we want to see as the fourth pillar. Therefore, as a watchdog agency, we have been more aggressive in that sense to pressurize the government." – Editor of an online news portal, interviewed virtually in October 2021

Public Reactions on The Media Coverage

The public reactions on the media coverage have often been what the media agencies have intended/expected. The key informants shared that the media literacy in both countries – India and Nepal, is quite limited and therefore the readers/audience are not able to decipher the intentions of the media outlets, the agenda/discourse they are eager to develop, and the reactions they expect from the public. In sensitive situations such as border conflict, several fake videos float around the internet, even posted by popular pages/groups which can create a lot of panic and therefore securitize the matter, unnecessarily. WhatsApp Forwards have been a serious problem for fact checkers in India with bombarding of fake news and videos. In the case with Nepal too, the scenario is similar. There have been efforts put in by some social media handles and websites such as Nepal Fact Check, Centre for Media Research (CMR) Nepal, My Sansar. However, the accessibility and awareness of these platforms have only reached a handful of media literate and educated community within Kathmandu and some urban areas.

"We cannot control public reactions. At best, what we can do is to educate people. Some efforts have been initiated. Nepal Fact Check is such initiative which constantly provides quick updates whenever any misleading or fake news is spreading around. Likewise, in India, what Dhruv Rathee does, explaining things in a very simple and easy way, is commendable. In the case of Nepal too, Youtubers like Random

Nepali and Binayak Kuikel are regularly posting informative videos. These efforts need to be appreciated and encouraged." – Media Scholar, interviewed virtually in September, 2021

While these efforts are welcome, the level and extent to which the social media 'mobs' operate is humungous, thereby making such efforts appear like 'needle in a haystack'.

You are literally like fighting a war where you are on a side with 5 people carrying swords while the other party has missiles and that too in plenty. We are just a small group funded with a limited budget and a zeal to address this issue. On the other hand, the social media 'army' of these 'patriots' are in thousands, and it takes a huge toll on us to go through several of these pages, understand the content, see the patterns and flaws. It is indeed an up-hill task." – Media Scholar/Fact checker, interviewed virtually in October, 2021

Knowledge and Capacity of Media Reporting Matters

The key informants have also shared that the capacity of journalists and the exposure to quality reporting also matters, to minimize the spread of misinformation and fake news. While the mushrooming growth of online media and YouTube channels have expanded the reach and quantity of media reporting/coverage, a close watch on the quality and the agenda-setting these outlets are doing, have not been monitored effectively. In this light, the key informants argue that alongside allowing the increasing market of the media sector, equal emphasis is also required for capacitating the journalists and the editors.

"The journalists and the editors go through various levels of training and exposure. In the online-digital context, the training curricula also needs to be updated as per the need of the hour. Some non-government agencies and umbrella organizations such as Federation of Nepali Journalists (FNJ) have initiated such trainings and orientations. However, they have been few and far between. Journalists, as they are specialists in various 'beats' also need to ensure that the information they are receiving are from authentic and credible sources." – Media scholar, interviewed virtually in November, 2021

The key informants also share sensitive issues such as national security and international relations require broader and in depth understanding about the geopolitics, diplomacy, global politics and international development, in order to frame any perspective around the issue. This also goes back to how journalism is studied or taught in Nepali context, and whether the degree courses match the standard of other global journalism courses.

"Teaching of journalism doesn't sit in isolation with the teaching standards of other disciplines. As we have witnessed about the teaching standards in other disciplines, journalism and media studies also need to be looked upon from the same bracket. The quality of our courses, teaching methodologies and the exposure that the students get is limited to the global academic practice. Therefore, topics such as national security, international relations, geopolitics are not given much attention in the journalism/media studies disciplines. We also have had very few Nepali researchers and scholars even from recognized universities, who are well versed in both journalism and national security. This has led a direct impact on the quality of media reporting on such topics." - International Relations scholar, interviewed virtually in November, 2021

CONCLUSION AND RECOMMENDATIONS

This study attempted to understand the nature of media reporting on national security issues in Nepal, particularly investigating the Lipulekh border dispute case and the extent of securitization applied by the mainstream and social media channels, while covering the story.

Though the paper has analyzed only a few media and social media content and only on the recent Lipulekh border dispute case, and therefore might not be entirely sufficient to make a comprehensive conclusion, given the high mainstream media and social media attention the story gathered, certain conclusions can certainly be drawn.

It has been observed that the reputed mainstream media outlets in general have chosen a cautious route towards threat neutralization and refrained from triggering highly charged reactions, from its readers/viewers. From the choice of words used for the title to the content, there was an attempt made to ensure that things do not get 'heated up'. In this regard, it can be deduced that a level of understanding and journalistic professionalism is maintained at least by mainstream media outlets.

However, especially in the online media space, blogs and other social media, there were sensationalist words and tone used to attract the audience. This drew the audiences towards such stories and triggered various sorts of emotional responses – thereby fulfilling the act of securitization. Particularly, in the YouTube videos, the securitization element was prominent with the titles being very provocative and usage of threatful language.

Through the key information interviews, it was also revealed that the mushrooming of online and social media globally and in Nepal with increased competition and trend of clickbait journalism, the securitization on sensitive issues such as national security seems to be 'natural' phenomenon. Specifically, India-Nepal border conflict over the last three decades is one of the hot topics in Nepal's political arena. During the elections too, the border security and national security management become one of the core strategies in the election manifestos. Therefore, the media coverage on India-Nepal border conflict become an obvious interest to the journalists.

However, this doesn't negate the fact that the capacity of journalists to report on national security and international relations issues needs to be improved. This is only a recent reform/improvement in the Nepali media sector to have a specialized reporting and specialist journalists. Otherwise, most of the media houses relied on a single journalist to cover a range of sectors from international relations, diplomacy, political affairs, economic affairs, entertainment, among others. This is still the case outside the capital, Kathmandu, where the media houses have limited journalists and resources. This scenario, obviously, puts the journalists into added pressure to understand multiple issues, which sometimes could be beyond the scope of understanding the depth of the context of national security and international relations issues.

Another less discussed scenario within the media sector in Nepal (also generally in other countries too in the current social media age) is the commercialization of journalism and the pressure to publish soon to compete in the market. This brings added pressure to the media house owners to cater to the 'interest groups' which helps in bringing revenue for the media houses. Strömbäck (2008, p. 34) discusses this phenomenon which he terms as mediatization of politics based on how:

1. media constitute the dominant source of information on politics and society;
2. media and its governance are independent from political control;
3. media content is governed by political or media logic; and
4. political actors are governed by political or media logic.

The higher the degree of the first two factors and greater the dominance of media logic in the last two factors outlined above, the larger is the degree of mediatization of politics. The mediatization of politics was very much prominent during the border 'encroachment' along the India-Nepal border region around Lipulekh and Limpiyadhura area, where the excessive media coverage dictated political discourses, parliamentary debates, marches and strikes. On the other hand, there is also politicization of media about how powerful people in politics dictate how media agencies work and cover debatable issues such as border encroachment and international diplomacy. An unfortunate incident happened with Jamim Shah, head of Space Time Network who was murdered in broad day light in Kathmandu in 2010, when he was reportedly killed by Indian underworld as he apparently had 'links with Pakistani intelligence' and the media reportedly sparking anti-Indian sentiments in Nepal. Other noted media editors also received death threats post the murder as a 'lesson' to the media industry (Dixit, 2010).

Furthermore, there is a tendency to make/manufacture sensationalist news that helps in triggering audience attention, which in media terms is often termed as *clickbait.* Online advertising revenue is a stable phenomenon as the revenue generated from advertisers is dependent on the number of times a unique visitor visits a webpage. Thus, the traffic of the visitors is crucial in this scenario than the quality of stories/media coverage. Search engines such as Google and social media sites including Facebook have also expanded options traditionally available to advertisers, putting more pressure on news sites to bring in traffic and compete for those advertisers.

Angele Christin (2018), in her article, *Counting Clicks: Quantification and Variation in Web Journalism in the United States and France*, puts this phenomenon aptly, "It is impossible to look at the recent evolution of journalism without looking at the evolution of online advertising because the two things are completely interconnected."

Christin further adds, "as online advertising became increasingly competitive, news organizations did what they had to do to survive in this new environment." This is very much true in Nepal and generally in the media world globally, that editors and journalists are now chasing 'sellable stories' such as stories about cats and celebrities instead of serious news topics such as foreign policy or the economy. In the context of Nepal, where nationalism is one of the hot topics for all seasons – as it is very much discussed and debated in the local tea shops, and scores of people hanging around in the newspaper outlets and stationery shops (where the newspapers are sold), passionately discussing about the nationalism/border encroachment issues.

The interest of media houses to capitalize on the nationalistic jingoism could also have triggered on the nature and extent of media reporting on such issues. Furthermore, with some level of realization and advocacy for the need for watchdog agencies, the ongoing initiatives by organizations such as FNJ, CMR-Nepal need to be encouraged and promoted. These efforts need to be rather owned by the government entities and the media houses, and institutionalized.

More often, the triggers resulting in a response become more important than the response itself. When these sensitive issues are reported purposefully in an unethical manner, without substantial facts, details and readers/viewers being misled, three major recommendations can be drawn from this study:

1. More awareness and understanding regarding fake news, misleading news and 'mission journalism' to improve media literacy at the public level and protect/prevent the consequences of securitization or threat building.
2. Capacity building of journalists and media professionals to better understand and report on national security, international relations, diplomacy related topics. This could be done in a systematic man-

Figure 2. Ideal national security and media interface

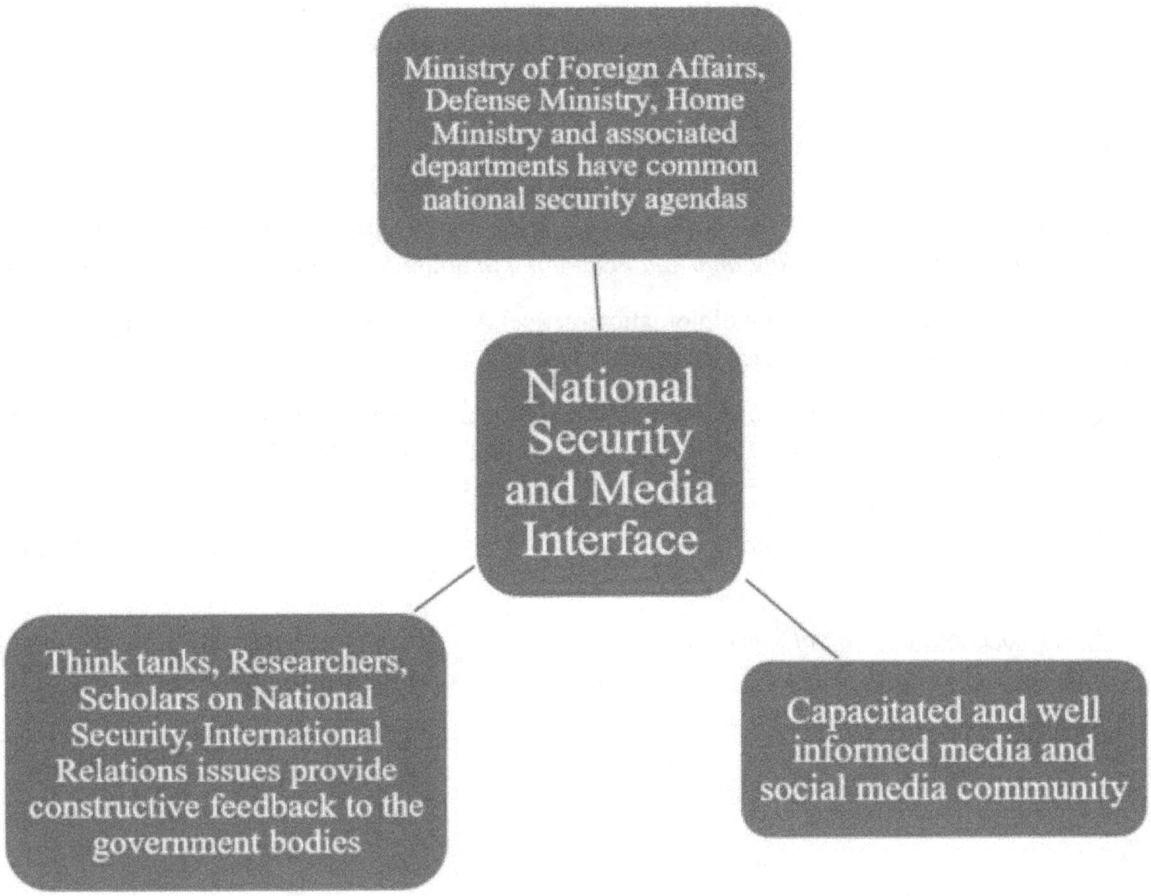

ner with tailored courses and orientations in collaboration with think tanks, research institutes, government departments under ministries of foreign affairs, defense and home affairs.

3. Development and proper implementation of media guidelines on reporting national security/international security/diplomacy issues.

Thus, these recommendations emphasize for multi-sectoral coordination between policy makers, media agencies and think tanks/organizations promoting better reporting and coverage, as presented in Figure 2 below. There is a need to have an interface between national security and media. To develop this interface, relevant ministries (such as Ministries of Foreign Affairs, Defense Ministry, Ministry of Home Affairs) need to come together to have a common interest around national security agenda. The ministries and the relevant government bodies should consult the academia and research/think tanks to identify the most pertinent national security agendas. For this, there needs to be regular consultation with the think tanks, researchers and scholars of national security and international relations. Furthermore, there needs to be a capacitated and well-informed media and social media community – which can track and identify fake, sensationalist news/stories and filter them out and contribute to the process of de-securitization.

This paper, thus advocates for the de-securitization of national security issues in Nepal to encourage threat neutralization, promoting more constructive and reformative discussions rather than ultra-patriotic jingoism, widely prevalent in current media and social media narratives.

REFERENCES

Adhikari, D. (2016). The Role of Media in Shaping Foreign Policy Discourse in Nepal. In P. Singh (Ed.), *The Role of Media in Promoting Regional Understanding in South Asia* (pp. 209–218). Pentagon Press.

Archetti, C. (2010). Media impact on diplomatic practice: An evolutionary model of change. *American Political Science Association (APSA) Annual Convention.*

Balzacq, T. (2005). The Three Faces of Securitization: Political Agency, Audience and Context. *European Journal of International Relations, 11*(2), 171–201. doi:10.1177/1354066105052960

Christin, A. (2018). Counting Clicks: Quantification and Variation in Web Journalism in the United States and France. *American Journal of Sociology, 123*(5), 1382–1415. Advance online publication. doi:10.1086/696137

Dixit, K. (2010, February). *Nepal's media brave threats in 'interesting times'*. Retrieved from Committee to Protect Journalists: https://cpj.org/2010/02/nepals-media-brave-threats-in-interesting-times/

EtvNepal. (2020, May 15). एक्कासी लपुलेक छरि्यो नेपालसिेना ।। नेपालसिेनापनिएक्सनमा उत्रयिो *Lipulek Kalapani Nepal*. Retrieved October 29, 2021, from Etv Nepal: https://www.youtube.com/watch?v=-A5I2fFlBJY

Explained: The Border Dispute Between India and Nepal | The Quint. (2020, June 18). Retrieved November 2, 2021, from The Quint: https://www.youtube.com/watch?v=WjITzeOcEhY

Fairclough, N. (1995). *Critical discourse analysis: the critical study of language*. Longman. Retrieved from https://www.felsemiotica.com/descargas/Fairclough-Norman-Critical-Discourse-Analysis.-The-Critical-Study-of-Language.pdf

Ghimire, B. (2020, June 13). *Constitution amendment bill to update Nepal map endorsed unanimously at the Lower House*. Retrieved November 9, 2021, from The Kathmandu Post: https://kathmandupost.com/national/2020/06/13/constitution-amendment-bill-to-update-nepal-map-endorsed-unanimously-at-the-lower-house

India vs Nepal Border Dispute | Explained by Dhruv Rathee. (2020, May 23). Retrieved November 1, 2021, from Dhruv Rathee: https://www.youtube.com/watch?v=ssUvFPn8DzQ

Janks, H. (n.d.). *Critical Discourse Analysis as a Research Tool.* Retrieved November 10, 2021, from https://www.uv.es/gimenez/Recursos/criticaldiscourse.pdf

KhabarNepal. (2019, November 21). भारतले *Kalapani Lipulek* नदयि जे पनहिुन सक्छ भन्दै *Jasmine Ojha Interview with Sheshmani*. Retrieved October 29, 2021, from ABCE Khabar Nepal: https://www.youtube.com/watch?v=4OiImIYxnKg

Lipulekh Border Dispute Case. (2019, November 9). Retrieved November 4, 2021, from Routine of Nepal Banda: https://www.facebook.com/officialroutineofnepalbanda/posts/3191843110848460

MoFA. (2020, May 9). *Press Release*. Retrieved November 10, 2021, from Ministry of Foreign Affairs: https://mofa.gov.np/press-release-regarding-lipu-lekh/

Nepal radio stations bombard border villages with anti-India songs. (2020, June 21). Retrieved October 29, 2021, from The Times of India: https://www.facebook.com/watch/?v=3055343814532794

Nepal's Kalapani border dispute with India: What is the crux of the issue. A detailed analysis. (2020, July 10). Retrieved October 29, 2021, from Bisbo: https://www.youtube.com/watch?v=ldYtV8pc9kE

Qadri, S. N. (2019). *Framing terrorism and migration in the USA: the role of media in securitization processes*. University of Glasgow.

Shakya, M. (2020). The politics of border and nation in Nepal in the time of pandemic. *Dialectical Anthropology*, *44*(3), 223–231. doi:10.100710624-020-09599-x PMID:32836686

Thapa, G. S. (2020, May 13). *Nepal confronts India in Lipulekh border dispute*. Retrieved November 3, 2021, from Asia Times: https://asiatimes.com/2020/05/nepal-confronts-india-in-lipulekh-border-dispute/

The Hindustan Mirror. (2020, May 17). Retrieved October 29, 2021, from Nepal Kalapani News | KalaPani Lipulekh | Kalapani Nepal news | Nepal Kalapani Border: https://www.youtube.com/watch?v=BmSe6jmtJAo

Tie, Y. C., Birks, M., & Francis, K. (2019). Grounded theory research: A design framework for novice researchers. *SAGE Open Medicine*, *7*, 1–8. PMID:30637106

Waever, O. (2007). Securitization and Desecuritization. In B. Buzan & L. Hansen (Eds.), *International Security: Widening Security* (Vol. 3, pp. 66–99). SAGE Publications.

Wagle, A. (2020, May 25). *The Kathmandu Post*. Retrieved October 30, 2021, from Return to the dialogue table: https://kathmandupost.com/columns/2020/05/25/return-to-the-dialogue-table

Williams, M. C. (2003). Words, Images, Enemies: Securitization and International Politics. *International Studies Quarterly*, *47*(4), 511–531. doi:10.1046/j.0020-8833.2003.00277.x

Zee News. (2020, May 20). Retrieved October 29, 2021, from DNA:नए नक़्शे से Nepal आखरि साबति क्या करना चाहता है? DNA Sudhir Chaudhary |Sudhir Chaudhary On Nepal: https://www.youtube.com/watch?v=FYUA70vDjBY

KEY TERMS AND DEFINITIONS

Desecuritization: The process of nullifying an issue, particularly related to politics or national affairs, that was securitized or considered a threat to human survival.

Diplomacy: Overall matters of a conduct of a country towards another country.

Discourse: Interchange, discussion, and conversation over an idea or topic.

Media: A communication channel through which we disseminate various forms of information such as news, music, movies, education, among others.

National Security: A broad concept encompassing a country's protection particularly related to territory and defense, internal and external politics, and economics.

Securitization: The process whereby an issue, particularly related to politics or national affairs, is considered a threat to human survival and therefore requires emergency actions or coercive means.

Speech Act: The process of analyzing the meaning behind the use of words in a particular manner.

Chapter 8
Evaluation of Websites as Digital Diplomacy Tools in Terms of Design Criteria:
In the Case of Sports Ministry of Turkey and Kyrgyzstan

Atilla Cakar
https://orcid.org/0000-0002-3564-3909
Kyrgyz-Turkish Manas University, Kyrgyzstan

Banu Erdogan Cakar
Kyrgyz-Turkish Manas University, Kyrgyzstan

ABSTRACT

The importance of digital diplomacy, which we encounter as public diplomacy activities on digital platforms, has been recognized more and more, and it has been actively used by many countries through applications such as social media accounts and websites. In the light of this information, the aim of the study is to reveal the ways in which the ministry of sports, which is responsible for sports and athletes, which increases the awareness and prestige of countries in national and international platforms, uses websites as a digital diplomacy tool. The official websites of the Ministries of Sports of Turkey and Kyrgyzstan, which were determined as the sample of the study, were analyzed with the categorical content analysis method, and the similarities and differences between the use of the websites of the ministries were determined.

INTRODUCTION

Digitization, which is an output of the information age, has increased both individual and public interaction with the digital world it has created. Of course, this communication medium, whose conductivity

DOI: 10.4018/978-1-6684-5822-8.ch008

and accessibility has increased, is not only used for communication purposes. In terms of foreign policy, digitalization has taken place and public diplomacy activities carried out with traditional media tools have also been carried out on digital platforms. These activities, which are specific to the digital field, have given birth to the concept of digital diplomacy. In particular, instant access and interactive communication offered by social media tools have been important in the emergence of digital diplomacy activities. Digital diplomacy is increasingly being applied in international politics and strategies are being developed for this purpose. Institutions exist in the digital world with their social media accounts and official websites. In this way, they gained a new field, a new tool to carry out their diplomatic activities; digital diplomacy.

Like many countries in the world, Turkey also wanted to adapt to the global digitalization process. For this purpose, it has done many studies and started an e-transformation project. One of the e-transformation projects was the attainment of a certain standard on the websites of public institutions. For this purpose, the criteria that should be on the web pages of public institutions have been specified by the public institutions transactions system. In these criteria, which are listed as 17 items, it is aimed that the sites reach a wider audience with the most appropriate content, and thus, benefit more efficiently from the opportunities provided by the digital world.

Based on this information on the literature, it is aimed to analyze the digital diplomacy activities of the ministries of sports, which are responsible for sports and athletes, which make a significant contribution to the promotion of countries in both national and international platforms. For this purpose, the sports ministries of Turkey and Kyrgyzstan were chosen as the sample of the study. The sports ministries of Turkey and Kyrgyzstan, which were selected as samples in the research, were named differently in the two countries. Names of the Ministry in Turkey; Ministry of Youth and Sports of the Republic of Turkey, in Kyrgyzstan; It is the Ministry of Culture, Information, Sports and Youth Policy of the Kyrgyz Republic. In the study, the ways in which the selected ministries use official websites as a digital diplomacy tool were evaluated. The websites were analyzed by categorical content analysis method within the framework of the design criteria determined by the public institutions transactions system. As a result of the analysis, the points provided and not provided by the design criteria of the sports ministries were determined and the similarities and differences between the web site usage of the two ministries were revealed.

WEBSITES AS A DIGITAL DIPLOMACY TOOL AND DESIGN CRITERIA FOR WEBSITES

When we look at the word diplomacy etymologically, it is seen that it comes from the Greek word "diploma". It got this name due to the fact that the documents belonging to the state during the Ancient Greek and Roman Empires were folded like diplomas. Over time, it has begun to be used in the sense of the science of examining documents. It gained the meaning of "conducting international affairs" today, when it was used by British Statesman Edmund Burke in 1796 (Baştan and Karagül, 2021:779). Since then, many definitions of diplomacy have been made. These definitions, which are the product of different perspectives, were actually made over two periods; old diplomacy and new diplomacy. The period defined as old diplomacy covers the period until the end of World War I. The process until the end of the Cold War in World War I was defined as new diplomacy (Acar, 2006:417). Over time, this foreign policy tool has given birth to the concept of public diplomacy as an activity to communicate not only with political representatives but also with citizens of the country. Public diplomacy, whose history dates back to the cold war period, is a style of public communication made to influence and change the feelings and thoughts of the people determined as the target audience in any country in the world (Manheim, 1990:4). In the new diplomacy period, that is, in public diplomacy, soft power has been realized. In other words, in classical diplomacy, strategy has become important by utilizing the power of political values, culture and foreign policy instead of threat, deterrence or propaganda during the war (Yücel, 2016:748).

With the effect of technological developments and the spread of information technologies, social transformations have been experienced and the new diplomacy period, which is the third period in diplomacy, has begun. New diplomacy includes digital diplomacy activities (Cercel and Saftescu, 2015:320-321). Digital diplomacy is defined as a country's use of information and communication technologies to carry out public diplomacy activities (Rashica, 2018: 75). Although there are opinions that digital diplomacy is a subdivision of public diplomacy, digital diplomacy has proven itself. Digital diplomacy has proven that it differs from public diplomacy by producing its own arguments with concepts such as twidiplomacy for diplomacy on Twitter, hashdag diplomacy for diplomacy with hashtags, cyber diplomacy, and e-diplomacy (Özlü, 2019:7); (Verrekia, 2017:14). In general, digital diplomacy should be considered under three headings in terms of its contribution to public policy. Listen and analyze, correct and influence, empower and transform. We should use social media as an effective tool through which we can collect and analyze information about what is happening in any country. In the edit and affect section, the situation that is desired to be changed can be corrected by taking advantage of the opportunity of social media to reach large masses. In the topic of empower and transform, foreign policy executives want to be effective in current events and support non-governmental organizations to strengthen. Support is received from them in the transformation to be experienced (Karagülle, 2015:53-54).

As Castells argues in the concept of network society, new communication technologies affect and transform the social structure. In digital diplomacy, states use social media to exercise their power. In this process, it has become inevitable for public institutions to use digital media as an alternative to traditional media tools. Many countries in the world have tried to take measures not to fall behind in the digital world (Akdoğan, 2014:54). In this context, many e-transformation projects have been initiated in Turkey in the process of adapting to the digitalizing world. One of these projects was to provide a certain level of content and design on the official websites of public institutions and organizations. For this purpose, a guide has been prepared for the websites of public institutions. While preparing this guide, samples from other countries were collected and taken as a basis. The first one was published in 2006 under the name of "public institutions website guide" and the second one was published in 2009 under the name of "public institutions website standards and recommendations guide". It has been made mandatory for all public institutions to comply with this guide (www.kakis.gov.tr).

The criteria that should be on the public web page in the guide prepared by Türksat; usability, accessibility, software and hardware, improvement of use, homepage, page structure, navigation, scrollbar and in-page navigation, in-page titles and website titles, links, post appearance, lists/tables, data entry-screen-based controls, It has been gathered under the headings of general qualifications and standards such as picture and multimedia elements, search, communication with the institution, metadata, archiving website content, privacy and security of personal information, website publishing, tests (Türksat, 2009). Among these criteria, the standards that fit the texture of the study were determined as follows: In the guide prepared by the public institutions transactions system, the criteria that should be on the public web page are stated as follows:

- Institution name, logo
- Purpose of the site
- Institutional structuring
- Institution's responsibilities and objectives
- Institution managers
- Sub-units of the institution and their duties
- Legislation related to the institution
- Pages describing the services offered by the institution
- Interactive services, if any
- Any kind of report that the institution is obliged to produce
- Statistical information
- Institutional announcements, news
- Press releases of the institution
- News about the institution in the press
- Any form that can be submitted over the Internet
- Institutional access information (phone, address, e-mail)
- Complaint and feedback mechanism
- Site-related help pages
- Frequently asked questions
- Data of the unionized personnel of the institution in accordance with Article 16 of the Law on Public Servants' Unions No. 4688
- Presentation of the institution, organizational structure, duties and responsibilities, etc., in a foreign language, if necessary.

Evaluation of Turkey and Kyrgyzstan Ministry of Sports Websites in Terms of Design Criteria

The criteria that should be on the official websites of public institutions and organizations published under the name of the Directory of Public Institutions Websites Standards and Suggestions are specified. In the study, categorical content analysis method was used in order to reveal how the sports ministries of Turkey and Kyrgyzstan use official websites as a digital diplomacy tool within the scope of these criteria. These criteria, determined by the public institutions transactions system, were grouped under five categories: institutional features, target audience, services offered, communication areas and foreign language options, and websites were evaluated on the basis of the elements in these categories (Cevher, 2015:391). In the study, some criteria of the categories made by Cevher were adapted according to the sports ministries, and the following findings were reached as a result of examining the web pages of the sports ministries of Turkey and Kyrgyzstan:

The name of the institution, which is one of the elements of the institutional features of the web pages, is included with their logos in both ministries. The most striking design of the logos on the top left of the page in both of them is the logo of The Ministry of Youth and Sports of Republic of Turkey includes the crescent and star on the flag of the Republic of Turkey, which shows that this logo belongs to Turkey. The colors of the logo are designed as red and white in harmony with the Turkish flag. While the logo of Ministry of Culture, Information, Sports and Youth Policy of the Kyrgyz Republic does not contain

Table 1. Institutional Features of the Web Pages of the Ministries of Sports of Turkey and Kyrgyzstan

Institutional Features	The Ministry of Youth and Sports of Republic of Turkey	Ministry of Culture, Information, Sports and Youth Policy of the Kyrgyz Republic
Name of Institution	Available	Available
Logo and Emblem	Available	Available
Slogan	Not available	Not available
Organization chart	Available	Available
Mission and Vision	Available	Not available
History	Available	Available
Administrator Information	Available	Available
Sub-Units of the Ministry	Available	Available
Related Legislation and Regulations	Available	Available
Institution Reports	Available	Not available
Statistical Data	Available	Not available

any symbols related to the flag of the country, it is used in the form of turquoise on a blue background, unlike the color of the flag of the country, which is red and yellow.

The slogan, which is a means of expressing the purpose of the institution with striking words or phrases, is not included in the web pages of both ministries. The organizational chart, which is another institutional feature, is on the pages of both ministries. However, on the page of the Ministry of Youth and Sports of the Republic of Turkey, the names and duties of the administrators, starting from the minister, are given with their photographs, while the page of the Ministry of Culture, Information, Sports and Youth Policy of the Kyrgyz Republic only shows the organization chart in tabular form. The names of the administrators are in a separate place under the title of the ministerial board.

While the mission and vision of the ministry is clearly stated on the page of the Ministry of Youth and Sports of the Republic of Turkey, there is no such sub-title on the page of the Ministry of Culture, Information, Sports and Youth Policy of the Kyrgyz Republic. Only the purpose and duties of the ministry are stated in the department of sports department.

The history of the institution, which is another of the institutional features, is included in the pages of both ministries. On the page of the Ministry of Youth and Sports of the Republic of Turkey, the law under which the ministry was established and the names that have changed in the process can be accessed. In the history of the Ministry of Culture, Information, Sports and Youth Policy of the Kyrgyz Republic, it is stated that the history of the ministry, including the pre-independence period, started in 1988 with the name of the Ministry of Culture of the SSR Kyrgyzstan, and it has been shown with the decrees whose name has changed 13 times in the process until today.

When you look at the manager information section on the pages of the ministries, it is seen that both are available. While the Ministry of Youth and Sports of the Republic of Turkey page contains only the information of the minister, the information of the two ministries differs from each other as the minister and then three of his deputy are present on the page of the Ministry of Culture, Information, Sports and Youth Policy of the Kyrgyz Republic.

Looking at the institutional characteristics of the sub-units affiliated to the Ministry, information on sub-units such as youth services general directorate, international organizations and foreign relations,

Table 2. Target Audience of the Web Pages of the Ministries of Sports of Turkey and Kyrgyzstan

Target Audience	The Ministry of Youth and Sports of Republic of Turkey	Ministry of Culture, Information, Sports and Youth Policy of the Kyrgyz Republic
Youth	Available	Available
Sportsmen	Available	Available
Volunteers	Available	Not available

strategy development directorate, social relations and communication department, youth and sports provincial directorates can be found on the page of the Ministry of Youth and Sports of the Republic of Turkey. On the page of the Ministry of Culture, Information, Sports and Youth Policy of the Kyrgyz Republic, although there is a link to the sub-units, the content of the page is empty. In the regional sub-units tab of the Ministry, the sub-units are given by categorizing them over the regions in the country. However, these categories included only the units covering the cultural part of the ministry.

Legislation and regulations of the ministries are located in both ministries. The legislation and regulations on the page of the Ministry of Youth and Sports of the Republic of Turkey; laws, decree-laws, decisions of the President/Council of Ministers, regulations, directives, circulars, implementation procedures and principles, institutional agreements/protocols, instructions and legislation are included in detail. The Ministry of Culture, Information, Sports and Youth Policy of the Kyrgyz Republic shared on its page the ministerial board regulation, which includes general provisions, purpose, job descriptions, and the rights of the ministry.

Although the institutional reports are included in the design of the web page of the Ministry of Youth and Sports of the Republic of Turkey, it is seen that the content is empty, and it does not exist in the Ministry of Culture, Information, Sports and Youth Policy of the Kyrgyz Republic. Statistical data were shared on the page of the Ministry of Youth and Sports of the Republic of Turkey, under the heading of statistics, within the scope of projects such as barrier-free sports schools, run while you can, and don't swim if you don't. On the page of the Ministry of Culture, Information, Sports and Youth Policy of the Kyrgyz Republic, no information on statistical data was found.

The target audience on the page of the Ministry of Youth and Sports of the Republic of Turkey; has opened separate headings for young people, athletes and volunteers. Youth can be informed and benefit from many opportunities such as youth camps, activity agenda, games and dormitory activities by logging in with personal data on the "we are young" page. In addition, the ministry also shares project calls to support youth projects under the name of project support for this target group. Sports news, support and announcements for athletes can be accessed on the "we are athletes" page, which is created for athletes, another target audience. The Ministry also chose volunteers as its target audience and created a "we are volunteers" page for them.

It is seen that the Ministry of Culture, Information, Sports and Youth Policy of the Kyrgyz Republic has determined the youth and athletes as the target audience and informed them accordingly. For this purpose, he shared the 2020-2030 youth policy on his page, which includes the discovery of new talents prepared for sustainable development in Kyrgyzstan, and the youth to have sufficient knowledge and skills. For the target audience of athletes, the Olympic awards, which started in 1976 under the name of the Olympic Games History, until 2008, were given in a chronological order with the names and branches

Table 3. Services Offered on the Web Pages of the Ministries of Sports of Turkey and Kyrgyzstan

Offered Services	The Ministry of Youth and Sports of Republic of Turkey	Ministry of Culture, Information, Sports and Youth Policy of the Kyrgyz Republic
Interactive Services	Available	Not available
Announcements	Available	Available
News	Available	Available
Search engine	Available	Available
Instant Access	Available	Not available
External Pages	Available	Not available

of the athletes. In addition, in order to inform the athletes, information on the prohibited substances and methods in the competitions was shared on the page of the ministry.

When we look at the services offered on the web pages of the ministries, it is seen that the interactive service is used on the page of the Ministry of Youth and Sports of the Republic of Turkey. Young people and athletes are provided to create a profile by entering their e-government or ID number. No interactive service was found on the page of the Ministry of Culture, Information, Sports and Youth Policy of the Kyrgyz Republic.

There are announcements and news on the pages of both ministries. While news and announcements appear on the main page without any title on the page of the Ministry of Youth and Sports of the Republic of Turkey, they appear under separate headings on the page of the Ministry of Culture, Information, Sports and Youth Policy of the Kyrgyz Republic. In addition, all the news can be seen here, as well as read by filtering through 7 regions in the country.

The search engine is on the pages of both ministries. However, while the search engine is used only for news on the page of the Ministry of Youth and Sports of the Republic of Turkey, it is used for the entire page on the page of the Ministry of Culture, Information, Sports and Youth Policy of the Kyrgyz Republic.

Instant access on the page of the Ministry of Youth and Sports of the Republic of Turkey is among the services offered. Instant access is designed for the ministry's target audience, which consists of youth, athletes and volunteers, to get information and log in quickly. There is no fast access service in the Ministry of Culture, Information, Sports and Youth Policy of the Kyrgyz Republic.

Looking at the external pages shared by the ministries; On the page of the Ministry of Youth and Sports of the Republic of Turkey, there are Atatürk corner, Presidential Communication Center, safe internet and secure web pages. On the page of the Ministry of Culture, Information, Sports and Youth Policy of the Kyrgyz Republic, there is no external page as a separate tab. However, the page contains information on the fight against corruption, including necessary information on the solution of corruption, and an action plan in the fight against corruption.

In the category of communication areas of the web pages, it was observed that the contact information of both ministries were shared as the ministry's address, phone number and e-mail address, while it was determined that the message of both ministers was not included. Information on access to the ministry The Ministry of Youth and Sports page of the Republic of Turkey clearly shows where the ministry is located by satellite mapping. It has been determined that there is no information about transportation

Table 4. Communication Areas of the Web Pages of the Ministries of Sports of Turkey and Kyrgyzstan

Communication Areas	The Ministry of Youth and Sports of Republic of Turkey	Ministry of Culture, Information, Sports and Youth Policy of the Kyrgyz Republic
Contact information	Available	Available
Message from the Minister	Not available	Not available
Transportation Information	Available	Not available
Suggestion and Wish Statement	Available	Not available
Information and Assistance Section	Available	Available
Social Network Communication	Available	Available
Frequently Asked Questions	Not available	Available
Photo Gallery Section	Available	Available

information on the page of the Ministry of Culture, Information, Sports and Youth Policy of the Kyrgyz Republic.

Notification of suggestions and wishes The Ministry of Youth and Sports of Republic of Turkey page offers a "write to us" form where they can write their suggestions and wishes digitally, with an entry written by the person's name, surname and e-mail address. On the page of the Ministry of Culture, Information, Sports and Youth Policy of the Kyrgyz Republic, no information could be found regarding the notification of suggestions and wishes.

Although information and help are on both pages, they differ from each other in terms of the method used. On the page of the Ministry of Youth and Sports of the Republic of Turkey, individuals are provided with the opportunity to apply through the information form prepared digitally and to inquire about the applications made here. On the page of the Ministry of Culture, Information, Sports and Youth Policy of the Kyrgyz Republic, the title of obtaining information is given by the work phone of the ministers and deputy ministers, and at what times they will meet, supported by the law on the reception of citizens. In addition, citizens were informed within the framework of the law created to prevent crimes envisaged under the hotline title and violations of legislation in the field of culture, information, sports and youth policy. The helpline phone number has been added, indicating the working hours.

It is seen that communication with the social network is provided on both ministry pages. Both ministries offer communication options via e-mail, Facebook, Twitter, Instagram and Youtube social networks.

Frequently asked questions are not on the page of the Ministry of Youth and Sports of the Republic of Turkey, but they are on the page of the Ministry of Culture, Information, Sports and Youth Policy of the Kyrgyz Republic. Frequently asked questions include answers to questions such as the degrees of medals and how they are earned, and how honorary titles and diplomas are received.

Although the photo gallery section is in different formats, it was found on the pages of both ministries. On the page of the Ministry of Youth and Sports of the Republic of Turkey, the photos appear in news archives. News and accompanying photos can be searched by filtering both by date and by tagging options used in digital media. There is a separate photo archive option on the page of the Ministry of Culture, Information, Sports and Youth Policy of the Kyrgyz Republic. In addition to the photo archive, there is also a separate video archive.

Looking at the foreign language support of the web pages of the ministries, it has been determined that there is no foreign language option.

Table 5. Foreign Language Options on the Web Pages of the Ministries of Sports of Turkey and Kyrgyzstan

Foreign Language Options	The Ministry of Youth and Sports of Republic of Turkey	Ministry of Culture, Information, Sports and Youth Policy of the Kyrgyz Republic
Foreign Language	Not available	Not available

CONCLUSION

In the digitalization process, countries carry out digital diplomacy activities with digital tools as an alternative to traditional media tools. In the study, the official websites of the sports ministries of Turkey and Kyrgyzstan were analyzed within the scope of these activities. As a result of the analysis, some differences as well as similarities were reached in the use of the websites of the two countries' ministries.

Looking at the websites of the ministries in terms of institutional features, it is seen that the names and logos of both ministries are included. However, there are some differences in the design of the logos.

In terms of institutional features, it is seen that the logo of the institution reminds the Turkish flag on the page of the Ministry of Youth and Sports of the Republic of Turkey and therefore directly represents Turkey. Representing Kyrgyzstan was not used in the logo of the Ministry of Culture, Information, Sports and Youth Policy of the Kyrgyz Republic. The use of slogans, which offers institutions the opportunity to explain their mission and vision with a striking phrase, was not preferred by both ministries. While the mission and vision are not specified in the Ministry of Culture, Information, Sports and Youth Policy of the Kyrgyz Republic, the mission and vision are given on the page of the Ministry of Youth and Sports of the Republic of Turkey. The mission on the page is "To bring our country's youth and sports to an innovative and competitive level that is compatible with today's requirements, prepared for the challenges of the future, sensitive to local values, not rejecting world culture; to ensure that Turkey is represented successfully and qualified in the international arena as sports.", and the vision is "To be a youth ministry that is the pioneer of change and development from local to universal." specified as. It is understood that the ministry will contribute to the image of Turkey in the international arena in the determined mission and vision. This aim is also seen in the presence of sub-units such as international organizations and foreign relations, strategy development department, social relations and communication department affiliated to the ministry. In terms of corporate identity, the most striking element on the website of the Ministry of Culture, Information, Sports and Youth Policy of the Kyrgyz Republic is the history of the ministry, not as of 1992 when the country gained its independence, but within the scope of the Kyrgyz Soviet Socialist Republic period. Therefore, the ministry did not ignore the successes achieved during the Soviet period. When we look at the institutional features in general, the institutional identities of both ministries; name, logo, organization chart, history, manager information, sub-units and legislative elements. The Ministry of Youth and Sports of the Republic of Turkey differed from the Ministry of Culture, Information, Sports and Youth Policy of the Kyrgyz Republic at this point by maintaining its corporate identity representation with the mission, vision, institution reports and statistical data elements on its page.

While the target audience is youth and athletes on both ministry pages, volunteers appear as the target audience in addition to youth and athletes on the page of the Ministry of Youth and Sports of the Republic of Turkey. Here, it is understood that the aim is to be more successful with the projects to be carried out with the support of the volunteers by including the volunteers in the target group.

In terms of the service offered on the web page, there are differences as well as similarities in the pages of the ministries. Both ministries offered announcements, news and search engine services to their visitors. Unlike traditional media tools, one of the most important features offered by digital media tools is interaction. However, the ministry websites differ from each other in terms of interactive communication service on the website. While interactive services are available on the page of the Ministry of Youth and Sports of the Republic of Turkey, such a service is not available on the page of the Ministry of Culture, Information, Sports and Youth Policy of the Kyrgyz Republic. In addition, the Kyrgyz Republic Ministry of Culture, Information, Sports and Youth Policy does not have a quick access option on the page, and it is seen that the opportunities offered by the digital world are not utilized.

In the use of the communication area on the official web pages of the ministries, both ministries; It has been seen that it includes contact information, information and help, social network and photo gallery options. However, the fact that the transportation information given on the page of the Ministry of Culture, Information, Sports and Youth Policy of the Kyrgyz Republic is not given over the digital map, and the lack of an option to notify suggestions and wishes as an interactive form of communication shows that the habit of using traditional media tools, not digital media tools, continues. This situation has also shown itself in the ministry's frequently asked questions option, which is one of the passive but practical methods of obtaining information, on its website.

When we look at the web pages of the Ministry in terms of the foreign language option, which is one of the most important criteria for digital diplomacy activities, it is seen that both ministries do not have any foreign language support. Although the page of the Ministry of Culture, Information, Sports and Youth Policy of the Kyrgyz Republic is designed in two languages, Kyrgyz and Russian, it is a result of the fact that the official language of this country is Russian and Kyrgyz, and the state language is Kyrgyz.

In general, in the study, it is suggested that the Ministry of Youth and Sports of the Republic of Turkey should develop a slogan in accordance with its mission and vision while promoting itself in the international arena, and add a foreign language option in order to announce the success of the athletes and thus the success of the country to a wider audience. The mission and vision of the Ministry of Culture, Information, Sports and Youth Policy of the Kyrgyz Republic should be stated and a slogan should be determined in this direction. In addition, it is recommended to include interactive services such as suggestion and wish notification, which will enable interactive communication with the target audience by taking advantage of the interactive communication opportunity offered by the digital world, and to add a foreign language option that will help increase its awareness internationally.

REFERENCES

Acar, D. Ş. (2006). Küreselleşen dünyada diploması. *Journal of Selçuk University Social Sciences Vocational School*, *9*(1-2), 417–440.

Akdoğan, I. (2014). *Dijital politik fanteziler*. İletişim Publishing.

Baştan, Y., & Karagül, S. (2021). Diplomasinin dönüşümü ve dijital diplomasi. *TroyAcademy International Journal of Social Sciences*, *6*(3), 777–803.

Cercel, M., & Saftescu, R. (2018). Digital diplomacy-perspectives and impact traditional diplomatic practices-case study: Digitization impact on Romanian and Belgian national diplomatic systems. *International Journal of Social Sciences and Education Research*, *1*(2), 318–328. doi:10.24289/ijsser.106416

Cevher, E. (2015). Kamu üniversiteleri web sayfalarının kullanılabilirliğinin içerik analizi ile incelenmesi. *Gaziantep University Journal of Social Sciences*, *14*(2), 387-402.

Kamu kurumları işlemleri sistemi. (n.d.). Retrieved June 18, 2022, from www.kakis.gov.tr

Karagülle, A. E. (2015). *Kamu dipolomasisi aracı olarak dijital medya, dijital diplomasi*. Marmara Üniversitesi, Sosyal Bilimler Üniversitesi.

Manheim, J. (1990). *Strategic public diplomacy: The evolution of influence*. Oxford University Press.

Official website of the Ministry of Culture, Information, Sports and Youth Policy of the Kyrgyz Republic. (n.d.). Retrieved June 27, 2022, from https://minculture.gov.kg/ru/

Official website of the Ministry of Youth and Sports of Turkey. (n.d.). Retrieved June 27, 2022, from https://gsb.gov.tr/anasayfa.html

Özlü, Ö. (2019). *Kamu diplomasisi oluşturulmasında dijital diplomasinin etkisi: Türkiye'de bulunan büyükelçiliklerin Twitter kullanımı*. Maltepe University, Institute of Social Sciences.

Rashica, V. (2018). The benefits and risks of digital diplomacy. *SEEU Review*, *13*(1), 75–89.

Türksat. (2009). Kamu kurumları internet siteleri standartları ve önerileri rehberi. *Sürüm, 1*(1).

Verrakia, B. (2017). Digital diplomacy and ıts effect on ınternational relations. *SIT Graduate Institute/ SIT Study Abroad SIT Digital Collections*.

Yücel, G. (2016). Dijital diplomasi. *TRT Akademi Issue: Digital Media*, *7*(1), 748–760.

KEY TERMS AND DEFINITIONS

Dıgıtal Dıplomacy: Digital diplomacy is the use of digital communication techniques for diplomatic purposes. It is seen that interstate relations are carried out strategically through digital platforms. These may include communications by officials working in embassies, government ministerial agencies, or other military, economic, or political institutions with their counterparts in other countries. The concept of digital diplomacy is a diplomacy process implemented in front of the public, with the internet being an open space. For this reason, it is also used to refer to public diplomacy. In this respect, digital diplomacy can be an expression that corresponds to the application of both interstate diplomacy and public diplomacy, which is called the diplomacy process between states and foreign public opinion, from digital platforms.

Dıgıtalızatıon: Digitization is the process of converting information into a digital (i.e. computer-readable) format. The result is the representation of an object, image, sound, document, or signal (usually an analog signal) obtained by generating a series of numbers that describe a discrete set of points or samples. The result is called digital representation or, more specifically, a digital image, for the object, and digital form, for the signal. In modern practice, the digitized data is in the form of binary numbers, which facilitates processing by digital computers and other operations, but digitizing simply means "the conversion of analog source material into a numerical format"; the decimal or any other number system can be used instead.

Ministry of Culture, Information, Sports, and Youth Policy of the Kyrgyz Republic: The Ministry of Culture, Information, Sports, and Youth Policy (Kyrgyz: Маданият, маалымат, спорт жана жаштар саясаты министрлиги, romanized: Madaniyat, maalymat, sport jana jashtar sayasaty ministrligi), previously known as the Ministry of Culture, Information and Tourism of the Kyrgyz Republic, is the ministry in charge of preservation and promotion of Kyrgyzstani culture in the republic and abroad. The ministry has its roots from the Soviet Union's Ministry of Culture, although the current ministry did not succeed directly from the Soviet ministry. Moreover, there were no ministries or state committees for tourism in the Soviet Union, because tourists to and from non-communist countries were highly restricted and few in numbers.

Ministry of Sports: A ministry of sports or ministry of youth and sports is a kind of government ministry found in certain countries with responsibility for the regulation of sports, particularly those participated in by young people. The ministry of sports plays an important role in gaining a positive image and increasing awareness of a country thanks to the achievements in the field of sports.

Ministry of Youth and Sports of Republic of Turkey: The Ministry of Youth and Sports of Republic of Turkey (Turkish: Türkiye Cumhuriyeti Gençlik ve Spor Bakanlığı) is a governmental agency within the Cabinet of Turkey in charge of regulating activities related to sports and youth development in Republic of Turkey. The ministry was established in 1969.

Network Society: Network society is the expression coined in 1991 related to the social, political, economic, and cultural changes caused by the spread of networked, digital information and communications technologies. The intellectual origins of the idea can be traced back to the work of early social theorists such as Georg Simmel who analyzed the effect of modernization and industrial capitalism on complex patterns of affiliation, organization, production, and experience. A network society refers to the phenomenon related to the social, political, economic, and cultural changes that have occurred due to the spread of the networks of digital and information technologies that have engendered the changes in the areas mentioned above. The network society is a social structure based on networks operated by information and communication technologies based on microelectronics and digital computer networks that generate, process, and distribute information via the nodes of the networks.

Web Design: Web design is a special designs that can be viewed by internet browsers in order to promote individuals or institutions. Web design has become the main and official information tool for businesses and individuals. It often helps to introduce people and institutions. Through web design, your designs become viewable in internet browsers. Today, with the increase in the use of internet and technology, the most important way of getting information and promotion has started to be web sites. The importance of web software and web design is increasing day by day. For most individuals and institutions, websites are already the primary means of promotion.

Chapter 9
Digital Public Diplomacy Social Media Use Tendency and Content Distribution of the Embassy of the Republic of Turkey in Bishkek

Erdoğan Akman
https://orcid.org/0000-0003-3781-4860
Institute of Social Sciences, Kyrgyzstan

Zeki Okyay
Institute of Social Sciences, Kyrgyzstan

ABSTRACT

The aim of this study is to investigate whether the Embassy of the Republic of Turkey in Bishkek uses social media effectively in the context of digital public diplomacy activities. The posts and contents of the official Facebook account of the Embassy of the Republic of Turkey in Bishkek between January 1, 2019 and February 21, 2020 were collected and analyzed in the context of digital public diplomacy. Accordingly, the posts made on the official Facebook account of the Embassy of the Republic of Turkey in Bishkek were analyzed by content analysis method in categories such as daily, monthly, posts by subject (bilateral relations, economy, trade, culture, education, health, activities, etc.), likes, comments, number of shares, etc. As a result of the research, it was observed that the Embassy of the Republic of Turkey in Bishkek does not use Facebook effectively.

INTRODUCTION

The digitalization process and the developments taking place in this process are affecting various fields, especially in areas such as the economy, military, political, social and cultural. Innovations in information

DOI: 10.4018/978-1-6684-5822-8.ch009

and communication technologies have also affected diplomacy itself, the way it works in international relations and the tools used in this process. Digitalization and digital communication have paved the way for public opinion and decisions by foreign countries to have influence on a global scale.

In this context, in today's increasingly digital world with the benefits of communication technology, states and all officials in the state are digitally integrated and have instant access to their citizens and have their feedback. Again, with the aforementioned advantages, it can reach citizens and intellectuals of foreign countries, produce instant strategic policies for foreign public opinion and get results from those policies. A country's government uses public diplomacy to influence foreign public opinion and adopt its policies. In this view, public diplomacy is an activity carried out by a government of a country to influence the citizens of another country to adopt its own ideological and political views. The traditional activities of public diplomacy transformed with the development of information technology, as in all other fields, and began to appear in various channels such as the Internet and social media., especially in the 2000s. The importance and place of social media in human life began to increase, and these platforms occupy an important place in the course of international relations. Thus, the power of digital diplomacy and digital public diplomacy has come to the forefront in the field of diplomatic relations and public diplomacy. Digital public diplomacy allows governments to get to know foreign citizens and Influencers who use social media channels, communicate with them interactively, and access various data.

In this context, digital public diplomacy can be defined as research on public diplomacy conducted using new communication technologies in a digital environment.

From this perspective, in the modern age, digital public diplomacy, which has as important an impact as traditional public diplomacy in international relations, makes a very important contribution to increasing the standing of countries in the international arena. Various strategies, techniques and campaigns targeting foreign peolple and Influencers are carried out via the internet and/or social media, and information can be transmitted synchronously, especially if it concerns various negative situations or issues that are not in the interests of a given country. Digital public diplomacy, in contrast to the traditional approach of public diplomacy, reveals a process that includes interactive communication, mutual views and dialogues. Social media platforms and channels play an important role in this process.

CONCEPTUAL FRAMEWORK

In the conceptual framework of this study, *diplomacy, traditional diplomacy, public diplomacy, traditional public diplomacy, tools used in traditional public diplomacy, digital public diplomacy and tools used in digital public diplomacy* are discussed.

Diplomacy

The need for mutual communication and agreement in inter-community relations has existed throughout human history. Diplomacy is an art of agreement that emerged from this need. In terms of origin, the word diplomacy dates back to ancient Greek and derives from the word "diploma". The word "diploma" meant "folded in two" in ancient Greek. In the ancient Greek and Roman Empire periods, all official documents belonging to the state were called diplomas because these documents were folded in half. After a while, the need to put the documents belonging to the state in a certain order became essential, and expert clerks started to work to meet this need.

Until the 18th century, diplomacy meant "the science of examining documents" (Tuncer, 2009:13). In the Turkish Dictionary of the Turkish Language Association, the word Diplomacy is defined as;

- The set of agreements regulating international relations,
- The work and art of representing one's country in a foreign country and at international meetings,
  -The position, profession of the person who works in this field,
  -This is the community of officials,
  -Power is explained in 5 different definitions as the skill and resourcefulness demonstrated during a negotiation (sozluk.gov.tr/).

In general, it is possible to define diplomacy as any attempt to resolve the issue between two or more states through mutual dialogue and negotiation on existing or potential problems.

The aim of diplomacy is to establish peace by preventing conflicts in unfavorable scenarios such as crises and wars that occur or are likely to occur between states. The diplomacy activities of countries are carried out by the foreign ministries and embassies.

Traditional Diplomacy

Since the early history of humanity, the advice and mediation activities carried out by the opinion leaders of the period, experienced people with reputation in order to find a common point through peace and negotiations in order to solve the problems experienced or likely to be experienced between societies, tribes or clans are accepted as the first examples of traditional diplomacy. In the following periods, the meetings of ambassadors sent as mediators or message transmitters in the kingdoms and city-states also appear as traditional diplomacy activities.

Traditional diplomacy activities have been carried out in various fields such as the use of natural resources between countries, the solution of border problems, the establishment of commercial agreements, etc.

Simultaneously with the developments in the world, there has been a change and transformation in diplomacy. Particularly with the developments in technology and with the globalization, there has been an expansion in the types of diplomacy. Today, it is possible to express the types of diplomacy as follows (Abdurahmanlı and Bağış, 2021:5):

- Mediation diplomacy
- Multilateral diplomacy
- Bilateral diplomacy
- Public diplomacy
- Civil diplomacy
- Summit diplomacy
- Conference diplomacy
- Parliamentary diplomacy
- Shuttle diplomacy
- Social diplomacy
- Conference diplomacy
- Nuclear diplomacy

- Preventive diplomacy
- Quiet diplomacy
- Cultural diplomacy
- Environmental diplomacy
- Humanitarian diplomacy
- Open diplomacy
- Coercive diplomacy
- Toothless diplomacy

Public Diplomacy

Before discussing the concept of public diplomacy, it is useful to scrutinize the word "public". In this context, the word public is defined in the Turkish Dictionary of the Turkish Language Association as "All of the state organs that provide public service, the whole of the people in a country, the public" (https://sozluk.gov.tr/).

When the literature is reviewed, it is possible to see various definitions of public diplomacy. With globalization and the development of information and communication technologies, especially the increase in the use of the internet and the widespread use of social media has brought about changes in many traditionally expressed terms. In this context, the traditionally known diplomacy has also changed and public diplomacy has emerged.

The question of when and by whom public diplomacy was first practiced in terms of its meaning is open to debate. However, the first use of public diplomacy as a concept can be found in American foreign policy. Public diplomacy gained notoriety for the first time with the concept of "softpower" (Kocabıyık, 2019:164). This concept was first used by Edmund Gullion in 1965 with the term "international flow of information and ideas" (Sancar, 2012:79).

Joseph Nye defines public diplomacy as: "In order for a country to achieve the results it wants in world politics, there are countries that admire its values, take it as an example, envy its welfare level and opportunities, and follow it" (Nye, 2005:14 cited in Kocabıyık, 2019:164).

According to another definition, Public diplomacy is defined as: "The efforts of states to influence international public opinion or the opinions of their constituencies in line with the interests of their countries" (Manheim, 1990:4 as cited in Yağmurlu, 2019:1269).

Following these definitions in the literature, it is possible to define public diplomacy in general terms as "all of the activities carried out by a government to influence foreign citizens, intellectuals and other governments abroad and to adopt their own policies without using hard (military) power".

As stated in this definition, today, governments, governmental institutions and non-governmental organizations carry out aid and investment activities in foreign countries in areas such as cultural, artistic, economic, commercial, medical, educational, etc. in order to influence the public opinion of other countries and increase their own prestige.

Traditional Public Diplomacy

Traditional public diplomacy is a stage that conveys messages in areas including cultural diplomacy, citizen diplomacy, faith diplomacy, lobbying and advocacy. The closest resemblance of traditional public diplomacy to public relations is its utilization of public relations tools. Traditional public diplomacy utilizes the tools of public relations in image, reputation and perception management to influence the governments and people of other countries. These tools are media relations and event management. In addition, traditional public diplomacy uses tools such as advertising and celebrity use, international publishing activities and national brands, publishing books on traditional public diplomacy, broadcasting films and series, organizing international tours of exhibitions of works of art, theater works, and other cultural activities (Fortner, 1994:279 cited in Sancar, 2014:185).

According to some scholars, traditional diplomacy is considered to be the efforts of governments to try to influence or direct publics, while public diplomacy, which is considered as a new generation diplomacy type, is a method that emerges directly between publics and uses actors among publics (Taylor, 2009: 6 as cited in Demirkol, 2020: 78).

Tools Used in Traditional Public Diplomacy

Unlike traditional diplomacy methods, it is an effort by governments to create public opinion in other countries and to do this through ***civil society, media, communication experts and cross-cultural interactions beyond diplomats.***

Tools Used in Digital Public Diplomacy

Since the 1990s, advances in information and communication technologies have led to massive change and transformation all over the world. The widespread use of computers and the internet, social media and the convenience of smart phones have also taken their place in the field of public diplomacy. It is seen that almost all of the official institutions, organizations, state administrators and officials of countries that have an important place in the world economy actively use social media channels such as facebook, twitter, instagram, odnoklassniki, vkontakte, etc. in public diplomacy, particularly in international relations and foreign policy activities.

Differences Between Traditional Public Diplomacy and Digital Public Diplomacy

The definition and approach of public diplomacy has gained a new dimension, especially with the concept of soft power, and a distinction has been made between traditional and new diplomacy. In this context, there have been differences in the criteria of actor, target, target audience, tools and methods in public diplomacy.

"While the main actor of traditional diplomacy is the state and relations are carried out between states on the axis of secrecy within closed systems, in public diplomacy, which is a new generation diplomacy type, it appears as diplomatic activities that are conducted openly in order to influence societies or societies that are dominated by non-governmental actors, in some cases bypassing states (Demirkol, 2020: 78)." While the main actors in traditional diplomacy are states, in public diplomacy, civil society, public opinion and individuals come to the fore in addition to the state.

Public Diplomacy Activities of the Republic of Turkey

The Ministry of Foreign Affairs is the main institution carrying out the diplomatic activities of the Republic of Turkey. The Ministry of Foreign Affairs of the Republic of Turkey was established by the Law on the Ministry of Foreign Affairs dated May 2, 1920, enacted by the First Turkish Grand National Assembly convened during the War of Independence. Although the Ministry of Foreign Affairs was established in the early years of the Republic, the origins of Turkish Diplomacy date back to the Ottoman Empire (www.mfa.gov.tr/).

In the Ottoman state organization, the Reis-ül Küttap, the head of the committee of scribes who conducted written records and paperwork, performed a duty similar to that of today's Foreign Minister. The first Reis-ul-Kuttap was officially appointed in 1523. On the 100th anniversary of the founding of the Republic of Turkey, Turkish diplomacy will celebrate its 500th anniversary (www.mfa.gov.tr/). The diplomatic mission of the Republic of Turkey has been spearheaded by the Ministry of Foreign Affairs since 1920. It also leads the country's public diplomacy activities.

According to the January 30, 2010 Prime Ministry circular, the Public Diplomacy Coordinatorship was established for the first time. With this circular, the concept of Public Diplomacy was given the name of an official organization for the first time in Turkey.

In the establishment circular of the Public Diplomacy Coordinatorship, the purpose of the department is stated as the international relations acquired a new dimension as a result of globalization, new diplomacy understanding gained importance as a more effective tool instead of traditional diplomacy, and informing the international community in the right direction through public diplomacy practices in order to change the negative perceptions towards Turkey in international platforms.

"The Public Diplomacy Coordinatorship continued its activities until the establishment of the Republic of Türkiye Directorate of Communications on July 24, 2018. With the establishment of the Republic of Türkiye Directorate of Communications, all activities of the Public Diplomacy Coordinator's Office were transferred to this institution (Aktaş, 2021: 67)."

In recent years, the Republic of Turkey has been conducting public diplomacy activities through its official institutions such as the Public Diplomacy Coordinatorship, the Republic of Türkiye Directorate of Communications, the Ministry of Foreign Affairs, the Presidency for Turks Abroad and Related Communities, Yunus Emre Institute, Turkish Radio and Television Corporation, Anadolu Agency, Maarif Foundation, Turkish Cooperation and Coordination Agency, and various non-governmental organizations, foundations and associations.

In this context, the Presidency for Turks Abroad and Related Communities has also been an important building block of Turkish public diplomacy with its efforts to improve social, cultural and economic relations with cognates and related communities and its programs on education.

Yunus Emre Enstitüsü has been conducting cultural and artistic activities for the promotion of Turkey, as well as teaching Turkish to foreigners in the centers it has established abroad since 2009 in order to "promote Turkey, Turkish language, history, culture and art, to present information and resources related to this subject to the world, and to provide services abroad for those who want to receive education in the fields of Turkish language, culture and art, and to support scientific studies. The Institute has 58 cultural centers in 48 countries. In addition to the Turkish language education provided at the cultural centers, Turkology departments and Turkish language teaching are supported through collaborations with educational institutions in different countries. Many activities are organized through the cultural centers

Figure 1. Turkey development assistance

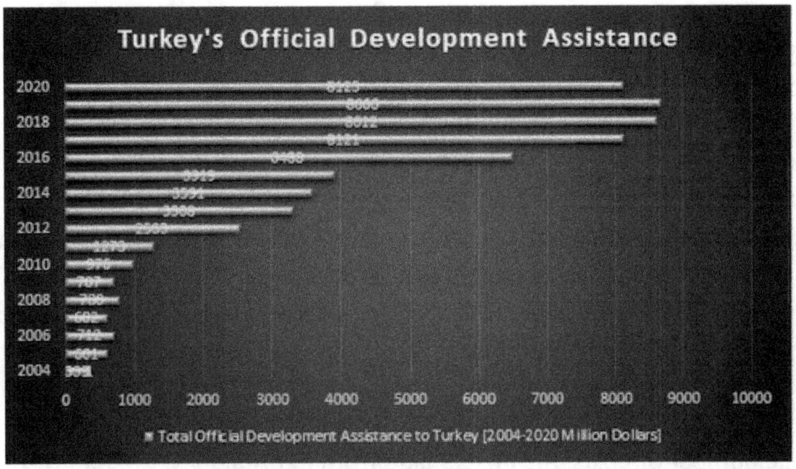

to promote Turkish culture and art, and Turkey is represented in national and international events. All these activities are within the scope of the Republic of Turkey's public diplomacy activities."

Another important institution in Turkey's public diplomacy is Turkish Radio and Television (TRT). Broadcasting to Turkey and the world with 14 television and 14 radio channels, trt.net.tr and www.trtvotworld.com websites in 41 languages, and 5 printed magazines, TRT's first overseas channel TRT-AVRASYA started broadcasting in 1993 with programs for the Caucasus and Central Asia. In 1998, the first foreign representative office was opened in Berlin, Germany. In the following years, representation offices were opened in Turkmenistan in 1999, Azerbaijan, Egypt and Belgium in 2000, the USA in 2002 and Uzbekistan in 2004. In 1999, TRT_SAYTEK was established and started broadcasting in order to provide viewing opportunities in countries where representative offices could not be opened. In 2008, www.trtvotworld.com was launched with news broadcasts in 31 languages. Today, it broadcasts in 41 languages, presenting the world public opinion with the latest developments from all over the world (Aktaş, 2021:79).

"Turkey, which conducts activities for friendly, brotherly and related countries through TIKA, has made significant changes in its foreign policy approach, especially with the economic development and the upward momentum in the level of prosperity it achieved (Turkey Development Assistance, 2020) after the 2000s. As an extension of its efforts to have a say in foreign policy and become an important actor in the world, it has aimed to be active in all regions. In this direction, TIKA, which is Turkey's humanitarian diplomacy implementer, expands its geography of activities every year and operates in 150 countries with 62 Program Coordination Offices in 60 countries (Aktaş, 2021:89)."

In the final analysis, it has been observed that the Republic of Turkey has been providing increasing levels of development assistance every year since 2004 in the context of public diplomacy activities in order to convey its policies to the public opinion of foreign countries and to adopt its opinions. In 2019, with an official development assistance of 8 billion 666 million US dollars, the Republic of Turkey became the largest humanitarian aid donor in the world in terms of national income (www.tccb.gov.tr).

RESEARCH METHODOLOGY

The research analyzes the social media posts of the Embassy of the Republic of Turkey in Bishkek in the context of public diplomacy, which include support, investment and cooperation activities in the fields of politics, economy, culture, trade, health, education, Turkey-Kyrgyzstan bilateral relations, etc. in Kyrgyzstan. Within this scope, the posts made by the official Facebook account of the Embassy of the Republic of Turkey in Bishkek in the last year between January 1, 2019 and February 21, 2020 were analyzed by the classification method of the content analysis technique. The posts of the Embassy of the Republic of Turkey in Bishkek were categorized into 4 categories: "Number of Posts, Number of Likes, Number of Comments and Number of Shares". It is seen that the Embassy of the Republic of Turkey in Bishkek shared 349 posts in total between the aforementioned dates and these posts received 41938 likes, 1830 comments and were re-shared 3988 times by its followers. In addition, the Embassy of the Republic of Turkey in Bishkek used a total of 1449 photos and videos in its posts.

In the table of the number of posts, the posts made from February 21, 2020 until January 1, 2019 are discussed in detail on a monthly basis. In this table, it is determined how many posts the Embassy of the Republic of Turkey in Bishkek made each month and how many photos were used in these posts. In addition, the topics of the posts (bilateral relations, economy, trade, culture, education, health, activities, etc.) were also included in the same table.

In the number of likes table, the posts made from February 21, 2020 until January 1, 2019 were considered on a monthly basis. The number of likes for the posts based on monthly basis is available in this table.

In the number of comments table, the posts made from February 21, 2020 until January 1, 2019 were considered monthly. The number of comments on posts based on monthly basis is available in this table.

In the number of shares table, the posts made from February 21, 2020 until January 1, 2019 were considered on a monthly basis. The numerical values of the number of times the monthly-based posts were re-shared by the followers are included in this table.

FINDINGS

According to Table 1, the Embassy of the Republic of Turkey in Bishkek shared a total of 349 posts between January 1, 2019 and February 21, 2020. These posts included a total of 1449 visual materials. Of the 349 posts shared by the Embassy of the Republic of Turkey in Bishkek, 128 were on Turkey-Kyrgyzstan bilateral relations, 41 on culture and arts, 38 on announcements, 34 on education, 32 on celebrations, 19 on commemoration programs, 17 on entrepreneurship, 13 on health, 10 on religious holidays, 9 on social responsibility, 6 on law and 2 on tourism. The Embassy of the Republic of Turkey in Bishkek posted the highest number of posts (48) in October 2019 and the lowest number of posts (9) in February 2020.

According to **Table 2**, the Embassy of the Republic of Turkey in Bishkek shared a total of 349 posts between January 1, 2019 and February 21, 2020. The posts made between the aforementioned dates were classified as monthly posts. The posts received 41938 likes in total. The highest number of likes to TIKA's posts was 5687 in September 2019 and the lowest number of likes was 537 in February 2020.

Table 3, according to the number of comments table, the Embassy of the Republic of Turkey in Bishkek shared a total of 349 posts between January 1, 2019 and February 21, 2020. The posts made between the

Table 1. Number of posts

Nº	Date of Postings	Number of Posts	Quantity of Photographs Used in Posts	Types of Posts by Subject
1	February posts from February 21, 2020 backwards	9	2 video 28 photos	Bilateral relations (3) Education (2) Law (2) Arts and Culture (1) Tourism (1)
2	January 2020	20	6 video 45 photos	Bilateral Relations (6) Education (3) Announcement (3) Culture and Arts (2) Celebration (2) Memorial Program (2) Health (1) Social Responsibility (1)
3	December 2019	17	4 video 70 photos	Bilateral relations (7) Announcement (3) Health (2) Entrepreneurship(2) Celebration (2) Social Responsibility (1)
4	November 2019	25	2 video 65 photos	Celebration (5) Bilateral relations (5) Commemoration Program (4) Culture and Arts (4) Education (3) Announcement (3) Entrepreneurship(1)
5	October 2019	48	16 video 66 photos	Bilateral relations (24) Culture and Arts (12) Announcement (5) Celebration (4) Education (2) Entrepreneurship (1)
6	September 2019	39	4 video 235 photos	Bilateral relations (11) Culture and Arts (8) Announcement (6) Entrepreneurship (4) Education (4) Celebration (2) Memorial Program (2) Social Responsibility (1) Health (1)
7	August 2019	27	7 video 83 photos	Bilateral relations (14) Entrepreneurship (3) Social responsibility (2) Religious Holidays (2) Celebration (2) Health (1) Culture and Arts (1) Announcement (1) Education (1)
8	July 2019	20	2 video 81 photos	Bilateral relations (6) Religious Holidays (5) Announcement (4) Memorial Program (3) Celebration (1) Entrepreneurship (1)
9	June 2019	24	5 video 72 photos	Celebration (6) Bilateral relations (4) Announcement (3) Education (2) Religious Holidays (2) Law (2) Tourism (1) Health (1) Social responsibility (1) Memorial Program (1) Culture and Arts (1)
10	May 2019	17	1 video 79 photos	Bilateral relations (4) Memorial Program (3) Education (2) Celebration (2) Social Responsibility (2) Culture and Arts (1) Health (1) Entrepreneurship (1) Religious Holidays (1)

continued on following page

Table 1. Continued

N°	Date of Postings	Number of Posts	Quantity of Photographs Used in Posts	Types of Posts by Subject
11	April 2019	27	2 video 213 photos	Bilateral relations (9) Culture & Arts (5) Announcement (4) Education (4) Entrepreneurship (2) Celebration (2) Law (1)
12	March 2019	35	3 video 163 photos	Bilateral Relationship (14) Culture and Arts (5) Memorial Program (4) Celebration (4) Education (3) Health (2) Entrepreneurship (1) Announcement (1) Law (1)
13	February 2019	28	169 photos	Bilateral relations (14) Education (7) Health (3) Social Responsibility (1) Entrepreneurship (1) Culture and Arts (1) Announcement (1)
14	January 2019	13	1 video 25 photos	Bilateral relations (7) Announcement (4) Health (1) Education (1)
15	**Total**	349	55 video 1394 photos	Bilateral relations (128) Culture and Arts (41) Announcement (38) Education (34) Celebration (32) Memorial Program (19) Entrepreneurship (17) Health (13) Religious holidays (10) Social Responsibility (9) Law (6) Tourism (2)

aforementioned dates were classified as monthly posts. A total of 1830 comments were made by the followers on the posts. While the highest number of comments on the posts of the Embassy of the Republic of Turkey in Bishkek was 249 in June 2019, the lowest number of comments was 21 in February 2020.

According to Table 4, the Embassy of the Republic of Turkey in Bishkek shared a total of 349 posts between January 1, 2019 and February 21, 2020. The posts shared between the aforementioned dates are classified as monthly posts. The posts were shared 3988 times in total by the followers. The posts of the Embassy of the Republic of Turkey in Bishkek were shared the most in October 2019 with 599 and the least in February 2020 with 32.

CONCLUSION

This research analyzes the posts made by the Embassy of the Republic of Turkey in Bishkek on its official Facebook page, one of the social media channels, in the context of public diplomacy through content analysis method. A total of 349 posts were shared on the official Facebook page of the Embassy of the Republic of Turkey in Bishkek between January 1, 2019 and February 21, 2020. These posts include posts on educational programs such as computer assistance, opening of Turkish language classes and laboratories, seminars, conferences, vocational courses, etc. conducted by various institutions and organizations of the Republic of Turkey throughout Kyrgyzstan. In bilateral relations, there are also posts on inter-institutional relations, including political relations between Kyrgyzstan and Turkey. In the posts made by the Embassy of the Republic of Turkey in Bishkek in the field of health, there are posts on many activities ranging from the provision of equipment to clinics in health institutions and organizations throughout Kyrgyzstan, especially the Kyrgyz-Turkish Friendship Hospital, to the restoration of buildings. In the field of social responsibility, there are posts by various institutions and organizations

Table 2. Number of likes

№	Post Sharing Dates	Number of Shares
1	February posts from February 21, 2020 backwards	32
2	January 2020	241
3	December 2019	152
4	November 2019	347
5	October 2019	599
6	September 2019	439
7	August 2019	368
8	July 2019	225
9	June 2019	325
10	May 2019	184
11	April 2019	284
12	March 2019	292
13	February 2019	391
14	January 2019	109
15	**Total**	**3988**

Table 3. Number of Comments

№	Post Sharing Dates	Number of Comments
1	February posts from February 21, 2020 backwards	21
2	January 2020	114
3	December 2019	98
4	November 2019	90
5	October 2019	197
6	September 2019	164
7	August 2019	150
8	July 2019	43
9	June 2019	249
10	May 2019	188
11	April 2019	89
12	March 2019	152
13	February 2019	219
14	January 2019	56
15	**Total**	**1830**

Table 4. Number of Shares

№	Post Sharing Dates	Number of Likes
1	February posts from February 21, 2020 backwards	537
2	January 2020	2038
3	December 2019	1524
4	November 2019	3485
5	October 2019	5481
6	September 2019	5687
7	August 2019	4183
8	July 2019	1823
9	June 2019	3300
10	May 2019	2812
11	April 2019	3017
12	March 2019	3621
13	February 2019	3124
14	January 2019	1306
15	**Total**	**41938**

of the Republic of Turkey on a variety of assistance and investments throughout Kyrgyzstan, such as raising public awareness about the lives of the disabled, providing generators that directly benefit the lives of poor citizens, building water channels, etc. The official Facebook page of the Embassy of the Republic of Turkey in Bishkek also shared posts on national days, religious holidays, mourning and commemoration days that are important for Kyrgyzstan and Turkey.

The posts included explanatory texts in both Turkish and Kyrgyz. The posts also occasionally used the official languages of Kyrgyzstan, Russian and English.

In conclusion, it is important to point out that the number of followers of the Embassy of the Republic of Turkey in Bishkek is 7658 as of March 11, 2020, this number should be increased and the posts on social media should reach a wider audience. In this context, it is important for the Embassy of the Republic of Turkey in Bishkek to maintain its promotional and advertising activities more actively, to make Turkey's strong support to Kyrgyzstan in every field known to a wider audience, and for Turkey's public diplomacy and diplomatic relations in Kyrgyzstan.

In this context, it would be beneficial for the Embassy of the Republic of Turkey in Bishkek to announce the important moments of the aid and investment activities carried out by the Embassy of the Republic of Turkey in Kyrgyzstan, including groundbreaking and opening ceremonies, in mass media tools as television, newspapers and radio. In addition, it is thought that the sponsorship of the Embassy of the Republic of Turkey in Bishkek in social responsibility and development activities conducted by various institutions and organizations in Kyrgyzstan will contribute to the recognition of the embassy. Furthermore, the official social media pages of the Embassy should be promoted in the ceremonies of the activities carried out by the Embassy of the Republic of Turkey in Bishkek by taking place in materials such as posters, brochures, etc.

REFERENCES

Abdurahmanlı, E., & Bagis, E. (2021). Definition of Diplomacy and Types of Diplomacy Available in the International Conjuncture. *Anadolu Academy Journal of Social Sciences*, *3*(1), 140–160.

Aktaş, A. (2021). *Tika's Studies in Kyrgyzstan as a Humanitarian Diplomacy Tool in the Context of Public Relations* [doctoral dissertation]. Kyrgyz-Turkish Manas University Institute of Social Sciences, Department of Communication Sciences.

Demirkol, F. (2020). Operation Peace Spring in the Context of Public Diplomacy. Bartın University Faculty of Economics and Administrative Sciences Journal, 11(21).

Kocabıyık, H. (2019). Changing Understanding of Diplomacy. *Public Diplomacy and Turkey, Eurasian Studies, 55*.

Sancar, G. A. (2012). *Public diplomacy and International Public Relations*. Beta Publications.

Sancar, S. A. (2014). *Public Diplomacy and International Public Relations*. Republic of Turkey Ministry of Foreign Affairs. Retrieved June 6, 2022, from https://www.mfa.gov.tr/site_media/html/disisleri-tanitim.pdf

The Presidency of the Republic of Turkey. (n.d.). *Turkey is the Country that Provides the Most Humanitarian Aid in the World Compared to its National Income*. Retrieved June 6, 2022, from https://www.tccb.gov.tr/haberler/410/102167/-turkiye-mill-gelire-oranla-dunyada-en-more-humanitarian-aid-the-country

Tuncer, H. (2009). *Old and New Diplomacy*. Ümit Publishing. Retrieved June 6, 2022, from https://sozluk.gov.tr/

Turkey Development Assistance. (2020). Retrieved June 6, 2022, from https://www.tika.gov.tr/upload/sayfa/Pictures/Turkiye%20Kalk%C4%B1nma%20Yard%C4%B1mlar%C4%B1%202020_tr.pdf

Yağmurlu A. (2019). Digital Diplomacy: Internet Applications of European Union Member States and Turkish Ministry of Foreign Affairs Within the Framework of Public Diplomacy. *e-Gifder, 7*(2).

KEY TERMS AND DEFINITIONS

Bilateral Relations: Consists of the political, economic, or cultural relations between two (2) sovereign/independent states.

Culture and Arts: Set of shared attitudes, values, goals, and practices that define a group of people, such as the people of a particular region. Culture includes the elements that characterize a particular peoples' way of life. Vast subdivision of culture, composed of many creative endeavors and disciplines. The arts encompass visual arts, literary arts, and the performing arts.

Embassy of the Republic of Turkey in Bishkek: Diplomatic representation of the Republic of Turkey in Kyrgyzstan.

Facebook: Is an online social media and social networking service owned by American company Meta Platforms. Founded in 2004 by Mark Zuckerberg with fellow Harvard College students and roommates Eduardo Saverin, Andrew McCollum, Dustin Moskovitz, and Chris Hughes, its name comes from the face book directories often given to American university students. Membership was initially limited to Harvard students, gradually expanding to other North American universities and, since 2006, anyone over 13 years old. As of July 2022, Facebook claimed 2.93 billion monthly active users, and ranked third worldwide among the most visited websites as of July 2022. It was the most downloaded mobile app of the 2010s.

Public Diplomacy Activities: Various government-sponsored initiatives aimed at communicating directly with foreign publics.

Social Media: Social media are interactive technologies that facilitate the creation and sharing of information, ideas, interests, and other forms of expression through virtual communities and networks.

Social Media Posts: Social media posts means any information or data submitted by a Third Party to a social media outlet or platform that is capable of then being displayed using the software or approved hardware.

Turkish Cooperation and Coordination Agency (TIKA): TIKA is a government department subordinate to the Ministry of Culture and Tourism (Turkey). Focusing on development cooperation, TIKA works in more than 150 countries.

Chapter 10
Understanding Digital Diplomacy Through Ukraine-Russia Events:
The Truth Behind Events in Ukraine and Donbass

Tolkun Bekturgan kyzy
Kyrgyz-Turkish Manas University, Kyrgyzstan

Niyazi Ayhan
Kyrgyz-Turkish Manas University, Kyrgyzstan

ABSTRACT

Digital diplomacy is a form of new public diplomacy that uses the internet, new information and communication technologies, and social media as a means to strengthen diplomatic relations. The main differences from classical public diplomacy are greater access to information, more interaction between people and organizations, and greater transparency. Diplomacy is radically transforming in front of our eyes. In the face of new challenges, its structure and methods are changing, and new directions are emerging. The chapter analyzes new opportunities and technologies for use by the diplomatic departments of the Russian Federation and Ukraine in the course of current activities in the field of international relations. The authors also presented a descriptive analysis of the document entitled "The Truth behind Events in Ukraine and Donbass (2014-2022)" published on the official website of the Ministry of Foreign Affairs of the Russian Federation.

INTRODUCTION

Jan Melissen argues that public diplomacy should be seen as "old wine in new bottles" (Melissen, 2005, p. 28), amphasizing that public diplomacy aims to communicate the positive aspects of a country to

DOI: 10.4018/978-1-6684-5822-8.ch010

a foreign public. In his article "The New Public Diplomacy: Between Theory and Practice," Melissen writes that three concepts that should be briefly considered in a discussion of public diplomacy are propaganda, nation-branding, and foreign cultural relations. Like public diplomacy, propaganda and nation-branding are concerned with the transmission of information and ideas with the aim of changing the attitudes of people in other countries towards their country or to strengthen the existing image. Cultural relations are much closer to the latest trends of the new public diplomacy than propaganda and nation-branding. The new public diplomacy as well as cultural relations focus more on interacting with foreign audiences rather than selling messages, building reciprocity and stable relationships rather than just political campaigns, securing "long term" needs rather than "short term" and "winning hearts minds" to build trust (Melissen, 2005, pp. 16-21).

In today's world, the informational effect is generally recognised internationally as 'soft power'. "Soft power" uses methods based on communication skills (Çaglar, 2019). "Soft power" is the opposite of "hard power", which includes military or economic power. The focus of soft power strategy is the use of persuasive techniques.

Diplomacy, which Bull defines as "the peaceful conduct of relations between states and other entities in world politics by official agents" (Bull, 1997, p. 156), continues to be the most widely used definition among diplomatic scholars. It follows Watson's characterization of diplomacy as a process of "negotiation between political entities that accept each other's independence" (Watson, 1984, p. 33).

The Internet, defined, as "a communication tool for publishing, sharing and storing information" (Westcott, 2008, p. 2), has become a hub for public and private communication. Facebook, Twitter, Qzone, Snapchat, VKontakte and other social networking platforms are used by over 2 billion people every day. Digital communication has shrunk the world and in the process changed the daily lives of billions of people (Adesina, 2017, p. 7). Web 2.0 technologies have paved the way for the development of social media. Online social networking tools allow users to create content, interact with other users and build communities (Payne et al., 2011, p. 54). The mediation and exchange of information between people from all over the world now takes place 24 hours a day, all year round. Social networks offer tremendous opportunities for governments and international organizations trying to participate in the new policy areas that are developing on the Internet.

Globalisation has affected not only the way people act and live, but also more importantly the way states and international actors act on the world stage (Westcott, 2008, p. 4). This rapid transformation of society has led to the emergence of various disciplines such as digital diplomacy or data diplomacy, also known as e-diplomacy. In the era of globalisation, diplomacy includes and promotes citizen participation, mass movements and people-to-people communication (Payne et al., 2011, p. 47).

Digital diplomacy makes active use of soft power through social media as a powerful tool for communicating with target audiences. In this case the social network acts as a platform on which social relations are built.

Marcus Holmes in The Theory and Practice of Digital Diplomacy (Corneliu Biola, Marcus Holmes, 2015, pp. 13-32) begins the first chapter on political innovation and digital diplomacy as an international practice. He challenges the common understanding of digital diplomacy as a purely cost-effective form of public diplomacy and argues instead that a more effective approach would be to explore the broader role of digital diplomacy in managing international change.

With the digitalisation of communication technologies, temporal and spatial constraints on individuals' communicative activities have disappeared and one-way interpersonal communicative activities have become very comfortable group communication (Dogan, 2013, p. 8). According to Westcott, the Internet provides a new platform for the old practice of persuasion in the international arena as well as in domestic politics (Westcott, 2008, p. 14). The most important change in diplomacy is the emergence of digital diplomacy. This is not the only term for the use of digital technology to achieve foreign policy goals. There are more than 20 similar terms and many different definitions, such as Twitter diplomacy, Internet diplomacy, data diplomacy. They are all centred around the process of digitalisation and datatization in foreign policy, which is very active. Datatization is a technological trend that transforms many aspects of social life into data, which is then translated into knowledge and realised as a new form of value.

Digital diplomacy provides data to influence audiences that cannot be reached through direct contact and interaction. Diplomats and consular officers can reach a wider audience within their diaspora more quickly and effectively. In addition, data diplomacy has shortened borders and time zones. Where once diplomats had to travel miles and days to deliver a message as plenipotentiaries, email and videoconferencing have accelerated the speed of interaction between government representatives. The work of diplomats and politicians has changed significantly with the advent of information technology and, more importantly, the digital society. Diplomats tend to reinvent their duties on a daily basis as they acquire more knowledge and master the tools available.

Every year, the topic of digitalisation and big data becomes more and more popular. Information technology is changing all aspects of our lives. Even a field as conservative as diplomacy is starting to take on new dimensions. Diplomacy as a profession in the world is adapting to new realities. Social media has become a new platform for politicians who no longer need to rely on television to make public statements. Today, everyone can get up-to-date information on international relations by subscribing to the social media pages of national leaders and their official agencies.

Diplomacy is being democratised in terms of simplified language of communication, accessibility and openness of diplomats and other officials. It is now targeting not only external audiences, but also internal audiences. Countries are building their brands on social media, it's called selfies-diplomacy. Thanks to digital communications, there are many opportunities to promote the messages of nations interacting with a wide range of foreign citizens. By analysing social media data, you can conduct diplomacy in a more intelligent, targeted and timely manner. It is now possible to communicate with influential users, follow current trends and not miss important events. Digital crisis response, for example, is already well developed. Technology has also made a number of consular duties easier. However, there are definitely negative trends, above all misinformation and political polarisation. The digitalisation of diplomacy in general is a long-term process, which has only just begun.

It is no coincidence that communication between leaders of countries and representatives of foreign ministries on social media is attracting a lot of attention. The possibility to directly address Internet users and follow lively debates involving diplomats increasingly distances diplomacy from the traditional model, in which it mainly functions as communication between heads of state. Foreign ambassadors used to address the people of the host country through newspapers, books and public speeches, but now they can do so interactively and often informally, round the clock, without intermediaries.

Digital diplomacy is not explicitly regulated by the Vienna Convention on Diplomatic Relations and other international legal instruments, so it can be said to have its own traditions. In fact, while the foreign ministries of various countries have developed guidelines for staff indicating the limits of what is permissible; today they contain more free communication than the official format. A careless tweet can at best cause a wave of criticism from commentators, and at worst cause a crisis in the real world. Nevertheless, forcing diplomats to use the language of protocol on social media seems unfair. It makes more sense for foreign ministries to try to strike a reasonable balance between benefits and risks and invest more resources in ensuring that communications are consistent and more effective.

So far, specialists have only become accustomed to the surface possibilities of the digital age. There is great potential for diplomacy in automating citizen services, analysing foreign audiences, processing and exchanging data, streamlining internal processes and possibly developing new formats for multilateral interaction.

When it comes to the theoretical basis for summarising the empirical evidence on digital diplomacy, it can be seen within the well-known concepts of "soft power". This also includes various concepts related to communication technologies, information transmission and perception.

In recent years, digital diplomacy has entered a new phase of its development. Instantly creating effective posts and counter-posts, generating compelling responses to user comments, finding sources of misinformation and trolls, identifying important and influential bloggers, etc. Today, big data processing and the use of artificial intelligence have become trends.

METHOD

The study focuses on the Donbass events between Ukraine and Russia since 2014. In this context, the study focuses on the way Russia tells the world about the incident and the digital diplomacy it has followed in this process. The digital diplomacy pursued by Russia with a focus on Donbass is carried out through the Russian Foreign Ministry. On the official website of the Ministry of Foreign Affairs, there is a separate link called "The Truth about Events in Ukraine and Donbass" (Russian Ministry of Foreign Affairs, 2022). In this context, the study will be analysed by descriptive analysis method through the content titled "The Truth about the Events in Ukraine and Donbass". Descriptive analysis is the presentation of the obtained data to the reader in an organised and interpreted manner (Yıldırım and Şimşek, 2008:224). It consists of summarising and interpreting the data under the predetermined general framework and themes related to this framework (Altunışık, 2010:322). In this study, the general framework is the content in pdf format published by the Ministry of Foreign Affairs of Russia over the Donbass events. Russia's views on the causes of the Donbass events, regime change, allegations of war crimes, allegations of human rights violations, Ukraine's armament and extreme nationalism are considered as the defining elements of the main themes. Summaries and interpretations have been formed based on these themes.

With the findings obtained as a result of the descriptive analysis, Russia's approach to Ukraine and Donbass events will be revealed. This data is revealing the messages that Russia gives to the world about its Ukraine policy throuhg digital diplomacy using the case study.

Russia's Digital Diplomacy

In the process of global digitalisation, the traditional understanding of geopolitical power is losing its meaning, and the ability to predict and use modern trends in digital technology is becoming almost more important for countries than the possession of the latest weaponry. Digital diplomacy tools are commonly referred to as the use of social media and online media platforms in the work of diplomatic missions. The use of such tools allows diplomats, with an appropriate approach, to practically contribute to the formation of a loyal public opinion towards the country they represent online.

The task of making digital diplomacy one of the instruments of foreign policy was set for the Russian Foreign Ministry by Russian President Vladimir Putin in 2012. At that time, the French agency AFP published the world's first ranking of the effectiveness of states in the field of digital diplomacy, using the Internet to promote foreign policy views and influence public opinion. The activities of diplomatic departments on the Internet (primarily on social networks), the number of subscribers to their accounts and citations were taken into account. Among 146 countries, the first place was taken by the United States. About 44 million people subscribed to the numerous accounts and blogs of the State Department. Turkey, Saudi Arabia, the United Kingdom, Japan and India were also in the top 10. Russia ranked 14th. In the Digital Diplomacy 2017 ranking, Russia ranked 4th, behind only the USA, the UK and France (Tsifrovaya Diplomatiya, 2018).

The topic in Russia was first announced by the head of the Department of American Studies, Doctor of Historical Sciences Natalya Aleksandrovna Tsvetkova. Web 2.0 methods of public diplomacy are "placing radio and television programmes on the Internet, distributing open access literature about the United States in digital format, monitoring discussions in the blogosphere, government in social networks, sending information via mobile phones, as well as creating personalised pages of US members" (Tsvetkova cited in Zinovyeva, 2013: p.213). In total, there are currently about 400 serious scientific papers devoted to digital diplomacy in the world, which is very few by the standards of world science. The study of digital diplomacy contributes to an objective understanding of political processes and the alignment of political forces in another state.

Russia is one of the world leaders in the field of digitalisation policy. In addition to ongoing digitisation programmes and strategies for the development of a digital society, digital services in Russia have developed astonishingly. In addition, Russia is setting trends in the digitalisation of politics at the regional and global level. At the regional level, we are primarily talking about the digital agenda of the Eurasian Economic Union. At the global level, Russia, together with the United States, are key actors in the negotiation process on responsible behaviour of states in cyberspace. In terms of digital diplomacy, Russian foreign ministries (primarily the Ministry of Foreign Affairs) are actively developing, are not afraid to be innovative, interact with the audience in social networks and release special mobile applications.

One of the most promising areas of Russian digital diplomacy appears to be the involvement of domestic technology enterprises in projects in the field of public diplomacy. The experience of the search company Yandex, which today processes most Russian-speaking Internet requests, of the popular VKontakte social network not only in Russia but also in many foreign countries, including the CIS countries, Israel, Germany and the USA, is successful.

In recent years, the integration of Russian Internet companies into the global information and innovation environment has accelerated. Examples include the creation of the DST Global fund with a global structure of IT assets, including accounts in Facebook, Twitter and Zynga, the acquisition of LiveJournal by SUP Media, the creation of a Yandex office in the US Silicon Valley.

Perviy Kanal and RTR, which also broadcast in the digital domain, make an important contribution to shaping a positive image of Russian politics and diplomacy. Blogs of Russian government officials and diplomats have already been created in Russian and English, and open data on their activities have been published on the portals of state institutions. At the same time, Runet companies can more actively engage in Russian digital diplomacy to popularise the Russian language and culture, effectively communicate Russia's vision of international problems to a global audience.

In mid-March 2014, following the annexation of Crimea, the United States, the European Union, Australia, New Zealand and Canada imposed the first set of sanctions (Makarchiev, 2022). These measures included asset freezes and visa restrictions on individuals on sanctions lists (there are US and EU lists), as well as a ban on companies in the sanctioning countries doing business with individuals and entities on the lists.

The subsequent expansion of sanctions (April-May 2014) was linked to the aggravation of the situation in eastern Ukraine. The organisers of the sanctions accused Russia of actions aimed at undermining Ukraine's territorial integrity, particularly in the supply of arms to pro-Russian rebels (Timofeyev, 2022).

The next round of sanctions was associated with the crash of a Boeing 777 in the Donetsk region on 17 July 2014, which, according to the leadership of a number of states, was caused by the actions of rebels supported by Russia (Interfax, 2022).

In August 2018, the US State Department announced the preparation of new sanctions against Moscow, the reason for which was the poisoning of double agent Sergei Skripal and his daughter Yulia in the UK with Novichok poison.

In the following years, the US and EU sanctions regime was expanded and new punitive measures were introduced following the poisoning of opposition politician Alexei Navalny by Novichik in Russia.

In February 2022, Russian President Vladimir Putin's declaration of a war against Ukraine, the so-called "special military operation in the Donbass", prompted a new round of sanctions from the European Union, Great Britain, the United States and Canada. Companies with world-famous brands suspended their activities in Russia (Krut', 2022, p. 96).

Another promising direction in the development of Russian digital diplomacy is the use of the Internet crowdsourcing potential. In this context, it is important to assess the ways in which the Russian Foreign Ministry uses digital diplomacy. In 2014, the first official account of the Russian Ministry of Foreign Affairs on the social network started working.

In 2014, the Russian Federation received significant pressure from Western agencies in the media sphere (Voronina, 2019).

On the website of the Russian Foreign Ministry there is currently a mobile application of the Ministry of Foreign Affairs, a consular information portal, a separate link on the Syrian chemical dossier of the Russian Foreign Ministry, "The Truth about Events in Ukraine and Donbas" on the page of the official website of the Foreign Ministry (Russian Foreign Ministry, 2022).

The Russian social network "vk.com" has a page of the Russian Foreign Ministry and is officially recognised. New content is constantly being published on this social network. A large number of photo and video materials providing information about the activities of the Ministry are provided. The site also features a general news feed, a section on foreign policy information, archive data, a section dedicated to consular and diplomatic representatives. Information on educational institutions is also presented here, and photo and video material is also available through links in the networks.

The Facebook information space concept is characterised by the following opportunities for diplomatic communication. Firstly, the page contains only official messages from the Russian Foreign Ministry. Secondly, the page contains additional materials on the topic of international relations. It is important that some messages are supplemented with additional comments by representatives of the Ministry of Foreign Affairs in an ironic or humorous way to attract the attention of users.

Texts published in the above social networks are provided with photo materials and multimedia. Adaptation of social networks to mobile applications makes them available for smartphones, tablets and other gadgets.

If we consider public diplomacy as a communication strategy, it is possible to establish a dialogue between certain politicians and influential bloggers in modern society. The younger generation in particular actively "subscribes" to popular bloggers who now manage their social pages.

In the field of active development of digital diplomacy, work was carried out to modernise the Internet portal of the Russian Foreign Ministry and promote it in the largest search engines. As a result, the popularity of the site has increased significantly, reaching the level of 600 thousand visitors and more than 2 million page views per month. The share of visits to the portal from mobile devices increased 4.5 times. Increased presence in leading social networks. The number of regular subscribers and readers of the accounts of the Russian Ministry of Foreign Affairs has increased many times - up to 2.3 million users. At the same time, the Facebook account reached 355 thousand subscribers, accounts on Twitter in Russian - 1.18 million, in English - 130 thousand, social network "Vkontakte" - 425 thousand Twitter @Russia designed to create a positive image of the state abroad, has 164,000 subscribers. Accounts were created on Instagram and Telegram messenger (Voronina, 2019).

Before the sanctions were imposed, the Russian Foreign Ministry actively used social networks such as Facebook, Instagram, Twitter and TikTok. Today domestic social networks Odnoklasniki, VKontakte, Periskop, Telegram, Rutube and Viber are more active.

Voronina (Voronina, 2019) writes that in November 2016 the Concept of Foreign Policy of the Russian Federation was published on the official website of the Russian Foreign Ministry. Section III, "Priorities of the Russian Federation in Solving Global Problems", it is indicated: foreign policy initiatives and actions, processes and plans for the socio-economic development of the Russian Federation, the achievements of Russian culture and science. It is noted that "wide use of new information and communication technologies" is necessary to objectively perceive Russia among a foreign audience (Decree of the President of the Russian Federation of 30 November 2016 N 640 "On Approval of the Concept of Foreign Policy of the Russian Federation"). The Ministry writes that it is necessary to strengthen the position of the Russian media in the global information space, "provide them with the necessary state support for this, actively participate in international cooperation in the information sphere, take the necessary measures to counter threats to information security".

As Yevgeny Panteleyev (Panteleyev, 2013) notes, the tasks of the diplomatic service in the public sphere remained the same - to achieve an objective perception of Russia in the world; to develop its own effective means of informational influence on public opinion abroad; to ensure the strengthening of the positions of the Russian media in the global information space and provide them with the necessary state support; to actively participate in international cooperation in the field of information, to take the necessary measures to repel information threats to the sovereignty and security of the country. It is also noted in the Foreign Policy Concept of the Russian Federation that the possibilities of new information and communication technologies will be widely used in diplomatic activities, and Russia will endeavour to create a number of legal frameworks.

Speech by the Minister of Foreign Affairs of the Russian Federation S.V. Lavrov at the plenary session "International Relations in the Context of Digitalisation of Public Life" of the International Scientific and Practical Conference "Digital International Relations 2022" (Lavrov, 2022):

Under the "skating rink" of the Western press, individual users of social networks and large `media outlets have the entire infrastructure for the distribution of news and assessments formed over the years. The heads of domestic media operators and ordinary employees are being prosecuted as part of the illegitimate sanctions action. We see how the global Western, especially American, Internet platforms *fanatically block the Russian information resource worldwide. They do it defiantly and without hesitation. The other day, the YouTube video hosting restricted access to the briefing of the official representative of the Russian Foreign Ministry M.V. Zakharova on 17 March of this year. The account of the State Duma of the Russian Federation was subjected to similar measures. Unreasonable restrictions are imposed on the publications of the Russian Foreign Ministry and foreign affairs organisations on the Twitter network simply because we tell the truth and back it up with facts.*

Lavrov says he believes that this is part of the culture of xenophobia, approved and fuelled by the Western world, which eliminates everything Russian and Russian.

Almost every day, powerful cyberattacks using advanced information technologies expose Russian state institutions, media, critical infrastructure facilities and the life support system. Describing all this as part of a coordinated information attack against Russia, Lavrov says that special attention should be paid to the tasks of protecting the relevant resources of the executive authorities, including the Foreign Ministry. It is necessary to constantly improve the measures taken for these purposes, to ensure daily control over the implementation of the relevant instructions of the Government. At the same time, he emphasises, it is necessary to do everything to take full account of the unique features of the diplomatic service, to reliably secure the truly invaluable and sometimes highly sensitive array of information accumulated in the diplomatic service.

Russia also said that certain legal and practical steps had been taken to further strengthen the state's technological digital sovereignty. The current crisis, as in any other area, offers additional opportunities for development, he said:

We constantly advocate the establishment of professional, constructive cooperation in the digital sphere, especially in the field of Internet governance and cybersecurity. It is now clear to all responsible politicians and professionals in this field that without universal agreements in the field of Internet regulation, the world risks falling into a state of cyberanarchy. The consequences of this, without exaggeration, could be catastrophic for the world economy, international security and even for the comfort and well-being of hundreds of millions of citizens (Lavrov, 2022).

Sergey Lavrov says that they will certainly continue to use their capabilities in information work within the framework of the legislation, but at the same time emphasises that domestic online services platforms and information and communication technology solutions are also working well. He recalls that in this sense he has been actively supporting and promoting Vkontakte for a long time, seven years ago in St. Petersburg I had a chance to personally launch the account of the Foreign Ministry on this service. He says that it is necessary to actively support Odnoklassniki and RuTube.

Successful promotion of political and diplomatic accounts serves as a proven strategy for competently conveying your messages. Many people pay attention not to general political pages devoted to diplomatic organisations, but to specific accounts of diplomats and politicians, because society is interested in the opinions of specific people, not impersonal ideas and messages. The aspect of page personalisation plays an important role in building a more informal relationship between the diplomat and the target audience, because it is important for users to know what kind of person this or that politician is, what views he or she holds. The impersonality of official pages can sometimes repel only a young audience, because they are used to more "live" accounts showing a person from different angles.

The importance of feedback is that users of social networks can also leave comments, participate in forums and thus express their interest in the diplomatic sphere.

Therefore, the communication strategy chosen by diplomatic bodies takes into account this convenient form of "fast" communication. Using social networks, the Ministry of Foreign Affairs of the Russian Federation informs citizens about the activities of the ministry, publishes constant messages about visits, meetings and other organisational events. Such a trend in communication with users strengthens the confidential aspect of the functioning of a diplomatic institution, where users can learn about an event occurring at any time not only by reading, but also by watching the event using the multimedia material provided.

In the modern world, the largest transnational corporations, together with states, play an important role as subjects of the global information space. Therefore, the prospects for digital diplomacy should be associated with leading multinational companies that can represent the country in the international arena. In Russia, these are public joint stock companies such as Gazprom, Lukoil, Sberbank, VTB, etc. Russia is one of the largest exporters of natural gas, so PJSC Gazprom, one of the leaders of transnational energy companies, is a new actor at the international level. As a result, a multi-level model of international diplomatic policy should be created with the participation of both state institutions and business structures.

The digitalisation of modern life has led to the fact that the audience of almost all ages has a genuine interest in social networks. The digital environment provides "soft power", which, as examined, is expressed in the implementation of a communication strategy. Modern diplomatic practice uses the resources of social networks to provide information content useful not only for members of the diplomatic community, but for all interested people.

FINDINGS

Digital diplomacy as a phenomenon in the Russian diplomatic community appeared not so long ago. However, in recent years, the Russian Ministry of Foreign Affairs has used popular social networks to communicate with the target audience, thereby increasing interest in its activities in terms of the development of a progressive society in the context of globalisation.

Today, the production and dissemination of information involves an international communication process. Communication and diplomacy are related to the fact that information fulfils the function of explaining a transnational policy or explaining the causes and consequences of events to the whole world.

When the circulation/opening of information takes place on digital platforms, the concept of digital diplomacy comes to the fore. The focus of digital diplomacy brings along a persuasion-based communication process. This study analyses an article published by the Russian Ministry of Foreign Affairs on the events in Donbass. In the analysis in question, it was analysed by descriptive analysis method. In this context, the causes of the Donbass events, ultra-nationalism, war crimes, media views on NATO's arming of Ukraine were tried to be explained through the main themes. In the light of these findings, it is aimed to reveal Russia's approach to Ukraine and Donbass events.

With the data obtained, it is seen that Russia does not favour the change of government in Ukraine. As it is known, Russia has a historical association with Ukraine. Until the Zelensky government, Russia-Ukraine relations have been carried out through this historical association. However, after Zelensky took over the government, a policy against Russia was pursued and warmer contacts were made with NATO and EU countries. Russia attributes the causes of the Donbass incidents to this change of government. It has stated that with the change of government, Ukraine has attempted to undermine the historical unity from the past. In this context, the destruction of the Lenin statue was interpreted as a distortion of history and an attempt to falsify history.

Another reason for Russia's intervention in Donbass is seen in the texts that Russia constructed/ constructed through discourses such as genocide and extreme nationalism. Accordingly, a policy of extreme nationalism was pursued in Ukraine and various racist groups put pressure on Russians living in Ukraine. Data on war crimes committed in the Donbass events were also shared. Another element of oppression was the language policies implemented by the Ukrainian government. While the official language of Ukraine was Russian, it became Ukrainian, which disturbed Russia. In addition, the text shared included visuals of children and texts stating that they wanted to speak Russian.

While the Russian government holds the current Ukrainian government responsible for all these incidents, it accuses European countries and the USA of provoking Ukraine. From Russia's point of view, the US and Europe are responsible for the events in Donbass by providing arms to Ukraine.

In this section, the findings of The Truth Behind Events In Ukraine & Donbass (2014-2022) in pdf format on the website of the Russian Ministry of Foreign Affairs are discussed. The Truth Behind Events In Ukraine & Donbass (2014-2022) consists of 46 pages. This content, in which the Donbass events are explained and described from the Russian perspective, is in English and Russian. The content published by the Russian Foreign Ministry will be interpreted through categories such as the causes of the Donbass events, regime change, allegations of war crimes, allegations of human rights violations, armament of Ukraine and extreme nationalism.

Russia: The Reason for the Donbass Events is the Regime Change in Ukraine

Russia attributes the main cause of the Donbass events to the regime change in Ukraine. As it is known, in 2013, the Ukrainian president Viktor Yanukovych announced that he would end his relations with the European Union. Following this announcement, demonstrations against Viktor Yanukovych and Russia started in the country. In February 2014, the protests turned into clashes in Donbass. This uprising ended with the impeachment of President Yanukovych on 23 February 2014. A new regime was established in Ukraine. In this section, Russia made references to the date when the Donbass events first started. It described the events with the discourses of armed clashes, blood and crisis. Underlining that Ukraine has undergone a major change, the article states that the most important reason for the change in Ukraine is the active provocation of European and US countries. The change that modern Ukraine has undergone is tried to be explained through norms. These norm changes are listed as human rights and freedoms, heroisation of Nazism, manifestations of neo-Nazism and radicalism, violation of the right to freedom of thought, conscience and beliefs, discrimination of citizens, torture of journalists and independent media, falsification of history. If we summarise this section briefly, it is stated that the changes and transformations that Ukraine has undergone have caused the Donbass events. The most emphasised phenomenon in the article, in which change has a negative meaning, is extreme nationalism.

Another criticism of Russia against the newly established government is that the new government deliberately distorts history and historical reality. In this context, Russia strongly opposed the demolition of the statue of Lenin, the founding leader of the USSR. In particular, the demolition of the statue of Lenin, the raising of the Ukrainian flag and the singing of the Ukrainian national anthem was interpreted as a distortion of history. Another argument presented as a distortion of history is that President

Zelensky did not give messages celebrating the victory in the Second World War. Russia attributes this to the new Ukrainian regime's desire to break the ties of historical unity.

Allegations of War Crimes

The Truth Behind Events In Ukraine & Donbass (2014-2022) also focuses on war crimes. In the said article, it is written that the Ukrainian government in 2014 exhibited behaviours that violated human rights and this idea was proven by eyewitnesses. In the article, it is stated that Ukrainian soldiers shelled and many people were killed. This was supported by an image of a person living in Donbass.

Another striking visual is the visuals of children who died under the title of "Children of Donbass". In the texts claiming that many children died in the Donbass attacks, the United Nations Report was also referred to. Another allegation made by Russia against war crimes was genocide. In the texts containing allegations of genocide against Russians by Ukraine, images such as elderly people, children, mothers and children were shared. This concept was supported with images of corpses, graves and cemeteries.

Another allegation of war crimes was the ceasefire violations committed by the Ukrainian army. Within a seven-year ceasefire period, many ceasefire agreements were made, but Ukraine did not comply with these agreements. The OSCE Special Monitoring Mission recorded more than 10,000 ceasefire violations. Russia has made such claims on the basis of independent international organisations.

Allegations of Human Rights Violations

Another justification given by Russia for the events in Donbass is the allegations of human rights violations. In this context, there are three issues that Russia addresses. The first of these is that they prevent the Russian population living in the Donbass region from speaking Russian. The oppression of Russian-speaking peoples was also supported by children's visuals. This oppression made sense to the reader in the form of the Ukrainian flag covering the mouth of a small child in order to prevent him from speaking. Under the Ukrainian flag, I want to speak Russian banners attract attention. In addition, it was stated that this process was accelerated by the law in 2019. In 2019, as it is known, Ukrainian was adopted as the state language in Ukraine. Another allegation of human rights violations is the pressure and restrictions on churches. News and visuals about the repression and restrictions on churches were included.

Another issue claimed by Russia is freedom of the press. Information on imprisoned journalists and restrictive information on journalists in Ukraine was mentioned, and the bans imposed on some media organisations were also mentioned. Thus, the Ukrainian people were deprived of their right to access to information. Perhaps the most talked about of the allegations of human rights violations by Russia is the rhetoric of Ukrainian leaders in the media about the residents of Donbass. It is worth noting that the speeches of Ukrainian Presidents, President Volodymyr Zelensky, Petro Poroshenko, Ukrainian Minister of Culture Yevhen Nyshchuk, etc., in their discourse on the residents of Donbass, have insulted the people of Donbass.

Armament of Ukraine

Another issue that Russia emphasises is the armament of Ukraine. Russia strongly opposes the arming of Ukraine, which is not a member of NATO, by NATO member states. It sees this situation as a threat to its territorial integrity. Russia's claim, which includes various visuals and data, is as follows:

- Lithuania played an active role in training Ukrainian soldiers. In addition, V has delivered arms to Ukraine free of charge.
- France has delivered radar vehicles and ammunition to Ukraine, and various simulators for the training of UAV operators.
- Canada, the United States, France, the United Kingdom and other Western countries supported extremists in Ukraine, and all these data were disclosed in a report by the Institute for Eurasian Studies (IERES) at George Washington University in September 2021.
- From the beginning of the year to the end of the second decade of February, about fifty military transport aircraft from various countries were sent
- In a joint statement by the Minister of Defence of Ukraine A. Reznikov and the head of the Armed Forces of Ukraine V. Zaluzhny, on 14 February this year, Ukraine received 2.000 tons of advanced weapons, ammunition and protective equipment per month last year.
- US President Biden approved an additional $ 200 million in military package aid for Ukraine in December 2021.
- According to the State Department, since 2014, the United States has provided $2.7 billion in military assistance to Ukraine.

Extreme Nationalism

The most important issue that Russia emphasises is extreme nationalism. In his statements, he stated that racism in Ukraine is on the rise. Visuals of extreme racist groups are given. In the visuals, people holding guns and symbols of extreme racist groups were included. It was also stated that such groups were banned in Russia. In fact, Russia associates the source of all the problems mentioned above with the ultra-nationalist policy of the Ukrainian regime.

Another issue mentioned was the attacks of racist groups against journalists. In the article where it is explained that many journalists have fallen victim to murder, it is supported with visuals of the dead journalists. It is also detailed that 250 journalists died between 2017-2019. And it is underlined that there is no progress in these murder investigations and investigations. In addition, attention was drawn to the perception management made by the mirotvarets website. It was targeted by stating that they published personal and private information of many people on the website. It was pointed out that journalists died after the publication of the personal information of the journalists mentioned on the website in question.

CONCLUSION

In “The Truth Behind Events In Ukraine and Donbas (2014-2022)”, published by the Russian Ministry of Foreign Affairs on its official website, Russia has worked on digital diplomacy. In this publication, the Ministry of Foreign Affairs tried to explain the events in Donbass from its own perspective. While explaining this, various data and reports were utilised, and at the same time, many visual texts were shared rather than written text, which is an attempt to persuade, which is indispensable for diplomacy activities.

In this study, a descriptive analysis was made on the texts mentioned. The main themes required for the descriptive analysis were determined by the researchers as the causes of the Donbass events, regime change, allegations of war crimes, allegations of human rights violations, armament of Ukraine and extreme nationalism, and the analysis was carried out within this framework.

As it is known, Russia and Ukraine have a historical unity. Both countries are participants of the Soviet Socialist Republics. After the dissolution of the USSR, Ukraine maintained its relations with Russia. However, when the foreign policies of Ukraine are analysed from time to time, it is seen that Ukraine is also in close relations with Europe and the USA.

The milestone of the Russia-Ukraine crises is 2013. In 2013, Viktor Yanukovych, the President of Ukraine at that time, announced that he had severed relations with the European Union. This means that Ukraine's relations with Russia will further tighten. The public criticised Yanukovych's policy on a large scale and as a result, Zelensky came to power through re-election. Unlike Yanukovych, Zelensky's policies have been closer to Europe, NATO and the EU, and his relations with Russia have come to a breaking point.

With this change, uprisings and riots were observed in Donbass. The Ukrainian army and the Russian army intervened in the events, and Russia became the first and only country to recognise the independence of Donbass. Based on the concept of digital diplomacy, this study focuses on Russia's narration of the Donbass events to other countries.

In the first part of the study, Russia's explanations about the causes of the Donbass events were focused on. Russia blames Ukraine's regime for the Donbass events. The government established in Ukraine used weapons to suppress the Donbass events and cost the lives of many innocent Donbass people. At the same time, the regime promoted racism, even to the point of human rights violations and genocide. Russia claims that the Russian population in Ukraine cannot speak their own language. The Ukrainian government has put various obstacles in the way of this. This presentation is supported by visuals in the texts in question. In the texts based on racism, there is also a claim of genocide. Stating that Ukraine is consciously and programmatically committing genocide, Russia has stated that it intervened in DOnbass in order to prevent this. Again, the texts about genocide were presented to the reader with visuals of children, women and cemeteries.

In general, in the context of digital diplomacy, some findings have been reached for the persuasion of the text in question. The text written for the Donbass events is presented to the reader in English and Russian. This is an indication that the Russian Ministry of Foreign Affairs wants to be heard by more countries. The text is also available on the website of the Ministry of Foreign Affairs and can be downloaded as a pdf. Another issue is the frequent use of figures and reports while explaining the reasons for the events in Donbass. Some of these reports are OSCE and UN reports. Russia has also tried to support its claims with visuals. There are visuals under each statement. This is the strategy of the Russian Ministry of Foreign Affairs to convince all countries of the world. Of course, within the scope of the Donbass events, Russia's digital diplomacy is not limited to this text. However, this text is an important data in terms of Russia's own perspective on its relationship with Ukraine and the arguments used in the narrative of the Donbass events.

REFERENCES

Abdurahmanli & Bagis. (2021). Definition of Diplomacy and Types of Diplomacy Available in the International Conjuncture. *Anadolu Academy Journal of Social Sciences*, 141-160.

Adesina, O. S. (2017). Foreign policy in an era of digital diplomacy. *Cogent Social Sciences*, *3*(1), 113. doi:10.1080/23311886.2017.1297175

Bjola, C., & Holmes, M. (2015). *Digital Diplomacy: Theory and Practice*. Routledge. doi:10.4324/9781315730844

Bull, H. (1997). *The Anarchical Society: A Study of Order in World Politics*. Macmillan.

Caglar, A. (2019). *Power: Hard Power, Soft Power and Smart Power.* http://www.alicaglar.net: Retrieved from http://www.alicaglar.net.tr/StaticFiles/file/guc-sert-yumusak-ve-akilli-guc.pdf

Dogan, M. (2013). *Digital Communication and New Media*. Anadolu University.

Interfax. (2022, January 30). *Voyna Sanksi*. Retrieved from interfax.ru: https://www.interfax.ru/story/111

Krut', V. (2022). Sanctions against Russia: Historical Background and Contemporaneity. *Topical Issues of Contemporary International Relations*, 95-99.

Lavrov, S. (2022, April 14). *Minister of Foreign Affairs of the Russian Federation S.V. Lavrov's "International Relations in the Context of the Digitization of Public Life" speech at the plenary session "Digital International Relations 2022" of the International Scientific and Practical Conference.* Retrieved from Russian Embassy: https://www.rus.rusemb.org.uk/fnapr/6175

Makarichev, V. (2022, March 9). *Istorii Sanksiy Antirossiyskih*. Retrieved from Morskiye Vesti Rossiya: http://www.morvesti.ru/analitika/1691/94407/

Manovich, L. (2018). *The Language of New Media*. Ad Marginem Press.

Melissen, J. (2005). The New Public Diplomacy: Between Theory and Practice. In J. Melissen (Ed.), *Studies in Diplomacy and International Relations* (pp. 3–27). Palgrave Macmillan.

Panteleev, E. (2013). Foreign Service: Modern Modes of Interaction with the Media. *Law and Administration. XXI century*, 94-104.

Payne, Sevin, & Bruya. (2011). Public Diplomacy in the Digital Age. *Comunicação Publica*, 45-70.

Russian Ministry of Foreign Affairs. (2022, April 6). Retrieved from www.mid.ru: https://www.mid.ru/

The Truth behind Events in Ukraine and Donbass. (2022). Retrieved from https://www.mid.ru/: https://russische-botschaft.ru/wp-content/uploads/2022/03/The-Truth-Behind-Events-in-Ukraine and-Donbass.pdf

Timofeyev, A. (2022, March 3). *History of Restrictions: Why Have There Always been Sanctions against Russia?* Retrieved from Gazeta.ru: https://www.gazeta.ru/social/2022/03/03/1596663.shtml

Tsifrovaya Diplomatiya: Vizovy i perspectivy. (2018, February 28). Retrieved from 2035.media: http://2035.media/2018/02/28/digital-diplomacy/

Voronina, D. (2019). The Development of Russian Digital Diplomacy at the Current Stage. *Journal of "International Communication"*, 1-11.

Watson, A. (1984). *Diplomacy: The Dialogue between States*. Methuen.

Westcott, N. (2008). Digital Diplomacy: The Impact of the Internet on International Relations. Oxford Internet Institute.

Yıldırım, A., & Şimşek, H. (2011). *Qualitative Research Methods in Social Sciences*. Seçkin Publishing.

Zinovieva, E. (2013). Digital Diplomacy, International Security and Opportunities for Russia. *Index Bezopasnosti*, 213-228.

KEY TERMS AND DEFINITIONS

Datatization: Datatization is a technological trend that transforms many aspects of social life into data, which is then translated into knowledge and realised as a new form of value.

Descriptive Analysis: Descriptive analysis is the presentation of the obtained data to the reader in an organised and interpreted manner.

Digital Diplomacy: Digital diplomacy, also referred to as Digiplomacy and eDiplomacy, has been defined as the use of the Internet and new information communication technologies to help achieve diplomatic objectives.

Internet: The Internet is the global system of interconnected computer networks that uses the Internet protocol suite to communicate between networks and devices.

Official Website: Official site or official website is the website of an institution to represent them online. All contents of the website must be accounted for because it represented the institution. This official website can be owned by anyone, individuals, companies, governments, and other organizations.

Public Diplomacy: In international relations, public diplomacy, or people's diplomacy, broadly speaking, is any of the various government-sponsored efforts aimed at communicating directly with foreign publics to establish a dialogue designed to inform and influence with the aim that this foreign public supports or tolerates a government's strategic objectives.

Russian Federation: Russian Federation is a transcontinental country spanning Eastern Europe and Northern Asia. It is the largest country in the world by area, covering over 17,098,246 square kilometres (6,601,670 sq mi), and encompassing one-eighth of Earth's inhabitable landmass.

Ukraine: Ukraine is a country in Eastern Europe. It is the second-largest European country after Russia covering approximately 600,000 square kilometres (230,000 sq mi).

Chapter 11
Reading Turkey's EU Accession Process Through Progress Reports in the Context of Public Diplomacy

Elifnur Terzioğlu
Ataturk University, Turkey

ABSTRACT

Public diplomacy, which is defined as an effort to influence the attitude and perception of the public in order to shape and implement the foreign policy in the desired direction, can also be evaluated as an effort to shape the public opinion of different countries in a positive and desired way. One of Turkey's most important goals in the international arena has been determined as membership to the European Union, and many governments have carried out activities in various dimensions in line with this policy for many years. The activities carried out by Turkey in the EU membership process are closely monitored by the EU and regularly reported since 1998. While evaluating the breakthroughs Turkey has made in terms of foreign policy in these reports, it is also possible to determine how the international community and the public perceive these efforts. Based on this foresight, in this chapter, Turkey's progress reports in the EU membership process will be evaluated in the context of public diplomacy, and a descriptive and analytical framework will be created in this context.

INTRODUCTION

Public perception, which affects foreign policy in international relations, is becoming more important for political actors day by day, and studies are being carried out on it in order to influence public opinion and the agenda. Understanding the importance of perception management, governments develop their policies by taking into account domestic and foreign public opinion. In this context, the policies developed are about creating a positive image on the target audience and influencing the target audience in the desired direction. Influencing the target audience without any pressure to support the foreign policy

DOI: 10.4018/978-1-6684-5822-8.ch011

brings the concept of public diplomacy to us. Although the classical diplomacy understanding is dominant in international relations, public diplomacy is gaining importance and becoming one of the effective factors in the position of countries in the international arena. Bringing new approaches in foreign policy, public diplomacy plays an active role in the field of international relations and it mostly does this with soft power. Contrary to the classical understanding of diplomacy such as international diplomatic relations, diplomatic declarations and negotiations between delegations, it is the aim of public diplomacy to influence the target audience with activities such as culture and art. Along with the transition to the digital world, public diplomacy activities increase its diversity and effectiveness in the political arena depending on the developments in the field of communication. Contrary to the classical understanding of diplomacy in international relations, in public diplomacy, countries try to influence and persuade not only the governments of other countries but also the citizens of the country, and determine their priorities in this direction. Considering the interests of national interests, it is not enough to persuade governments and officials of international organizations alone. States or governments have to directly inform the foreign public, thereby positively influencing their perceptions. With the development of technology, the classical understanding of diplomacy is not sufficient in the international arena, and political actors cannot get the results they want. For this reason, influencing foreign societies by winning their hearts has brought a new dimension to international relations and demonstrated the importance of public diplomacy. Governments are starting to no longer communicate with foreign societies without public diplomacy. In summary, public diplomacy has become the most active and strategic method used by developed states to create a positive image on foreign countries. In this chapter, progress reports that play an important role in EU and Turkey relations will be evaluated in the context of public diplomacy.

BACKGROUND

When the literature on public diplomacy is reviewed, it is possible to see many definitions related to the subject. The first of these is that Mark (2002:8) states that public diplomacy aims to establish deep-rooted relations, to understand the culture and people of other countries, to identify their needs, to share their perspectives, to create a positive perception, and to create a positive environment for the image and awareness of a country. It is the definition that expresses power. Manheim (2002:75), on the other hand, defines public diplomacy as the art of managing perceptions and directing foreign institutions in line with targets. According to Nye (2005: 14), who is one of the most important people who caused public diplomacy to be known and used frequently in the context of international relations, public diplomacy is a field of use of soft power. Although the relations in countries that have adopted democracy are carried out through political actors, the important target audience is the foreign public opinion. Influencing political leaders doesn't make sense if governments can't positively influence the foreign population. When we look at the concept of diplomacy, it is defined as all of the intergovernmental relations and the methods used in establishing these relations (Riggins, 1998: 4). Before the Second World War, diplomacy targeted only the states that are the actors of the international system, but after the war, especially with the development of technology, international organizations and non-governmental organizations started to play an active role in the political arena. Due to these innovations, the public has started to be seen as an important actor in diplomacy (Akçadağ, 2010: 3). While military and economic power are the most effective power elements used in diplomacy, with the globalization after the Cold War, the world has begun to move to a multipolar power system and the ability to direct and persuade the public appears as an effective power. Today, the harsh sanctions that exist in the classical diplomacy understanding are losing their power and importance, and governments are trying to influence the foreign public opinion through public diplomacy (Aydoğan and Aydın, 2011: 13). Nye (2005:14) states that soft power as a public diplomacy element means that in order for a country to achieve the desired results in world politics, foreign public opinion should voluntarily admire its values, take it as an example, and countries that aspire to their welfare level and opportunities should follow it. According to Kalın (2011:163), contrary to hard power, soft power is beyond military and economic indicators, such as culture, education, art, written and visual media, film, poetry, literature, architecture, higher education (universities, research centers, etc.), non-governmental organisations, science and technology infrastructure and innovation capacity, tourism, economic cooperation platforms, and diplomacy. In addition, soft power reveals the depth of social capital of a country. Countries that can bring together soft power elements such as culture, art, education and science and position them on the communication strategy draw attention in the international system, creating a positive image. Thus, the processes carried out in diplomacy are diversified, and new areas are opened to the countries at the point of persuading the target audience, apart from the traditional understanding of diplomacy (Nye, 2005: 54). After the Second World War, Western states carried out many public diplomacy activities by conducting educational, cultural and artistic activities in order to establish cultural relations with foreign states. Organizations such as the Alliance Française of the French, the British Council of the English, and the Goethe Institute of the Germans, which were established to carry out language and cultural activities in the target countries, can be given as examples for these studies (Akçadağ, 2010:14). Applications such as international roaming scholarship programs especially provided for students also have an important place for public diplomacy activities. Erasmus+, College of Europe, Jean Monnet, Chevening scholarship programs, which offer education opportunities in Europe, and Fulbright Program in the USA, play a very active role in public diplomacy. The aim of this program, created on behalf of Arkansas Senator William Fulbright in 1946, is defined as "to introduce freedom and democracy" to youth, experts, trade unionists and artists in "totalitarian" countries (Öztürk, 2009:5). The increasingly transformed world is becoming more and more digital, and every information becomes accessible to everyone thanks to the developing information network. This allows countries to directly manage the processes related to their image in the context of foreign policy. It is possible to say that European countries have an older tradition in international relations compared to the USA and they allocate more budget to this field. Many European countries have cultural attractions. According to Nye, the closest competitor of the USA in terms of power resources is Europe. The languages of many European countries are widely spoken in the world. The most spoken European languages in the world are English, Spanish, Portuguese, Russian and German. Some European countries have national agency networks operating for the dissemination of their languages and cultures in the field of public diplomacy (Akgün, 2009: 3). The European Union's development of policies that give importance to issues such as international law, climate problems, democratization, freedom of the press, and human rights, and its activities in this direction both for the domestic and foreign public, contributes to its positive image around the world. Announcement to the public through the media and the pressures for the adoption of the International Criminal Court, abolition of the death penalty, arms control agreements and approval of the Kyoto protocol can be given as an example in this context (Bostancı, 2012:79). In addition, the structures of European cities that have preserved their historical texture for centuries and accordingly being the center of attention of tourists throughout the world offer important opportunities in the field of tourism and cultural diplomacy (Akçadağ, 2010:16). Although each country has its own methods in public diplomacy activities, the language and tools used differ significantly. These differences are closely related to the policies pursued by the countries, as well as their historical and cultural backgrounds. This is related to cultural diplomacy approaches that differ from country to country in terms of both their political priorities and their cultural codes (Kalın, 2012:168). When Turkey's public diplomacy studies are examined, it is seen that the post-Cold War period has gained momentum. Since the 1990s, Turkey's public diplomacy activities have become active, especially through humanitarian aid activities and non-governmental activities carried out abroad in the field of education, as well as official institutions such as the Turkish Cooperation and Coordination Agency (TIKA) (TIKA, 2022). In addition, studies such as the establishment of units such as the Presidency for Turks Abroad and Related Communities, Yunus Emre Foundation, Public Diplomacy Coordinatorship, Anadolu Agency's multi-lingual broadcasting, TRT's emphasis on international broadcasts and opening new channels for this purpose have made Turkey more public in the field of public diplomacy assertive and effective. The Presidency Government System and the establishment of a Communications Department directly subordinate to the Presidency and the association of media institutions and organizations with this Presidency shows the importance given to public diplomacy. In addition, the fact that cultural diplomacy institutions are gathered under the Ministry of Culture and Tourism in a way that will allow them to work in closer coordination with each other reveals once again the importance given to this issue (Özkan, 2015: 8). There is a lot of discussion about the aims, fields of activity, actors and dimensions of public diplomacy. However, it is seen that public diplomacy aims to directly change the behavior of the target audience by influencing them. Köksoy (2014:215), referring to Hans Tuch's definition of "creating an understanding against the ideals, thoughts, values, cultures, institutions, goals and policies of nations", emphasizes that public diplomacy adopts purposes such as increasing two-way dialogue, resolving conflicts, and managing total communication. Nye (2005:109) discusses public diplomacy in three dimensions in his book Public Diplomacy and Soft Power. Accordingly; The first dimension is "daily communications" which includes conveying local and foreign policies, the second dimension is "strategic communications" where a series of simple themes are developed, as in a political campaign or an advertising campaign, and the third dimension is "exchange programmes, internships, seminars, conferences" "Developing long-term relationships with important people over the years through access to cultural activities and media channels". While the source of public diplomacy was the government when it first emerged, with the development of communication technologies and globalization, the target audience became more accessible and other actors such as multinational companies and non-governmental organizations stepped in, communication tools have diversified and the source in public diplomacy is no longer just the state. Now, public diplomacy activities are carried out by other actors apart from the relevant institutions of the state, these actors sometimes get involved in the work of governments, sometimes they can carry out their own work completely independently from the state (Özkan, 2015:8). While public diplomacy tries to influence the public, it uses political communication tools. Karadağ (2012:61), political communication; defines it as the use of various communication types and techniques by political actors in order to impose certain ideological aims on certain groups, masses, countries or blocs, and to put them into action and put them into practice when necessary. When it comes to the elements of the political communication process, five points are important: the one who conveys the message, the receiver of the message (target audience), the vehicle used, the message/message and feedback. In order for political communication to take place fully, these five elements must be used effectively (Aziz, 2011:4). In addition to this, cultural, educational, technological and economic instruments are used in public diplomacy activities. When we look at the international public diplomacy studies, it is seen that the cultural and educational activities are predominant. The reason for this can be considered as the prominence of cultural and educational activities as an element of soft power. Looking at the historical process of the relations between the European Union and Turkey, it is seen that especially in recent years, the relations are not only about the economy, but also the cultural and educational interaction has gradually intensified. Exchange programs carried out to increase the international recognition, reliability and prestige of countries, foundations and institutes established to establish ties with all parts of the world play an important role in this area.

TURKEY EU MEMBERSHIP PROCESS

Although the relationship between the Republic of Turkey and the European Union has turned into a snake story, cultural and educational cooperation, especially economic, is an indication that the bond between them cannot be broken. The most important feature of Turkey-EU relations, which has a long history, is that it has always followed a fluctuating course from the beginning and the parties have maintained their will to maintain this relationship despite the problems experienced from time to time. As a matter of fact, membership to the EU continues to be one of Turkey's most important strategic goals, despite all the difficulties encountered during the negotiation process. Turkey, after Greece, is the second country to apply for partnership with the European Economic Community on 31 July 1959. With this partnership application, Turkey, as a member of the North Atlantic Treaty Organization (NATO), supported its position in the Western Bloc with economic integration, and did not want to benefit from EU financial aids and lose its market share in EU member states (Terzi, 2019:131). Turkey's economic expectation from this partnership is to gain the opportunity to enter the EU market and to contribute to the increase of foreign direct investment from EU countries; therefore, it can be said that the EU, seen as a 'market power' or a 'commercial power', is attractive to Turkey. In the same period, Turkey was seen by Western countries as a country that could cooperate to prevent the spread of the Union of Soviet Socialist Republics (USSR) to Eastern Europe and to develop relations with the Middle East (Eralp, 2009: 152). These reasons have brought Turkey and the EU closer together. As a result, the Ankara Agreement was signed on September 12, 1963, and entered into force on December 1, 1964 (Arıkan, 2006: 54). The main purpose of the Ankara Agreement is expressed as making the improvement of living standards in Turkey and the EEC countries continuous, thanks to accelerated economic development, regular expansion of trade, and the elimination of differences between the Turkish economy and the community economy (Baç, 2001:25). When the processes known as milestones in EU-Turkey relations are mentioned, it is noteworthy that Turkey's application for full membership on 14 April 1987. However, in its opinion dated 18 December 1989, the European Commission stated that Turkey is not yet ready for EU membership (European Commission, 2022). Customs Union negotiations started between the EU and Turkey in 1993, and the Customs Union entered into force on 1 January 1996. In fact, Turkey expected to become an EU member shortly after the Customs Union was established in accordance with Article 28 of the Ankara Agreement. However, its candidacy was not proposed in Agenda 2000, which was presented to the EU Council of Ministers on 16 July 1997 by the European Commission (European Commission, 1997:57). On 10-11 December 1999, the European Council granted Turkey the status of a candidate country for EU membership at the Helsinki Summit. After being declared a candidate, Turkey made some adjustments in its domestic policy in order to adequately comply with the Copenhagen political criteria and thus to start accession negotiations. It was expected that Turkey would sufficiently comply with the Copenhagen political criteria to start accession negotiations (mfa.gov.tr, 2022). For this reason, the first amendments to the Constitution were adopted in 2001, and the second amendments were adopted in 2004. At the Copenhagen Summit in September 2001, the European Council decided to increase the financial support through the 'Instrument for Pre-Accession Financial Assistance (IPA)' system. A total of six harmonization packages were adopted in 2003 and 2004, and these packages regulated issues such as shortening the duration of pre-trial detention, abolishing the death penalty, making it more difficult to close political parties, improving freedoms of assembly and expression, human and minority rights, and strengthening gender equality (Baç, 2005:19). After the Council of Europe decided to start membership negotiations with Turkey in 2004, Turkey's accession negotiations to the EU started on October 3, 2005 (Kaygusuz, 2012: 161). Although the process of joining the membership gained momentum during the 1999-2005 period, it is observed that the harmonization efforts slowed down after 2005 and almost stopped after 2011 (Yılmaz, 2016: 92). When the course of Turkey-EU relations in the historical process is analyzed, it is seen that this relationship is directly affected by the developments in the international system and European integration. Just as the developments in the Cold War or its aftermath were decisive in the past, today Turkey-EU relations are affected by changes in the international system, developments in our region or the situations the EU is facing. The refugee crisis in 2015 can be given as an example. The fact that the Syrian civil war caused an intense wave of immigration and this wave had a deep impact on Europe in the recent period revealed the need for cooperation with Turkey (Kutlay and Yılmaz, 2015:5). Turkey-EU relations, which had been relatively stagnant until this date, witnessed important developments after that, and within the framework of the Turkey-EU Summits on 29 November 2015, 7 March 2016 and 18 March 2016, where concrete decisions were taken on irregular migration, progress was made at every stage of relations (European Commission, 2016: 108). However, Turkey-EU relations have been damaged due to the cold and critical attitude of the EU towards Turkey after the 15 July coup attempt and a mutual trust problem has arisen (European Commission, 2016: 6). Varna Summit on March 26, 2018 plays an important role in normalizing relations. The leaders of Turkey and the EU, who came together in Varna on the said date, confirmed the importance of Turkey-EU cooperation and Turkey's candidacy (IKV, 2018). With the transition to the Presidency Government System of the Republic of Turkey, the state of emergency was lifted on 19 July 2018. After three years, the Reform Action Group Meetings (RAG), which was established in order to follow the reforms carried out within the scope of the work required to fulfill the Copenhagen criteria, at the highest level and to ensure the effective implementation of the reforms, during the European Union accession process was held on 29 August and 11 December 2018 and 9 May 2019. During the meetings, the determination to accelerate the reform process was shared with the public, and many important decisions were taken regarding the steps to be taken in the political reform process (EU, 2022). On the other hand, Turkey continues its efforts to update the Visa Liberalization Dialogue and the Customs Union, which is beneficial for both the EU and itself. With regard to visa liberalization, the European Commission has confirmed that as of 8 December 2018, Turkey has fully met 66 of the 72 obligations in the Visa Liberalization Roadmap. In this framework, there are 6 obligations to be met for visa liberalization. Working Groups were established for each remaining obligation in the Visa Liberalization Dialogue in line with the REG decisions (Avrupainfo, 2022). Cooperation between Turkey and the EU continues within the framework of the Financial Facility for Refugees. Turkey hosted 2.5 million refugees in 2015, and in the same period, with Germany's decision to open its borders to asylum seekers, negotiations began between Turkey and the EU to control the migration flow. At the Turkey-EU Summit on 18 March 2016, an agreement was reached on the "Turkey-EU Summit Statement". With this agreement, it was planned to control irregular migration and to deter human smuggling (European Council, 2022).

At this Summit, which is also known as the 18 March Agreement, the EU has committed 3+3 billion Euros to be used for Syrians in Turkey. In order to transfer this amount to our country, the EU Facility for Refugees in Turkey (FRIT) mechanism has been established (Europa, 2022). Contacts between Turkey and the EU continue in every field and level, and the negotiations held with the EU in key areas such as foreign policy, economy, energy, transportation and the fight against terrorism support the membership process. In this context, the High Level Economic Dialogue Meeting was held on 28 February 2019. In the meeting, it was aimed to strengthen the cooperation and revitalize the economic relations in the face of the slowing global trade and geopolitical uncertainties between Turkey and the EU (Avrupainfo, 2022). Considering the current uncertainties and risks in the international arena, it can be said that Turkey will continue to be an important stakeholder for the EU in order to strengthen existing partnerships, strengthen cooperation and dialogue.

PROGRESS REPORTS

Progress Reports are the reports that the Commission regularly submits to the Council and the Parliament, by monitoring and evaluating the positive or negative developments of the candidate country in the membership process. The reports in question "*were named Progress Report until 2016, and then Country Report*" (EU, 2022). These reports, which are prepared regularly for candidate countries, including Turkey, include assessments such as the past and current state of relations, the political and economic criteria to be fulfilled for membership, regional issues and international obligations, and the capacity to fulfill membership responsibilities (Özcüre, 2014: 457-458). In this chapter, the reports for the years 2011 and 2016 will be briefly mentioned, as they form an idea among the progress reports prepared for Turkey in 1998, but the years 2018 and 2019 will be analyzed in detail, excluding 2017[1], because they are both up-to-date and constitute the sample of the study.

2011 Progress Report

In the 2011 Progress Report, it has been stated that Turkey is politically competent in the process of harmonization with the EU, but there is a lack of fundamental rights and freedoms such as lawsuits filed against writers and journalists in Turkey, internet restrictions, especially freedom of expression, and these developments are worrisome. Along with the Sledgehammer and Ergenekon Trials of the period, the opportunity to expose the crimes against the rule of law and democracy in Turkey was not used, and the defendants' detention periods were long. It has been argued that the judiciary progressed slowly due to the overcrowding of the prisons and it was stated that the conditions needed to be improved. However, it was added that the expected progress on the fight against corruption and parliamentary immunity did not materialize. A proposal was made for the continuation of the Kurdish Initiative issue and the construction of a new constitution to resolve the Kurdish issue. Turkey's civilian oversight over the army has been stated as a progress issue (European Commission, 2011: 23-26). When we look at the 2011 Progress Report, it was emphasized how important the constitution and the rule of law are in the path of democratization, and it was stated that despite the criticism of freedom of expression, it made progress contrary to expectations. It has been suggested that progress should definitely be made on the Kurdish issue, which is the subject of constant discussion. Despite the criticism of the report from Turkey, the belief that relations with the EU should continue, has started structuring studies on the specified issues.

2012 Progress Report

33 chapters within the scope of harmonization with the EU acquis were discussed in the last chapter of the 2012 Progress Report, which covers the titles of political, economic and capacity to assume the obligations of full membership in general. According to this report, it was stated that Turkey did not cooperate enough in the illegal immigration agreement signed with the EU in May 2012. In the second half of 2012, Turkey decided not to participate in the meetings due to the Greek Cypriot Administration's coming to the EU Presidency. Another point that has been criticized is that Turkey has not fully implemented the customs union and there are still some articles in the legislation that violate the commitments regarding the customs union. The length of pre-trial detention and the right to defense were criticized and their legality was questioned. It has been stated that the laws regarding the dissolution of political parties and the financing of election campaigns do not comply with European standards, therefore no progress has been made in this regard. Briefly, the Turkish judicial system was criticized (European Commission, 2012: 70-72). It has been added that not enough progress has been made in the protection of fundamental rights, the Third Judicial Reform and the protection of the administration of justice. It has been argued that the presence of a household name showing religious knowledge on identity cards does not comply with the European Convention on Human Rights and that the 2010 decision of the ECtHR should be applied in this regard. Emphasizing that women's employment should be strengthened, the report stated that unregistered employment continues as a significant problem. In the report, in which positive impressions were given as well as criticism, it was added that 856 million Euros was allocated to Turkey from the Instrument for Pre-Accession Financial Assistance (IPA[2]) (European Commission, 2012: 5-6). The fact that Turkey has extended a helping hand to its neighbor countries, especially to approximately 100,000 Syrians fleeing the war, has been expressed with praise. However, the 8.5% growth of the Turkish economy and the decrease in the unemployment rate to 8.9% have been expressed as positive developments (European Commission, 2012: 38). In summary, the 2012 Progress Report contains similar issues to the 2011 Progress Report. While it is stated in the report that Turkey's economy is getting stronger, especially with the decrease in unemployment rate, political criticisms continued.

2013 Progress Report

Turkey 2013 Progress Report can be considered as one of the harshest and most critical texts written by the EU since the past. It was stated that serious steps should be taken in order to establish and sustain democratic foundations, especially on issues such as freedom of expression, independence of the internet and media, human rights and the judiciary. In the report, it was mentioned that the 23rd (Judiciary and Fundamental Rights) and 24th (Justice, Freedom, Security) chapters could only be opened, but that Turkey had to undergo a serious reform process and criticized the violent events in the Gezi resistance (European Commission, 2013: 51-71). The report also stated that there are serious problems regarding Turkey's Cyprus policy and emphasized the necessity of removing the veto that Turkey brought on EU-NATO cooperation, including the Greek Cypriot Administration (European Commission, 2013: 4). The 2013 Turkey Progress Report, especially for Turkey, which went through the process of 17 December, is considered as a report that unilaterally handles the political agenda of Turkey from the perspective of the EU. Looking at the past reports, it is seen that democracy is the most important issue. It would not be wrong to say that the European Union is concerned about the fundamental rights and freedoms experienced in Turkey, expresses this and expects reforms to correct this situation as soon as possible.

2014 Progress Report

The 2014 Progress Report draws attention to the positive developments in Turkey-EU relations compared to other years. In the report, the importance of the sustainability of the Positive Agenda efforts, which was a positive step for the relations between Turkey and the EU started in 2012, was mentioned, and even the then Prime Minister Recep Tayyip Erdoğan's declaring 2014 as the "EU Year" was perceived as a positive and concrete step in terms of relations (European Commission, 2014: 11). The issues of signing the Turkey-EU Readmission Agreement and mutual development of visa liberalization dialogue were discussed. However, in the report, Turkey was commended for refugees from Syria and Iraq, and it was added that Turkey would continue to play an active role in EU programs within the framework of financial aid. In the report where there were positive developments regarding the Kurdish Question, it was stated that the Solution Package accepted by the TBBM in June 2014 is important for the democratic resolution of the Kurdish issue (European Commission, 2014: 13). The judicial system is one of the most critical issues in the 2014 report. Issues such as the internet law, the closure of Youtube and Twitter, the murder of Hrant Dink, the MIT law, the HSYK regulation were criticized in this context, and it was emphasized that these problems limited the freedom of thought and expression. Regarding the freedom of expression, the Armenian issue and the Kurdish issue, which have been going on for years in Turkey, were reiterated in the report and it was emphasized that some legal changes were needed, such as Article 314 of the Turkish Penal Code, which restricts freedom of expression (European Commission, 2014: 17-25). It has been observed that in the 2014 Progress Report, similar issues were discussed, especially the functioning of the judicial system, freedom of expression, the fight against corruption, the Cyprus problem, the Kurdish problem, the Armenian issue. Despite this, Turkey's interpretation of the report, which still expressed a positive opinion compared to other years, was also positive.

2015 Turkey Report

In the 2015 Progress Report, which supports the accession negotiations due to the common interests of the EU and Turkey, it is seen that the contacts between Turkey and the EU on foreign relations and security continue. In the report, it was stated that the process carried out regarding the Kurdish issue should be further improved, and that Turkey continued political dialogues with necessary points in the field of foreign and security policy in the fight against terrorism. Due to the progress Turkey has made in the field of economy, it has been named as a positive development that steps have been taken for the opening of the 17th chapter, "*Economic and Monetary Policy*" (European Commission, 2015: 4). However, the report also touched upon the struggle with the PKK and criticized the fact that the peace process came to a standstill despite the positive developments in the past. In the report, it was emphasized that within the framework of the visa liberalization dialogue initiated in December 2013, cooperation in the fields of visa, mobility and migration continues, and a consensus was reached to accelerate the cooperation in the field of energy (European Commission, 2015: 4-9). As it can be understood, the 2015 Progress Report, like other reports, provides a roadmap for full membership to Turkey. To date, the Commission has written 20 reports on Turkey, but these reports have started to be thought that they do not contribute to Turkey's progress on the EU path, moreover, the Commission has been constantly criticizing Turkey through these reports. This further strengthened the already existing "Euroscepticism[3]" and further reduced support for the EU perception.

2016 Turkey Report

The key issue of the 2016 Progress Report is undoubtedly the coup attempt of July 15. Although its fight against ISID is praised in the report, Turkey has been severely criticized for the measures it has taken in the fight against FETO and its actions in the fight against the PKK/supporters. The fact that the definition of Fetullah Terrorist Organization (FETO) was not included in the report, which referred to the coup attempt as the "Gulen Movement", caused strong reactions from Turkey. It has been criticized that many civil servants were dismissed, companies, including media outlets, were closed for this reason, most of them were detained and arrested, and the state of emergency was extended (European Commission, 2016: 5-8). It was emphasized that arrangements regarding the rule of law and fundamental rights regarding the detention of HDP members were urgently needed, and it was suggested that the problem in the Southeast could be resolved through a political process. In addition, by emphasizing that the independence of the judiciary is getting worse and worse, issues such as the dismissal of judges and prosecutors from their duties and the confiscation of their assets, which were carried out within the scope of the Gülen Movement, were criticized. Regarding freedom of expression, it was stated that the closure of media outlets, the detention and arrest of journalists, writers and social media users caused by the coup attempt raise concerns (European Commission, 2016: 17-25). In the report, which supports Turkey's efforts to find a solution to the Cyprus issue, the relations between Russia and Turkey were also mentioned and the improvement of the relations, which were disrupted by the downing of the Russian jet on the grounds that it violated the Turkish airspace, in November 2015, with the Joint Syria Mechanism established between Turkey and Russia, was interpreted positively. In addition to these, Turkey, which is the fifth largest trading partner of the EU, hosting approximately 3 million refugees, has created a positive image towards the EU, and it has been stated that economic and commercial integration has increased (European Commission, 2016: 17-25).

2018 Turkey Report

In the report, it was stated that events such as dismissal, arrest and detention decisions taken under the state of emergency (OHAL) declared after the coup attempt on 15 July 2016, and their collective and disproportionate implementation, are a serious concern and that this state of emergency should be lifted without delay. In this report, which states that the 31 decree laws that were enacted under the state of emergency, have serious shortcomings, it is stated that the decrees have not been subject to the rigorous and effective inspection of the parliament. These decree-laws have not been open to judicial review for a long time and have not been subject to a decision of the Constitutional Court yet. Certain civil and political rights, such as freedom of expression, freedom of assembly and procedural rights, have been significantly restricted by these decrees. In total, more than 150,000 people were detained, 78,000 people were arrested and more than 110,000 civil servants were dismissed during the State of Emergency. Officials stated that approximately 40,000 of them were reinstated, 3,600 of them by decree (European Commission, 2018: 5-13). With the referendum held in April 2017, constitutional amendments bringing the presidential system in Turkey were accepted. It has been expressed that these changes do not contain enough balance and control, and even endanger the executive and the judiciary. It was emphasized that the powers transferred to the Presidency through the emergency decrees increased the role of the President over the executive. It has been stated that the appointment of trustees instead of mayors and elected representatives weakens local democracy to a large extent (European Commission,

Figure 1. Word Cloud of 2018 Turkey Report
Source: Prepared with data taken from European Commission (European Commission, 2018).

2018: 15-19). In the report, it was stated that the legal framework in Turkey includes respect for human rights and fundamental rights, but these were weakened and damaged by the emergency decrees. Criminal cases brought against journalists, academics, human rights defenders, writers and social media users, the withdrawal of press cards and the closure of many media outlets at the same time cause serious concerns, as there is a serious decline in freedom of expression, which is one of the weakest areas in Turkey (European Commission, 2018: 30-33). As can be seen in Figure 1, the judiciary system and the fight against corruption are among the prominent topics in the 2018 Turkey Report word cloud. It has been stated that preparations for Turkey's judicial system are still at the initial stage, and there has been a serious setback in 2017, especially in terms of the independence of the judiciary. Constitutional amendments regulating the Council of Judges and Prosecutors (HSK) entered into force, and the HSK continued to suspend judges and prosecutors and change their positions. However, it was stated in the report that the country has a certain level of preparation in the fight against corruption, where it has not made any progress. It was emphasized that it is important to further align the legal and institutional framework with international standards, as undue influence is allowed in the investigation and execution of corruption cases followed by the public. It was stated that Turkey's investigation, prosecution and conviction performance in corruption cases, especially in high-level corruption cases, remained weak (European Commission, 2018: 28).

Another notable title in the word cloud is that Turkey has made progress in the field of migration and asylum policy. It continues to implement the EU-TR Declaration by effectively managing Turkey's migration movements towards the Eastern Mediterranean in March 2016. On Visa Liberalization, Turkey submitted a work plan to the European Commission at the beginning of February explaining how Turkey will meet the seven unmet visa liberalization criteria, and this plan has been taken into consideration by the Commission. The report clearly states that Turkey has made some progress in dealing with competitive pressures and market forces within the EU (European Commission, 2018: 42).

2019 Turkey Report

In the report, it was first criticized that the state of emergency (OHAL) regime ended on 18 July 2018 with the end of the last extension period, but immediately afterwards, the TGNA approved a law to

Figure 2. Word Cloud of the 2019 Turkey Report
Source: Prepared with the data from the European Commission (European Commission, 2019)

protect many elements of the state of emergency regime for three years. The law has limited certain fundamental rights, especially with practices such as dismissal of public servants, extension of detention periods, restriction of freedom of movement. During the state of emergency, Turkey has been criticized for issuing 36 decree laws that limit the rights of defense and extend the powers of police and prosecutors in order to prolong the investigation processes, and stipulate the dismissal of 152,000 civil servants such as academics, teachers and public servants. It was underlined that many human rights defenders, civil society activists, LGBTI (lesbian, gay, trans and intersex individuals), media members, academics, doctors, judges are still in detention and exposed to smear campaigns (European Commission, 2019: 5-9). It has been stated that with the new presidential system, the power is concentrated in the hands of the executive and the TGNA has greatly restricted the legislative and audit functions. In the report, it was stated that the growing political polarization prior to the municipal elections in March 2019 prevented constructive dialogue from forming in the parliament, and even the detention of many HDP deputies, especially the Peoples' Democratic Party (HDP), was a cause for concern. It is observed that there is still a serious regression in Turkey's judicial system and the recommendations given in previous reports are ignored or not applied. In addition, it was stated in the report that the continuing pressure on judges and prosecutors and the relocation of a large number of judges and prosecutors without their consent adversely affected the independence and quality of the judiciary (European Commission, 2019: 5-9). It has been stated that Turkey continues its great humanitarian aid and support efforts to at least 3.6 million registered Syrian refugees and approximately 370,000 registered refugees from other countries, thus, it should be praised as the country that hosts the largest refugee community in the world. At the same time, seven working groups were formed to carry out technical studies on the remaining criteria in the field of Turkey visa liberalization dialogue, but no progress was made (European Commission, 2019: 20). A serious regression continues in the field of Human Rights and Fundamental Freedoms as well. Although Turkey's legal framework includes key sentences on respect for human rights and fundamental freedoms, it needs to be aligned with the laws of the European Convention on Human Rights (ECHR) and the European Court of Human Rights (ECHR). There has been serious backsliding in the areas of freedom of expression, freedom of assembly, freedom of association, procedural rights and property rights (European Commission, 2019: 8).

It can be seen in the word cloud of the 2019 Turkey Report in Figure 2, the words fighting organized crime, fighting corruption and regression come to the fore, similar to 2018. The report states that Turkey has a certain level of preparedness in the fight against organized crime, but progress is limited overall. Data protection in Turkey is still not up to European standards, and the country needs to make improvements in cybercrime, seizure of assets and witness protection legislation (European Commission, 2019: 43). In the economic field, it was stated in the report that the recession in the Turkish economy continued and serious concerns were raised about the functioning of the country's market economy. The currency crisis and years of high credit growth caused the inflation rate to decline in the economy. Turkey has made some progress and reached a good level of preparedness in dealing with market forces and competitive pressures within the EU. It is stated that Turkey is in good cooperation with the EU market in terms of trade and investment. Improvements were made in the energy sector; It has also been emphasized that some progress has been made in expenditures for physical capital, research and development and education. However, in the report, it is seen that the deficiencies in education quality and gender equality continue (European Commission, 2019: 9-10).

2020 Turkey Report

In the 22nd Turkey Report and Enlargement Package published on October 6, 2020, it has been clearly stated that although the state of emergency (OHAL), which is said to have a serious impact on democracy and fundamental rights, ended in 2018, its effects were felt for two years and this situation is worrying. It has been stated that the continuation of the centralization of the legislative, executive and judiciary at the Presidential level has led to a decline in the rule of law, democratic standards and fundamental freedoms. In the report, it is stated that although the Istanbul metropolitan mayoral elections on June 23, 2019 were professionally organized, the attitude towards the opposition candidate who won the elections was not fair (European Commission, 2020: 16-22). In the report, in which the views on the southeast were also stated, it was stated that the reason why the 31 March 2019 local elections became questionable despite the improved security environment was the appointment of trustees from the center, the arrest and dismissal of party representatives, instead of the 47 HDP mayors elected democratically. It has been argued that with this attitude that harms local democracy, civil society comes under pressure, free working areas continue to be restricted, and civil society activities are prevented. In this report, in which the Gezi trial was also criticized, it was stated that Turkey's judicial system had regressed significantly, and that concerns regarding the independence of the judiciary continued. It has been stated that the 2019-2023 Judicial Reform Strategy announced by the President in May 2019 is insufficient to eliminate the fundamental deficiencies regarding the independence of the judiciary, and even that no measures have been announced to address the concerns identified in the annual country reports of the European Commission (European Commission, 2020: 36). It has been stated that although Turkey has a certain level of preparation in the fight against organized crime in the fight against corruption, which has also come to the fore in the 2019 progress report, its progress in this area is generally limited, no progress has been made, and the country does not have preventive institutions in this regard. As can be seen in the word cloud of the 2020 Progress Report in Figure 3, human rights and fundamental rights are among the topics frequently mentioned in the report. It is stated that the deterioration in these issues continues, and that most of the measures introduced during the state of emergency remained in force, causing deep and devastating consequences. Although the legal framework includes general guarantees regarding the observance of human rights and fundamental rights, it has been stated that this framework needs to be harmonized with the European Convention on Human Rights (ECHR) and the ECHR (European Commission, 2020: 28).

Figure 3. Word Cloud of the 2020 Turkey Report
Source: Based on data from the European Commission (European Commission, 2020)

In the word cloud created with the data taken from the 2020 Progress Report, it is seen that one of the issues where the word "*backsliding*" is frequently used is freedom of expression. It has been stated that the regression on this issue continues, and the disproportionate application of restrictive measures adversely affects freedom of expression and the spread of dissident voices. The continuation of criminal proceedings and convictions of journalists, human rights defenders, lawyers, writers and social media has been severely criticized (European Commission, 2020: 78). In the report, it was mentioned that as Turkey has made some progress in the field of migration and asylum policy, it is important that throughout 2019, it remains committed to the implementation of the Turkey-EU Accord of March 2016 and plays a key role in ensuring the effective management of migrant flows along the Eastern Mediterranean route. Turkey is an important country with the largest refugee population in the world, hosting more than 3.6 million registered Syrian refugees and about 370,000 registered refugees from different nationalities. In March 2020, it was stated in the report that this attitude of Turkey, which took an active role in helping immigrants and refugees use the land route to Europe via Greece, was supported (European Commission, 2020: 42). Regarding the economic criteria, which constitute the important pillar of the progress reports, it has been stated that the Turkish economy is at an advanced level, but no progress has been made in the reporting period, and this situation has raised concerns about the functioning of the economy. With the emergence of the COVID-19 crisis, a series of measures have been taken by the authorities in order to alleviate the economic impact of the epidemic. However, it was stated that these measures were limited due to a limited policy space and institutional weaknesses, especially on the financial side. The European Commission recommended that emergency measures be proportionate, implemented within a limited time frame, and in this context respecting the rule of law and democratic and human rights standards, given the limited measures taken in light of the impact of the pandemic on employment, particularly informal employment (European Commission, 2020: 55). It can be said that the progress reports are an important text that shows the current status of the Copenhagen political and economic criteria and the harmonization with the EU acquis, and the extent of the developments between the European Union and the candidate country to the European Union. Therefore, the countries that want to become a member of the EU have to take into account the criticisms brought in the harmonization process and draw a road map accordingly. Progress reports have an important place in terms of being one of the most important links of Turkey's EU enlargement strategy, stating that the accession negotiations process is continuing, and confirming that it is a key partner. Developments in Turkey in recent years, the ups and downs of relations have unfortunately negatively affected Europe's perception of Turkey-Turkey's Europe, and bilateral relations have come to an impasse again. In the reports published in recent years, Turkey's negative approach to Turkey, rather than suggestions for reviving the accession process, has caused the Turkish public to approach the EU critically. For this reason, in order to take a positive step in the EU process, Turkey needs to carefully examine some deficiencies, suggestions and progress points identified in the reports, and the European Commission should also play a guiding, mediating and facilitating role in the process.

CONCLUSION

Public diplomacy has a very important place in the field of international relations and plays such an active role as to affect the image and reputation of countries. Activities such as culture, arts, sports and education, which are among the soft power elements, are seen as indispensable elements of public diplomacy and the studies carried out in this context positively affect the international interactions. Looking at the relations between Turkey and the EU in this context, it is seen that there is a fluctuating process within the negotiation process that has been going on for years. Although the membership process has been prolonged and caused negative thoughts, it is obvious that the relations will not end because of mutual benefits. Progress reports constitute important milestones in the process of membership to the European Union. In these reports, Turkey's current position in the EU membership process and the transformations that it needs to be realized are expressed in details. In each progress report, the progress of the country in the accession process compared to the previous reporting period is presented. In these reports, Turkey's situation in many fields from economy to democratization, from domestic political developments to diplomacy is revealed from the perspective of the EU. Although many issues have been discussed in the reports as detailed above, important determinations have also been made on the subjects of international relations and public diplomacy, which are the subject of this study. In this context, for example, in the 2011 Progress Report, it was emphasized that Turkey needed to reach international standards by making various arrangements on human rights. As it is known, fundamental human rights and freedoms are not seen as internal issues of countries today, but are accepted as issues with an international context. In this context, the emphasis on this issue can be understood as one of the prerequisites for Turkey to have a position that is accepted by other countries and the international community. Another issue emphasized in the 2012 Progress Report regarding international relations and public diplomacy is the issue of immigration. Migration, which has become a prominent problem all over the world in recent years, is of great importance in terms of affecting the demographic structures of countries and revealing the problems of coexistence of different societies, as well as being a diplomatic issue. This problem is important because it is an issue with international dimensions and a country's relationship with societies in different geographies, and it is an important area in which international organizations make mandatory regulations. In the 2012 Progress Report, Turkey's hosting of the large-scale refugee influx, especially from Syria, was praised. This attitude of Turkey has caused it to create a positive image both in the Middle East geography that it is neighbour to and in the Western world, which may be affected by this problem. In the 2013 Progress Report, the issue of human rights, which is also of international importance, was re-emphasized, and especially issues such as freedom of expression, internet and media independence were highlighted as areas that need to be developed urgently. As it is known, with digitalization, especially the media field has become an issue that needs to be addressed on a global scale, and the performances of countries in this regard are of great importance in terms of image and reputation. In the 2014 and 2015 Progress Reports, the issue of asylum seekers, which is also a current issue, was discussed, Turkey's stance on this issue was appreciated and the active role of the EU Financial Aid programs was linked to the positive attitude it has taken in this issue. In the report, it was emphasized that Turkey's collaborative stance on this issue is an important part of the dialogue at the international level. It can be stated that all these approaches will have important contributions to Turkey in terms of public diplomacy. In the 2016 Progress Report, Turkey's international position, in particular, its relations with Cyprus and Russia have been discussed. In this context, the requirements foreseen for Turkey to establish and maintain diplomatic positive relations are emphasized. Progress Reports are also of great value in terms of public diplomacy, as they suggest the necessary arrangements for Turkey to become an indispensable actor in both its close environment and the international society it is a part of. Human rights and refugee issues, which had been emphasized in the 2018, 2019 and 2020 Progress Reports as well as in previous reports, were reconsidered, the dimensions of the developments in these issues in Turkey were emphasized, and recommendations were made regarding new regulations that Turkey should make. When we look at the progress reports, which are a summary of the problems Turkey has experienced in the EU membership process and the developments it has made, it is seen that the most emphasized issues in international processes and public diplomacy in the nearly 10-year period covering the years 2011 and 2020 are focused on democratization, human rights and migration. Thanks to the progress and developments it will make in these matters, Turkey will be able to gain a rightful reputation in the international arena, and thus, it will be able to carry out a positive public diplomacy strategy by creating a positive image in the eyes of the public opinion of different countries.

REFERENCES

AB'den Türkiye'ye bir yıl süre. (2021). https://www.milliyet.com.tr/dunya/ab-den-turkiye-ye-bir-yil-sure-2441174

Akçadağ, E. (2010). *Dünya'da ve Türkiye'de Kamu Diplomasisi*. https://www.kamudiplomasisi.org/makaleler

Akgün, B. (2009). Türk Dış Politikası ve Uluslararası Örgütler. *Akademik Orta Doğu, 3*(2).

Arıkan, H. (2006). Turkey and the EU: An Awkward Candidate for EU Membership. Ashgate.

Avrupa Birliği ve Dış İlişkiler Genel Müdürlüğü. (n.d.). *IPA*. https://www.ipa.gov.tr/IPA_1070

Avrupa Komisyonu. (2016). *AB Genişleme Politikasına İlişkin 2016 Bildirimi*. Brüksel.

Aydoğan, B., & Aydın, H. (2011). Güç Kavramı, Kamu Diplomasisi ve Güvenlik. *Ekopolitik, 11*(2), 13.

Aziz, A. (2011). *Siyasal İletişim*. Nobel Yayınları.

Baç, M.M. (2001). *Türkiye ve Avrupa Birliği; Soğuk Savaş sonrası İlişkiler*. İstanbul: Alfa yayınları.

Baç, M. M. (2005). Turkey's Political Reforms and the Impact of the European Union. *South European Society & Politics, 10*(1), 17–31. doi:10.1080/13608740500037916

Bostancı, M. (2012). *Stratejik Bir İletişim Aracı Olarak Kamu Diplomasisi - Kamu Diplomasisinde Medyanın Rolü ve Önemi*. Anahtar Kitaplar.

Eralp, A. (2009). The Role of Temporality and Interaction in the Turkey-EU Relationship. *New Perspectives on Turkey*, *40*, 152. doi:10.1017/S0896634600005252

European Commission. (1997). Agenda 2000: For a Stronger and Wider Union. *Bulletin of the European Union*, COM(97) 2000 final, Supplement 5/97.

European Commission. (2011). Commission Staff Working Document. Turkey 2011 progress report. SEC (2011) 1201 final.

European Commission. (2012). Commission Staff Working Document. Turkey 2012 progress report. SWD (2012) 336 final.

European Commission. (2013). Commission Staff Working Document. Turkey 2013 progress report. SWD (2013) 417 final.

European Commission. (2014). Commission Staff Working Document. Turkey 2014 progress report. SWD (2014) 307 final.

European Commission. (2015). Commission Staff Working Document. Turkey 2015 Report. SWD (2015) 216 final.

European Commission. (2016). Commission Staff Working Document. Turkey 2016 Report. SWD (2016) 316 final.

European Commission. (2018). Commission Staff Working Document. Turkey 2018 Report. SWD (2018) 153 final.

European Commission. (2019). Commission Staff Working Document. Turkey 2019 Report. SWD (2019) 220 final.

European Commission. (2020). Commission Staff Working Document. Turkey 2020 Report. SWD (2020) 355 final.

European Commission. (n.d.). Commission Opinion on Turkey's Request for Accession to the Community. *Bulletin of the European Communities*, SEC (89) 2290 final, Brussel, 20 December 1989, par. 13. http://aei.pitt.edu/4475/

European Council. (2016). *EU-Turkey Statement.* https://www.consilium.europa.eu/en/press/press-releases/2016/03/18/euturkey-statement/

Helsinki Zirvesi. (1999). https://www.mfa.gov.tr/helsinki-zirvesi-10-11-aralik-1999.tr.mfa

Hobolt, S. B., Van der Brug, W., De Vreese, C. H., Boomgaarden, H. G., & Hinrichsen, M. C. (2011). Religious Intolerance and Euroscepticism. *European Union Politics*, *12*(3), 359–379. doi:10.1177/1465116511404620

Kalın, İ. (2011). *2000'li Yıllar: Türkiye'de Dış Politika*. Meydan Yayıncılık.

Karadağ, H. (2012). *Bir Dış Politika Tekniği Olarak Kamu Diplomasisi: Karar Verem Sürecine Etkisi.* Gazi Üniversitesi Sosyal Bilimler Enstitü, Uluslararası İlişkiler Anabilim Dalı, Doktora Tezi.

Kaygusuz, Ö. (2012). Democracy Anchored in the Presidential System: The 'Solution Process', Constitution Making and the Future of Europeanization in Turkey. *The Turkish Yearbook of International Relations*, (43), 159–196.

Köksoy, E. (2014). Kamu Diplomasisi ve Halkla İlişkiler İlişkisi: Kuramsal Bir Değerlendirme. Marmara İletişim Dergisi. *Sayı*, *22*, 211–231.

Kutlay, M. & Yılmaz, Ö. (2015). Mülteci Krizi ve Türkiye-AB İlişkilerinde Eksen Kayması Riski. *Uluslararası Stratejik Araştırmalar Kurumu, 29.*

Manheim, J. (2002). Talking Points for Meeting with Staff of Senate Foreign Relations Committee. *The Washington Quarterly*, 75.

Mark, L. (2002). *Public Diplomacy*. Foreign Policy Center.

Nye, J. (2005). *Soft Power*. Elips Kitap.

Özcüre, G. (2014). *Avrupa Birliği'nin İstihdam ve Sosyal Politikası*. Derin Yayınları.

Özkan, A. (2015). *21. Yüzyılın Stratejik Vizyonu Kamu Diplomasisi ve Türkiye'nin Kamu Diplomasisi İmkânları, Rapor no:70*. Tasam Yayınları.

Öztürk, T. (2009). *Dış Politikadaki Etkin Unsur: Kamu Diplomasisi ve Türkiye'nin Kamu Diplomasisi Etkinliği*. Academic Press.

Reform Action Group Meetings. (n.d.). https://www.ab.gov.tr/49767_en.html

Riggins, J. (1998). *A Strategic Assessment of Public Diplomacy*. USAF.

Terzi, Ö. (2019). The EU-Turkey Customs Union. Shortcomings and Prospects for Modernization. In *The Proliferation of Privileged Partnerships between the European Union and its Neighbours*. Routledge.

The EU Facility for Refugees in Turkey. (n.d.). https://ec.europa.eu/neighbourhood-enlargement/enlargement-policy/negotiations-status/turkey/eu-facility-refugees-turkey_en

Türk İşbirliği ve Koordinasyon Ajansı Başkanlığı (TİKA) Tarihçe. (n.d.). https://www.tika.gov.tr/tr/sayfa/tarihce-222

Turkey-EU High Level Economic Dialogue Joint Press Communique. (n.d.). https://www.avrupa.info.tr/en/pr/turkey-eu-high-level-economic-dialogue-joint-press-communique-9286

Varna Zirvesi Sonuçlarini Olumlu Olarak Değerlendiriyoruz. (n.d.). https://www.ikv.org.tr/ikv.asp?id=3140

Visa Liberalisation Dialogue. (n.d.). https://www.avrupa.info.tr/en/visa-liberalisation-dialogue-6896

Yılmaz, G. (2016). From Europeanization to de-Europeanization: The Europeanization Process of Turkey in 1999–2014. *Journal of Contemporary European Studies*, *24*(1), 86–100. doi:10.1080/14782804.2015.1038226

KEY TERMS AND DEFINITIONS

Communication Process: The communication process is made up of four key components. Those components include encoding, medium of transmission, decoding, and feedback.

Diplomacy: The art and practice of conducting negotiations between nations.

European Union: The European Union (EU) is a political and economic union of 27 member states that are located primarily in Europe.

International Relations: International relations, international studies or international affairs is the scientific study of interactions between sovereign states.

Progress Reports: The European Commission has been publishing annual reports evaluating the progress achieved by the candidate countries with respect to the Copenhagen criteria since 1998. These reports were called "Progress Report" until 2016, and have been called "Country Report" afterwards.

Public Diplomacy: In international relations, public diplomacy, or people's diplomacy, broadly speaking, is any of the various government-sponsored efforts aimed at communicating directly with foreign publics to establish a dialogue designed to inform and influence with the aim that this foreign public supports or tolerates a government's strategic objectives.

Public Perception: A belief or opinion, often held by many people and based on how things seem.

Turkey: Officially the Republic of Türkiye is a transcontinental country located mainly on the Anatolian Peninsula in Western Asia, with a small portion on the Balkan Peninsula in Southeast Europe. It is also a candidate country for EU.

ENDNOTES

1 EU Foreign Ministers stated that a progress report will not be published in 2017 in Valletta, the capital of Malta, which assumed the EU term presidency, and that time would be given to Ankara instead of interrupting the negotiations. (https://www.milliyet.com.tr/dunya/ab-den-turkiye-ye-bir-yil-sure-2441174 Access Date 15.03.2021)

2 The Instrument for Pre-Accession Assistance (IPA) has been designed by the European Commission to provide financial and technical assistance in support of reforms in EU candidate countries ("enlargement countries") for the period 2007-2013. (http://www.ipa.gov.tr/IPA_1070 Access Date: 15.04.2021)

3 Euroscepticism, translated as the European Union or European Skepticism, is a political view that expresses those who reject and criticize European policies (Hobolt, Van der Brug, De Vreese, Boomgaarden & Hinrichsen, 2011: 367).

Chapter 12
Diplomatic Transformation of Series Narrative:
Velvet Evolution of Representation From Valley of the Wolves to Valley of the Wolves-Ambush

Savaş Keskin
Bayburt University, Turkey

ABSTRACT

In addition to what the studies on the discourse and character modeling of the Valley of the Wolves series say, this chapter argues that there has been a Neo-Ottomanization and religiosity evolution in terms of the discourse and the hero's semiosis. The thesis of this section is that Valley of the Wolves series has evolved in terms of narrative and character since it began to appeal to international target audiences. It is the main assumption of the section that there is a parallel transformation with the public diplomacy practices of the Republic of Türkiye in the process following the fact that the audience groups, especially in Arab geography, Afghanistan and Pakistan, where Islamic influence is dominant, become fans of the Valley of the Wolves. In this section, it is aimed to explain the velvet evolution, which exemplifies the transition from the Republican ideology to the Neo-Ottoman ideology in diplomatic media narratives, through the historical rupture of the Valley of the Wolves.

INTRODUCTION

This text reinterprets the process of diplomatic transformation in the narrative/discourse of a television series as 'velvet evolution' with reference to the velvet effect of 'soft power' instrument. Because the narrative of *Valley of the Wolves*, which is constructed with the aim of appealing to the Turkish market as a 'Mafia Series', becomes more politicized as its sphere of influence expands to cross-border areas and the discourses of its new versions begin to resemble the dominant diplomatic discourse. The narrative transition takes place in 'soft' tones and phases, just as it is an instrument of soft power. The series

DOI: 10.4018/978-1-6684-5822-8.ch012

Valley of the Wolves: Ambush, which constructs a political semiology of the world according to the narrative representations of the 'Neo-Ottoman' discourses around which the government's discourse policies have orbited in the last few decades, epistemologically breaks away from the early *Valley of the Wolves* narrative and acts as a trans-media instrument that paves a diplomatic context of consent to Neo-Ottomanist policies. However, the smooth transition that causes us to call this rupture a velvet evolution is the preference for a gradual transition rather than a sharp transition from the *Valley of the Wolves* series to the *Valley of the Wolves: Ambush* series. Because in the narrative/discourse structure of the first seasons of the *Valley of the Wolves* (before *Valley of the Wolves: Iraq*), codes of violence and killing, nationalism, flag, identity, family order, masculinity, respect for traditions, good and bad women were dominant (Gültekin, 2006), while in the last seasons the discourse mode of nationalism shifts from the Republican narrative to the Neo-Ottomanist narrative. Although there is a discourse shift in the deep state-mafia dichotomy that covers the Middle East order, a new discourse is constructed in the series The *Valley of the Wolves: Ambush* that focuses on capital and terrorism, which becomes evident in the state-global order dichotomy. This discourse construction maximizes the political salience of the series and makes it clear that the narrative cannot be reduced to a mafia story. Günerbüyük (2009), as claimed in this text, attempts to confirm the thesis that the *Valley of the Wolves* legitimizes a discourse parallel to the state/government policy, dominant public nationalist discourse and ownership structure.

The influence of *Valley of the Wolves* in the Arab, Balkan and Near Asian geography, which constitutes the scope of nostalgic emulation in the historical hinterland of neo-Ottoman discourses, makes the diplomatic discourse construction of this series more valuable. This text, which aims to explain the relationship between the discourse of the series and the organizations of political discourse through the story of this politicization and 'velvet evolution' towards the diplomatic instrument, also attempts to provide a critical commentary on the trans-mediatic structure and multi-semiotic collaborations of the dominant public discourse.

The main issue of this text is that soap opera narratives/discourses work as ideological devices that reshape/represent historical, geopolitical and diplomatic realities in line with hegemonic purposes and biasedly. The signifiers in the representational world of TV series control the masses' consciousness of historical reality as they are the contexts in which reality is encoded and codified. Therefore, this paper also aims to analyze ideology through a systemic functional approach. While investigating the meaning that emerges through the use of linguistic and visual images in representation, O'Halloran (2008: 443) defines the work of creating layers of content and expression as a system. The dominant discourse, organized by the semiosis in each layer, is assembled as an ideological system assembly in which the parts work in coordination with each other. This text also examines the working principle of multimodal signs by comprehending the systemic construction of the discourse transformed in the transition from *Valley of the Wolves* to *Valley of the Wolves: Ambush* with a systemic functional approach. As an audio-visual cultural force (Jabbour, 2015), *Valley of the Wolves*, which appeals to its viewers over a wide period of time like all TV series due to its genre characteristic, controls the way audiences experience reality and can cause irreparable ruptures in the way the instrumental reason it creates perceives reality. These ruptures, in turn, may cause unpredictable problems in the future of Türkiye's public diplomacy and foreign policy. After all, just as Türkiye has changed its diplomatic discourse in the last quarter century, there is always the possibility of a new paradigm shift according to realpolitik.

Neo-Ottomanism, which is of ideological interest in the *Valley of the Wolves* versions of the text, is a system of historical thought first articulated by David Barchard. Defined as a consciousness of the Ottoman past, which is assumed to be a more influential force in Türkiye than Islam, this ideological system of thought and discourse imagines Türkiye as an attractive country that has regained its economic power and proven itself (Yavuz, 2020: 3-4). Neo-Ottomanism, which is widely agreed to have begun to establish its original base with the politics of Turgut Özal and Necmettin Erbakan, was essentially presented as a prescription for a way out of the crisis of the poles of thought in Türkiye (traditionalism-modernism, sharia-secularism, Orientalism-Occidentalism). Neo-Ottomanism, also defined as a pluralist and populist Islamic ideology (Yavuz, 1998: 22) that seeks to deal with the complexities and challenges of a state that has reached a level of economic and political development that is not quite comparable to most Muslim-identified countries, includes an alternative modeling of identity and state to the theses of the Republic and the discursive apparatus of Kemalism. The theses of Neo-Ottomanism, formulated in the literature with the slogan 'Make Türkiye Great Again' in reference to Donald Trump's slogan 'Make America Great Again', advocates the ideal of realizing the desire to become an expansionist and global actor. Indeed, increasing political participation in the Middle East and claims of becoming a regional superpower (Taşpınar, 2008) are integrated with the teachings of leadership of the Islamic geography and enter public circulation as new dominant discourses.

In the last few decades, Türkiye has been adapting the theses of Neo-Ottomanism to concrete policies as a form of diplomatic relations in Intergovernmental Organizations (IGO), on the one hand, and 'soft power' systems at the Non-Governmental Organization (NGO) civil society level within the framework of cultural diplomacy instruments, on the other. Among these systems, one of the most popular ones in the literature is undoubtedly the Turkish TV series. Establishing the cultural outlets of the Turkish diplomacy model in Arab, Balkan, Near East, Far East and Latin countries, TV series enlarge the sphere of influence of the Neo-Ottomanist discourse as a lifestyle and consent generator. Indeed, the main thesis of this text is that an Islam-oriented discourse set expressing cultural affinity is used to create a nation-branding strategy that will find a response in the Arab geography. As a matter of fact, the effective rise of the *Valley of the Wolves* versions in the Arab geography and the transformation of the dominant discourse took place with historical synchronicity. The use of TV series as a public diplomacy instrument to influence audiences in various geographies serves to realize the goal of 'building reputation in the eyes of other nations'. In Nye's terms (2008: 97), the political values that states defend at home and abroad, as well as their cultures that are attractive to others, are part of soft power. This requires the export of cultures that are manufactured as historical and contemporary lifestyles in media channels and whose semiosis is shaped by the modes of political discourse. Dissemination through media channels, which is an easier and more accessible method than exporting cultural products as tangible commodities, is an effective choice in terms of both the multilayeredness created by the diversity of content and mobilization. For this reason, content such as visual arts, literature, theater, dance and music, which are elements of cultural diplomacy all over the world, are served as popular culture products (Mark, 2009: 5). As multimodal representations that incorporate many forms of literature, music, drama and visual arts, *Valley of the Wolves* versions serve as powerful mediators in the use of Türkiye's Neo-Ottomanist diplomatic discourse as 'soft power'. Because a transnational audience that accepts the historical reality narrated in the series will indirectly act as the perpetrator of Türkiye's discursive ideology. Therefore, in this text, TV series are referred to as an instrument of soft power (Nye, 1990: 197) secured by cooperation based on common will and consent. A cultural diplomacy promoted by mutual understanding between people of other nations (Lenczawski, 2007: 3), however unrecognized at the level of nations, benefits Türkiye's political influence. Some governments in various Arab countries (Saudi Arabia, United Arab Emirates, Egypt, etc.), which have recently adopted anti-Turkish TV series policies, aim to create resistance to this influence. Otherwise, it is inevitable that a Neo-Ottomanist sentiment spreading in the

Arab geography through media, public opinion, public relations and branding will support Türkiye's thesis of becoming a regional power.

With the exception of violence and representations of masculinity (Gültekin, 2006), the literature of academic studies on the series versions of the *Valley of the Wolves* generally expands in terms of its public diplomacy impact. Studies arguing that the *Valley of the Wolves* series played a role in the establishment of Turkish soft power, especially in the Arab geography (Cerami, 2013; Ghazanfar et al., n.d.; Anaz & Özcan, 2016), focus on the role of Islamic discourse emphasis and alternative historical narratives. The Ottoman denominator underlying the Islamic discourse is discussed as an implicit image indicator in the series. Indeed, the message that the salvation offered by the series as a prescription against the 'Western' danger is the Neo-Ottomanist. Kılıçaslan (2021) confirms that Türkiye's claim to be a regional power has become an important soft power in the Arab world in the context of political marketing. Rising as a 'hero' in Arab countries, Polat (Murad) Alemdar represents a Türkiye-oriented symbol in the struggle of the Islamic geography against the West as a role model for whom brands are produced. This symbol intersects Türkiye's diplomatic objectives due to the politicization of Turkish television series marketed to the Arab geography (Emre-Çetin, 2014) and the objectives of Arab viewers who are part of the admirer culture. Because the fact that viewers want to be like Polat (Murad) Alemdar means that they indirectly want to be a Turk, and the discursive dimension of being a Turk requires defending Türkiye's diplomatic interests.

Another context of the *Valley of the Wolves* series' soft power influence in the Arab world is its contribution to the cultural dissemination of a modernized Islamic way of life touted as the 'Turkish Model' (Mohapatra, 2008). Transforming social life traditions in the Arab world around a cultural dynamic in which Türkiye is a role model, the influence changes lifestyles as well as worldviews. This is because the Turkish style of men, women, nationalism, religiosity, patriotism, etc. is a continuation of a code system that naturally includes Türkiye's political arguments. Every Arab viewer inspired by the Turkish Model increases their sensitivity to the Neo-Ottoman idea through a kind of cultural assimilation. The effectiveness of the Turkish Model in the Arab audience also points to the success of the 'culture/nation branding' strategy in the Turkish television series market, including the *Valley of the Wolves* series (Yalkın, 2018, Al-Ghazzi & Kraidy, 2013). Brand equity that highlights Türkiye and Turkish culture as a model serves to gain a prominent position in the competition within the cultural industries. The attractiveness of the Turkish brand would also mean the attractiveness of the Neo-Ottoman system of thought. This marketing strategy, which complements foreign policy, will establish a mass network where cultural diplomacy activities at the intellectual level will be supported at the popular culture level. As a matter of fact, The *Valley of the Wolves: Ambush* is important in terms of being presented as one of the most powerful popular culture limbs of Turkish foreign policy (Yukaruç, 2017). However, the tendency of Turkish TV series, and particularly the *Valley of the Wolves* versions, to establish more cultural similarities and Islamic affinities in order to resonate with Arab audiences also involves the possibility of a reverse expansion of an Arabism movement called Pan-Arabism (Carelli, 2015). This is because the Neo-Ottoman identity advocates a plural and Islamist concept of identity instead of a singular Turkism. This argument has the potential for a hybridity in which Arab influence also finds a place in the new perception of nationalism.

BACKGROUND: NEO-OTTOMANIST TURKISH TV SERIES EFFECT IN THE ARAB WORLD

Turkish TV series and soap operas are generally discussed within the framework of a Neo-Ottomanist soft power effect in the Arab world (Berg, 2017; Alankuş & Yanardağoğlu, 2016; Carney, 2018). Arısoy (2016: 137) even characterizes this power as 'Soap Power', creating a new conceptual space to discuss the issue. Thinking of 'Soap Power' alongside the various information-based factions of power in public diplomacy is a key to understanding the complexity of Turkish soap operas' effectiveness in the Arab, Balkan, Latin American and Asian markets. This influence is so strong and so intertwined with Neo-Ottomanist thinking that Buccianti (2010) interprets the current situation as a kind of 'Concquering' in the Arab world. This conquering effect, which emphasizes the perception of subordinate nations in the Ottoman period, indicates that Neo-Ottomanist thought is being discussed as a visible problematic in international studies.

Yeşil (2015), who attributes the ability of Turkish TV series to establish a market outside the country to transnationalization and local-global convergence, makes a critical political economy reading within the framework of state support, export facilities and marketing opportunities for TV series that tend to build a diplomatic context for state policies. The government support provided in budgeting and marketing increases the production quality of the series and paves the way for its politicization in accordance with the principle of narrative autonomy. Therefore, it can be said that there is a common axis between the discourses of the government, which are prominent in public diplomacy, and the discourses of the series. Moreover, the Turkish TV series sector, which correctly manages the capitalization that global consumer culture has spread to all relations, writes a transnational success story that it owes to the flexibility in its capital structure and export-oriented production approach (Khan & Ulrike, 2020). The fact that the production and marketing plan of transnational market-oriented TV series is not only limited to the Turkish audience, but is also designed according to the consumer performances and demands of the audience in target markets sheds light on the discursive transformation made public in *Valley of the Wolves: Ambush*. Because Polat Alemdar's Turkishness, masculinity, patriotism, his relationship with religion, women, his family and the enemy should appeal not only to the domestic market but also to the foreign market. As a matter of fact, the *Valley of the Wolves* has done the job with limited modifications instead of sharp metamorphoses in order to fully adapt to the Arab world it appeals to by nature.

The soft power impact of Turkish TV series cannot be limited to the Arab world or other countries as a public diplomacy target. The mechanisms of public discourse at work in Türkiye's domestic politics also strive to produce the ground for the establishment of a Neo-Ottomanist perception. The effort of Neo-Ottoman political discourses to establish a historical bloc in the public sphere has occurred almost simultaneously on the stage of mediatic struggle in Turkish domestic politics and foreign policy. While the modernization effect experienced in the transition from the Ottoman Empire to the Republic of Türkiye was comprehending the struggle of various currents of thought in Türkiye's domestic politics, a new era began in which the dominance of secular approaches in the foreign policy representation of the nation brand faded. This new era offers many new perspectives for understanding the clash between Neo-Ottomanism and Kemalism in Türkiye's Middle East policy, as well as the response of the synthesized Turkish Model in the Arab world (Taşpınar, 2008). While the Turkish Model was a modern role model for the Middle East until the beginning of the second millennium, touted through a discourse modalized by Kemalism and a plane of signifiers, the Neo-Ottomanist Turkish Model that emerged in the foreign policies of the Justice and Development Party government demonstrates the enactment of an alternative historical and geopolitical role model in the Middle East. The development of satellite broadcasting in the Arab world indicates a shift in the axis of modernization influence focused on Türkiye (Yanardağoğlu & Karam, 2013). The dominance of Turkish TV series in the Arab world, which evolved from Silver to *Valley of the Wolves* or *Resurrection: Ertugrul*, symbolizes a paradigm shift in the modernization model. Moreover, this paradigm shift expands the axis of Middle East policies towards the Balkans. Because the scope of Neo-Ottomanist discourses includes the Balkans as much as the Middle East. The academic research on the impact of Turkish Soap Operas and Telenovelas in the Balkan world (Panjeta, 2014) illustrates the limits of the area addressed by the Neo-Ottomanist discourse.

According to Çevik (2017), Turkish TV series and soap operas contain Neo-Ottomanist messages that can directly or indirectly influence Arab audiences to establish Turkish soft power. Audience perceptions also indicate a relative success. Berg (2020) explains the success of Turkish drama series with Arab audiences on the grounds of cultural affinity. He draws the boundaries of cultural affinity within the framework of common historical past, Islamic identity and interactions in the Middle East geography. This framework, which constitutes the main basis of Neo-Ottomanist discourses, constructs the idea of historical unity, Islamic unity and geographical unity as the discourse of the series in a rapprochement process in which Türkiye is at the center. Anaz (2014), while questioning the success of Turkish TV series in Middle Eastern countries through a reception study on Egyptian viewers, finds that in addition to reasons such as professionalism in technical equipment, lack of alternatives, dramaturgical success in the script, the Islamic success story, which is exemplary in terms of gender equality, democratization, human rights and freedom of expression, is emphasized. Indeed, Yiğit (2013) also draws attention to the influence of a secularizing model of Islam based on gender equality and relations. The Neo-Ottomanist worldview, where the modern Islamic model intersects, can be considered as the key principle of success in the Arab world. However, despite this Neo-Ottomanist influence, it is important to keep in mind that the fact that Turkish TV series contain only popular culture images is among the reasons why they are very successful in their geographies of influence (Pothou, 2020).

While the Kemalist model of modern Türkiye, as an example of modernization in the Arab world, faces opposition from some traditionalists, as in Türkiye, the discourse of the series, which includes a context of signs in which Neo-Ottomanist thought is cynically encoded, certainly holds possibilities for greater integration with Arab audiences. However, the overt form of Neo-Ottomanism is also likely to encounter oppositional resistance on the basis of Arab nationalism, and this possibility has been realized recently.

Samaan (2013), questioning the rise and fall of the Turkish Model in the Arab world, which was recoded with a Neo-Ottomanist discourse, opens parentheses to the ruptures in intergovernmental organizations (IGOs) and Turkish foreign policy, on the one hand, and on the other hand, cites the intensity of overly political TV series and aggressive discourses that directly emphasize regional power. The rise of the Telenovelas, followed by TV series such as the *Valley of the Wolves*, *Resurrection: Ertugrul, Magnificent Century,* etc., brought about counter-propaganda from Arab countries against Türkiye's breakthroughs in the struggle for regional power and calls for boycotts. This is because Türkiye has increasingly used the Turkish TV series industry as a foreign policy tool in its struggle to become a regional power (Ayata, 2014) and has created a huge public opinion in the Arab world, which has increased the anti-Türkiye political consensus of local governments.

Studies focusing on the 'other' side of the Turkish TV series influence in the Arab world emphasize the negativization approach in representation. Erkazancı-Durmuş (2016), who examines how Turkish TV series are represented in Saudi Arabian newspapers, concludes that in contrast to the overtly negative image, a positive self-construction is being done in the Turkish media. As a matter of fact, some prominent news in the Turkish media recently announced that Turkish TV series have started to be banned in countries such as the United Arab Emirates, Afghanistan, Egypt and Saudi Arabia (Yeni Şafak, 2018; Takvim, 2021; T24, 2018; CNN Türk, 2012). The shutdown reflex, which is a natural consequence of intergovernmental tensions affecting intercultural relations as well as diplomatic activities, can also be seen as an engagement by the Arab world to offset the disadvantageous position of its organic ties with Türkiye and to defend authentic identity. Buccianti (2020) argues that Turkish TV series, which are dubbed to create localization opportunities, should be questioned in the dilemma of social emancipation or cultural alienation for the Arab world. This is because, on the one hand, the TV series that spread Türkiye's cultural hegemony undermine the authenticity of Arab identity, while on the other hand, the Turkish Model modernization paradigm triggers a socially liberated Arab identity. The *Valley of the Wolves* has a mission that needs to be questioned in the dilemma of 'awakening/awareness raising' and 'sleeping/deluding the masses' while sowing a Neo-Ottomanist discourse system summarized above in the Arab world.

METHODOLOGICAL DESIGN

The main issue examined and questioned in this text is the evolutionary process of the use of series discourses as a diplomatic instrument that controls the viewer's perception of reality and all emotional relations with reality. Because this process demonstrates that TV series are not just a content of entertainment consumption and that the reality represented in TV series can be too politicized to be simply a fiction. For this reason, the narrative/discourse of the TV series *Valley of the Wolves* and *Valley of the Wolves: Ambush* has been analyzed not only at the linguistic level but also at all semiological layers that constitute the discourse system. In the text, multi modal discourse analysis method was used in the interpretation and analysis of the data/codes. This is because the multimodal social semiological theory approach is a rich theoretical ground for research involving multimedia representations, data analysis, code storage and retrieval periods (O'Halloran, 2013: 42-43).

O'Halloran (2011: 120-136) describes the multimodal or multi semiotic approach to discourse analysis as a way of understanding the semiotic sources and modes (visual, auditory, tactile, olfactory, gustatory and kinaesthetic) of multimodal phenomena in the discourse and plot of multimodal texts. This practice of understanding requires analyzing the camera angles, the symbols used and the framing approach. Since the multimodal discourse in the TV series *Valley of the Wolves* and *Valley of the Wolves: Ambush* is a structure in which many symbols and signs interact at different layers, it can be understood by looking at many different semiotics, from the characters' clothes to their words, from their social positions to their facial expressions and gestures. For example, while Polat Alemdar's foster mother Nazife Candan was not a character whose religious identity was as prominent as her husband Ömer Candan in the period from the *Valley of the Wolves* to the last episodes of the *Valley of the Wolves: Ambush,* her adoption of the image of a religious woman wearing a hijab, especially in the last period, is a modal dimension that indicates the aforementioned discursive transformation.

In his multimodal discourse analysis approach, Kress (2011: 136) argues for a three-dimensional approach to ideology and discourse integrity. Accordingly, the material diversification of textual particles (gestures, words, moving or motionless images, text, music, etc.) indicates a multimodal semiological design in each layer between the upper and lower dimensions. Each subsidiary dimension between main and secondary characters, upper and lower spaces, class representations, capitalistic superiority and inferiority, friend and enemy dimensions, etc. are the structures of a seemingly unified discourse. In the case of the *Valley of the Wolves*, the transformation of representation in each of these dimensions will mean the transformation of the discourse of the series. The transformation of the characters from individuals in the ranks of the mafia to individuals in the ranks of intelligence organizations means that the discourse of the series gives up the emphasis of 'This is a mafia series'. Because the discourse dimension of the relationship between Polat Alemdar and Laz Ziya character and the discourse dimension of the relationship between Polat Alemdar and Amon are different in terms of the signs and behavioral symbols in representation. Therefore, different dimensions of discourse establish the situational structure of the middle ground between foreground and background where modal density is distributed (Norris, 2004: 102-110). Between the discursive indicators in the foreground and the supporters in the background, there is also a middle plan as an event horizon that describes the situational flow and ordinariness. The characters in the middle plan, where events take place between Polat Alemdar in the foreground and the extras in the background, constitute the social flow universe of the narrative weave.

This text focuses not only on what and how people, the actors of discourse in representation, say, but also on what visual signs say about them. This is because the ways in which visual semiotic resources represent people guide feelings about how to relate to them. The universe of representation positions the viewer in relation to the people in the image. It establishes the relationship between discourse and reality through representational strategies focused on individualization and collectivization (Machin & Mayr, 2012: 96). How the characters appear in the versions of *Valley of the Wolves* helps us to grasp the discursive sub-dimensions of political hegemony. After the 'hood' event in Iraq, the *Valley of Wolves: Iraq* rupture occurs in the mafia narrative. The character Muro, who appeared in the series during the government's Kurdish Initiative, the so-called 'solution process', is presented as a 'sympathetic and legitimate' person despite being portrayed as a PKK terrorist, and cooperation is established with a comedy-oriented cinematic universe that deviates from the serious narrative of the series (*Valley of Wolves: Muro*). After the 'Mavi Marmara' incident with Israel, Polat Alemdar, whose main duty is to fight against the mafia, is seen contributing to the liberation struggle for the Palestinian people and taking revenge (*Valley of Wolves: Palestine*). During the period of anti-structuring policies, which were publicly referred to as 'Ergenekon', the character of İskender Büyük was brought to the forefront and the movie *Valley of the Wolves: Gladio* was fictionalized. Finally, after the July 15 Coup Attempt, *Valley of Wolves: Homeland,* which represents a discourse structure in the cinematographic universe in which the character Polat Alemdar is on a mission to suppress the coup, exemplifies the political framing that changes according to the transformations in the character's position.

In the analysis phase of this text, the multimodal cooperation between macro-semiosis and micro-semiosis at the character and narrative level is explained. The discourse difference between the two versions of the *Valley of the Wolves* series (transition to Neo-Ottomanist discourse) is firstly explained through the layers of the protagonist (Polat Alemdar) in the discourse system and the evidence/indicators of these layers. In the second stage of the analysis, the evidence/indicators of deuteragonist and antagonist discourse systems were analyzed comparatively. In the third stage, the layers of Neo-Ottomanist discourse in the discourse system of Old Türkiye and New Türkiye were excavated and multiple signifiers were revealed.

The Velvet Evolution of Neo-Ottomanist Discourse from *Valley of the Wolves* (VoW) to *Valley of the Wolves: Ambush* (VoWA)

The *Valley of the Wolves* (VoW), the second work on a similar concept by a team that achieved ratings success with the series Deli Yürek on the axis of mafia-state relations, has realized a velvet evolution in its discourse and claim over time, even if it started its screen adventure with the simple claim of being a 'mafia series'. The basic questions of the viewers watching this transformation were asked by the character Memati to the character Abdulhey in a dialog in the very first episode (Episode 4) of the *Valley of Wolves: Ambush* version. This dialog can be considered among the most important generics of the series in terms of containing the transformation in discourse at a basic level.

Abdulhey: Brother! You know the Karahanlıs, Laz Ziyas, Testeres, Hüsrev Aghas, they are nothing compared to this. [...] It was the first time we sat at such a long table.

Memati: And what was this council Abdulhey? I thought we had become Barons.

Abdulhey: Brother, the council was Karahanli's council. Karahanli was only one of the great ones.

Memati: Then what are these?

Abdulhey: In the international arena there is not only one big one. There is the biggest, and then there are the big ones who are its competitors. [...] These are arms dealers. These are the men who start and end wars. Laz Ziya was a transporter, a custodian.

The transformation and metamorphosis of the enemies means that the discourse of the series also evolves. The scope of the previous series is minimized due to a problem specific to Türkiye. There are now 'big' enemies, thrones, money, goals and victories. By using person, group and event semiotics (Templar-Mason, Amon-Rockefeller, Gladio-Ergenekon, etc.) that are very close to historical and current political reality, The *Valley of the Wolves* versions have started to build the first pillar of the Neo-Ottomanist discourse through the capital owners and the Templars in Türkiye.

As the first layer where the discursive difference between VoW and VoWA is constructed, the position of the Protagonist in the discourse system is analyzed. Since Polat Alemdar is the subject of discourse and the ideology embodied in discourse, there is a strong relationship between who he is and the discourse of the series. Because the protagonist, which is a combination of the concepts of Proto (first) and Agonist (Actor) (Gaikwad, 2017), is the most important symbol at the center of the narrative. It acts as the practical component of the symbol for every layer of the discourse.

Although Polat Alemdar is a kind of persona/mask in the narrative of the series, he essentially functions as an alter ego. Because Polat Alemdar is more like a state of integration and jouissance (satisfaction) rather than a role. As a matter of fact, after a while Ali Candan turns into Polat Alemdar's alter ego. Polat Alemdar is now the main personality and protagonist. Although the signifiers/symptoms of the discourse system in the character have an important place in this stage of analysis, Ali Candan also acts as a 'sinthome' (Lacan, 1975: 1-2) as a soothing/compensation mechanism. Because the gaps in Polat Alemdar's imaginary-symbolic-real triangle that cause psychoses are compensated and soothed by the ideal of Ali Candan. In this respect, he assumes an important role in the Neo-Ottomanist discourse

Table 1. Layers of the Protagonist's Semiotic Discourse in VoW: What Does the Character Tell Us in All Its Forms?

1st Layer: Public/Open Ego Representation	2nd Layer: Secretive/Alter Ego Representation
Civilian - Pure Mafia - Councilor - Baron	*Government Official - Agent*
Evidence / Demonstrators: • Name-Polat Alemdar • Uncertainty of the source of money • Luxury cars • Spending in dollars • Clothing style • Unregistered use of weapons • Bouncers / men • Relationship with Escorts • Alcohol and smoking • Gambling games • Unlawful killing • Threatening the police • Attempt to kill a prosecutor • Threats and ostentatious speech • Partnerships with Mafia members • Becoming a member of the Council • Barony vs.	*Evidence / Demonstrators:* • Appearing as Ali Candan • Discussions and cooperation with the Public Security Organization • Negotiations and collaboration with the character Aslan Akbey

as a synthome. Because Polat Alemdar is also a synthome, that is, a catharsis mechanism that acts as a sedative in the political traumas of the Turkish Nation.

The diversity and multiplicity in the evidence of the Mafia identity indicates that the dominant discourse in VoW is based on this identity. There are few discourses of evidence that Polat Alemdar is a state official and he is generally seen as a mafia. A third layer, Efe Karahanli layer, is not used to construct a clear discourse set in the series. For this reason, we have reduced the character's discourse strategy to the level of dilemma in two layers instead of three layers, because the third layer, 'Son of the Mafia', can actually work as a sub-layer of the first layer. However, even though the discourse system in layer 2 is suppressed as a neurosis, it also emerges as serious psychoses when the 'synthome' fails to maintain its function. Polat Alamdar's jeopardizing the Valley of the Wolves operation after he executes 6 mafia bosses in one night following the murder of a mafia boss named Süleyman Çakır is questioned by Aslan Akbey. In this interrogation, apart from Polat Alamdar's psychoses, we can also observe a discourse construct in which he confesses his true identity.

Aslan Akbey: I am the state and you serve for the state. [...] Don't give me the same treatment you give to everyone else. It doesn't work for me. You are not a mafia boss. You are a state official.

Polat Alemdar: According to what, according to whom?

Aslan Akbey: According to me, according to you.

Polat Alemdar: Look Mr. Aslan! I'm a mafia boss. Admit it! I am the father of the mafia!

Table 2. Protagonist's Semiotic Discourse Layers in VoWA: What Does the Character Tell Us About Himself?

Single layer: Mafia - Government Official	
Evidence / Demonstrators: • Name-Polat Alemdar • Uncertainty of the source of money • Luxury cars • Spending in dollars • Clothing style • Unregistered use of weapons • Bouncers / men • Unlawful killing • Threats and ostentatious speech	• Negotiations and Cooperation with the Council of Elders • Negotiations, cooperation and struggle with bureaucrats and politicians • Partnerships with Mafia members • Caliphate • Leadership of the Council of Elders • Dynasty • Negotiations and cooperation with the Public Security Organization, etc.

As reinforced in the dialog above, the journey of the character Polat Alemdar reveals that he is indeed first a mafia boss, council member and baron, and then a state official. The state is limited to Mr. Aslan who says 'I am the state'. The state's sphere of struggle and existence does not go beyond the mechanisms occupied by the mafia and the establishment of public security. In the series, the state has as much horizon as its enemy, the mafia (the council). In fact, the mafia (Mehmet Karahanlı), in a meeting with the 'state' (Aslan Akbey), says the following to belittle it:

- *What is the state! Isn't it me, you, him?*

In VoWA, the discourse system represented by the character is synthesized in a single layer and modeled in accordance with the diversity and multiple modal structures in the state symbols of Neo-Ottomanist discourse. The transition that starts towards the last chapters of VoW is now completely evident in VoWA. The table below presents the ideological framework described by the protagonist's semiotic discourse codes in VoWA. In this situation, which can be interpreted as the convergence of layers and the realization of unity in discourse, there is now a fluid discourse in which opposites coexist.

In VoWA, Polat Alemdar's identity shifts from multi-layeredness and hidden codes to a clear identity. Polat Alemdar possesses kinaesthetic accents and symbolic signifiers that produce the discourse of both mafia boss and state official together. There has been a unity and intertwining in identity. Apart from the intertwining of the entire mafia narrative with the identity of the statesman, the only thing that has changed in the discourse is that some codes of religiosity, such as praying, have replaced escort relations, alcohol, smoking and gambling. In any case, indicators that could contradict Islam have been removed from the public eye. While there is no public discomfort within the framework of the 'ethics of intended outcome' or Macchiavellian understanding when situations such as unfair gain and manslaughter are based on a holy purpose, some sharp indicators that cannot be compensated for have been removed from the visual discourse. The character of Polat Alemdar has become ideal to be the role model of Neo-Ottomanist thought, which is a plural and hybrid concept. The state identity is synthesized with the mafia identity, which is further demonstrated, and there is no longer a conflict in identity. In fact, the emphasis on religion and the imperialist deep state has reached a sacred dimension with Ronald's Caliphate offer and Amon's dynasty offer.

Ustad Ronald: Polat Alemdar. It is not a question of binding Türkiye. We made a very big mistake in the 20th century. We compelled you to abolish the caliphate for fear that Muslims would unite. We fragmented Islam as much as we could, but this move did more harm than good. In order to integrate Islam with the world, we need to connect it to a center somewhere.

Polat Alemdar: [...] Now you are promising me the caliphate?

Ustad Ronald: Let's call it a modernized version.

The prominence of Neo-Ottomanist discourse, which comes to the fore with the dialog about the Caliphate, is strengthened in the dialog of Amon, the imperial dynasty that is claimed to rule the world, with Polat Alemdar.

Amon: Now the battle is being fought over which power will come to power in the new world order.

[...]

Polat Alemdar: In the past, states established dynasties. Now dynasties form states.

Amon: Turks talk about their dynasty being left stateless. However, your homeland was left without a dynasty. But you know, it wasn't us who did it.

Polat Alemdar: Last time you offered me the caliphate with Ustad. Now will you offer me a dynasty and ask me to establish a state that you will rule?

Amon: No, I have more of him. [...] The real question is: Do you want to be the new Ra next to Amon in the newly formed world?

Apart from these dialogues in which the Neo-Ottomanist discourse is explicitly transferred to the discourse between strong characters, Polat Alemdar's religious personality model is implicitly presented. For example, Polat Alemdar, who defends himself and takes cover in the conflict scenes in the first episodes of VoW, does not feel the need to protect himself in the conflicts as the episodes progress in VoWA. The bullets ricochet to other places as if he was being protected. The perception of a sacred identity is established through a system of symbols in the lower layers. Not only his Neo-Ottomanist duties and rituals, but also his personality are constructed as a substratum of a religious sacred discourse.

The construction of the system of semiotics as character modeling in the representation of discourse includes the narrative of the Other/Alter as well as the narrative of the 'I/We'. Because hegemonic discourse is generally constructed through the position of the other (van Dijk, 2011: 397-398). In order to understand the discourse system, the semiotic representation layers and signifiers of the antagonist positioned against the protagonist and the deuteragonist supporting the protagonist were analyzed in this phase of the analysis.

In VoW, from the beginning to the end of the narrative, there is not much change in the categorical and collective structure of the friend (deuteragonist), whereas the collective and categorical structure of the enemy has undergone a change of globalization and internationalization in line with the Neo-

Table 3. Sublayers of the Deuteragonist and Antagonist (with Tritagonist) Discourse System in VoW

1st Layer Deuteragonist (Friend)	2nd Layer Antagonist (Enemy)
Intelligence Bully Family Mafia State	Mehmet Karahanli Mafia Council Intelligence Family State America Templars

Ottomanist discourse. In the early episodes and middle episodes, the antagonist discourses of the series are expressed on the mafia-council level. However, the identity contradiction, which demonstrates the categorical inseparability of enemy and friend, only differentiates individually. The discourse of the series conforms to the concept of 'This is a Mafia Series'. While there is confusion in collective identities, the discursive equivalent of the strategy of affirmation and negation, accusation and justification can be found at the level of individual characters. The propositions "Mafia is bad but Memati is good", "Drug dealers are bad but Uncle Halo is good", "The intelligence people are good but the mole is bad", "Ömer Baba (Father) is good but Mehmet Karahanlı (Father) is bad", "Testere Necmi is bad but Süleyman Çakır is good" indicate that identities are constructed individually rather than collectively and that there is not really a distinction between good and bad. Family is good but also bad.

In VoWA, on the other hand, it can be determined that the discursive expression of the enemy begins to match the antagonist categories on which the Neo-Ottoman identity is built, and this resemblance is getting stronger.

While the 'We' category of the discourse retains its discursive scope in general, only some deepened identities are articulated in response to the strengthening and deepening of the enemy. In VoWA, unlike VoW, there is an extra imperial deep state organization called the Council of Elders in the 'We' category. However, the enemy has evolved from the mafia to the enemies of the Neo-Ottoman discourse, which

Table 4. Sublayers of the Deuteragonist and Antagonist (together with Tritagonist) Discourse System in VoWA

1st Layer Deuteragonist (Friend)	2nd Layer Antagonist (Enemy)
Intelligence Bully Family Mafia State Council of Elders Muslims	Mafia Capital Holders America England ISIS PKK Foreign Intelligence Organizations Templars Putschist Soldiers FETO Gladio Russia West Iran The Vatican and Western Christians

Table 5. Türkiye-Oriented Discourse Layers in VoW

Layer 1 **What kind of a country is Türkiye?**	**Layer 2** **What kind of a country should/will Türkiye be?**
The Mafia has taken over A government ruled by those who collaborate with the mafia Unsafe - Illegal "Dark and Misty" Internal security issues Economically dependent on the West The US is trying to put it under the control of the Focus of Global Powers Weakening of state power Surrendered to drugs It is a country where politicians are incompetent.	Cleaned from the mafia Cleared of collaborators Economically independent Liberated from America Standing Up to Global Powers No illegal activities It should/will be a country governed by a strong political context.

has gained popularity in terms of its relationship with the global imperialist system. The enemies are here global and regional powers. For the establishment of the Neo-Ottomanist discourse, it is important that the enemy becomes globalized and generally meets the Western-Christian synthesis or the Arab-Shiite synthesis as opposed to the Turkish-Islamic synthesis. Because the 'We' identity that the Neo-Ottoman discourse constructs through enemies is demonstrated in the deuteragonist layers represented in and around Polat Alemdar. The enemies are the 'others' who are the antagonists and tritagonists of the Neo-Ottoman identity.

The Turkish collectivity represented in VoW and VoWA and spread across various semiotic layers at the discourse level is analyzed within the framework of the systemic discourse approach. This is because the Neo-Ottomanist discourse expands on the discourses of 'Old Türkiye' and 'New Türkiye'. Old Türkiye is portrayed as weak, captured and not independent. Polat Alemdar fights for a new and strong Türkiye.

The social and organizational model of Türkiye presented in the early chapters of VoW evolves from the Kemalist/Republican state model to the Neo-Ottoman state discourse towards the end. But state discourse / narrative in early period of VoW series highligts the Modern Türkiye. For example, the membership of the European Union, blessed by Kemalist Turkey as a modernization policy, has been among the most important discourses of the state, which aims to be a part of the West. In the early period of the VoW series, unlike VoWA, the European Union / West is presented as a 'salvation solution' to the governing order and human rights problems in the Türkiye. The most important discursive indicator of this presentation is seen in the dialogue between Polat Alemdar and Abdulhey Çoban.

Abdulhey: If this European Union does not have a good side, why are we trying to enter it?

Polat Alemdar: Who said it has not a good side, Abdulhey? It doesn't matter whether you enter or not. The criteria proposed by the European Union are important criteria for a humane life. Those who govern us have never given sovereignty and wealth to the people/citizens. Now the citizen has the right to demand at least this. Look, the EU has given you the right as an ordinary citizen to keep one of our rulers waiting at the door.

Abdulhey Çoban: I'm sorry, man.

Table 6. Layers of Neo-Ottomanist Discourse on Türkiye in VoWA

Layer 1 **What kind of a country is Türkiye?**	**Layer 2** **What kind of a country should/will Türkiye be?**
Republican Democratic Secular Focusing on territorial integrity Exploited Withdrawn Under pressure Under the control of foreign powers Downsized Powerless state	Empire Dynastic / Monarchical Secular Expansionist Imperial Reclaimed occupied territories Open to the Outside Capable of external forces Overgrown Strong state With a caliph Dynastic rule Economic Superpower Leader of the Islamic world Great Türkiye!

Essentially, while modern Kemalist ideology argues that getting rid of the Ottoman Empire is the vision of a 'great state', Neo-Ottomanist ideology presents a nostalgic and imperial vision of a return to roots as a prerequisite for becoming a 'great state'. In the early period of VoW, the goals and ideals presented as a prescription for solutions to the state's problems are shaped by the position of the mafia. In the later period, when relations between the mafia and the global power background are established, the context of the Neo-Ottomanist discourse is established. The discursive construction of Türkiye in VoWA, in which this context realizes itself, is expressed on the level of the indicators in the table below.

The 'opposition' on the syntagmatic signifier plane of the series is shaped as Neo-Ottoman discourse 'against' Kemalist discourse. There is a sharp transformation towards representations that openly and without any indirection propagate the Neo-Ottoman discourse. The dialogue that exemplifies and summarizes this situation in its most obvious and precise form is between the Chairman of the Council of Elders / Aksaçlı and Polat Alemdar.

Head of the Elders [...] The state is being rebuilt. Our priority is to achieve the goal without any accidents while creating this new structure of the state.

Polat Alemdar: What is the goal?

Head of the Elders: The Republic of Türkiye was founded with the fear of Sevres. All our institutions were organized in order not to experience Sevres again. This is changing. Our institutions will now be designed in accordance with the imperial vision. Not closed inwards, but open outwards. Self-confident, not fearful.

Polat Alemdar: That's why I wanted to meet with you [...] The only way to destroy Gladio is to make a revolution. If you cannot make the revolution, we will perish. Türkiye will even be looking for Sevres. If there is to be a revolution, Türkiye needs to change from a laic system to a secular system. [...] Religious groups need to be organized independently. [...] Laicism was a temporary goal, the real goal was secularism. [...] The social cement of this society is religion. If this social cement is removed, society will collapse.

The dialog above is a discourse construction that contains and exemplifies VoWA's Neo-Ottomanist discourse transformation in almost a few sentences. Because the dialog, which begins with the discourse "This is a mafia series" and expresses the final point of the series, also proves the sharpness and flexibility of the change over a long period of time.

INSTEAD OF CONCLUSION: BETWEEN POST-NEO OTTOMANIST DISCOURSE AND POST-POST-KEMALIST DISCOURSE

Polat Alemdar, who emerges in an organization representing the state system of Kemalist Türkiye in order to protect this system, later begins to construct a state discourse against this system. However, this contrast is not perceptible. The state that appears and is sanctified in the early period of the *Valley of the Wolves* is the Kemalist state in all its aspects and manifestations. State officials are also inspired by these people (Doğu Bey, Aslan Akbey, etc.). However, later this state is portrayed negatively and the Neo-Ottomanist state discourse is presented as if it is being celebrated.

While the discourse of the series, which started with the ideology that founded the Republic, was able to control the effect of a velvet transition in its evolution to Neo-Ottomanist discourse, it was supported or criticized for expressing this effect with a sharp and incisive system of symbols in the final stages.

As summarized in the dialogue between Aksaçlı and Polat Alemdar at the last stage of the analysis, the social change required by the Neo-Ottoman discourse is a 'revolution'. This revolutionary discourse, which is unpredictable whether it will be like the Velvet Revolution or not, is reactionary for some and a return to the essence for others in terms of being called a kind of counter-revolution. On the one hand, while establishing a legitimate context for Türkiye's domestic politics, on the other hand, messages of transformation and rapprochement are given to the Arab world and a call for reconciliation is made. This is because the discourse of Mustafa Kemal Atatürk in contemporary Arab nationalism has a similarity with the Post-Kemalist discourse that inspired Neo-Ottomanism. The VoWA discourse, which emphasizes that the Republic of Türkiye, which was founded by an anti-Ottomanist revolution, is in the process of an anti-Kemalist counter-revolution, seems to be more compatible with the post-Kemalist discourse, that is, with a state model in which the Kemalist Republic is reformed and retouched.

The main problem here is that the current foreign and domestic policy synthesis tends to shift towards a post-Neo-Ottomanist framework. This is a consequence of the rise of what is referred to as post-post-Kemalism, which claims that post-Kemalism has triggered its own 'orthodoxy' movement (Aytürk & Esen, 2022). As scholars discussing the rise and fall of the Turkish Model in the Arab world develop the critical base of post-Neo Ottomanism, it is inevitable that this discursive transformation between the versions of *Valley of the Wolves* in Türkiye will be discussed on a similar academic base. The series, which is the subject of daily media conspiracy theories and rumors that it will return to the screens with a new series (*Valley of the Wolves: Chaos*), has the potential to exhibit more dominant forms of post-post-Kemalism as a discursive route in the next phase. However, the combination of changes in foreign policy also holds the strong possibility of a post-Neo Ottomanist transformation in the series discourse. Because the difficulty of the government in establishing its hegemonic and historical bloc or the policy changes that will take place within the framework of a possible change of power will manage the metamorphosis adventure of the *Valley of the Wolves* discourse in new 'post-' or 'neo-' phases. Perhaps the series, which expresses the dominant discourse, will shift to the position of oppositional discourse. In any case, it will continue to be among the important examples of public diplomacy and ideological series reality as an alternative school in the historiography.

REFERENCES

T24. (2018, March 14). *Wall Street Journal: Suudi Arabistan'da Türk dizileri yasağının arkasında Selman var*. https://t24.com.tr/haber/wall-street-journal-suudi-arabistanda-turk-dizileri-yasaginin-arkasinda-selman-var,580819

Al-Ghazzi, O., & Kraidy, M. (2013). Neo-Ottoman cool 2: Turkish nation branding and Arabic-Language transnational broadcasting. *International Journal of Communication*, *7*, 2341–2360.

Alankuş, S., & Yanardağoğlu, E. (2016). Vacillation in Turkey's popular global TV exports: Toward a more complex understanding of distrubution. *International Journal of Communication*, *10*(17), 3615–3631.

Anaz, N. (2014). The geography of reception: Why do Egytptians watch Turkish soap operas. *Arab World Geographer*, *17*(3), 255–274.

Anaz, N., & Ozcan, C. C. (2016). Geography of Turkish soap operas: Tourism, soft power, and alternative narratives. In I. Egresi (Ed.), *Alternative Tourism inTurkey: Role, Potential Development and Sustainability* (pp. 247–259). Springer. doi:10.1007/978-3-319-47537-0_15

Arısoy, C. (2016). Turkish series: Products of popular culture and tools for inclusive globalization. *Online Journal of Communication and Media Technologies*, *6*(1), 129–142. doi:10.29333/ojcmt/2543

Ayata, B. (2014). Turkish foreign policy in a changing Arab World: Rise and fall of a regional actor? *journal of European Integration*, *37*(1), 95–112. doi:10.1080/07036337.2014.975991

Aytürk, İ., & Esen, B. (2022). *Post-Post Kemalizm / Türkiye çalışmalarında yeni arayışlar*. İletişim.

Berg, M. (2017). Turkish drama serials as a Tool for soft power. *Participation Journal of Audience and Perception Studies*, *14*(2), 32–52.

Berg, M. (2020). Turkish drama serials and Arab audiences: Why Turkish serials are succesfull in the Arab World. In Y. Kaptan & E. Algan (Eds.), *Television in Turkey* (pp. 223–244). Palgrave Macmillan. doi:10.1007/978-3-030-46051-8_12

Buccianti, A. (2010). Dubbed Turkish soap operas conquering the Arab World: Social liberation or cultural alienation? *Arab Media & Society*, *3*, 1–7.

Carelli, P. (2015). Pan-Arabism through television: Arab TV series between national identities and transnational media. *Communicazioni Sociali*, *2*, 218–229.

Carney, J. (2018). Resur(e)recting as spectacular hero: Diriliş Ertuğrul, necropolitics, and popular culture in Turkey. *Review of Middle East Studies*, *52*(1), 93–114. doi:10.1017/rms.2018.6

Cerami, C. (2021). Rethinking Turkey's soft power in the Arab World: Islam, secularism and democracy. *Journal of Levantine Studies*, *3*(2), 129–150.

Çevik, S. B. (2019). Turkish historical television series: Public broadcasting of Neo-Ottoman illusions. *Southeast European and Black Sea Studies*, *19*(2), 227–242. doi:10.1080/14683857.2019.1622288

Emre-Çetin, K. B. (2014). The 'politicization' of Turkish television dramas. *International Journal of Communication*, *8*, 2462–2483.

Erkazancı-Durmuş, H. (2016). The representation of Turkey through narrative framing-Saudi Arabian and Turkish Newspapers' coverage of the Arabic dubbed Turkish series noor. *Moment Dergi. Sinema ve Politika*, *3*(2), 483–507. doi:10.17572/mj2016.2.483507

Gaikwad, K. B. (2017). Protagonist: A prime mover of the plot of a literary work. *An International Multidiciplinary Journal*, *2*(6), 1–8.

Ghazanfar, S., Zeeshan, M., Ullah, K., Shehnaz, S., & Hussain, M. (n. d.). Changes in family values due to information communication Technologies. *The Explorer Islamabad: Journal of Social Sciences*, *1*(10), 385–389.

Gültekin, Z. (2016). Irak'dan önce: Kurtlar Vadisi dizisi. *İletişim Kuram ve Araştırma Dergisi, 22*(9), 9-36.

Günerbüyük, C. (2009). *Kurtlar Vadisi dizisinde politik söylem* [Unpublished Master Thesis]. Marmara University.

Jabbour, J. (2015). An illusionary power of seduction? An assesment of Turkey's cultural power in the Arab World in light of its audio-visual presence in the region. *European Journal of Turkish Studies, 21*(2015).

Khan, M., & Ulrike, R. (2020). Transnationalization, exportation, and capitalization of Turkish television and its impact on the audience of the Egypt and Pakistan. *European Journal of Soil Science*, *59*(2), 123–137.

Kılıçaslan, E. (2021). Bölgesel güç olma bağlamında siyasal pazarlama açısından kamu diplomasisi: Kurtlar Vadisi dizisi söylem analizi. *Meriç Uluslararası Sosyal ve Stratejik Araştırmalar Dergisi*, *5*(14), 167–185.

Kraidy, M. M., & Al-Ghazzi, O. (2013). Neo-Ottoman cool: Turkish popular culture in the Arab public sphere. *Popular Communication*, *11*(1), 17–29. doi:10.1080/15405702.2013.747940

Kress, G. (2011). Multimodal discourse analysis. In J. P. Gee & M. Handford (Eds.), *The Routledge Handbook of Discourse Analysis* (pp. 35–50). Routledge.

Lacan, J. (1975). Le sinthome. *Seminar*, *23*. https://www.lacanonline.com/wp-content/uploads/2014/11/Seminar-XXIII-The-Sinthome-Jacques-Lacan-Thurston-translation.pdf

Lenczowskı, J. (2008). Cultural diplomacy, political influence, and integrated strategy. In Strategic Influence: Public Diplomacy, Counterpropaganda and Political Warfare (pp. 3-30). The Institute of World Politics Press.

Machin, D., & Mayr, A. (2012). How to do critical discourse analysis: A multimodal introduction. *Sage (Atlanta, Ga.).*

Mark, S. (2009). A greater role for cultural diplomacy. In Discusion Papers in Diplomacy (pp. 1-44). Netherlands Institute of International Relations 'Clingendael'.

Mohapatra, A. K. (2008). Democratization in the Arab world. *International Studies*, *45*(4), 271–294. doi:10.1177/002088170904500401

Norris, S. (2004). Multimodal discourse analysis: A comceptual framework. In P. LeVine & R. Scollon (Eds.), *Discourse and Technology: Multimodal Discourse Analysis* (pp. 101–115). Georgetown University.

Nye, J. S. (1990). Soft power. *Foreign Policy*, *80*(80), 153–171. doi:10.2307/1148580

Nye, J. S. (2008). Public diplomacy and soft power. *The Annals of the American Academy of Political and Social Science*, *616*, 94–109. doi:10.1177/0002716207311699

O'Halloran, K. L. (2008). Systemic functional-multimodal discourse analysis (SF-MDA): Constructing ideational meaning using language and visual imagery. *Visual Communication*, *7*(4), 443–475. doi:10.1177/1470357208096210

O'Halloran, K. L. (2011). Multimodal discourse analysis. In K. Hyland & B. Paltridge (Eds.), *Companion to Discourse* (pp. 120–137). Continuum.

O'Halloran, K. L. (2013). Multimodal analysis and digital technology. In E. Montagna (Ed.), *Readings in Intersemiosis and Multimedia* (pp. 35–53). IBIS Editions.

Panjeta, L. (2014). The changing soaps and telenovela genre: Turkish series impact. *Epiphany Journal of Transdisciplinary*, *7*(1), 137–168. doi:10.21533/epiphany.v7i1.89

Pothou, E. (2020). Why so successful? An audience research on the Turkish TV series in Greece. *VIEW Journal of European Television History and Culture*, *9*(17), 62–78. doi:10.18146/view.211

Samaan, J. L. (2013). The rise and fall of the 'Turkish Model' in the Arab World. *Turkish Policiy Quarterly*, *2013*(Fall), 61–69.

Takvim. (2021, November 22). *Taliban'dan yeni yasak! Türk dizileri de etkilenecek. Kadınların oynadığı yapımların gösterilmesi yasaklandı*. https://www.takvim.com.tr/dunya/2021/11/22/son-dakika-talibandan-yeni-yasak-turk-dizileri-de-etkilenecek-kadinlarin-oynadigi-yapimlarin-gosterilmesi-yasaklandi

Taşpınar, Ö. (2008, October 7). *Turkey's Middle East policies: Between Neo-Ottomanism and Kemalism.* Carnegie Endowment for International Peace. https://carnegieendowment.org/2008/10/07/turkey-s-middle-east-policies-between-neo-ottomanism-and-kemalism-pub-22209

Türk, C. N. N. (2012, August 23). *Mısır'dan Türk dizilerine yasak!* https://www.cnnturk.com/2013/dunya/08/20/misirdan.turk.dizilerine.yasak/720165.0/index.html

van Dijk, T. (2011). Discourse and ideology. In T. Van Dijk (Ed.), *Discourse Studies. A Multidisciplinary Introduction* (pp. 379–407). SAGE. doi:10.4135/9781446289068.n18

Yalkın, C. (2018). A brand culture approach to managing nation-brands. *European Management Review, 15*(1), 137–149. doi:10.1111/emre.12129

Yanardağoğlu, E. & Karam, I. N. (2013). The fever that hit Arab satellite television audience perceptions of Turkish TV series. *Identities, 19*, 561-579.

Yavuz, M. H. (1998). Turkish identity and foreign policy in flux: The rise of Neo-Ottomanism. *Journal for Critical Studies of The Middle East., 7*(12), 19–41. doi:10.1080/10669929808720119

Yavuz, M. H. (2020). *Nostalgia fot the empire: The politics of Neo-Ottomanism*. Oxford University. doi:10.1093/oso/9780197512289.001.0001

Yeni Şafak. (2018, March 7). *Türk dizilerinin yasaklanmasının ardındaki kirli oyun*. https://www.yenisafak.com/hayat/turk-dizilerinin-yasaklanmasinin-ardindaki-kirli-oyun-3166022

Yeşil, B. (2015). Transnationalization of Turkish dramas: Exploring the convergence of local and global market imperatives. *Global Media and Communication, 11*(1), 43–60. doi:10.1177/1742766515573274

Yiğit, A. (2013). *Turkish drama in the Middle East: Secularism and cultural influence*. IEMED Mediterranean Yearbook 2013. https://www.iemed.org/publication/turkish-drama-in-the-middle-east-secularism-and-cultural-influence/

Yukaruç, U. (2017). *A constructivist approach to popular culture and foreign policy: The case of Turkey and Valley of Wolves: Ambush* [Unpublished Doctorate Thesis]. University of East Aglia.

KEY TERMS AND DEFINITIONS

Dıscourse: Discourse is a multi-layered structure of expression and representation that encodes the reality that dominates the series. The discourse that establishes the reality that dominates the public consciousness and shows it to the audience as a representation works together with the systemic structure of the Neo-Ottomanist ideology in this study. In this study, discourse is the constructive power that defines events and phenomena within the framework of the dominant ideology.

Neo-Ottomanısm: Neo-Ottomanism is an academic name given to government policies that reflect Turkey's economic, cultural, and political re-taking an imperial position and its desire to become a 'great regional power' again.

Publıc Dıplomacy: Public diplomacy is a comprehensive influencing activity that aims to create a positive image and a context of consent among the goverments and publics of other countries.

Representatıon: Representation is a show style that includes the events shown in the TV series replacing real events, showing them as real and transforming reality. Reproduction of reality through actors pretending to be real in serials claiming to show reality is referred to as representation.

Soft Power: Soft power is defined as the work of countries to influence the people of other countries by using nation branding and other public relations activities and to popularize their own culture and policies.

Valley of the Wolves (VoW): VoW is a 'mafia series' that started broadcasting in 2003 and lasted for four seasons. Centering on the protagonist of Polat Alemdar, the series deals with the struggle between the state and the mafia. The series, which started with the Kemalist state narrative, has moved to the Neo-Ottomanist narrative in recent seasons.

Valley of the Wolves (VoWA) Ambush: VoWA is the continuation of the VoW series. In the series, unlike the VoW series, the struggle between the state and global powers is described entirely from a Neo-Ottomanist perspective. The series, which includes representations and discourses that legitimize the state's foreign policy, is about Turkey's adventure of becoming a great power again in the face of global powers.

Chapter 13
Twitter as a Digital Channel of Public Diplomacy in Turkey

Ömer Alanka
Hatay Mustafa Kemal University, Turkey

Ülhak Çimen
Atatürk University, Turkey

ABSTRACT

Governments want to create foreign public opinion by spreading credible information to achieve their national goals, objectives, and interests. In the global balance of political power, it is important for a country to use the tools of public diplomacy. In the 21st century, Turkey intensively uses cultural values as a tool of public diplomacy. In this context, Turkey actively uses social media as a digital medium while promoting its cultural heritage as a soft power. Turkey, which has analyzed the impact of digital diplomacy well in the historical process, is using this field more and more widely. In this study, examples of the Republic of Turkey's public diplomacy practices on social media are presented and how it uses public diplomacy as soft power is investigated. In this context, four Twitter pages where public diplomacy is most widely used (The Republic of Türkiye Directorate of Communications, Turkish Maarif Foundation, TIKA, and Yunus Emre Institute) were analyzed through content analysis technique.

INTRODUCTION

Public diplomacy, also termed as soft power, reveals the changes that countries make by using their cultural values to achieve their foreign policy goals. In public diplomacy, countries conveying their own messages to the target audience is one of the most important stages of this soft power. Indeed, with the attraction created by soft power, countries can both influence target countries and ensure the voluntary participation of people in the target country to the messages and values of the source country. Recently, it has been observed that Turkey has frequently resorted to the tool of public diplomacy as a soft power. In this process, it is understood that Turkey has intensively used its heritage of cultural and historical values as a public diplomacy tool.

DOI: 10.4018/978-1-6684-5822-8.ch013

The concept of public diplomacy was first recognized with the concept of soft power. The concept was first used by Edmund Gullion in 1965 in the sense of "international flow of information and ideas" (Sancar, 2012: 79). Joseph Nye, on the other hand, made the concept more comprehensive by stating that in order for a country to achieve the results it wants in world politics, there must be countries that admire the values of that country, take it as an example, envy its prosperity and opportunities, and follow it (Nye, 2005:14). As the phenomenon of communication has become widespread and more sophisticated in the globalizing world, this concept has also transformed into a new form. Since the second half of the twentieth century, communication and communication channels have become widespread due to the development of mass communication technologies, and accordingly, public diplomacy activities have increased and diversified.

The difference between diplomacy and public diplomacy is that diplomacy involves relations between representatives of countries and other international actors, while public diplomacy targets the entire public or informal groups, organizations and civil society organizations in a foreign society (Melissen, 2007: 12-13). Public perception is becoming increasingly important in international relations. Countries have to take into account both domestic and foreign public opinion while developing policies. In this context, in order for the policies developed to be accepted, it is necessary to win the hearts and minds of the target audience. In addition, states resort to the tools of public diplomacy to develop a positive image (Kocabıyık, 165). In general terms, public diplomacy refers to interacting with foreign public opinion. The main reason for the process of interaction with foreign public opinion is to change the behavior of that country in favor of national interests. In this process, other countries need to be educated, informed and included in the processes. At this point, public diplomacy has become a strategic communication tool (Efegil, 2018).

In addition to the classical diplomacy methods of delegation negotiations, official statements and diplomatic declarations, public diplomacy plays a supporting role in protecting national interests. Today, countries have started to use public diplomacy, which is defined as "winning hearts and minds", in addition to classical diplomacy. This new public diplomacy is a new component of general diplomatic practices and is more than a form of propaganda conducted by diplomats. In this respect, public diplomacy is a new type of diplomatic relationship network that requires different skills, techniques and attitudes. For example, this situation was revealed in a report published in 2002 by Auswärtiges Amt, the ministry responsible for Germany's foreign policy and relations with the European Union. According to this report, public diplomacy in Europe was ranked as the number one priority among all fields (Melissen, 2005:11). As can be seen from this example, in addition to economic and political relations, interconnections at the civil society level are becoming increasingly important in inter-state relations. In this context, the international system has transformed into a structure in which the need for increasing international integration has emerged in the last quarter of the twentieth century (Keohane, 2002: 27-29). Thus, public diplomacy has become an important practice of international relations.

Understanding the cultures, people and needs of other countries is among the main objectives of public diplomacy. In addition, public diplomacy also aims to share the perspectives of other societies, correct misperceptions and find common grounds. In this context, public diplomacy is based on the assumption that it positively changes the image and recognition of states (Mark, 2002:8-9). Public diplomacy refers to a communication process. Countries are obliged to use the media effectively while developing public diplomacy activities in foreign public opinion.

THE IMPORTANCE OF TWITTER USE IN PUBLIC DIPLOMACY

The impact of the media on societies is an undeniable fact. In this respect, mass media have important functions in the context of public diplomacy. Today, the digital technology field, which is called new media, is a powerful communication channel that countries use while developing their public diplomacy policies. Especially the importance of social media is seen in political election processes. In many countries, politicians use social media effectively in political elections. The same situation is also seen when countries develop their public diplomacy policies.

Digital diplomacy is a relatively new concept for Turkey. The concept of digital diplomacy, which came to the agenda in 2009, has gradually gained importance for Turkey and the whole world and has started to gain a place in diplomacy activities. Today, social media offers new opportunities for public diplomacy as it enables interaction with the general public and specific audiences beyond national borders (Vergeer & Hermans, 2013). The fact that social media opens new doors for public diplomacy reveals the importance of the digital world. In this process, public officials use social media to communicate with audiences in a direct, continuous and unlimited way, avoiding financial and bureaucratic barriers (Graham et al, 2013).

Digital technologies provide unlimited opportunities for public diplomacy, which is also characterized as soft power. In contrast to conventional mass media, new media's features of asynchrony, demassification and interactivity allow a country to directly reach the public opinion of other countries and share its public diplomacy policies directly with that country.

At this point, researchers believe that it would be useful to analyze the micro-blogging platform Twitter in terms of public diplomacy. Twitter is a popular social media tool for politicians, diplomatic actors (twitplomacy), government representatives and public relations experts. In terms of public diplomacy, Twitter can provide important data for academic studies (Waters & Jamal, 2011). In this context, Twitter is a micro-blogging service that has quickly become the most frequently used social media service in strategic communication campaigns (Stelzner, 2009). Thus, the phenomenon called "Twiplomacy" or "hashtag diplomacy" emerges. "Twiplomacy" or "hashtag diplomacy" refers to the use of Twitter, a microblogging service, by heads of state, leaders of intergovernmental organizations (IGOs) and diplomats to conduct public diplomacy and diplomatic outreach.

The use of Twitter for diplomatic purposes increased after 2014. In this respect, it is possible to see Twitter diplomacy as a prominent example of digital diplomacy. Thus, it is understood that Twitter is an important tool for public diplomacy. One of the responsibilities of embassy and consulate staff in foreign policy is to promote and represent the country of origin by interacting with host governments, local businesses and civil society organizations, media, educational institutions and private citizens (Rose, 2007). Twitter is ideally suited for these purposes. This is because Twitter offers ambassadors and embassies communication opportunities not available in mainstream media. Social networks can enable direct connection and interaction between stakeholders and individuals at lower costs and with less effort (Waters & Williams, 2011).

In addition to communicating, social networking sites such as Twitter also engage with businesses and government agencies, for example by asking specific questions or lodging complaints on Twitter. Therefore, social media sites such as Twitter facilitate the core activities of embassies in various ways by creating and developing rich relationships and networks (Kietzmann et al., 2011). In this context, the field of digital diplomacy deals with issues such as soft power, data visualization, digital diaspora, digital cultural diplomacy and digital country branding.

Furthermore, concepts such as futurism, online chat and cyber security are also within the scope of digital diplomacy. The USA sees digital diplomacy as a new type of democratic diplomacy based on technology that requires internet freedom, cares about the wishes of the people, deals with cyberactivism. The United Kingdom, on the other hand, considers the solution of classical diplomacy's problems via the internet and the transfer of classical diplomacy to the internet as digital diplomacy (Aslan & Göksu, 2016: 5).

The Republic of Turkey has recently taken important steps in the field of digital public diplomacy. It can be said that these studies have started to be handled in a regular and systematic manner compared to previous periods. For example, in 2009, Namık Tan, the Deputy Undersecretary of the Ministry of Foreign Affairs at the time, stated that embassies would have a presence on social networks such as Twitter and Facebook in the context of public diplomacy.

The first example of digital diplomacy in Turkey was the rescue of four US journalists detained in Libya in 2011 through Turkey's efforts. Turkey's Ambassador to Washington, Namık Tan, announced the rescue of the journalists on Twitter and posted their pictures on this platform. This was an example of Turkish diplomacy's presence in the new media. Another example was Ahmet Davutoğlu's announcement on Twitter of the overthrow of Egyptian President Hosni Mubarak in Batumi, where he was on an official visit during his term as Foreign Minister. These examples demonstrate that new media sometimes surpasses conventional media (Aslan & Göksu, 2016:11). In this part of the study, the public diplomacy activities carried out by the Republic of Turkey are analyzed.

THE IMPORTANCE AND OBJECTIVE OF THE STUDY

Public diplomacy, which has become self-evident that it is extremely important in the image of countries, has become more important for country policies, especially with the effective use of social media platforms. The Republic of Turkey has been successfully using public diplomacy especially in the last 20 years and has been announcing it to the world through social media in the last 10 years. The study aims to demonstrate how Twitter, a social media platform, is used in the use of public diplomacy for Turkey. Again, the study is considered important in terms of demonstrating the impact of the relationship between public diplomacy and the social media platform Twitter.

The Method of the Research

Conceptual components were defined through a literature review. On the basis of communication science, other related fields such as technology, sociology and politics were also benefited from. Content analysis technique was used to analyze Twitter posts in the study. The posts were analyzed systematically in written and visual form.

Scope and Limitations of the Research

The study covers 4 Twitter pages (The Republic of Turkey Directorate of Communication, Turkish Maarif Foundation, TIKA and Yunus Emre Institute) where public diplomacy is most widely used. Apart from these, some other pages (such as Foreign Relations, Afad Directorate, Turkish Red Crescent) were excluded from the study due to their limited posts on public diplomacy. The posts between 09.05.2022 and 09.06.2022 were analyzed in the study. The reason for choosing this date range is that Twitter does not provide a retrospective view of the posts before 09.05.2022.

Hypotheses of the Research

- Public diplomacy, which refers to the process of communicating with foreign publics to explain the ideas and ideals of Turkey, its institutions and culture, as well as its national goals and current policies, has been successfully used on Twitter.
- Turkey's public diplomacy efforts are occasionally subject to bureaucratic obstacles. Twitter offers an example of successful use in demonstrating Turkey's public diplomacy achievements to the masses in a direct, continuous and unlimited way.

FINDINGS AND INTERPRETATION

The official accounts of the Turkish Republic Directorate of Communications (T.R. Presidency of Communications of the Republic of Turkey), Turkish Maarif Foundation, Yunus Emre Institute, Turkish Red Crescent and TIKA (Turkish Cooperation and Coordination Agency Presidency) were analyzed in the study. While analyzing the content of the pages, both the direct posts and quotations of the pages were analyzed in the context of public diplomacy. The Turkish Republic Directorate of Communications was established in September 2010. The page has 1.3 Mn followers and follows 97 other pages. Turkey Maarif Foundation was established in September 2016. The page has 35.1 thousand followers and follows 18 other pages. Yunus Emre Institute was established in April 2010. The page has 96.5 thousand followers and follows 310 other pages. TIKA was established in 1992. The page has 264.7 thousand followers and follows 122 other pages. On all 4 pages, there is no limit on commenting, retweeting and liking, and anyone can follow the pages. It is also understood that 5 pages use a positive language in terms of public diplomacy in all of their posts.

The Turkish Republic Directorate of Communications Content Production

The official account of the Turkish Republic Directorate of Communications produced 9 pieces of content related to public diplomacy between 09.05.2022 and 09.06.2022. These contents were commented 150 times, retweeted by 7018 pages and received 6682 likes. The official page of the Turkish Republic Directorate of Communications produced content in the form of photos, photos+posts, posts and links.

The Turkish Republic Directorate of Communications Citation

The page retweeted a total of 13 retweets from 5 different pages related to public diplomacy. The content shared is related to both public diplomacy content and public diplomacy pages. The hashtag status of the posts is shown in the table. The page mainly retweeted the posts of the President and the Director of Communications.

Table 1. The Turkish Republic Directorate of Communications Content Production

Content	Contents Number	Number of Content Comments	Number of Content Retweets	Number of Content Likes	Type of Content
Turkey Africa Media Summit	3	63	6111	2043	3 Photos+Writing 2 Writing 1 Photo
Teknofest Azerbaijan	2	24	407	1685	7 Photo
Turkish American Day Parade	1	11	142	812	4 Photo
The History and Future of Turkey-US Relations	1	10	93	514	Link
Pakistan Milgem Project	1	31	191	1173	1 Photo
TRT French	1	11	74	455	1 Photo+Writing 2 Writing

Maarif Foundation of Turkey Content Production

Between 09.05.2022 and 09.06.2022, the official account of the Maarif Foundation of Turkey produced 24 public diplomacy-related content (almost all of them related to education). These contents were commented on 12 times, retweeted by 342 pages and received 1485 likes. The official page of the Maarif Foundation of Turkey also produced content in the form of videos, photos and graphically supported text.

Maarif Foundation of Turkey Citaion

The page retweeted a total of 12 retweets from 11 different pages related to public diplomacy. The content of the posts covers educational activities outside Turkey, which is one of the important pillars of public

Table 2. The Turkish Republic Directorate of Communications Citation

Content	Date	From Whom It is Made	Hashtag
Yunus Emre Institute	8 June 2022	Recep Tayyip Erdoğan	
Maarif Foundation of Turkey	8 June 2022	Recep Tayyip Erdoğan	
TİKA Venezuela	8 June 2022	Recep Tayyip Erdoğan	
Pakistan Milgem Project	1 June 2022	Recep Tayyip Erdoğan	
Teknofest Azerbaijan	28 May 2022	Recep Tayyip Erdoğan (3 Sharing)	#TEKNOFEST #TeknofestAzerbaycan
Africa Day	25 May 2022	Emine Erdoğan	#AfrikaGünü #AfricaDay
Africa Day	25 May 2022	Fahrettin Altun	
Pakistan Milgem Project	20 May 2022	T.C. Presidential	
TRT French	12 May 2022	Fahrettin Altun	
TRT French	11 May 2022	TRT Français	
TIKA Syrian Housing Project	9 May 2022	Fahrettin Altun	

Table 3. Maarif Foundation of Turkey Content Production

Content	Contents Number	Number of Content Comments	Number of Content Retweets	Number of Content Likes	Type of Content
Educational Activity of Venezuela	1	None	19	57	Video
Diplomatic Relations with Friendly and Sister Countries	1	None	16	75	4 Photos
Educational Activity of Columbia	1	None	8	35	2 Photos
Educational Activity of Albania	1	None	15	44	Video
Educational Activity of Ethiopia	1	None	17	76	4 Photos
Africa Educational Activity	2	None	27	106	2 Graphic Supported Text 4 Photos
Educational Activity of Kenya	1	None	16	61	4 Photos
Educational Activity of Dakar	1	None	17	78	1 Photo
Turkey Africa Media Summit	1	2	25	96	1 Photo
Teknofest Azerbaijan	1	None	14	60	4 Photos
Educational Activity of Palestine	1	2	44	159	Video
Educational Activity of Albania	1	1	15	67	2 Photos
Educational Activity of Senegal	1	None	11	65	4 Photos
Educational Activity of Kyrgyzstan	1	None	16	59	4 Photos
Educational Activity of Romania	1	None	4	41	4 Photos
Educational Activity of Gabon	4	2	28	131	4 Photos
Educational Activity of Liberia	1	2	25	72	2 Photos
Educational Activity of Congo	1	None	9	51	Video
Educational Activity of Venezuela	1	1	10	63	1 Photo
Educational Activity of Sudan	1	2	6	89	1 Photo

diplomacy. The hashtag status of the posts is shown in the table. The page mainly re-shared the content of the maarif foundation pages outside Turkey.

Table 4. Maarif Foundation of Turkey Citation

Content	Date	From Whom It is Made	Hashtag
Erbil Educational Activity	8 June 2022	T.C. Erbil BK	#erbil
Educational Activity of Afghanistan	2 June 2022	Afghan-Turk Maarif Schools	#paintings #calliography
Educational Activity of Afghanistan	30 May 2022	Afghan-Turk Maarif Schools	
Educational Activity of Guinea	30 May 2022	Les Ecoles Maarif Turco-Guieennes	#tmaarifvakfi#EcolesMaarif TurcoGuieennes
Educational Activity of Senegal	29 May 2022	Foundaition Maarif de 'Türkiye au Sênêgal	
Educational Activities of Chad	29 May 2022	Complexe Maarif Tchado Turc	
Somali Educational Activities	27 May 2022	Tmfsomalia	#somalia #university
Rwandan Educational Activities	25 May 2022	TurkishEmbassyKigali	
Educational Activities of Ethiopia	23 May 2022	International Maarif Schools of Ethiopia	#intmaarifschools
Educational Activities in Algeria	16 May 2022	Mahinur Özdemir Göktaş	
Educational Activities in Albania	11 May 2022	University of New York in Tirana	
Educational Activity of Senegal	9 May 2022	Foundaition Maarif de 'Türkiye au Sênêgal	

Yunus Emre Institute Content Production

The official account of Yunus Emre Institute produced 46 content related to public diplomacy between 09.05.2022 and 09.06.2022. These contents were commented 7 times, retweeted by 864 pages and received 2190 likes. The Yunus Emre Institute official page also produced content in the form of photographs, graphically supported photographs, videos and links.

Yunus Emre Institute Citation

The page retweeted a total of 28 retweets from 17 different pages related to public diplomacy. The content of the posts covers different parameters that feed public diplomacy. The hashtag status of the posts is shown in the table. The page re-shared versatile sharing content.

TIKA (Turkish Cooperation and Coordination Agency) Content Production

TIKA's official account produced 53 public diplomacy-related content between 09.05.2022 and 09.06.2022. These contents received 31 comments, were retweeted by 864 pages and received 2407 likes. TIKA's official page produced content in the form of photos, link links, photos + text, photos with graphic support, videos, and links.

Table 5. Yunus Emre Institute Content Production

Contents	Number of Contents	Content Comments	Number of Content Retweets	Content Likes	Content Type
Ethnosport Culture Festival	1	None	14	27	4 Photos
Ömer Seyfettin Commemoration Program	1	None	11	30	Link
Introducing Turkish TV Series	4	None	106	227	Link, 5 Photos
Turkish Promotion in Argentina	1	None	20	50	Link
Nazım Hikmet Commemoration Program in Moscow	1	None	4	3	Link
Jordanian Turkish Miniature Love	1	None	15	38	1 Graphic Supported Photo
Turkish Cuisine in Hungary	1	None	18	47	Video
Contribution to Language Education in Croatia	1	None	18	41	Link
Teknofest Azerbaijan	4	2	106	423	3 Videos
Concert in Ireland	1	None	16	47	Link
Turkey-South Korea Diplomatic Relations	1	None	15	40	Video
Turkish Culture Workshop in Serbia	3	None	44	128	2 Links 3 Photos
Communication in the Digital Age in Serbia	11	None	173	354	11 Photos 2 Links
Turkey-Africa Relations	1	None	27	67	1 Link
Austrian Alienation and Different Cultures	2	None	31	69	1 Graphic Supported Photo 1 Link
Concert in Hungary	1	None	16	38	1 Graphic Supported Photo
Turkish Tastes in Morocco	1	None	15	30	1 Link
Ukrainian Orphans Learn Turkish	2	None	37	100	1 Link 4 Photos
Yunus Emre Institute in Mexico	1	2	30	80	1 Link
Turkish in Somalia	1	None	24	50	1 Link
Turkish Cuisine in South Africa	1	None	20	55	1 Graphic Supported Photo
Burundi'de Türkçe	1	None	24	50	Video
2nd Balkan Archery Tournament	1	None	17	34	Video
Turkey-Georgia Turkology Cooperation Protocol	1	None	20	43	4 Photos
Turkish Cuisine in London	1	None	17	53	Video
Turkish Coffee in South Korea	1	None	23	66	1 Link

TIKA Citation

The page retweeted a total of 2 retweets from 2 different pages related to public diplomacy. Shared content covers the topics of culture and aid that feed public diplomacy. The hashtag status of the posts is shown in the table. While the page mostly produced content itself, it made a limited number of re-shares.

Table 6. Yunus Emre Institute Citation

Contents	Date	From whom	Hashtag
Ethnosport Culture Festival	09 June 2022	Serdar Çam (Corporate - Contact Account)	
Macedonian Theater Show	08 June 2022	Yunus Emre Institute – Skopje	
Turkish Series	07 June 2022	Mehmet Nuri Ersoy	#rtukkurumsal
Turkish Promotion in Argentina	05 June 2022	Prof. Dr. Şeref Ateş	
Romania Children's Festival	03 June 2022	Ahmet Çiçekler	
Romanian Turkish Language History	03 June 2022	Yunus Emre Institute – Constanţa	
Music Festival	02 June 2022	TİKA	#BaşkentKültürYolu
Music Festival	02 June 2022	Serdar Çam (Corporate - Contact Account)	#FestivalBaşkentte
Music Festival	02 June 2022	Prof. Dr. Şeref Ateş	#FestivalBaşkentte
Romania Training Program for Trainers	02 June 2022	Yunus Emre Institute – Constanţa	
Mexican Turkish Cultural Center	02 June 2022	Prof. Dr. Şeref Ateş	#Türkiye
World Language Turkish	01 June 2022	Prof. Dr. Şeref Ateş	
Turkey-South Korea Diplomatic Relations	30 May 2022	Yunus Emre Institute – 튀르키예 문화원	#BasındaBiz
Hungarian Turkish Cuisine	30 May 2022	Yunus Emre Institute -Budapeşte	#BasındaBiz
Teknofest Azerbaijan	28 May 2022	Yunus Emre Institute – Bakı	#Teknofestazərbaycan
Communication in the Digital Age in Serbia	28 May 2022	RTÜK	
Teknofest Azerbaijan	28 May 2022	Recep Tayyip Erdoğan	#TeknofestAzerbaycan
Palestinian Diplomats	28 May 2022	Jerusalem Yunus Emre Turkish Cultural Center	
Turkish Education in Georgia	25 May 2022	Ahmet Misbah Demircan	
Turkish in Azerbaijan	23 May 2022	Serdar Çam (Corporate - Contact Account)	#Azerbaycan
Multicultural Heritage	20 May 2022	Yunus Emre Institute - Madrid	
On the Trace of Multi-Cultural Heritage	20 May 2022	Yunus Emre Institute -Amsterdam	#Sevilla
Agreement on Cultural Centers of Turkey and Algeria	16 May 2022	Serdar Çam (Corporate - Contact Account)	
Turkish Music in Hungary	16 May 2022	Yunus Emre Institute - Budapest	
Balkan Archery Tournament	12 May 2022	Archers Foundation	
Turkish Concert	11 May 2022	Yunus Emre Institute - México	
Lost Works of Abdulhamid Khan	10 May 2022	Yunus Emre Institute - Warszawa	#BasındaBiz
Skopje Book Fair	09 May 2022	Yunus Emre Institute - Skopje	

Table 7. TIKA (Turkish Cooperation and Coordination Agency) Content Production

Contents	Number of Contents	Content Comments	Number of Content Retweets	Content Likes	Content Type
Healthcare in Afghanistan	1	None	11	54	3 Photos
Ethnosport Culture Festival	1	None	4	48	4 Photos
Support to Beekeeping in the Balkans	1	1	20	92	4 Photos
Cyprus Film Screening	2	None	67	215	4 Photos 1 Link 1 Photo
Kosovo Hymns	2	None	26	106	3 Photos 1 Photo + Writing
Support to Nutrition in Afghanistan	1	1	12	46	1 Photo
Support for Food Education in Bosnia and Herzegovina	1	1	15	83	4 Photos
Art Education in Tajikistan	1	2	15	88	4 Photos
Support to Science in Tunisia	1	None	12	65	4 Photos
Music in Africa	1	None	6	50	4 Photos
Support for the Karabakh Symposium	1	None	4	41	3 Photos
Women in the Digital World	1	None	5	32	4 Photos
Support for Tourism Education in Namibia	1	None	7	39	3 Photos
IT Education in Tajikistan	1	None	5	61	3 Photos
586 Projects in Pakistan	1	1	35	99	1 Graphic Supported Photo
Support for Health Education in Serbia	1	None	13	69	3 Photos
Cultural Heritage Symposium in Mongolia	1	1	35	103	3 Photos
Pharmacy Education in Azerbaijan	1	2	19	96	3 Photos
Girls' High School in Afghanistan	1	5	24	127	3 Photos
Laboratory in the Republic of South Africa	1	None	22	110	4 Photos 1 Link
Media Education in Serbia	1	1	7	49	Video
Support for Oral and Dental Health in Tanzania	1	1	14	90	3 Photos
Free Health Care in Chad	1	None	8	52	3 Photos
Support for Television Installation in Macedonia	1	None	4	23	Video
Support to Colombian Dairy Production Facility	1	1	9	55	3 Photos
Turkey Africa Media Summit	1	1	13	83	1 Photo
Theater Festival in Kosovo	1	None	8	53	4 Photos
Child Health Education in Uzbekistan	1	2	16	93	2 Photos
Support to Indian Ocean Coastal Countries	1	1	14	57	4 Photos
Support to African Countries	2	2	37	137	4 Photos 1 Graphic Supported Photo
Search and Rescue Training in Bosnia and Herzegovina	1	1	12	71	Video
Multimedia Education in Azerbaijan	1	None	9	66	4 Photos
Support to Flower Producers in Peru	1	None	15	63	3 Photos
Support for the Development of Livestock in Uzbekistan	1	1	13	70	4 Photos
New Media Education in Serbia	2	1	22	117	8 Photos
127 projects in Colombia	1	1	22	85	1 Graphic Supported Photo
Support for Dental Services in Tanzania	1	None	11	58	3 Photos
Robotic Coding Workshop in Kazakhstan	1	None	11	85	2 Photos
Stationery Support to Guatemala	1	None	12	66	3 Photos
Technology Support to Azerbaijan	1	None	23	88	3 Photos
Mosque Restoration in Algeria	1	3	27	107	Video
106 Projects in Algeria	1	None	26	94	1 Graphic Supported Photo
Drone Training in 10 Countries	1	None	9	42	3 Photos
Women's Education in Cameroon	1	1	12	71	3 Photos
Support for Spring Festivals in Macedonia	1	None	10	66	4 Photos
Food Aid in Laos	1	None	14	102	2 Photos
Support for Cambodia Disaster Victims	1	1	13	609	2 Photos
452 Projects in Kazakhstan	1	None	16	101	1 Graphic Supported Photo
Support for Bosnia and Herzegovina Language Course	1	None	13	72	2 Photos

Table 8. TIKA Citation

Contents	Date	From whom	Hashtag
Ethnosport Culture Festival	08 June 2022	Serkan Kayalar	#EtnosporFestivali
Aid Projects to Venezuela	08 June 2022	Recep Tayyip Erdoğan	

CONCLUSION

Web 2.0 technologies have transformed individuals from passive viewers into active content producers. Social media users, who are active content producers in the digital space, freely express their opinions about the policies of countries. In this process, states desire to influence active social media users in the digital world to their own advantage. It has become a necessity for states to use social media effectively, especially in the context of promoting their own image positively to the world public opinion, which is one of the most important functions of public diplomacy. Social media-based diplomacy studies increase the importance of empirical field studies. In this respect, the Republic of Turkey is obliged to give importance to empirical field studies while conducting public diplomacy activities. In this respect, fields such as political communication or advertising, which are more established scientific disciplines, can provide a theoretical framework for digital media-based public diplomacy studies.

Public diplomacy is one of the most prominent examples of soft power (Tuch, 1990), which refers to the process of communicating with foreign publics in order to explain the ideas and ideals of a government, a nation, its institutions and culture, as well as its national goals and current policies. In the conceptual framework drawn by Tuch for public diplomacy, Twitter extends far beyond the borders of the state in the processes of establishing public relations, which have a strategic importance, and carries the classical idea of diplomacy to a richer and more cultural field. As countries communicate their national goals and policies to foreign public opinion, they also strengthen their state image in a positive sense.

Between May 09, 2022 and June 09, 2022, 4 Twitter pages directly related to public diplomacy produced 132 pieces of content. The number of comments on this content is 200. Page posts were re-shared 9068 times in a one-month period and the posts were liked by 12764 people. 4 pages re-shared 55 content due to public diplomacy content. It is understood that the qualitative and quantitative data obtained as a result of the content analysis support Hypothesis 1 (Public diplomacy, which refers to the process of communicating with foreign publics in order to explain Turkey's ideas and ideals, institutions and culture, as well as national goals and current policies, is successfully used on Twitter) and Hypothesis 2 (Twitter offers an example of successful use in demonstrating Turkey's public diplomacy achievements to the masses in a direct, continuous and unlimited way).

REFERENCES

Aslan, P., & Göksu, O. (2016). Digital Diplomacy, Global Perception and Turkey. *14th International Symposium Communication in the Millennium*, 573-590.

Efegil, E. (2018). *Türk Dış Politikası ve Kamu Diplomasisi*. Kamu Diplomasisi Enstitüsü. https://www.kamudiplomasisi.org/makaleler/makaleler/94-tuerk-di-poltkasi-ve-kamu-dplomass

Graham, T., Broersma, M., Hazelhoff, K., & van't Haar, G. (2013). Between broadcasting political messages and interacting with voters. *Information Communication and Society*, *16*(5), 692–716. doi:10.1080/1369118X.2013.785581

Keohane, R. O. (2002). *Power and Governance in A Partially Globalized World*. Routledge.

Kietzmann, J. H., Hermkens, K., McCarthy, I. P., & Silvestre, B. S. (2011). Social media? Get serious! Understanding the functional building blocks of social media. *Business Horizons*, *54*(3), 241–251. doi:10.1016/j.bushor.2011.01.005

Kocabıyık, H. (2019). Değişen Diplomasi Anlayışı, Kamu Diplomasisi ve Türkiye. *Avrasya Etüdleri*, *55*(1), 163–196.

Koyuncu, S. (2017). *Bir İletişim Pratiği Olarak Kamu Diplomasisi: T.C. Başbakanlık Basın Yayın ve Enformasyon Genel Müdürlüğü'nün Türk Kamu Diplomasisindeki Yeri* [Unpublished PhD Thesis]. Gazi University Institute of Social Sciences.

Mark, L. (2002). *Public Diplomacy*. Foreign Policy Center.

Melissen, J. (2005). The New Public Diplomacy: Between Theory and Practice. In J. Melissen (Ed.), *The new public diplomacy: soft power in international relations* (pp. 3–28). Palgrave Macmillan. doi:10.1057/9780230554931_1

Nye, J. (2005). *Yumuşak Güç, Çev. Reyhan İnan Aydın*. Elips Kitap.

Rose, A. K. (2007). The foreign service and foreign trade: Embassies as export promotion. *World Economy*, *30*(1), 22–38. doi:10.1111/j.1467-9701.2007.00870.x

Sancar, G. A. (2012). *Kamu Diplomasisi ve Uluslararası Halkla İlişkiler*. Beta Yayınları.

Stelzner, M. A. (2009). *Social media marketing industry report*. Retrieved online February 26, 2010 from http://www.socialmediasummit09.com/

Tuch, H. N. (1990). *Communicating with the world: U.S. public diplomacy overseas*. St. Martin's. doi:10.1007/978-1-349-60512-5

Vergeer, M., & Hermans, L. (2013). Campaigning on Twitter: Microblogging And Online Social Networking As Campaign Tools in The 2010 General Elections in The Netherlands. *Journal of Computer-Mediated Communication*, *18*(4), 399–419. doi:10.1111/jcc4.12023

Waters, R. D., & Jamal, J. Y. (2011). Tweet, tweet, tweet: A content analysis of nonprofit organizations' Twitter updates. *Public Relations Review*, *37*(3), 321–324. doi:10.1016/j.pubrev.2011.03.002

Waters, R. D., & Williams, J. M. (2011). Squawking, tweeting, cooing, and hooting: Analyzing the communication patterns of government agencies on Twitter. *Journal of Public Affairs*, *11*(4), 353–363. doi:10.1002/pa.385

KEY TERMS AND DEFINITIONS

Digital Diplomacy: Also referred to as digiplomacy and ediplomacy (see below), has been defined as the use of the internet and new information communication technologies to help achieve diplomatic objectives. However, other definitions have also been proposed. The definition focuses on the interplay between internet and diplomacy, ranging from internet driven-changes in the environment in which diplomacy is conducted to the emergence of new topics on diplomatic agendas such as cybersecurity, privacy and more, along with the use of internet tools to practice diplomacy.

Diplomacy: Is the art and science of maintaining peaceful relationships between nations, groups, or individuals. Often, diplomacy refers to representatives of different groups discussing such issues as conflict, trade, the environment, technology, or security. People who practice diplomacy are called diplomats.

Government: Is the system or group of people governing an organized community, generally a state. In the case of its broad associative definition, government normally consists of legislature, executive, and judiciary. Government is a means by which organizational policies are enforced, as well as a mechanism for determining policy. In many countries, the government has a kind of constitution, a statement of its governing principles and philosophy. While all types of organizations have governance, the term government is often used more specifically to refer to the approximately 200 independent national governments and subsidiary organizations.

New Media: Are forms of media that are computational and rely on computers and the Internet for redistribution. Some examples of new media are computer animations, video games, human-computer interfaces, interactive computer installations, websites, and virtual worlds. New media are often contrasted to "old media", such as television, radio, and print media, although scholars in communication and media studies have criticized inflexible distinctions based on oldness and novelty. New media does not include analog broadcast television programs, feature films, magazines, or books – unless they contain technologies that enable digital generative or interactive processes.

Public Diplomacy: In international relations, public diplomacy or people's diplomacy, broadly speaking, is any of the various government-sponsored efforts aimed at communicating directly with foreign publics to establish a dialogue designed to inform and influence with the aim that this foreign public supports or tolerates a government's strategic objectives.

Social Media: Is a collective term for websites and applications that focus on communication, community-based input, interaction, content-sharing, and collaboration. People use social media to stay in touch and interact with friends, family, and various communities.

Turkey: Officially the Republic of Türkiye, is a transcontinental country located mainly on the Anatolian Peninsula in Western Asia, with a small portion on the Balkan Peninsula in Southeast Europe. It shares borders with the Black Sea to the north; Georgia to the northeast; Armenia, Azerbaijan, and Iran to the east; Iraq to the southeast; Syria and the Mediterranean Sea to the south; the Aegean Sea to the west; and Greece and Bulgaria to the northwest. Cyprus is located off the south coast. Ankara is Turkey's capital, while Istanbul is its largest city and financial centre.

Twitter: Is an online news and social networking site where people communicate in short messages called tweets. Tweeting is posting short messages for anyone who follows you on Twitter, with the hope that your words are useful and interesting to someone in your audience. Another description of Twitter and tweeting might be microblogging. Some people use Twitter to discover interesting people and companies online, opting to follow their tweets.

Chapter 14
Application of Public Diplomacy in New Media Platforms:
The Case of TIKA

Mehmet Ferhat Sönmez
Fırat University, Turkey

ABSTRACT

Public diplomacy practices carried out by states and non-state actors are instantly presented to the public of other countries thanks to the new media. This makes it easy to determine the level of influence of a public diplomacy practice on the public opinion of countries and helps states to produce new public diplomacy policies and to improve existing policies. In addition, new media allows one state to spy on public diplomacy practices conducted by another state and provides tips for taking action against it. This study aims to answer the question of how the practices of public diplomacy are shaped in new media environments. For this purpose, the Twitter account of the Turkish Cooperation and Coordination Agency (TIKA) was chosen as a case study and a netnographic study was conducted.

INTRODUCTION

Regarding etymological origins, the concept of diplomacy, which comes from the ancient Greek language and derives from the verb *"diplo,"* meaning *"folded in two,"* over time came to be used as *diplōma* (noun). Diploma, which means a document granting certain privileges to the bearer, had a function similar to that of modern passports. In the following period it was used to describe any document granting a privilege (Costantinou, 1996). Diplomacy, whose sphere of influence in the historical process is constantly expanding, has become a conduit for new actors, subjects and forms of interaction. It is now associated not only with interstate relations, but also with supranational organizations, multinational companies and even insurgent groups (Leira, 2016).

The concept of diplomacy represents all activities involving the conduct of relations between sovereign states through officials at home or abroad. It is seen as the communication system of the international society, as it is a tool that allows states to communicate with each other. The concept of diplomacy in

DOI: 10.4018/978-1-6684-5822-8.ch014

its current meaning was first used by British statesman Edmund Burke in 1796. According to Burke, based on the French word for "diplomat," diplomacy allows for the development and implementation of foreign policy (Berridge & James, 2003). Public diplomacy, on the other hand, has a meaning beyond traditional methods in politics and international relations. It is a multidimensional communication process that includes cultural interaction studies, public management activities, habit and behavior formation, perception-image management processes along with political information (Bostancı, 2012).

A Brief Overview of the Historical Development of Diplomacy

The emergence of structured diplomacy dates back long before the concept in consideration began to be used along with the state and politics. It is known that even before written record history there were negotiations to end wars and to negotiate peace in order to help the wounded. The practice of sending mutual envoys to conduct these negotiations is considered the first example of diplomacy (Nicolson, 1941). Thus *ad hoc (concerned with a particular purpose)* diplomacy emerged the first method of diplomacy in history. In ad hoc diplomacy, it is aimed at finding a solution to a problem, and representatives (ambassadors) are temporarily sent abroad to achieve a specific goal or task (Artunç, 2021). Within the scope of this practice, the messengers started to carry some introductory signs, and the relations between societies, especially trade and marriage, also improved (İskit, 2007).

In the 15th century the method of continuous diplomacy emerged and was first used by the Italian city-states. These city-states adopted the method of continuous diplomacy to eliminate possible risks of war. The method of continuous diplomacy was adopted throughout Europe in the following period, and a model method of diplomacy was developed (Tuncer, 2009). *"With the method of continuous diplomacy, defined as "the presence of diplomatic representatives in another country for a significant period of time to carry out diplomatic activities on behalf of their country, to obtain information about the country they are in, and to report to their country"* (Anderson, 1993), diplomatic relations became institutionalized and permanent. Thus, ad hoc diplomacy was replaced by time- and subject-independent embassies, and diplomatic representation became important instead of diplomatic representation (Watson, 1982). In the 17th and 18th centuries, French understanding of diplomacy had influence in the field of diplomacy, and continental Europe was influenced by French diplomacy until the French Revolution of 1789 (Tören, 2021). In the 19th century, England was at the forefront of diplomacy. Taking advantage of the Industrial Revolution, this country became a rising power and achieved significant world domination on the international stage (Kennedy, 2001). When we look at the historical development of diplomacy prior to the 18th century, we can say that the form of diplomatic communication was bilateral and of limited quality. However, this situation began to change from the 19th and especially from the 20th century. It turned into multilateral communication through international organizations, which not only multiplied, but also diversified their interests. Thus, the traditional understanding of diplomacy lost its meaning and the concept of public opinion gained importance (Gönlübol, 1993). Eventually, the concept of public diplomacy emerged, which expanded the boundaries of diplomacy and diversified the actors and subject.

Public Diplomacy and Soft Power

The concept of "soft power" refers to the ability of a country to influence the public opinion of another country and persuade the people of another country to act according to their will without using elements of pressure and without resorting to money. According to Joseph Nye, who introduced the concept of "soft power" into the field of diplomacy, "*hard power*" and "*soft power*" are interrelated because they both seek to influence the behavior of others. The difference between them lies in the nature of the behavior and the clarity of the sources. Hard power (command power) is the ability to change the behavior of others through coercion and direction. Soft power (cooperative power) is the ability to shape what others want and involves a process of manipulation (Nye, 2004).

Public diplomacy is also an element of soft power and is characterized as a set of actions carried out by a state to influence the public opinion of another country or countries. Public diplomacy, tailored to the interests and priorities of states, is also a mechanism of proactive protection against possible threats and potential risks. The subjects of public diplomacy, which are carried out to support the traditional diplomatic activities of states with states, are the state and institutions acting on behalf of the state. Public diplomacy differs from traditional diplomacy in that it is not aimed at foreign governments, but at nongovernmental actors and elements. Understanding, informing and influencing the public opinion of other countries as well as expanding relations between countries by eliminating misunderstandings are among the goals of public diplomacy (Doğan, 2012). From this perspective, public diplomacy covers a broader field than diplomatic communication. Unlike propaganda, it aims to create a language of strategic communication based on objective data and facts (Kalın, 2010). Because the phenomenon of diplomacy has become more complex and fragmented with globalization, paving the way for the inclusion of new actors in the international political scene (White, 2005). Globalization and the development of communication technologies have not destroyed the existence of diplomacy itself, but have affected the rules of the game, the playing field, the style of play, and the actors (Hamilton & Langhorne, 2011). In the new diplomacy, the playing field overflowed from the corridors of the Foreign Ministry. Along with diplomats, businessmen, civil society representatives, opinion leaders, famous names, and even tourists joined the game. Thus, in the new understanding of public diplomacy (Cull, 2009):

- The importance of nongovernmental organizations has grown.
- The processes used by actors of public diplomacy to communicate with the people of the world have evolved into new, real-time and global technologies such as the Internet.
- Concepts of propaganda were replaced by concepts based on marketing, and communication theory was used.
- The relationship between actors and people during the Cold War was abandoned, and the emphasis was on human communication, with the international actor playing the role of a mutually informative mediator.

Digital Diplomacy

With the ubiquity of the Internet and social media, virtually all social institutions and practices of everyday life, from education to health care, from economics to politics, have undergone major transformations. These transformational processes were also reflected in international politics, so that politicians and public diplomacy actors alike had to shift their actions, discourses and activities to social media platforms. The reason for this is that the Internet and social media have opened up unlimited movement and wide application area in the field of international relations, as in every field. In this virtual universe, various elements of public diplomacy, such as the state and institutions acting on behalf of the state, politicians, international NGOs, think tanks, company representatives, opinion leaders, and academics have created their own ecosystems.

In classical diplomacy ((Diplomacy 1.0) the practice of hard power prevailed, there was negotiation, sovereignty, mutual agreements, propaganda, and hierarchical structures within international relations. Statesmen, foreign ministers and diplomats were the most important actors. In public diplomacy (Diplomacy 2.0), the principle of soft power was adopted and strategic communication took the place of propaganda, especially during the Cold War, and public opinion of other countries was tried to be influenced by soft tools such as culture, art and tourism. .Digital diplomacy (Diplomacy 3.0) is the requirement that statesmen are also present in the online world and closely follow what happens on digital platforms (Yücel, 2016).

Digital diplomacy is a fairly new concept and does not have a long history. The concept of digital diplomacy, based on having social media and foreign policy on the same platform, began to attract attention after an analysis entitled "Public Diplomacy in the Computer Age," written by Allen S. Hansen in 1984. In 1994, the first e-mail was sent between Swedish diplomat Carl Bildt and former U.S. President Bill Clinton. Since the 2000s, digital diplomacy applications have become more diverse. The first virtual embassy was opened by the Maldives in 2007, followed by Sweden (diplomacy data, 2022).

Digital diplomacy is defined as the use of the Internet and information technology by state and non-state actors to manage international exchange processes. Digital diplomacy has enriched the ways in which the message and/or image interacts with the foreign public, and has simplified the ways in which actors' information resources are structured and organized. Moreover, digital diplomacy provides diplomatic actors with the necessary data to analyze changes and changing trends in international relations (Bjola, 2015). The transformative goals of digital diplomacy, which pave the way for a more effective use of diplomatic methods in an online world that is becoming more and more saturated by the day, are as follows (Hanson, 2012):

Knowledge Management: protecting, sharing, and effectively using information to protect national interests abroad.

Information Management: combining information flows to anticipate social and political change.

Public Diplomacy: using new means of communication to ensure continuity of communication with the masses on the Internet.

Consular Intervention: establishing personal channels of communication to communicate with citizens abroad in crisis situations.

Disaster Response: harnessing the power of online technology in natural disasters.

Outsourcing: establishing digital mechanisms to leverage external expertise in line with national goals.

Internet Freedom: establishing Internet freedom to protect free speech and democracy.

Policy Planning: developing policy plans for effective oversight and rapid decision-making.

Social Media and Twitter in Digital Diplomacy

Since the early periods of the twenty-first century, the Internet and new media have acquired a universal quality as a tool for versatile communication, and at the same time have created their own historical content, adapting to the emergence of practices, hierarchies and structures (Papacharissi, 2015). Social networks have merged written, verbal and audiovisual forms of human communication into one system, created a meta-language through hypertextuality, and completely changed the nature of communication by allowing interaction from different points in a given period of time (Castells, 2008). A network society, whose raw material is information, in which individual and collective existence is shaped by new technological tools, and these tools establish a system or set of relationships has emerged (Castells, 2008).

Through the development of Internet technology, many people living in different parts of the world and working in different jobs have been able to cooperate or compete as equals, and the equal conditions of different platforms have made the world flat (Friedman, 2005). This situation has brought diplomacy into the online field, and traditional methods of diplomacy have been updated to fit the online field. Diplomatic practices such as letters, invitations, telegrams, in-person conferences, announcements and statements in traditional media have evolved into cell phones, emails, teleconferences, Youtube channels, online events and even virtual embassies on social media platforms (Abbasov, 2007). Thus, the state control inhibiting international decision-making processes has decreased, the number of stakeholders in the process of international policy strategies has increased, information about an issue, event or situation has been accelerated, and traditional diplomatic services have been provided to the domestic public as well as the public of other countries quickly (Wescott, 2008). With social media democratizing the access and dissemination of information by removing geographic, cultural, and linguistic barriers, anyone with a laptop or cell phone has the ability to influence the masses (Armstrong, 2009). In this respect, social media performs a transformative function in international politics and not only takes diplomacy beyond hierarchical chains of relationships, it has also brought ordinary people into the political world, making them potential practitioners of diplomacy (Seib, 2012).

One of the applications of social media used in digital diplomacy is Twitter, and Twitter has become a diplomatic barometer, especially for international relations analysis and forecasting (Lüfkens, 2022). As an important building block of new media, Twitter plays an increasingly important role in political communication. It is very convenient for politicians because it is a source of first-hand news for journalists and politicians. It is also easy and useful to connect to more sophisticated platforms such as Youtube and Facebook (Lakomy, 2014). Moreover, users can access content that requires little attention and interaction in less time. This advantage makes the Twitter app attractive to diplomats who are already busy enough (Yepsen, 2012).

The fact that Twitter has become a functional tool for diplomatic activities has led to some necessary changes in traditional diplomacy. First, through these platforms, leaders mandated to represent their countries are freed from dependence on classical methods of reaching their interlocutors and addressing the public. Of course, leaders have not completely eliminated diplomats and foreign affairs services, but the need for special couriers, encrypted telegrams, and specially authorized spokespersons to convey their foreign policy instant messages and views has been greatly reduced. Twitter has removed the spatiotemporal restriction, and thus messages prepared by seasoned diplomats with great difficulty have become unimportant. With the "Send" button, hundreds of thousands of people can be contacted at the same time. Moreover, with the advent of the Internet and social media, confidentiality, the most important principle of classical diplomacy, became irrelevant. In addition, personal and mostly personal relationships of politicians and diplomats have been added to the forms of relationships that are formed in an impersonal and online environment (Ovalı, 2020).

METHOD

Social media platforms have seriously changed public life. It has given a more functional quality to applications in areas such as education, health care, public relations and marketing. This is also evident in the fields of politics and international relations. Social media is very functional both for implementing public diplomacy practices and for creating an image by promoting the practices that have been implemented. For this reason, social media is widely used by states, institutions acting on behalf of the state, and non-state actors.

In this context, this study attempted to find out how the @Tika_Turkey account managed by TIKA is used on the Twitter platform. To do this, the following questions are sought to be answered:

Research question 1: What issues related to public diplomacy are discussed on the @Tika_Turkey account?

Research question 2: What elements and methods of public diplomacy are emphasized in the @ Tika_Turkey account?

To answer these questions, this study used a netnographic research method. Netnographic analysis refers to Internet ethnography and is a qualitative interpretive research methodology that adapts traditional anthropological ethnographic research methods face-to-face to the study of online cultures and communities (Jupp, 2006). Netnographic analysis helps us understand the context of the online world of social interaction and is an applied approach that combines communicative research with digital forms of data collection, data analysis, and data research (Kozinets, 2010). In the netnography method, where the online interaction space is viewed as an extension of the field of communication in people's everyday lives, there are publicly available observation resources such as forums, websites, and blogs. Therefore, this method is less visible in terms of observation and allows the researcher to "snipe" (Kozinets, 2010). In doing so, all user actions and messages are recorded in virtual channels, which are the social spaces of online communities. From this perspective, websites, forums, blogs, or social networks subjected to netnographic research represent an important pool of data (Varnalı, 2012).

The netnographic method of research allows for a variety of research designs. In this study, the flexibility of the netnographic method was used, and a mixed-method study was preferred. One of the most distinctive features of a mixed-method study is that data collected by different methods are used to corroborate each other and strengthen the validity of the study. According to the mixed research approach, each phenomenon has both quantitative and qualitative dimensions, and it is important to use different methods together, especially in the social sciences. In a mixed research approach, it is acceptable to use different methods in the same study based on this principle. There are many types of mixed research approaches, and exploratory research design is among them. In exploratory design, the qualitative aspect of the research data is handled first and then the quantitative part of the research is started according to the results obtained from the qualitative data (Yıldırım & Şimşek, 2013). From this point of view, in this study, depending on the research design, attempts were made to obtain qualitative data by participant observation and quantitative data by content analysis.

Sample

In a netnographic study, one of the communities suitable for the purpose of the study should be chosen as the sample. When selecting the sample, the criteria of finding a group suitable for the research topic, intensive communication traffic in the group, detailed and rich content, and a high level of communication between the participants should be considered (Çomu & Halaiqa, 2014).

In this study, @Tika_Turkey, the Twitter account of TIKA (Turkish Cooperation and Coordination Agency), was chosen as a sample suitable for the study. TIKA, founded in 1992, is an element of public diplomacy acting on behalf of the Republic of Turkey. Established to develop a more active understanding of Turkey's foreign policy, TIKA is an element of Turkey's foreign policy implementation in many regions and countries. TIKA, which has 62 program coordination offices in 60 countries, carries out development-oriented cooperation studies in 150 countries. At the same time, it carries out various activities in cooperation with government agencies, universities, nongovernmental organizations and private enterprises. It reflects Turkey's development aid (TİKA, 2022).

Scope and Limitations

All social media platforms can mediate the elements and principles of public diplomacy in new media environments. Considering this aspect, social media platforms have digitized public diplomacy and opened up suitable areas for the implementation of diplomacy. On the other hand, social media is an ever-expanding universe, and therefore it is very difficult to include all social media platforms in social media studies. Thus, in this study, TIKA's Twitter account (@Tika_Turkey), which was identified as a sample, was included in the scope of the study, sample accounts/pages on various social media platforms were excluded. Similarly, there are no limits on the time or amount of content created on social media. Therefore, in social media-focused research, it is very difficult to examine all of the content created by the sample defined for the study and requires a long time frame. For this reason, the content created in the @Tika_Turkey account is limited to the period from March 1, 2022 to March 31, 2022.

FINDINGS AND ANALYSIS

The first of the research methods identified in this study is participant observation. As we know, the method of "observation" is often preferred in social research. Observational research is based on collecting data about situations such as attitudes, behaviors, phenomena, characteristics, and relationships using charts and scales. Observation through the senses or by technical means can be done both once and several times at intermittent intervals. From this perspective, the observation method is a complex research method and requires the researcher to play some roles and use a number of techniques, including their five senses, to collect data (Baker, 2006).

Participatory observation, on the other hand, is identical to ethnographic studies that aim to identify a particular culture from the inside. In this method, the goal is to describe in detail the culture or subculture being studied. Therefore, it is necessary to be included in the culture/subculture being studied. Participatory observation involves accessing sources of information by entering the community/culture that is the subject of the study. From this perspective, participatory observation facilitates the observation of cultural practices in everyday life and forms the basis of field research (Kawulich, 2005). In netnographic research, where ethnographic methods are adapted to online research, the stages of participatory observation are *"exploring the online field and cultural input - collecting and analyzing data - analyzing and interpreting - providing research ethics - getting feedback"* (Çomu & Halaiqa, 2014).

In this study, a participatory observation was made on the characteristics of new media. First, the @ Tika_Turkey Twitter account was subscribed and the page was followed. The study period (March 1, 2022 to March 31, 2022) was determined to understand the structure and operation of @Tika_Turkey's Twitter account, as well as the quality of content created on the page. Observations made to study the content created by @Tika_Turkey were recorded during the defined period of the study, the collected data was analyzed and interpreted. Research ethics were followed throughout the study. As a result of the included observation, the following can be said about @Tika_Turkey:

Figure 1. @Tika_Turkey Background Picture

- @Tika_Turkey account; The practices of public diplomacy implemented by TIKA are promoted, shared and published. In this respect, @Tika_Turkey is an example of an online community where digital public diplomacy practices are demonstrated.
- The @Tika_Turkey Twitter account has Twitter pages that publish content in English (@tika_english1), French (@tika_fr), German (@tika_deutsch) and Arabic (@tika_arabic). The content created on these pages in different languages also focuses on the practice of public diplomacy and aims to reach out to different cultures, regions and countries.
- There is a website that is published to promote TIKA's public diplomacy practices. The website provides information on TIKA's organizational structure, activities, coordinating offices in various countries, publications, and reports on public diplomacy.
- The content created in the Twitter account @Tika_Turkey is supported by visuals (photos and videos). In this way they tried to improve the quality and attractiveness of the content. This approach aims to increase the level of interaction by reaching more people/pages.
- @Tika_Turkey Twitter account has the phrase "FROM THE HEART OF THE TURKISH PEOPLE" in the background image. In our opinion, the purpose of adding this phrase to the background image is to point out some positive characteristics of the Turkish nation and to create a positive image/perception of the Turkish nation in the public opinion of different nations. (See Figure 1).

The second method used to increase the validity of this study is content analysis. As it is known, the purpose of content analysis is to reach the concepts and contents that can explain the collected data. The analysis process for the data obtained through observation, interview or document review consists of four stages: *"coding the data, finding the themes, organizing the codes and themes, defining and interpreting the findings"* (Yıldırım & Şimşek, 2013).

In the data coding stage, which is the first step of content analysis, the information received must be analyzed and divided into meaningful sections, and the conceptual meaning of each section must be found (Yıldırım & Şimşek, 2013). Because the coding process is an analytical process used by the researcher

Table 1. Public Diplomacy Orientation List

Public Diplomacy Categorical Orientation List	
Orientation	Mutual meetings and visits by the authorities, signed agreements, panels, conferences, symposiums, press conferences, wish messages for important days/events
Orientation	Humanitarian aid practices in different regions/countries
Orientation	Support given in different regions/countries and on various subjects
Orientation	Presentation of public diplomacy practices to the public

and there are three basic coding formats: open coding, axial coding and selective coding (Corbin & Strauss, 1990). In this study, preference was given to *"open coding,"* which is one of the three coding styles described by Corbin and Strauss. In the process of open coding, events/actions or interactions are compared according to their similarities and differences and grouped by creating categories/subcategories (Corbin & Strauss, 1990). To this end, first of all, a general conceptual framework regarding the concept of diplomacy was created and a list of orientations related to the concepts that make up diplomacy was prepared. The table below provides a list of orientations prepared for this study.

Table 1 contains a list of orientations created to create a "coding within a general framework" list. The orientation list is preliminary for finding codes and topics. However, the orientation list is not sufficient for coding and classifying data. To make up for this deficiency and conduct a qualitative content analysis, it is necessary to find themes that can explain codes at a general level. Finding themes will help identify commonalities between the codes. In order to do thematic coding, the first thing to do is to identify similarities and differences. Then, it is necessary to identify themes that can unite codes related to each other (Yıldırım & Şimşek, 2013). In this study, the units of analysis corresponding to the categorized themes were determined by analyzing the data based on a pre-prepared list of orientations, and a list of codes was prepared accordingly. The following table contains the list of codes prepared for this study.

Table 2 contains the categorical list of codes created for this study. In order to create the list of codes, various units of analysis were prepared to help explain the data at a general level. The thematic coding of the units of analysis was then performed. As a result of the coding performed, the thematic coding of public diplomacy was defined as *"diplomacy, humanitarian aid, support, and self-promotion."* Mazıcı (Mazıcı, 2020) and Uysal & Schroeder (Uysal & Schroeder, 2019)) studies were used in defining the categories. New categories were added according to the content of the study.

In content analysis, the next step after editing codes and themes is the identification and interpretation of findings. At this stage, the defined findings are interpreted and the researcher has to make sense of the data he collects, explain the cause-effect relationships between the findings and make evaluations for the results obtained (Yıldırım & Şimşek, 2013). The following section provides evaluations regarding the conclusions determined based on the data obtained for this study.

The @Tika_Turkey page, which was determined as a sample for this research, is followed by 262,541 accounts during the research period. @Tika_Turkey account follows 122 accounts during the research period. In the @Tika_Turkey account, the distribution of the contents produced during the research period by categories is as follows.

When we examine Graphic 1, we see the distribution of the content created in @Tika_Turkey's account by topic. Accordingly, there is a total of 92 items in the period between March 1 and March 31. Diplomacy-themed content constitutes the first place in the distribution of these contents according to their

Table 2. Public Diplomacy Categorical Code List

Public Diplomacy Categorical Code List	
Analysis Unit	**Code**
• Event (conference, panel, symposium, press conference, forum) • Celebration • Agreement • Visit • Meeting	Diplomacy
• Basic needs aids (food, clothing, drinking water), • Basic health aids (medicine, surgery, hospital, infirmary, doctor)	Humane aid
• Educational support • Project support • Material/hardware support • Infrastructure support • Development/employment support	Support
• Presentation of public diplomacy applications • Corporate promotion	Self-promotion

subjects. The rate of diplomacy-themed content is 50% and it constitutes half of the content produced in @Tika_Turkey account. In the second place is support-themed content with 24%. In the distribution of the contents according to their subjects, TIKA's self-promotion is in the third place with 17%. In the last place, there is humanitarian aid-themed content, and the rate of humanitarian aid-themed content is 8%.

When we make a general assessment of the distribution of the content produced in the @Tika_Turkey account according to their topics, it is possible to say that TIKA focuses on traditional diplomacy practices. The traditional practices of diplomacy are mutual visits and talks between officials and various activities carried out by government officials. TIKA also focused on traditional diplomacy methods and these practices were shared with the public on the @Tika_Turkey account.

The support given by a country to different regions and on different issues is another one of the most functional elements of public diplomacy. This practice of public diplomacy increases a country's prestige in the eyes of the international community and ensures a positive image in global public opinion. However, these applications need to be implemented in more countries. Ultimately, public diplomacy is a kind of marketing activity, and effective marketing depends on influencing a large audience. The practice of public diplomacy, even if it is properly planned and implemented, will not go beyond the national dimension if it is not nourished by universal propaganda. Social media platforms are the most

Figure 2. Distribution of Contents Produced on @Tika_Turkey Twitter Account by Topic (March 1, 2022-March 31, 2022)

Public Diplomacy Categorical Orientation List	
Orientation	Mutual meetings and visits by the authorities, signed agreements, panels, conferences, symposiums, press conferences, wish messages for important days/events
Orientation	Humanitarian aid practices in different regions/countries
Orientation	Support given in different regions/countries and on various subjects
Orientation	Presentation of public diplomacy practices to the public

Table 3. Content Analysis Evaluation of @Tika_Turkey Twitter Account (March 1, 2022-March 31, 2022)

DIPLOMACY	f	%
Vizit	20	43,5
Meeting	3	6,5
Congratulation	14	30,4
Activity	8	17,4
Agreement	1	2,2
Total	46	100
HUMANE AID	f	%
Basic Needs Aid	3	42,9
Basic Food Aid	4	57,1
Total	7	100
SUPPORT	f	%
Project Support	4	18,2
Education Support	9	40,9
Material/Hardware Support	2	9,1
Infrastructure Support	3	13,6
Development/Employment Support	4	18,2
Total	22	100
SELF-PROMOTION	f	%
Presentation of Public Diplomacy Applications	6	35,3
Corporate Promotion	11	64,7
Total	17	100

convenient means of presenting diplomatic activities to the global public. TIKA also preferred social media to present its public diplomacy practices to the international public, and 19% of the content on the @Tika_Turkey account was reserved for self-promotion.

Although the public diplomacy categorical code list prepared for this study consists of four main themes (see Table 2), different sub-titles (analysis units) were determined for each theme. The analysis units corresponding to the categories were analyzed and interpreted on the basis of frequency and percentage values. The table below provides the distribution of analysis units according to the categorical code list created.

When we evaluate the contents of @Tika_Turkey between March 1 and March 31, it is seen that almost half (43.5%) of the contents in the diplomacy category are mutual visits between government representatives of different countries and TIKA officials. Congratulatory tweets for important days and events take the second place (30.4%). Important dates such as the independence days of countries, women's day or the day of the disabled were remembered by TIKA and an example of public diplomacy was displayed by sending congratulatory messages. In the third place of the diplomacy category, there are events such as panels, forums and conferences with 17.4%. In the last place of this category, there is content with the theme of agreement and its rate is only 2.2%.

Figure 3. Geographical Orientation of TIKA's Aids in @Tika_Turkey Account (March 1, 2022-March 31, 2022)

Public Diplomacy Categorical Code List	
Analysis Unit	**Code**
• Event (conference, panel, symposium, press conference, forum) • Celebration • Agreement • Visit • Meeting	Diplomacy
• Basic needs aids (food, clothing, drinking water), • Basic health aids (medicine, surgery, hospital, infirmary, doctor)	Humane aid
• Educational support • Project support • Material/hardware support • Infrastructure support • Development/employment support	Support
• Presentation of public diplomacy applications • Corporate promotion	Self-promotion

When we look at the contents in which TIKA's humanitarian aid activities are shared, it is seen that the rate of content in which basic needs aids are provided is 42.9%, while the rate of basic health aids is 57.1%. Sharing the humanitarian aid provided by TIKA to underdeveloped countries on the @ Tika_Turkey account is an example of digital diplomacy, and thus, it is aimed to reach wider audiences. Especially in the Ukraine crisis, aid to the Ukrainian refugees who took refuge in Moldova is extremely important for Turkey's public diplomacy. The geographical orientation of the humanitarian aid provided by TIKA in the specified period is shown in the figure below.

When we look at the contents of the support category, which is another component of public diplomacy, it is seen that education supports are in the first place with 40.9%. Educational support provided by TIKA in different geographies and on various subjects was presented to the world public via the @ Tika_Turkey account. In the second place of this category, there are content with the theme of project support and development/employment support. In the third place is infrastructure support (13.6%), and the infrastructure support provided by TIKA was shared on @Tika_Turkey account. In the last row of this category, there are tweets about material/hardware support with 9.1%.

In @Tika_Turkey account, the content in the self-promotion category was created on two different themes. The first is that all kinds of public diplomacy practices carried out by TIKA are published on @Tika_Turkey account and this rate is 35.3%. The second theme is TIKA's corporate promotion. 64.7% of the content in this category consists of messages containing corporate promotion.

CONCLUSION

This study is based on the problem of the use of social media in digital diplomacy and @Tika_Turkey account is determined as a sample. Based on the evaluations made on the data obtained, it is possible to say that the @Tika_Turkey account is predominantly shared with traditional diplomacy methods. The traditional methods of diplomacy are carried out through government officials and persons appointed by governments. In general, reciprocal visits and negotiations are carried out in the form of memorandums of understanding and between officials or in the form of public events. In @Tika_Turkey, the reflections of the traditional diplomacy approach can be seen clearly. The number of tweets about the visits of the TIKA president and meetings with representatives of different countries is relatively high. In our opinion, the reason for this situation is to preserve the interaction and coordination between the sub-units of the states and to carry it to higher levels in the future.

It is important to share messages containing humanitarian aid activities on the @Tika_Turkey account. Because studies in the field of humanitarian aid are among the public diplomacy practices that give results in a short time to influence the public opinion of other countries. In the @Tika_Turkey account, tweets promoting such applications were posted. Sharing the humanitarian aid made during the Ukraine crisis with the international public through the @Tika_Turkey account will make serious contributions to Turkey's public diplomacy efforts.

Another functional theme in the execution of public diplomacy is the support given in various subjects. Supports provided under the titles of education, materials and infrastructure help the active conduct of public diplomacy. The presence of messages on the @Tika_Turkey account about the support given by TIKA in different countries will also contribute to Turkey's public diplomacy. In addition, the promotion of TIKA's public diplomacy practices on the @Tika_Turkey account will attract the attention of the world public.

Social media has transformed all social institutions and politics has also been affected by this transformation. This is particularly evident on Twitter. On different social media platforms, more mundane and entertainment-oriented topics are predominant. On the other hand, Twitter is a platform where more serious issues are discussed. TIKA also aims to increase Turkey's prestige in the world by sharing Turkey's public diplomacy practices with the online world via the @Tika_Turkey account. For this purpose, it uses the unlimited range of action opened by social media, thus trying to keep up with the developments in digital diplomacy.

REFERENCES

Abbasov, A. (2007). *Digital Diplomacy: Embedding Information and Communication Technologies in the Department of Foreign Affairs and Trade.* Australian National University.

Anderson, M. S. (1993). *The Rise of Modern Diplomacy.* Longman Press.

Armstrong, M. (2009). Social Media as Public Diplomacy. *Perspectives, 1*(2).

Artunç, R. T. (2021). Ad Hoc Diplomasi (Ad Hoc Diplomacy). In M. Güneş (Ed.), *Diplomasi Kavramları Sözlüğü* (pp. 22–24). SDE Publications.

Baker, L. M. (2006, Summer). Observation: A Complex Research Method. *Library Trends, 55*(1), 171–189. doi:10.1353/lib.2006.0045

Berridge, G. R., & James, A. (2003). *A Dictionary of Diplomacy*. Palgrave Macmillan. doi:10.1057/9780230501348

Bjola, C. (2015). Making sense of digital diplomacy (Introduction). In C. Bjola & M. Holmes (Eds.), *DIGITAL DIPLOMACY Theory and practice*. Taylor&Francis Group. doi:10.4324/9781315730844

Bostancı, M. (2012). *Kamu Diplomasisinde Medyanın Rolü ve Önemi - Stratejik Bir İletişim Aracı Olarak Kamu Diplomasisi*. Anahtar Books.

Castells, M. (2008). *Enformasyon Çağı: Ekonomi, Toplum ve Kültür: Ağ Toplumunun Yükselişi*. İstanbul: Publications of Bilgi University.

Çomu, T., & Halaiqa, İ. (2014). Web İçeriklerinin Metin Temelli Çözümlenmesi. In M. Binark (Ed.), *Yeni Medya Çalışmalarında Araştırma Yöntem ve Teknikleri* (pp. 27–87). Ayrıntı Publications.

Corbin, J., & Strauss, A. (1990). Grounded Theory Research: Procedures, Canons, and Evaluative Criteria. *Qualitative Sociology, 13*(1), 3–21. doi:10.1007/BF00988593

Costantinou, C. M. (1996). *On the Way to Diplomacy*. University of Minnesota Press.

Cull, N. J. (2009). *Public Diplomacy: Lessons from the Past*. Figueroa Press.

diplomacy data. (2022). *History of Digital Diplomacy and Main Milestones*. Retrieved April 3, 2022, from http://diplomacydata.com/history-of-digital-diplomacy-and-main-milestones/

Doğan, E. (2012). Kamu Diplomasisinin Sunduğu Fırsatlar ve Kısıtları Üzerine. In A. Özkan & T. E. Öztürk (Eds.), *Kamu Diplomasisi Enstitüsü Serisi: 1* (pp. 13–30). TASAM Publications.

Friedman, T. L. (2005). *The World is Flat A Brief History of The Twenty-first Century*. Farrar, Straus and Giroux.

Gönlübol, M. (1993). *Uluslararası Politika: İlkeler, Kavramlar, Kurumlar*. Attila Bookstore.

Hamilton, K., & Langhorne, R. (2011). *The Practice of Diplomacy: Its Evolution, Theory and Administration*. Taylor&Francis Group.

Hanson, F. (2012). *Revolution @State: The Spread of Ediplomacy*. Lowy Institute for International Policy.

İskit, T. (2007). *Diplomasi, Tarihi, Teorisi, Kurumları ve Uygulaması*. İstanbul: Publications of Bilgi University.

Jupp, V. (2006). *The Sage Dictionary of Social Research*. Sage Publications.

Kalın, İ. (2010). *Türk Dış Politikası ve Kamu Diplomasisi*. MÜSİAD.

Kawulich, B. B. (2005). Participant Observation as a Data Collection Method. *Qualitative Social Research, 6*(2).

Kennedy, P. (2001). Büyük Güçlerin Yükseliş ve Çöküşleri (8. b.). İstanbul: Türkiye İş Bankası Cultural Publications.

Kozinets, R. (2010). *Netnography: Doing Ethnographic Research Online*. Sage Publications.

Lakomy, M. (2014). *Tweety na szczycie. Polityka responsywna. In Studia Medioznawcze Media*. Wydział Dziennikarstwa i Nauk Politycznych Instytut Dziennikarstwa Uniwersytetu Warszawskiego.

Leira, H. (2016). A Conceptual History of Diplomacy. C. M. Constantinou. In P. Kerr & P. Sharp (Eds.), *The SAGE Handbook of Diplomacy* (pp. 28–38). SAGE Publications.

Lüfkens, M. (2022). *Twiplomacy*. Retrieved February 27, 2022 from https://twiplomacy.com/blog/twiplomacy-study-2012/

Mazıcı, E. T. (2020). Covid-19 Pandemi Sürecinde Dijital Diplomasi: T.C. Dışişleri Bakanlığı Üzerine Bir Araştırma. *Turkish Studies*, *15*(4), 1087–1104.

Nicolson, H. (1941). *Diplomacy*. Oxford University Press.

Nye, J. S. (2004). *Soft Power*. PublicAffairs.

Ovalı, A. Ş. (2020). Türkiye-ABD İlişkilerinde Twitter Diplomasisi. *Uluslararası İlişkiler*, *17*(65), 23–45.

Papacharissi, Z. (2015). *Affective Publics: Sentiment, Technology, and Politics*. Oxford University Press.

Seib, P. (2012). *Real-Time Diplomacy, Politics and Power in the Social Media Era*. Palgrave Macmillan.

TİKA. (2022). *TİKA*. Retrieved March 13, 2022, from https://www.tika.gov.tr/tr

Tören, D. (2021). *Diplomasi ve Tarih Boyunca Geçirdiği Evrim*. Retrieved February, 16, from tuicakademi.org/diplomasi-ve-tarih-boyunca-gecirdigi-evrim/

Tuncer, H. (2009). *Diplomasinin Evrimi*. Kaynak Publications.

Uysal, N., & Schroeder, J. (2019). Turkey's Twitter public diplomacy: Towards a "new" cult of personality. *Public Relations Review*, *45*(5), 1–9.

Varnalı, K. (2012). *Dijital Kabilelerin İzinde: Sosyal Medyada Netnografik Araştırmalar*. MediaCat Publications.

Watson, A. (1982). *Diplomacy: The Dialogue Between States*. Routledge.

Wescott, N. (2008). *Digital Diplomacy: The Impact of the Internet on International Relations*. Oxford Internet Institute.

White, B. (2005). Diplomacy. In J. Baylis & S. Smith (Eds.), *The Globalization of World Politics: An Introduction to International Relations* (pp. 387–403). Oxford University Press.

Yepsen, E. A. (2012). Practicing Successful Twitter Public Diplomacy: A Model And Case Study Of U.S. Efforts. In *Venezuela*. Figueroa Press.

Yıldırım, A., & Şimşek, H. (2013). *Sosyal Bilimlerde Nitel Araştırma Yöntemleri*. Seçkin Publications.

Yücel, G. (2016). Dijital Diplomasi. TRT Akademi Dijital Medya Sayısı, 1(2), 748-760.

KEY TERMS AND DEFINITIONS

Digital Diplomacy: The use of the Internet and various social media tools to carry out diplomatic objectives.

Diplomacy: The activity of managing relations between different countries and the skill in doing this.

Globalization: The act of globalizing or extending to other or all parts of the world.

New Media: Different forms of electronic and interactive communication like the internet, web sites, computer games, e-mail, social networks, blogs, wikis.

Public Diplomacy: Public diplomacy, also called people's diplomacy, any of various government-sponsored efforts aimed at communicating directly with foreign publics.

Soft Power: A way of dealing with other countries that involves using economic and cultural influence to persuade them to do things, rather than military power.

Twitlomacy: Twiplomacy refers to the use of Twitter and other social media sites by government agencies and officials to engage with the public, disperse information and even leverage global influence.

Chapter 15
Reflecting Turkey's Attitude and Benevolence Towards Syrian Refugees to the World Through Digitalized Public Diplomacy

Selver Mertoğlu
Atatürk University, Turkey

Ömer Alanka
Hatay Mustafa Kemal University, Turkey

ABSTRACT

In 2011, Syrians fleeing the civil war in Syria tried to migrate to neighboring countries. While some countries did not accept Syrian refugees, others opened their doors to immigrants. Currently, Turkey is known as the country with the highest number of Syrians. These citizens, who left their countries and homes and migrated to other countries to protect their lives and children, faced different problems in the countries where they settled. Turkish authorities are taking steps to solve these problems. The aid and problem-solving steps taken for Syrian refugees are exhibited to the citizens of other countries through digitalized public diplomacy. In this study, firstly, information about the concept of migration is given and the migration from Syria to Turkey is discussed. Then, two different news published on the website of TRT World news channel were examined through critical discourse analysis to demonstrate how Turkey's attitude and benevolence towards Syrians is reflected to the world through digitalized public diplomacy.

INTRODUCTION

Turkey, which is located in an important region in terms of its geopolitical position, has an immigrant and emigrant structure. Turkey, which has opened its doors to people of many different races, religions and languages for centuries, today has approximately 5 million 506 thousand 304 foreign nationals. The vast majority of these are migrants fleeing the Assad regime in Syria. Syrian citizens who tried to save

DOI: 10.4018/978-1-6684-5822-8.ch015

their lives due to the bloody attacks of the Assad regime sought refuge in Turkey. Turkey opened its doors to migrants in difficult situations and took them under temporary protection. Some Turkish citizens criticize the authorities for granting Syrian migrants many of the same rights that they grant to their own citizens. The aid provided to migrants, who are often prioritized in hospitals, schools and government offices, also attracts attention. There are citizens who use social media to publicize their criticism, as well as those who support the aid provided to Syrians. However, there are also news websites that try to create a positive perception by presenting Turkey's attitude towards migrants.

The concept of migration is first explained in this study and then information about migration from Syria to Turkey is given. Then, 2 different news published on the website of TRT World news channel were examined through critical discourse analysis to demonstrate how Turkey's attitude and benevolence towards Syrians is reflected to the world through digitalized public diplomacy. The selected news items were determined in accordance with the objective of the study by purposive sampling method. The news articles titled "Syrian refugee children get education in Turkey" and "Syrians living in Turkey to become citizens, Erdogan says" were analyzed.

Concepts, Reasons, and Types of Migration

The history of migration dates back to the existence of humanity. In mass population movements, migrants have sought places where living standards are the most favorable for them. According to Akgür, who defines the concept of migration, which is influenced by many factors, migration is the settlement of a certain segment of the population living in a certain settlement area to another place for various and different reasons (Akgür, 1997, p. 41). According to Bruce and Yearley, migration is the movement of people from one country to another with the intention of staying (Bruce & Yearley, 2006, p. 197). Fichter (1990, p. 154) defines it as "any movement or migration of people through time, physical space or social structures".

The concept of refugee, which is considered within the scope of protection in Turkey, is defined in Article 1 of the United Nations (UN) Geneva Convention Relating to the Status of Refugees. Article 1 of the Geneva Convention on the Status of Refugees defines refugee as "any person who, owing to well-founded fear of being persecuted for reasons of race, religion, nationality, membership of a particular group or political opinion, is outside the country of his nationality and is unable or, owing to such fear, is unwilling to avail himself of the protection of that country, or who, having no nationality and being outside the country of his former habitual residence as a result of such events, is unable or, owing to such fear, is unwilling to return to it" (UNHCR). Migration can be caused by many reasons such as political, economic and educational reasons. Migration by people who do not like the living conditions where they live can be either forced or voluntary. Turkey is a country receiving migration as it is seen as an attractive region for citizens of other countries in terms of its climate and geopolitical location. Turkey, which is home to many people from different languages, religions and nationalities, is also known as a country of immigration.

Types of migration are as follows:

1. Internal migration: Internal migration is the movement of a person within a country. In general, migration from villages to cities is called internal migration. Internal migration that does not change the country's population can also be experienced from city to village or from city to city.

2. External migration: Unlike internal migration, external migration is the movement to settle in a different country by crossing the borders of the country. In addition, there is a decrease in the country's population in foreign migration and this movement causes serious problems in sending and receiving countries (Özyakışır, 2013, p. 8).
3. Free migration: Free migration, also called voluntary migration because it is carried out voluntarily, is done to improve living conditions. In short, it is a voluntary migration movement made by people in search of better financial and educational opportunities.
4. Forced migration: These are migrations that take place against people's own will. In these migrations, migrants flee persecution and oppression or may be exiled.
5. Labor migration: Labor migration can be inward or outward. In this type of migration, which can also be defined as the relocation of labor, people go to work in countries or regions with better conditions.
6. Seasonal Migration: The movement of people to travel or work at certain times of the year is called seasonal migration.
7. Brain drain: The migration of scientists, experts or those who want to get a better education to different regions is called brain drain.
8. Legal migration: According to this migration, people carry out migration movements in accordance with the law.

The phenomenon of migration, which has existed since the emergence of humanity, can occur for many reasons. While some fled from war, others had to leave their region to protect themselves from epidemics. Especially the chaos in the region where they live and the existence of conflict environment push people to look for different places where they can live. People who try to protect their lives for security reasons try to start a new life by migrating. In addition to these, there are also economic reasons. People living in underdeveloped regions try to gain economic benefits by migrating to developed countries. Natural disasters and invasions are also among the causes of migration. People who lose their homes as a result of events such as earthquakes move to safer regions for life safety. In addition to these, there are migrations for education, and these migrations are made to places where education conditions are higher. As can be seen, those who move as migrants leave the region they are in for different reasons.

Different theories have been developed by scholars trying to understand the concept of migration. The reason why there are more than one of these theories is due to the confusion in the concept of migration. The theories developed for the concept of migration, which has different types, are divided into early migration theories and contemporary migration theories. Ravenstein's Laws of Migration, Stouffer's Cross-Cutting Opportunities Theory, Lee's Push and Pull Theory are among the migration theories that center on economy, distance and opportunities (Bulut & Bimay, 2020, p. 18). In the contemporary period, it is seen that the theories have differentiated with the effect of globalization. A few of these are as follows: Neo-Classical Theories, New Economics of Labor Migration Theory, Split Labor Market Theory, World Systems Theory, Migration Systems Theory, Network Theory, Institutional Theory, Cumulative Causation Theory.

Migration from Syria to Turkey

Syria, officially known as the Syrian Arab Republic, is a country located in Western Asia. Syria has geopolitical importance as it is both a Mediterranean and a Middle Eastern country. In March 2011, chaos erupted in the country as a result of movements that started in March 2011 and spread across the country a month later. Demonstrators demanded the resignation of the ruling Bashar al-Assad. As the Syrian army opened fire on the people in April 2011, the Syrian migration movement from Syria to Turkey began in April 2011. Fleeing the civil war in Syria, the people of the country started to search for safe zones. These forced migrations took place both inside and outside the country (Orhan, The Situation of Syrian Refugees in the Countries Neighboring Syria: Findings, Conclusions and Recommendations, 2014, p. 5). A significant number of migrants fleeing the conflict in Syria have migrated to Turkey. In 2011, during this wave of migration, Turkey not only hosted Syrian refugees under the open door policy but also protected them under temporary protection status.

According to the report published by the Directorate of Migration Management on August 25, 2022, Syria was the nationality that migrated to Turkey the most from 2014 to 2017. According to the report, the migration fluctuating by years continues until today. As of August 18, 2022, there are 3 million 652 thousand 813 Syrian migrants in Turkey (Mülteciler Derneği, 2022). Syrian migrants who fled their country and sought refuge in Turkey are accommodated within the borders of the country under temporary protection status. While some Turkish citizens have a negative attitude towards the immigration of Syrians into the country, others have a positive attitude towards this situation. In addition to Syrian citizens who have temporarily settled in Turkey, there are also those who have obtained residence permits and settled in the country without leaving. Turkey has become the country with the highest number of refugees in the world by opening its doors to Syrians. Syrian migrants face problems such as shelter, health, education and finding a job, and they also face problems of integration. Legal regulations on the situation of Syrian asylum-seekers in Turkey were issued in 2013. Until this date, it is seen that they were positioned as immigrants by the Decree of the Council of Ministers and special laws. Those who entered Turkey illegally were labeled as illegal (Başak, 2011, p. 5). Based on Article 91 of Law No. 6458, known as the "Law on Foreigners and International Protection", the "Temporary Protection Regulation" was prepared and the legal deficiency regarding the situation of migrants was tried to be eliminated. In October 2011, Syrian migrants registered in Turkey were granted "temporary protection status". This provided Syrians with indefinite stay, protection against detention, and protection and assistance to respond to urgent needs (Orhan & Gündoğar, 2015, p. 7). Thus, Syrians in Turkey are secured and protected.

The continuous growth of the Syrian population causes many problems within the country. Due to these problems, xenophobia has also increased within the Turkish society. Hate speech is generated due to the problems arising from the differences between the two societies. However, there are posts and publications on social media and media to prevent prejudices against Syrians. In addition, social media also contributes to diplomatic relations between the two countries. The easy circulation of all kinds of information in the new media, where violence-promoting, humiliating and polarizing content is quite common, poses a threat to Syrian migrants.

Burhan Yildirim
@BurhanY04608152

"Isn't the country's lack of resilience evident from this? We have become slaves. Work, earn, pay taxes, and Syrians get salaries from our taxes. For some reason, Syrians are more valuable than Turks. We took this land by shedding blood, Syrians take it from us by paying money."

yiKar55:GOD PROTECT THE TURKISH
@YILDIRAYKARGUN

"Tomorrow, if someone somewhere in the country gets fed up with them, if they attack them, if we respond to them, it is very likely that the country will become like Syria because of the Syrians. Why don't you see this, it means that you have an interest in them, you don't protect the son of the homeland so much."

Ozlem Yilmaz
@ozlemvemeraki35

"When will these so-called refugees be sent out of Turkey, when will we be the only ones in our country, and why did we turn some of these refugees, who are of no use to us, into citizens of Turkey and why do we think that they will be given the right to vote?"

The posts quoted above were taken from Twitter, one of the social media channels with the highest number of users. The number of tweets containing such negative meanings and hate speech accessed by using the word "Syrians" is quite high. On the other hand, there are also constructive steps taken by civil society organizations regarding Syrian refugees and efforts to erase the disinformation spread in the society. The stories created about Syrians using public diplomacy are communicated to target audiences through appropriate forms of communication.

EVALUATION OF DIGITALIZED PUBLIC DIPLOMACY IN TERMS OF SYRIAN MIGRANTS

Two different news items on the TRT World news website selected for the study were examined through critical discourse analysis method to demonstrate how Turkey's attitude and benevolence towards Syrians is reflected to the world through digitalized public diplomacy.

News 1

Headline: Syrians living in Turkey to become citizens, Erdogan says (3 JUL 2016) (TRT World, 2016).

Turkish President Recep Tayyip Erdogan announced that millions of Syrians living in Turkey will have a chance to become citizens.

1. *Macro Structure*

The title of the news article includes the words of Turkish President Recep Tayyip Erdoğan. The headline, which provides information about the news and conveys the main topic of the news to the reader, increases credibility as it includes a direct quote. In the news spot, the title is reinforced by emphasizing again that Recep Tayyip Erdoğan announced that millions of Syrians living in Turkey will have the chance to become citizens. With the expressions in the title and the spot, Turkey's benevolence towards those in need of help is emphasized and an image is tried to be created. When we look at the photograph used in the news article, the image of Recep Tayyip Erdoğan is included along with the Turkish flag representing Turkey. The photograph of a Syrian refugee sitting in a tent waving a Turkish flag in front of his tent camp in Turkey suggests that Turkey is accepted as a homeland by refugees due to its independence. The presence of Erdoğan in these photographs depicting Turkey's independence indicates that he represents Turkey, and the fact that his name is mentioned in the news was also effective. The other photograph depicts a refugee carrying the message "Thank you to the EU for closing the border" during a protest demanding the opening of borders in a makeshift camp on the Greek-Macedonian border near the village of Idomeni in Greece. The implication here is that the EU is cruel to refugees but Turkey is on their side. Another photograph depicts Syrian refugees working in a clothing factory owned by Syrians in Gaziantep, Turkey. Here, it is indicated that Syrians are employed and that Turkey is doing its best to prevent them from being victimized. The last photo depicts refugee tents in Kilis province in southeastern Turkey. Turkey is portrayed as a country that also considers the refuge of Syrian citizens.

Ideology is seen to be at work in the presentation of the main news event. The main event of the news article, which tries to create a positive perception about Turkey, is that works are being carried out on the possibility of Syrians becoming Turkish citizens. In the presentation of the main news event, Recep Tayyip Erdoğan's words about the millions of Syrians living in Turkey will have the chance to become citizens of the country that provides them shelter are included. The news event was constructed according to newsworthiness criteria. There is no background information in the news. When the comments of news sources on the event are analyzed, it is seen that only Recep Tayyip Erdoğan's speech is included. Erdoğan's condemnation of other countries for not opening their doors to Syrians in difficult situations is also included in the news, while it is demonstrated that Turkey lends a hand to the fallen and other countries remain silent.

2. *Microstructure*

Syntactically, the news report uses sentences with active voice. This situation increases credibility. When we look at the words used, the words "Turkish citizenship" and "refugee" draw attention. In the news article emphasizing that Syrians will be granted Turkish citizenship, the word "refugee" makes the reader intuit that Turkey protects refugees with its power and independence. The news article contains credible and convincing information. Especially direct quotes from Recep Tayyip Erdoğan constitute credibility.

As a result, the photographs of message chosen to create a positive image of Turkey in the news article demonstrate Turkey's benevolent attitude towards Syrian refugees. It is also conveyed in the main theme of the news article that many problems of Syrians will be solved as Turkish citizens.

News 2

Headline: Syrian refugee children get education in Turkey (19 AUG 2018) (Radhakrishnan, 2019)

Spot: Education program in Turkey aims to prevent what the UN calls a lost generation of Syrian children.

1. *Macro Structure*

The title of the news article informs the readers that Syrian refugees are receiving education in Turkey and conveys the main subject of the news article. The headline refers to Syrians as refugees and tries to show the importance Turkey attaches to education and the services it provides for Syrian citizens. In the news spot, it is stated that the education program in Turkey aims to prevent what the UN calls a lost generation of Syrian children. The spot reinforces the title by showing that Turkey is reaching out to the victimized Syrian citizens and helping them with education, which even the UN does not care about.

In the photograph selected for the news item, balloons symbolizing the Turkish flag are seen in the hands of Syrian children. While showing the importance of Turkey for Syrian generations, Turkey's independence and greatness were also emphasized. In the photograph reinforcing the image of benevolent Turkey, smiling children convey that they are happy to be in Turkey.

The main event is presented in the news spot and headline. While Syrians being able to receive education in Turkey is the subject of the news item, its presentation includes data and expressions that prove the information in the spot. In addition, the news article lacks background information. Why Syrians seek refuge in Turkey and why they are called refugees are information that is not included in the news. The context of the news item is Turkey, which attaches importance to education. The parties to the incident are not included in the news report.

2. *Microstructure*

Syntactically, sentences are presented with an active structure. The sentences used with numerical data that increase credibility have a transitive feature. "There are at least 1.5 million Syrian refugee children in Turkey, and over 610,000 are enrolled in school. But according to Turkey's ministry of national Education, more than 350,000 Syrian children are not getting any formal education." Sentence structures like this draw the reader's attention to the news. The word refugee draws attention in the news article. By choosing the word refugee for Syrians who fled the conflict in their own country and took refuge in Turkey, their need for help is emphasized.

The news article contains credible and convincing information. The fact that examples are shown in relation to the issue also changes the reader's approach to the issue. It was tried to show to all TRT World readers that with the aid provided to Syrians, their economic, cultural and social problems were tried to be solved. As a result, the reporter reconstructed and presented reality in the news report. The image of benevolent Turkey was reinforced in the news report where ideological production was realized.

CONCLUSION

In 2011, Syrian migrants fled the Assad regime and migrated to Turkey. This study first provides information about the background of the event. Then, in order to demonstrate Turkey's attitude towards Syrians to the citizens of other countries through digitalized public diplomacy, 2 different news on TRT World news website were examined with critical discourse analysis. In the critical discourse analysis developed by Teun A. Van Dijk, the news text was divided into macro and micro structures and the meaning behind the sentences was tried to be revealed. In this study, which tries to demonstrate how Turkey's attitude and benevolence towards Syrians is reflected to the world, the sample was selected in accordance with the objective.

The first news article analyzed was titled "Syrians living in Turkey to become citizens, Erdogan says". The headline includes the words of the President of Turkey Recep Tayyip Erdoğan and the rest of the news text follows this pattern. The main event is the efforts to enable Syrians to become Turkish citizens by obtaining citizenship in Turkey. In this way, many problems of Syrian refugees will be solved. While processing the event in the news text, Turkey's benevolence and justice in the eyes of the citizens of other countries are portrayed. In the news article, which provides a positive perspective, a government that does not differentiate the people who seek refuge from its own people is shown. The news report contains credible and convincing information. Especially direct quotes from Recep Tayyip Erdoğan create credibility. As a result, the photographs of message chosen to create a positive image of Turkey in the news report demonstrate Turkey's benevolent attitude towards Syrian migrants. It was also conveyed in the main theme of the news article that many problems of Syrians would be solved as Turkish citizens.

The title of the second news item analyzed is "Syrian refugee children get education in Turkey". Again, Turkey's benevolent behavior towards Syrian refugees is demonstrated. The news article includes information that Syrian children living in Turkey can receive education and learn Turkish. With the photographs and expressions used in the news article, the reader is made to intuit that Syrian children are happy in Turkey. The credibility of the news is increased by giving examples related to the subject. It was tried to be demonstrated to all TRT World readers that with the aid provided to Syrians, their economic, cultural and social problems were tried to be solved. In this news, the image of benevolent Turkey was reinforced. Like every country, Turkey is trying to increase its prestige by taking advantage of the opportunities offered by digitalized public diplomacy. They actively use social media and websites to do this.

REFERENCES

Akgür, Z. G. (1997). *Migration from Rural Areas to Urban Areas and Imbalances between Regions in Turkey*. T.C. Ministry of Culture Publications, Prime Ministry Press Office.

Başak, C. (2011). *Refugees, Asylum Seekers and Illegal Migrants*. Republic of Turkey Ministry of Interior Publication.

Bruce, S., & Yearley, S. (2006). *The Sage Dictionary of Sociology*. Sage Publications. doi:10.4135/9781446279137

Bulut, Y., & Bimay, M. (2020). In Y. B. Akin (Ed.), *The Problem of Migration And Refugees With Local, National And Global Dimensions* (pp. 9–33). Çizgi Publishing House.

Derneği, M. (2022). *Number of Syrians in Turkey August 2022*. https://multeciler.org.tr/turkiyedeki-suriyelisayisi/#:~:text=T%C3%BCrkiye'de%20kay%C4%B1t%20alt%C4%B1na%20 al%C4%B1nm%C4%B1%C5%9F,652%20bin%20813%20ki%C5%9Fi%20oldu

Fichter, J. (1990). *Sociology Nedir?* Selcuk University Publication.

Orhan, O. (2014). *The Situation of Syrian Refugees in the Countries Neighboring Syria: Findings, Conclusions and Recommendations*. ORSAM Publication.

Orhan, O., & Gündoğar, S. Ş. (2015). *The Effects of Syrian Refugees on Turkey*. ORSAM Publication.

Özyakışır, D. (2013). *Migration (Theory and Regional Practice)*. Nobel Publications.

Radhakrishnan, R. (2019, AUG 19). *Syrian refugee children get education in Turkey.* TRT World. Retrieved from https://www.trtworld.com/turkey/syrian-refugee-children-get-education-in-turkey-19676

Syrians living in Turkey to become citizens, Erdogan says. (2016, July 3). *TRT World.* Retrieved from https://www.trtworld.com/mea/syrians-living-in-turkey-to-become-citizens-136720

UNHCR. (2022). *What is a Refugee?* The UN Refugee Agency. Retrieved from https://www.unhcr.org/what-is-a-refugee.html

KEY TERMS AND DEFINITIONS

Migration: It is the act of settling in another place by leaving the area where communities or individuals are located for any reason.

Public Diplomacy: Public diplomacy is a process that describes how the government of a country tries to influence the citizens and intellectuals of another country in line with their own political and ideological views.

Refugee: A person who has been persecuted in his own country for certain reasons and has taken refuge in another country.

Syria: Syria, also known as the Syrian Arab Republic, is a country located in Western Asia. Its language is Arabic.

TRT World: It is an international television channel founded by TRT and replacing TRT int.

Turkey: Turkey, or officially the Republic of Turkey, is a country with most of its territory in Anatolia and a small part in Thrace, the southeastern extension of the Balkan Peninsula.

Assad Regime: When Bashar Assad, son of Hafez Assad, took over the administration in Syria, he created his own regime. The name of this regime is known as Assad or the Assad regime.

Chapter 16
The Role of Social Media in Digitalized Public Diplomacy:
An Example of Turkish Image in TRT World's Twitter Account

Selver Mertoğlu
Atatürk Universitesi, Turkey

ABSTRACT

Developments experienced in communication technologies have caused digitalization by changing and transforming all areas of life. Especially thanks to the opportunities and possibilities provided by new communication technologies, the authorities of different countries can convey their political and ideological thoughts to the citizens of other countries quickly and effectively. Social media is one of the most important digital communication networks with the power to influence the international agenda. Countries that take their place in digital diplomacy can more easily manage public perceptions with social media environments, which have an important place in international relations. In this study, by emphasizing the importance of social media channels in the digitalization of public diplomacy, the authors have shown the Turkish image displayed based on the posts made on TRT World's Twitter account. For this, the shares and comments selected by the purposeful sampling method will be analyzed with discourse analysis and the reflected Turkish image will be revealed.

INTRODUCTION

With the rapid development of communication technologies, significant changes and transformations have been experienced on societies. The new generation communication technologies, which make their effects felt from the economy to politics, from the social field to the cultural field, oblige everyone to participate in the world they create. In the 21st century, when everything has become digital and virtual, joining the network has become a necessity. Public diplomacy has also taken its share of the changes and transformations experienced. Countries have started to benefit from the environment offered by new

DOI: 10.4018/978-1-6684-5822-8.ch016

communication technologies in order to get an idea about each other. Digitization, interaction, multimedia, hypermedia, simulation, speed and the trivialization of the concept of space are the most important features of new media. These features make this area attractive for users. Now, not only do states communicate with each other, but also citizens of countries can participate in this communication. Prestige, image and prestige are essential in digital public diplomacy, which is carried out on a voluntary basis. Countries use new media effectively to increase their prestige and prestige.

Social media has become an environment that government officials, non-governmental organizations and the country's media actively use together with brands. In this study, firstly, information about public diplomacy is given under the title of *"The Role of Social Media in Digitalized Public Diplomacy: An Example of Turkish Image in TRT World's Twitter Account"*. Then, unlike traditional public diplomacy, digital public diplomacy and new media are emphasized. After giving general information about Twitter, which also constitutes the sample of the research, four different posts selected from TRT World account were analyzed with discourse analysis. The posts selected for analysis from the posts on TRT World's page between 13 June and 31 May are as follows:

@trtworld (10 May 2022) (https://twitter.com/trtworld/status/1535237909502107649)

President Recep Tayyip Erdogan says Turkey is aiming to become a global hub for healthcare services

@trtworld (31 May 2022) (https://twitter.com/trtworld/status/1531595091978108928)

Turkey's Defense Minister Hulusi Akar reiterates Ankara's determination to continue fighting against terrorism, saying the country does not accept any terror presence along its borders

@ trtworld (2 June 2022) (https://twitter.com/trtworld/status/1532217947778781186)

UN says it will use the name "Turkey" effective immediately after Ankara sent a letter to the international body asking it to drops using " Turkey " in official documents, languages

@ trtworld (13 June 2022) (https://twitter.com/trtworld/status/1536366536986095616)

Turkey continues defending the rights of its citizens and the Turkish Cypriots ' within the framework of its "entrepreneurial and humanitarian foreign policy", Turkish FM Cavusoglu says

As these sharings taking the place were examined in TRT World 's Twitter account, it was seen that most of the news made was linked to trtworld.com. For this reason, the news on the site was included in the analysis by going to trtworld.com in the linked posts. As a result of the analysis, it has been shown that a positive perception of the Turkish image is tried to be created in the shares made by TRT World on its Twitter account, so that there are posts and visuals aimed at increasing Turkey's image and reputation.

PUBLIC DIPLOMACY

Countries need public diplomacy in order to have an idea about each other. Many thinkers have defined public diplomacy based on solid relations by evaluating it from their own perspective. According to

Leonard, the main purpose of public diplomacy is to understand the cultures and lifestyles of countries by building deep-rooted relations and to correct any misunderstandings (Leonard, 2002, s. 8-9). Strategic communication, which is used especially in the formation of deep-rooted relations between countries, brings the countries closer to each other and ensures the realization of perception management. The media, on the other hand, mediates the formation of perception by providing information flow between countries.

To Tiedeman, who draws attention to the fact that public diplomacy is a communication process, the process of transferring the ideas, culture and policy of a country's government to other countries is called public diplomacy (Tiedeman, 2004, s. 6). With the spread of the internet, which has a network-based interactive feature with the invention of web 2.0 rather than a one-sided information flow, the sovereign powers of the countries can easily present their information, including their own policies, to the public of other countries. With the loss of importance of the concept of time and space, access to information has become easier. Another thinker who defined public diplomacy is Hans N. Tunc. He also emphasizes the communication aspect of public diplomacy and states that it covers all activities related to understanding, informing and influencing the public (Tunch, 1990, s. 3). Definitions made on public diplomacy implemented using soft power meet on common ground as a strategic communication method applied to protect the sovereignty of the governments of the countries. Edmun, who uses public diplomacy to show the influence of the public on foreign policy Gullion was the first to use the concept.

Public diplomacy, which is an important form of communication for foreign policy in gaining image and prestige, has started to become network-oriented with the development of information and communication technologies. There is now a more effective and successful digital public diplomacy against the practices of traditional public diplomacy. Szondi distinguished the traditional public diplomacy from the public diplomacy of the 21st century as follows: While conflict and tension prevailed in the traditional Public Diplomacy, there is an atmosphere of peace in the 21st Century Public Diplomacy. While the aim of traditional public diplomacy is to provide political change by influencing the target audiences, 21st-century public diplomacy aims to create a favourable environment and positive impression that will raise the country's political and economic interests abroad. While persuasion and the administration of the public are preferred as a strategy in traditional public diplomacy, it is essential to establish and develop relationships and mingle with the public in 21st-century public diplomacy. Traditionally, communication was one-way and monologue, but now there is two-way communication, dialogue. When evaluated as research, very little research is preferred in traditional public diplomacy, while scientific research and feedback evaluation are available in the 21st century. In addition, ideologies and interests are at the forefront of the content of the message in traditional public diplomacy. On the other hand, thoughts and values constitute the content of the message in 21st-century public diplomacy. When looking at the target audience, there is the general public of the target country in the traditional (public) and classified publics in the 21st century. As a channel, one prefers traditional mass media and the other prefers old and new mass media together. The last distinction is the budget. Traditional public diplomacy uses public resources. 21st-century public diplomacy prefers public and private partnerships (Szondi, 2009, s. 305). It is no longer just the state that has a say in public diplomacy. In addition to the state, many sectors, institutions and individuals are also involved in public diplomacy. Substituting communicative action for the interests in traditional public diplomacy also builds trust between countries. In addition, while ideologies were tried to be imposed on the public in the past, today thoughts and values are given priority, thus perception management is getting stronger.

There are two different approaches to public diplomacy a hard and a soft approach. According to the so-called strict approach, the purpose of public diplomacy is to persuade the people of other countries and to change their behaviour by resorting to propaganda. It uses traditional media tools for this (Signitzer & Coombs, 1992, s. 140). The soft or flexible approach, on the other hand, is based on the establishment of long-term relationships by establishing mutual interaction. For this, it brings more culture and knowledge to the fore. In flexible public diplomacy, where new communication tools are preferred, it is tried to establish permanent relations with lifestyle, politics and economy, together with artistic activities, in order to realize the transfer of culture. In public diplomacy used in a country, different units convey political information and cultural activities (Signitzer & Wamser, 2006, pp. 438-439). Soft power applied in public diplomacy, which is closely related to the concept of power, operates based on persuasion and consent. Now, influence is created with different strategies by giving importance to the thoughts and ideas of the public, rather than imposition. Rather than traditional public diplomacy, the public, not the states, is prioritized.

In public diplomacy, which cares about the existence of the public, it is tried to reach the goal by influencing the thoughts and behaviours of the citizens of other countries on foreign policy issues with appropriate tools and public relations activities. In this way, Nations are trying to realize perception management in line with their own interests. While each country fulfils its mission of promoting its own interests, it can expect public diplomacy to achieve many tasks and goals. Pratkanis summarizes (Pratkanis, 2009, s. 114) some of these tasks and objectives as follows:

- To declare the appropriateness and validity of an action,
- Editing the opposition structure
- Changing the thinking and actions of both enemies and neutrals and collaborators
- Gaining support to achieve the goal
- Eliminating others by forming strategic alliances
- Creating a perception of dictator, tyrant and terrorist by opposing propaganda
- To put pressure on the world and condemn rogue states
- Ending structures of ethnic genocide and cleansing
- Encouraging warring states to cease fire
- Justifying causes of war in the eyes of important neutrals
- demoralize the enemies
- To raise the morale of one's own country
- Persuading an enemy to surrender
- Supporting war conditions (allowing house searches, gaining support from local leaders, soliciting information, keeping civilians off the battlefield, spreading rumours, supporting them with faith-building efforts)
- Reducing the perception of the security dilemma (increasing security elements within the nation)
- To prevent a war from breaking out and resolve a conflict where it first occurred
- To allocate negotiation conditions by changing the image and expectations of structures in conflict, in other words, to replace conflict with conflict resolution.
- Creating an environment for reconciliation not only in wartime but also in peacetime,
- Supporting international organizations and getting support from them is making agreements that will provide peaceful conditions.

Along with public diplomacy, each country tries to create a positive perception in the world by influencing its own public opinion. Thus, it is expected from the public to acquire the desired behavior through perception management.

It is possible to divide some of the public diplomacy models, which have an important place in foreign policy, into five main headings. In the model designed by Cowan and Arsenault, which was first described as a three-stage model, there are stages in the form of a monologue, dialogue and cooperation. In the stage called a monologue, the purpose is persuasion, while the means are statements, press releases, and speeches, and the flow is one-way. In the stage called dialogue, the aim is the exchange of information and ideas. Conversation at the dialogue level as a tool, while using discussion platforms, the flow is two-way as it is interaction. Finally, the purpose of the cooperation is to develop relationships, the tool is to jointly carry out projects, and the flow is bidirectional and multidirectional (Çevik, 2014, s. 39). In the model developed by Cowan and Arsenault, the model in which one-sided information flow is provided has passed to the stage where mutual interaction and information exchange take place. The second public diplomacy model is called Integrated. In the integrated public diplomacy approach, public diplomacy is also divided into three groups: short and medium-term mediated public diplomacy, medium and long-term nation branding and country reputation approach, and public diplomacy based on relations based on soft power (Golan, 2014, s. 418-424). In public diplomacy, which Golan talks about and examines under three headings, first of all, there is public diplomacy that takes place through an intermediary. In the medium and long-term approach, an image is created with the branding system. Finally, there is a long-term and sustained effect in the relationship-based approach.

The third public diplomacy model is described as reactive and proactive. According to this approach, it is in question that the crises that may occur or occur in public diplomacy should be resolved as soon as possible. Proactive public diplomacy intervenes by anticipating possible crises. Reactive public diplomacy, on the other hand, is trying to solve the emerging crises immediately. In this way, the resulting damage is minimized. In the fourth public diplomacy model, cooperation and competition are emphasized. Leonard et al. When examining competitive/collaborative public diplomacy, it classifies it according to countries, interests and ways of working. G-20 countries, EU countries, permanent members of the UN Security Council, NATO Diaspora are included in the competitive system. They apply competitive public diplomacy to create political influence, to provide military cooperation, to create trade, investment, tourism and policy exchange and to ensure intergovernmental cooperation. In addition, there is both bilateral and multilateral work in the competitive system. In the collaborative system, all developing countries are targeted. While ensuring human rights, democracy and good governance, ensuring regional stability is the area of interest in collaborative public diplomacy. Compared to the competitive system, a multilateral working style is seen in cooperative public diplomacy (Leonard, Stead, & Smewing, 2002, s. 25). Finally, among the public diplomacy models, it is possible to describe them as rigid and flexible. As mentioned before, when public diplomacy is implemented with a strict approach, its results create short-term effects. However, when a flexible approach is applied, its effects are more permanent and long-term.

Whatever the model, public diplomacy has certain implementation tools. It is tried to reach the goal by using the most effective tool according to its content. Culture, belief, education, sports and now media and social media diplomacy as one of the most important tools are seen as tools of public diplomacy. Through cultural diplomacy, nations try to create an image against each other. For this reason, it tries to provide cultural transfer by using cultural fields such as art, science and education. Like culture, belief is among the tools most frequently used by states in creating and managing perception. Again, it is seen that sports provide rapprochement between countries. In education diplomacy, it is tried to create public opinion for the interests of the nation by providing information transfer between countries. Therefore, training programs are one of the best ways of knowledge transfer. Finally, media and social media diplomacy are also used by public diplomacy as a tool.

First, propaganda was made using traditional media in public diplomacy. Media, like other tools, is preferred as an important tool in public diplomacy. II. The media was used effectively during World War II and the Cold War. Newspaper, television and radio, which are traditional media tools that provide unilateral information flow, are the most frequently used tools in public diplomacy by countries. However, with the invention of the internet in the 21st century, the dimension of public diplomacy has also changed. Public diplomacy has also been transformed through the internet, which provides instantaneousness in the network-oriented global village. Statesmen are now involved in social media channels. Because governments have had to use social media to create their policies on the network (Ekşi, 2014, s. 117). Twitter is the preferred choice of governments on social media such as Twitter, Instagram, Facebook. In addition to their personal accounts, accounts are created on behalf of many ministries such as foreign affairs, and posts translated into English are made, and an image is tried to be created by informing the people of other countries.

Digitalized Public Diplomacy and New Media

In the United States, the Defense Advanced Research Projects Agency (DARPA) invented ARPA for military research in 1969. Thus, the foundations of the Internet were set up. The usage area of the internet has expanded especially with the computers starting to enter private property. The inventions that came, in turn, caused everyone to take their place in the virtual network. While the possibilities offered by smartphones have influenced people, they have opened the doors of a different world for them. Anyone who has an internet network and a device in that world have the right to participate. The digital environment, which is often seen as a democratic environment, has become attractive without the restriction of time and space by creating the virtual public space.

Advances in technology have led to the emergence of many concepts such as artificial intelligence, digital money, and virtual reality, and have caused radical changes in different areas from the way of life of societies to their habits. This network was later used to interconnect computers in universities and research institutions in the United States. With the entry of computers into private properties, the use of the Internet has expanded. In particular, the invention of smartphones has created a network society that connects almost the whole world. We are According to the report published by Social in 2022, global internet users have increased to 4.95 billion at the beginning of 2022, making up 62.5 per cent of the world's total population. In addition, while it is stated in the report that there are 4.62 billion social media users worldwide in January 2022, this figure is equal to 58.4 per cent of the world's total population (Kemp, 2022). As the number of users increases day by day, the impact rate of the internet and social media is also increasing.

Social media, which emerged with the introduction of web 2.0 technology after web 1.0, which allows one-way data flow, provides its users with the opportunity to intervene in the content and exchange information in a mutual interaction environment. While the universe has evolved into a global village, it has also caused transformations in the social sphere. Today, when everything is digitized, transferred to digital and made accessibly, public diplomacy has also taken its share. Traditional public diplomacy and the digitalized public diplomacy of the 21st century are clearly separated from each other. Digital diplomacy helps to establish communication between countries. Realizing the power of the Internet, government officials started to invest in this area and provided the necessary equipment. The United States is also among those who realize the power of the internet. In 2002, the first e-Diplomacy Taskforce was established in the USA.

For Bjola and Holmes, digital diplomacy is not only state but also non-state actors managing international exchange using the internet and information communication technologies (Bjola & Holmes, 2015, s. 1272). Different qualifications are made for this digitalized diplomacy, such as electronic diplomacy, cyber diplomacy, twiplomacy or web 2.0 diplomacy. Cyber diplomacy, which tries to create public opinion by using soft power without the need for military support, is seen as the most important tool in the image creation actions of governments. The virtual medium, in which a large part of the world's population is located, provides multiple information flows, helping not only the transfer of information between the states but also between the state and the public. Thus, virtual public spaces are created and perception management is carried out in these environments. Governments using social media try to influence the thoughts and behaviours of societies with strategic communication. Elements belonging to the public are now integrated with each other.

Communication on the virtual network, known as new media, has certain characteristics. The seven important features of the digital environment where geographical boundaries are unimportant are as follows (Lister, Dovey, Giddings, Grant, & Kelly, 2009, s. 13):

1. **Numeracy:** In the new media, all data is included as 1 and 0. Digital data, which is divided into small pieces with mathematical codes, includes many different data such as audio, video, photographs, and text.
2. **Interaction:** new media allowing mutual feedback now also allows the receiver to intervene in the content.
3. **Multimedia:** In new media, more than one media is gathered on a single platform. For this reason, it is also called multimedia.
4. **Hypermedia**: Unlike traditional media, the hypermedia feature of new media enables data to be connected to each other.
5. **Interface:** Thanks to the interfaces, information is transferred between devices in the new media.
6. **Simulation**: It is the representation of reality in new media. There are simulated truths in virtual reality.
7. **Network access:** One of the features that distinguish new media from traditional media is network access.

With the opportunities it has provided, the new media has taken its place in almost everyone's life and continues to do so. Network media, where everyone can make their voices heard, has also changed foreign policy. Thus, diplomatic structures have also been transformed. The effect of social media, which is included in the scope of new media, on public opinion formation, perception management and image formation is quite large. Generally preferred for digitalized public diplomacy are social media channels such as Facebook, YouTube, Twitter, Instagram and TikTok, where the number of users is high. Twitter, in particular, is a sharing site where government officials inform the public by announcing all kinds of developments in the country. Thanks to Twitter, information and news about foreign policy are instantly accessible. On Twitter, the agenda is created thanks to the feature known as Trend Topic. Trend Topic, known as Short TT, consists of the most mentioned topics. This can be a word, phrase or tag. The trending topics used with the # sign, commonly known as hashtags, change daily. Thanks to the TT feature, government officials, individuals or brands try to win them by influencing the feelings and thoughts of the citizens of other countries by sharing foreign policy. In addition to these, media organs also try to influence the thoughts and feelings of the people of other countries by sharing their own country's policies through social media. In this way, media organs also support image formation.

, information about Twitter was given because the shares on TRT World 's Twitter account were examined. Twitter in 2006 by Jack Dorsey, Biz Stone, Noah Founded by Glass and Evan Williams. Twitter, whose number of users has increased over time, is now in fifteenth place among the most preferred social networking sites in the world. Twitter is a verb meaning to tweet and tweet to tweet. Therefore, there is a bird figure in the logo of the social networking platform. The bird figure with its head slightly upturned means freedom. Biz Stone stated that Twitter helps to overthrow despotic regimes and that this bird figure will be found on the crackling walls of tyranny (Stone, 2014: 104). Defending the freedom of expression, Twitter has added many different features to its interface with the work of its programmers. Due to its structure, it is seen as one of the most comfortable virtual environments where diplomacy is practised. According to January 2022 data, Twitter has 436 million active users (Kemp, 2022).

Your twitter the features available in the interface are as follows (Mertoğlu, 2021, p. 162-163):

1. **Twetter Polls:** Twitter Polls create questions and help other users to express their opinions.
2. **TBT:** " Throw " in English back TBT, which is the abbreviation of "Thursday", is translated into Turkish as a return to Thursday. Users share their old photos with the hashtag #TBT.
3. **Snapchat, Whatsapp and Instagram Tweet Sharing:** tweeter offers the opportunity to share Tweets on other social networks.
4. **Parental Consent:** Twitter requires parental consent to create an account under the age of 13. The system detects and locks the accounts of children under the age of 13. Parental consent is required for the account to be used again.
5. **Bidwatch:** Bidwatch, which is currently an application used only in the United States, allows users to identify misleading information.
6. **DM Dock:** This feature helps to navigate the main page while messaging on Twitter.
7. **TweetDeck:** TweetDeck allows viewing multiple timelines in a single window.
8. **Fleets:** Fleets are instant tweets that disappear after 24 hours.
9. **Moment Creation:** With the Twitter Moments feature, Twitter users can create their own news and stories and transfer them to other users.
10. **QR Code:** Thanks to the QR code, people can find and follow each other more easily.
11. **Lists:** Lists are groups created on Twitter.
12. **Topics: With the** Twitter topics feature, it customizes the topics determined according to the user's interests.
13. **Media Studio: The** media studio feature provides editing of Twitter content.
14. **Livecut: It** is a feature used in Media Studio. Videos to be broadcast on Twitter can be edited with Livecut.
15. **Direct Message:** The Direct Message feature, abbreviated as DM, enables private messaging on Twitter. However, mutual follow-up with the person to whom the message is to be sent is a must.
16. **Trend Topik**: The most talked about topics are listed thanks to the feature abbreviated as TT.

Twitter, which has the features that attract users to the network, acts as an important news source around the world. Elon right now On Twitter, purchased by Musk, the news reaches millions of people instantly through 280-character tweets and retweets. Twitter, which is also used for diplomacy. Also called Twiplomacy or Twitter Diplomacy. Those who use Twitter as a tool for public diplomacy also help create an environment for discussion on foreign policy issues, enabling everyone to express their opinions. Twiplomacy covers "the work of governments, authorities, non-governmental organizations or individuals on behalf of the state to communicate, chat, interact with citizens in the international arena, and increase reputation" (Aydın, 2022, s. 36). Those who share about country politics using Twitter try to create an image by reaching the target audience faster.

METHOD

The Role of Social Media in Digitalized Public Diplomacy: An Example of Turkish Image in TRT World's Twitter Account", the data selected by purposive sampling method were analyzed with discourse analysis to achieve the purpose. Thus, by showing the role of social media in public diplomacy, its role in creating an image has been revealed. Critical discourse analysis will be made in this study, which tries to reach the Turkish image displayed based on the shares TRT World has made on its Twitter account.

Van Dijk makes discourse analysis under two headings. In this analysis, known as synthetic and semantic analysis, he aimed to reach the meaning of the discourse with semantic analysis while examining the grammatical structure of sentences with syntactic under the title of synthetic (Van Dijk, 1988, p. 71, 91-92). Critical discourse analysis, which consists of macro structure and microstructure, is divided into macro and microstructures. Under the name of macrostructure, "thematic" and "schematic" analyses are carried out. In the microstructure, syntactic analysis, regional harmony, word choices, and news rhetoric are tried to be reached (Özer 2015: 247). The fact that language is loaded with ideologies is the most important basis of critical discourse analysis. Ideologies are also dominant in the language used in the news. These ideologies are imposed on societies by producing consent through mass media, as Althusser points out with the ideological apparatus of the state. The discourses that dominate the mass media are instantly transferred to the target audience and naturalized and reproduced with different strategies. Especially the emergence of the internet and the opportunities it provides have made perception management easier. News agencies and newspapers instantly share their news with their readers without worrying about speed and space. Ideologies embedded in the discourses in the news are also revealed with the help of critical discourse analysis. In this study, Twitter shares in the determined sample were analyzed with critical discourse analysis and the creation of a Turkish image in the context of foreign policy and public diplomacy was tried to be shown.

The posts selected for analysis from the posts on TRT World's page between 13 June and 31 May are as follows:

@trtworld (10 May 2022) (https://twitter.com/trtworld/status/1535237909502107649)

President Recep Tayyip Erdogan says Turkey is aiming to become a global hub for healthcare services

@trtworld (31 May 2022) (https://twitter.com/trtworld/status/1531595091978108928)

Turkey's Defense Minister Hulusi Akar reiterates Ankara's determination to continue fighting against terrorism, saying the country does not accept any terror presence along its borders

@ trtworld (2 June 2022) (https://twitter.com/trtworld/status/1532217947778781186)

UN says it will use the name "Turkey" effective immediately after Ankara sent a letter to the international body asking it to drops using " Turkey " in official documents, languages

@ trtworld (13 June 2022) (https://twitter.com/trtworld/status/1536366536986095616)

Turkey continues defending the rights of its citizens and the Turkish Cypriots ' within the framework of its "entrepreneurial and humanitarian foreign policy", Turkish FM Cavusoglu says

TRT World 's Twitter account, it was seen that most of the news made were linked to trtworld.com. For this reason, the news on the site was included in the analysis by going to trtworld.com in the linked posts.

RESULTS

In the study, which aims to show the Turkish image displayed based on the shares of TRT World on its Twitter account, a post dated 10 May 2022 was first examined.

1. *President Recep Tayyip Erdogan says Turkey is aiming to become a global hub for healthcare services.*

the text added to the post on TRT World 's Twitter account, it is stated that President Recep Tayyip Erdoğan said that Turkey aims to become a global centre for health services. In the news about Turkey, President Recep Tayyip Erdoğan's words and photos are generally included. In this analyzed post, Turkey and Recep Tayyip Erdogan are identified. TRT World has added a link to its website in this post so that its followers can read the rest of the news. Thus, the curiosity of TRT World followers is tried to be satisfied easily. The photo provided with the link includes the image of Recep Tayyip Erdoğan making a speech on the podium. The development of the health sector in Turkey was tried to be emphasized in the title with the information missing, and the attention of the followers was tried to be attracted.

When the link in the post is clicked, the Twitter user is directed to the news site. The macro and microstructure in the news here is as follows:

TITLE: ERDOGAN: TURKEY AIMING TO BECOME GLOBAL HEALTHCARE HUB

Turkey expects to serve 1.5 million patients next year and is aiming to receive $10 billion in revenue from the global healthcare market, says President. _

Macro Structure

In the headline of the news, there is a direct quotation from the words of Turkish President Recep Tayyip Erdogan. Giving the title, which is stated that Turkey aims to be a global health centre, as a direct quote increases credibility. In the spotlight, the title is given by opening a little more. The title and spot highlighting Turkey's success in health care emphasize that it will develop globally as well. The title and the spotlight consisted of the words of the President, and it was tried to create a positive image of Turkey's success and future success in the health sector in the eyes of the citizens of other countries. Looking at the photos used in the news, there is a visual of Recep Tayyip Erdoğan making a speech on the podium. It consists of discourses that will create a positive impression about Turkey in the presentation of the main event. The language of expression is simple. In the study, which does not have any background information about the event, has been tried to create an image in the public in the context of public diplomacy by showing Turkey's success in health.

Micro Structure

The sentences in the news are presented with active structure. There is no implicit meaning in the news. The reporter refrained from adding his comments with the direct quotations he used in the news. According to the words of the President, Turkey is also preferred by the citizens of other countries in the field of health. In the news, which states that billions of dollars are transferred by foreign patients, it is tried to ensure that the citizens of other countries trust Turkey's health sector.

2. *Turkey's Defense Minister Hulusi Akar reiterates Ankara's determination to continue fighting against terrorism, saying the country does not accept any terror presence along its borders*

Twitter post, which was chosen as the second in the study, shows the determination of Turkey's defence minister Hulusi Akar on terrorism. Akar said that Ankara reiterated its determination to continue the fight against terrorism and that terrorism can never be accepted within the borders of the country, and the reader's perception is that Turkey is a safe country. The image shared in the Twitter post includes the image of Hulusi Akar and the Turkish flag. This image was used to support the sharing of the defence minister's words. In this Twitter post, as in the other shared post, the follower was directed to TRT World's own web page.

HEADLINE: TURKEY VOWS TO CONTINUE ITS FIGHT AGAINST TERRORISM

Turkish defense Minister Hulusi Akar says Ankara will not hold back from protecting its borders and is ready to act at any time " until the last terrorist is neutralized "

Macro Structure

In the headline of the news, it is emphasized that Turkey takes a stance against terrorism and is determined to do so. According to the news headline and spot that tries to create a positive image for Turkey, it is touted as a safe zone. Turkey's success in the military field, as well as in terms of health, is tried to be demonstrated. The spot consisting of the words of Hulusi Akar, the Minister of Defense of Turkey, provides summary information about the general content of the news. The photo used in the news is the same as the image in the Twitter post. Hulusi Akar's stance in this photograph makes the reader feel his determination on the subject. The presentation of the main event included the words of the Minister of Defense. In general, the creation of the news in the form of direct quotations increases its credibility. In addition, there is no background information in the news.

Micro Structure

The sentences in the news are presented actively and effectively. Among the words and sentences used in the news, "neutralised", and "For us, there is no ethnic, religious, or sectarian discrimination between terrorism and terrorists" draw attention. By trying to convey that there is no discrimination in Turkey, it is shown that everyone from different languages, religions and races is respected. Again, the use of the word "deactivated in case of killing of terrorists" demonstrates Turkey's goodwill.

3. *UN says it will use the name "Turkey" effective immediately after Ankara sent a letter to the international body asking it to drops using " Turkey " in official documents, languages*

TRT World on its Twitter account, it is explained that Turkey has requested the United Nations to change the name of the country to "Turkey". The photo in the post shows the waving of the Turkish flag. It is also seen that the Turkish flag is shown in the news about Turkey in particular. The waving Turkish flag is trying to emphasize the independence of Turkey in a way. Trying to display Turkey's image to the citizens of other countries, TRT World benefits from digitalized public diplomacy while doing this. In this way, positive perceptions are created. As with other posts, this tweet was directed to TRT World's own page.

HEADLINE: UN TO USE 'TURKEY' INSTEAD OF ' TURKEY ' AFTER ANKARA'S REQUEST

UN spokesman Stephane Dujarric says the country's name change became effective, in all foreign languages and documents, from the moment the letter from Ankara was received.

Macro Structure

It has been tried to arouse the curiosity of the reader by deducting the information in the title of the news. It was stated that Ankara applied for such a change by making a name transfer in the title of the news, which states that an application was made from Ankara, the capital of Turkey, to use the Turkish name in all foreign languages and documents. In the spotlight, it was continued as a continuation of the bond. The fact that the letter sent by the authorities in Ankara for exchange is stated as Ankara sent it also shows the emphasis on the capital of the country. In addition, it is stated in the spot that this application is effective. The photograph used in the news also includes the image used on Twitter. The sun and the sky rising above the waving flag show the brightness and independence of the country. UN spokesperson

Stephane at the presentation of the main event Dujarric ‘s words and Turkish Foreign Minister Mevlüt Çavuşoğlu’s statements are included. There is no background information in the news.

Micro Structure

There are active and passive sentences together in the news. Turkish Foreign Minister Mevlüt Çavuşoğlu’s statement about the event was given in quotation marks, increasing credibility. The words chosen for the news are important in the formation of Turkey-oriented perception. The emphasis on the word Turkey makes the name of the country come to the fore. In addition, it was tried to show that the UN was not indifferent to Turkey’s applications in the news text.

4. *Turkey continues defending the rights of its citizens and the Turkish Cypriots ‘ within the framework of its “entrepreneurial and humanitarian foreign policy”, Turkish FM Cavusoglu says*

tweet chosen to be analyzed for the study It is stated that Turkish Foreign Minister Mevlüt Çavuşoğlu said that Turkey continues to defend the rights of its citizens and Turkish Cypriots within the framework of its “entrepreneurial and humanitarian foreign policy”. In the post, which creates a profile of a country that takes care of its own people, there are pictures of Turkish Foreign Minister Mevlüt Çavuşoğlu and the President of the Turkish Republic of Northern Cyprus Ersin Tatar making speeches at the rostrum. Directing its followers to its own page in the last post, TRT World glorifies Turkey in the eyes of the readers with the Tweets it shares.

Title: Impossible for Ankara to neglect rights of TRNC and its people: Cavusoglu

Turkish Foreign Minister Cavusoglu reiterated support for a two-state solution for Cyprus in a visit to Nicosia, capital of the Turkish Republic of Northern cyprus.

Macro Structure

In the last news of the research, it is seen that Mevlüt Çavuşoğlu stated that it is not possible for Ankara to neglect the rights of the TRNC and its people. Spot is a continuation of the title. The title is the Turkish government and the Turkish people, referred to as Ankara by name transfer. It is tried to be shown that Turkey, which is stated to continue to defend the rights of Turkish Cypriots, protects and protects the rights of Turkish citizens. The photo used in the news is the same as the image on Twitter. The images of both Turkish Foreign Minister Mevlüt Çavuşoğlu and President of the Turkish Republic of Northern Cyprus Ersin Tatar inform the reader about who the parties are. The reader, who looks at the photo before the news, will be able to sense what the content of the news is about. While presenting the main event of the news, Mevlüt Çavuşoğlu was made to speak in general. In the presentation of the main event, it is stated that Turkey and the TRNC will maintain positive relations in peace and relations. In the news, which does not have background information, the words of Çavuşoğlu, one of the parties to the incident, are in a way to emphasize peace and unity.

Micro Structure

The sentences in the news are presented with active structure. There is no implicit meaning in the news. In the text, there are word sentences that provide unity and integrity with the TRNC. In the eyes of the reader, Turkey's protective and peaceful attitude towards its neighbouring countries and citizens is displayed. In general, the reporter tried to be objective by not adding his own interpretation of the event. The news text stating that Çavuşoğlu tweeted about the incident shows that social media, which has become an important tool in public diplomacy, is also used by government officials.

CONCLUSION

Digitized Public diplomacy keeping up with the world is seen as an important form of communication for countries in foreign policy in gaining image and prestige. With the invention of Web 2.0, countries conduct their relations on a voluntary basis. In contrast to traditional public diplomacy, there is public diplomacy that prioritizes dialogue by being digitalized. Especially since social media channels have turned the world into a global village, it is an environment preferred by the country's authorities. Power holders, brands, etc., try to influence the people of different regions by developing certain strategies. creates public opinion through digital public diplomacy.

The Role of Social Media in Digitalized Public Diplomacy: An Example of Turkish Image in TRT World's Twitter Accounts", the importance of social media channels in the digitalization of public diplomacy was emphasized, and the Turkish image on display was tried to be shown, based on the posts made by TRT World on Twitter. For this, the shares and comments selected by the purposive sampling method were analyzed by discourse analysis and the reflected Turkish image was revealed. The tweets of the four different TRT World pages analyzed include news about Turkey. It is seen that TRT World redirects to its own web page in each of the analyzed Tweets. In this way, it is ensured that the followers read the whole news. According to the findings obtained from the news analyzed by discourse analysis, TRT World enabled the reader to look at the events with a positive perspective in the news about Turkey. While trying to show how successful Turkey is in the fields of military and health, the news generally made the Ministers and Presidents talk. The credibility of the news is increased, especially with direct quotations. The independence of Turkey, which is shown to the people of other countries with an image that protects and protects its own citizens as a pro-peaceful, was emphasized.

As a result, in the social media, which gained importance with the digitalization of public diplomacy, posts are made to ensure the Turkish image and prestige in the eyes of the citizens of other countries. It is reported that every country is against terrorism, which is an important issue, and has a President who tries to protect his country, homeland and nation from external threats. In the news trying to create a positive image for Turkey, it is touted as a safe zone. Thoughts and behaviours produced based on consent, rather than thoughts imposed by force, are now included in public diplomacy. Public diplomacy, it is tried to reach the goal by influencing the thoughts and behaviours of citizens of other countries on foreign policy issues, with appropriate tools and public relations activities. Thus, it is seen that the governments of countries that try to gain a reputation by managing negative perceptions in the eyes of the people of other countries benefit from digital public diplomacy. By explaining Turkey's own values, views and ideas to the citizens of other countries, the importance of new media and especially social media in establishing positive relations with these countries and providing perception management have been tried to be demonstrated once again with this study, thus contributing to the field.

REFERENCES

Agile, B. S. (2014). *Humanitarian Aid in International Public Relations: Public Diplomacy Dimension*. Institute of Strategic Thinking.

Aydin, A. (2022). *The Effect of Public Diplomacy Practices in Digital Environment on Perceptual Processes: The Example of Digital Natives* [Doctoral Thesis]. Marmara University Institute of Social Sciences.

Bjola, C., & Holmes, M. (2015). *Digital Diplomacy: Theory and Practice*. Routledge. doi:10.4324/9781315730844

Dijk, T. A. (1988). *New Analysis: Case Studies of International and National News in the Press*. Lawrence Erlbaum Associates Publishers.

Ekşi, M. (2014). *Public Diplomacy and Turkish Foreign Policy in the Ak Party Era*. Political Bookstore.

Golan, G. J. (2014). An Integrated Approach to Public Diplomacy. In International Public Relations and Public Diplomacy (pp. 417-440). Peter Lang.

Kemp, S. (2022). *Digital 2022: Another year of bumper growth.* Retrieved from https://wearesocial.com/uk/blog/2022/01/digital-2022-another-year-of-bumper-growth-2/

Leonard, M. (2002). *Public Diplomacy*. Center for Foreign Policy.

Leonard, M., Stead, C., & Smewing, C. (2002). Public Diplomacy. London: The Foreign Policy Center.

Lister, M., Dovey, J., Giddings, S., Grant, L., & Kelly, K. (2009). *New Media: A Critical Introduction*. Routledge.

Mertoglu, S. (2021). *The Genealogy of Views from Paganism to Neo-Paganism: The Rise of Eye Cult in the Age of Social Media*. Ataturk University Press.

Ozer, O. (2015). Critical discourse analysis in the case of Teun Adrian van Dijk. In B. Yıldırım (Ed.), *Methods in Communication Studies* (pp. 197–287). Literaturk.

Pratkanis, A. (2009). Public Diplomacy in International Confilcs. In *PM Nancy Snow, Routledge Handbook of Public Diplomacy* (pp. 111–154). Routledge.

Signitzer, B., & Wamser, C. (2006). Public Diplomacy: A Specific Governmental Public Relations Function. In *Public Relations Theory II* (pp. 435-465). Lawrence Erlbaum.

Signitzer, B., & Coombs, T. (1992). Public Relations and Public Diplomacy: Conceptual Covergences. *Public Relations Review*, *18*(2), 137–147. doi:10.1016/0363-8111(92)90005-J

Szondi, G. (2009). Central and Eastern European Public Diplomacy. In N. S. Taylor (Ed.), *Routledge Handbook of Public Diplomacy* (pp. 292–314). Routledge.

Tiedeman, A. (2004, May 4). *US Public Diplomacy in the Middle East.* Seminar on Geography, Foreign Policy and the World Order.

Tunch, H. N. (1990). *Communicating With the World: US Public Diplomacy Overseas*. St. Martin's Press.

KEY TERMS AND DEFINITIONS

Digital Diplomacy: Digital diplomacy, also referred to as Digiplomacy and eDiplomacy (see below), has been defined as the use of the Internet and new information communication technologies to help achieve diplomatic objectives.

Digitalization: Digitization is the process of converting information into a digital format . In this format, information is organized into discrete units of data (called bit s) that can be separately addressed (usually in multiple-bit groups called byte s). This is the binary data that computers and many devices with computing capacity (such as digital camera s and digital hearing aid s) can process.

Public Diplomacy: In international relations, public diplomacy, or people's diplomacy, broadly speaking, is any of the various government-sponsored efforts aimed at communicating directly with foreign publics to establish a dialogue designed to inform and influence with the aim that this foreign public supports or tolerates a government's strategic objectives.

Social Media: Social media are interactive technologies that facilitate the creation and sharing of information, ideas, interests, and other forms of expression through virtual communities and networks.

TRT World: TRT World is a Turkish public broadcaster international news channel which broadcasts in English 24 hours a day, operated by the Turkish Radio and Television Corporation (TRT) and based in Istanbul. It provides worldwide news and current affairs focusing on Turkey, Europe, Africa, and Western and Southern Asia.

Turkish Image: Image means the general opinion formed in the minds of others about something. The Turkish image also defines the thought patterns formed in the minds of citizens of other countries about Turkey.

Twitter: Twitter is a microblogging and social networking service on which users post and interact with messages known as "tweets", owned by American company Twitter, Inc. Registered users can post, like, and retweet tweets, however, unregistered users have the ability to only read tweets that are publicly available. Users interact with Twitter through browser or mobile frontend software, or programmatically via its APIs. Prior to April 2020, services were accessible via SMS. Tweets were originally restricted to 140 characters, but the limit was doubled to 280 for non-CJK languages in November 2017. Audio and video tweets remain limited to 140 seconds for most accounts.

Chapter 17
An Analysis of Eskisehir Metropolitan Municipality Activities in the Context of Public Diplomacy and City Diplomacy

Yasemin Özçakıl
Ankara Hacı Bayram Veli Üniversitesi, Turkey

ABSTRACT

The process of diplomacy and public diplomacy activities is known as ensuring communication from state to state or from state to public. However, with the global world formed with the increase in technological developments, diplomatic relations have started to be carried out between cities as well as states. The organization of activities to ensure the interests of cities in the international arena and to increase the recognition of their countries is explained as city diplomacy. It carries out activities through local governments and municipal organizations to establish and develop permanent relations between cities and other countries. In this study, the activities carried out by Eskişehir Metropolitan Municipality are examined in the context of public diplomacy and city diplomacy.

INTRODUCTION

Diplomacy is the establishment of peaceful and long-lasting relations with other countries. Over time, diplomacy has become public diplomacy, encompassing issues such as gaining the sympathy of other countries and ensuring the interests of countries against other foreign countries. Public diplomacy is defined as *"influencing people in target countries and controlling them to change their domestic and foreign policies in order to defend countries' foreign policy objectives and national interests"* (Sancar, 2012). Public diplomacy has emerged to establish relations based on goodwill towards countries in order to influence the target public opinion and to create a positive image. City diplomacy, a type of

DOI: 10.4018/978-1-6684-5822-8.ch017

public diplomacy, is explained as organizing activities to ensure the interests and recognition of cities in the international arena. City diplomacy carries out activities through local governments and municipal organizations to establish and develop permanent relations between cities and other countries. With the globalization period in the world, the recognition of some cities has left countries behind. This situation indicates that the importance of cities as well as countries in diplomatic relations has increased. Recognized cities are known as economically developed places with high standards of quality of life. City diplomacy, which is accepted as a type of public diplomacy, is today seen as the diplomatic relations of local governments. Municipalities, which are one of the important institutions of local governments, were first carried out at the national level according to the wishes and needs of the people with the increase in migration to cities as a result of industrialization and the increase in the population living in the city, and this situation has changed in the international context over time with the emergence of technological innovations. This situation has changed over time in the international context with the emergence of technological innovations. Municipalities have carried out activities related to public diplomacy and city diplomacy in order to develop themselves institutionally, and have attached importance to relations with other countries. The aim of this study is to explain the activities of city diplomacy and to examine how diplomacy is carried out through local governments. In the global world, local governments come to the forefront in international politics with their municipal activities, and the activities of Eskişehir Metropolitan Municipality are examined under the sub-headings of city diplomacy.

PUBLIC DIPLOMACY AND CITY DIPLOMACY

Public diplomacy first emerged in the United States during the Cold War. Prof. Edmund Gullion, Dean of the Fletcher School of Law and Diplomacy at Tufts University, addressed it as a scientific subject (Sancar, 2012).

According to Szondi, public diplomacy is defined as the promotion of developed countries' political and ideological views to the citizens and intellectuals of other countries. Through these promotions, developed countries create a public opinion in rival countries that is culturally and ideologically foreign to that country (2008).

Public diplomacy is explained as the implementation of a country's own ideas as a communication process in accordance with the interests of other countries (Doğan, 2012). Although countries that suffered economic and social losses after World War II could not gain economic and military superiority over other countries that entered the war, they attempted to establish a relationship with public diplomacy tools (Erzen, 2012). Public diplomacy application areas are known as non-governmental organizations, international organizations, universities and schools, and municipalities. Public diplomacy is practiced through tools such as traditional and new media and international events. City diplomacy is considered as one of the sub-branches of public diplomacy.

City diplomacy is defined as the implementation of public diplomacy activities at the local level. Cities have started to prioritize diplomatic relations as a result of globalization. Cities that want to be recognized as brand cities have carried out efforts to improve their economic and quality of life, and have benefited from city diplomacy activities to replace conflicts and tensions with other countries with an environment of peace and trust. Turkey, Asia and Africa, North-South America, Europe and many other countries benefit from city diplomacy activities in their relations, country policy understanding and communication activities (Esenler Municipality, n.d.). City diplomacy is a new concept. Unlike public diplomacy, city diplomacy reveals its activities for domestic policy practices. These studies cover all country diplomacy beginning from local diplomacy. City diplomacy carries out the activities of establishing international political, social and economic relations, activities in the field of culture and art, work to improve tourism potential, and the promotion of these values to other countries. These practices are organized by local governments. The main purpose of these practices is to help cities create a positive image and become a brand for foreign countries (Yalçın, 2021).

METHOD

In the theoretical part of the study, a literature review was conducted, and in the practical part, the activities of Eskişehir Metropolitan Municipality and the information obtained from the website and the municipality were examined in accordance with the qualitative content analysis method. Due to the time limitation of the study, the activities of the municipality in 2011, 2015 and 2019 were examined in accordance with qualitative content analysis by randomly spacing four years apart. The activities of Eskişehir Metropolitan Municipality, news from the website and sources obtained from the municipality were analyzed by creating categories such as sister city relations, foreign relations, political, social, culture-arts.

DISCUSSION

Eskişehir took part in the İnönü Wars and Eskişehir-Kütahya battles during the national struggle period and started to develop with industrial investments made during the Republican period. Today, Eskişehir is a city developed in the field of industry with factories established in the field of food, textile, national defense industry. Eskişehir is known as an important city because it is close to cities such as Istanbul and Ankara and is on the transportation route of important developed cities. In addition, Anadolu University and Osmangazi University in the city have created the image of a democratic city with a high number of students, a high level of education and an emphasis on culture and arts. When we look at the political history of Eskişehir, the Republican People's Party and Democratic Party administrations were effective in the administration of the city between 1946 and 1960. Afterwards, Hicri Sezen, İlhan Hakman, Şefik Aktuğlu in 1960 and 1980, and Aydın Arat in 1994, ran for mayor from the True Path Party and won the mayorship (Sarı, 2018). In 1999, Yılmaz Büyükerşen, who ran for the Democratic Left Party, was elected as mayor. In 2019, Büyükerşen, who ran again from the Republican People's Party, was elected as mayor and is still in his position. With these developments, the city has become active in local politics (Bozkurt, 2021). This study aims to investigate the fact that Eskişehir has become a developed city for cultural, artistic and economic reasons through public diplomacy and city diplomacy activities specific to the Metropolitan Municipality. The aim of the study is to explain how the activities of the municipality stand out in international politics in the global world and how this situation affects public diplomacy and city diplomacy. In this study, Eskişehir Metropolitan Municipality has made a name for itself in the international arena with its activities in the fields of culture, arts and sports. It has established communication ties with various countries of the world through sister city relations. The city has been represented in the international arena through municipal activities in the aforementioned fields.

FOREIGN RELATIONS OF THE MUNICIPALITY OF ESKİŞEHİR

Eskişehir Metropolitan Municipality has worked to promote the city with foreign countries and to establish lasting relations with local and international representatives of these countries. The city defines itself as a student city due to the presence of two well-established universities in Eskişehir, Anadolu University and Osmangazi University. According to a news article published on the website of Eskişehir Metropolitan Municipality on March 25, 2011, students from the CIEE (Council on International Education Exchange) student exchange program visited Eskişehir. *"CIEE (Council on International Education Exchange) student exchange programs have brought together students from various parts of the world to create an international and intercultural bridge"* (CIEE Mission, n.d.). According to the news dated April 9, 2015 on the Eskişehir Metropolitan Municipality website, foreign students visited Eskişehir within the scope of the International Youth Cultural Interaction Program between Eskişehir Municipality and Frankfurt Municipality of Germany. Eskişehir and Frankfurt became sister cities in 2013. Through educational programs, Eskişehir Metropolitan Municipality introduced the city to visiting students. Thus, foreign students learned about both Turkish culture and the local culture of Eskişehir. This contributed positively to the development of public diplomacy and city diplomacy. Eskişehir was ranked first in the Student Friendly University Cities category by the University Research Laboratory in 2018, 2019, 2020 (Student Friendly University Cities, 2020).

Eskişehir Metropolitan Municipality received visits from Embassies of various countries. Embassies of 21 different countries visited the municipality between 2015 and 2019. The visits of ambassadors to Eskişehir paved the way for cooperation between countries in the fields of culture, arts, economy and through international events, and enabled the development of city diplomacy (Özçakıl, 2022). Consul General and Ambassadors of the countries visiting Eskişehir Metropolitan Municipality participated in the cultural and artistic activities of the municipality and had the opportunity to get to know the city through these programs. It is reported in the news published on the municipality's website on May 28, 2019 that the Consul General of Croatia attended the *14th International Eskişehir Children and Youth Theaters Festival.* It is reported in the news published on the Municipality's website on 14 May 2019 that the Greek Consul General visited Eskişehir for the concert of Greece's popular artist Alkistis Protopsalti organized by Eskişehir Metropolitan Municipality. The Consulate General and Ambassadors of the countries visiting Eskişehir and getting to know Eskişehir's culture and the activities of the municipality contributed to the city diplomacy activities and facilitated the execution of diplomacy practices.

ESKIŞEHIR MUNICIPALITY'S SISTER CITY RELATIONS

Sister cities are defined as commercial, economic, peace-oriented, cultural, long and deep relationships established with cities, districts or states of different cultures. Eskişehir Metropolitan Municipality has attached importance to sister city relations. Eskişehir Municipality has signed 11 sister city agreements. These are: Tatarstan (Kazan), Linz (Austria), Changzhou (China), Paju (South Korea), Frankfurt (Germany), Saint Jose Ten Noode (Belgium), Kyrenia and Nicosia (Turkish Republic of Northern Cyprus), Cluj Napoca (Romania) (Eskişehir Metropolitan Municipality Sister Cities, n.d.).

Sculpture artists from Paju Province of South Korea took part in the Turkish-Korean Friendship Monument project in Eskişehir City Park (Bizim Şehir, 2007: 15). After the signing of the sister city agreement with Paju, many Korean artists/groups came to Eskişehir and organized events. Guest soloist-

recital- Traditional Korean Music concerts were given in Eskişehir Municipality symphony orchestra and Eskişehir participated in the Traditional Ginseng Festival afterwards.

According to a news article published on EMM's website on March 8, 2015, Mayor of Frankfurt, Feldmann held a meeting with Eskişehir Metropolitan Municipality, businessmen and civil society representatives of the city on cooperation between Eskişehir and Frankfurt. It is seen that Frankfurt and Eskişehir have developed projects for educational, cultural, artistic and economic cooperation with the sister city agreement. According to the news article published on Eskişehir Municipality's web page on March 20, 2015, students from Frankfurt participated in painting workshops organized by the Children's Rights Unit of EMM and visited Eskişehir with city guides. Subsequently, in the news article dated October 14, 2019 on the web page of EMM, it was stated that students from Frankfurt who came with the exchange program visited Eskişehir. In the news dated December 10, 2019 on Eskişehir Metropolitan Municipality's web page, it was stated that the theater play *"Who Came"* was performed together with the actors from Frankfurt and Eskişehir City Theater actors. In 2015 and 2019, Eskişehir Metropolitan Municipality and Frankfurt Municipality hosted students from Frankfurt in Eskişehir with cultural and art activities. With all these events, Eskişehir Metropolitan Municipality has promoted the cultural and social promotion activities to Frankfurt. It is stated in the news article dated August 18, 2019 on Eskişehir Municipality's website that Frankfurt Municipality decorated its trams with Eskişehir's city visuals. The visuals of Eskişehir were seen on the trams by the people of Frankfurt, which aroused the curiosity and recognition of the city by foreigners and led to the development of Eskişehir's concept of city diplomacy. It is stated in the news article published on Eskişehir Municipality's website on August 19, 2019 that a *"Sister Cities Football Tournament"* was organized in Frankfurt and a tournament was organized between Frankfurt football teams *"Tus Makkabi"* and *"Fv Saz-Rock"* and *"Eskişehir Anadolu University Football Team"*. Eskişehir Municipality contributed to city diplomacy by renewing its sister city image with Frankfurt through the football tournament organized in Frankfurt.

According to the news published on the website of Eskişehir Municipality on May 23, 2015, EMM organized a *"Turkish-Korean Friendship Concert"* with the participation of famous South Korean musicians. Culture and arts events were organized to strengthen Eskişehir's relations with its sister city Paju.

Joint international projects developed with sister cities have increased Eskişehir's recognition in foreign countries, thus facilitating the conduct of city diplomacy. Activities in the fields of language, education, culture and arts, as well as lifestyles, ideas, aesthetics and artistic understandings have enabled the development of city diplomacy between cities.

It is reported in the news published on Eskişehir Municipality's website on September 20, 2019 that a *"Green Fitness"* sports event was organized with sister city Kazan. The Green Fitness sports event was conducted in parks such as Kentpark, Sazova Science, Culture and Art Park, Kanlıkavak Park and Dede Korkut Park, thus introducing important touristic areas to Tatarstan. The organization of sports events such as Green Fitness by Kazan Municipality and Frankfurt Municipality's friendship football tournament in Eskişehir has brought Eskişehir to the forefront in countries such as Frankfurt and Tatarstan, thus promoting peace and friendship dialogues and supporting city diplomacy. Permanent relations have been established between cities that are culturally close to each other.

INTERNATIONAL CULTURE, ART AND ORGANIZATION ACTIVITIES OF ESKİŞEHİR MUNICIPALITY

City diplomacy activities are used by cities to reflect and promote their historical and cultural values. It works to carry out city diplomacy activities through subjects such as art, literature, traditions and customs, and the social structure in which they live (Kurtuluş, 2020).

According to the strategic plan of Eskişehir Metropolitan Municipality:

"Eskişehir will continue to be a leading city in Turkey in the field of culture, arts and education, the activities of the City Theaters and Symphony Orchestra will be continued, Eskişehir will be an model city in terms of museology, Eskişehir will be a city of festivals, Eskişehir will be a city of art galleries and exhibitions". In order to create the image that Eskişehir exists with art and artists, Eskişehir Metropolitan Municipality has attached importance to international culture and arts activities and has implemented activities accordingly. Eskişehir was named "Capital of Intangible Cultural Heritage" in 2011 and "Capital of Culture of the Turkic World" in 2013 by UNESCO, and these achievements have contributed positively to its reputation both nationwide and internationally.

Eskişehir Metropolitan Municipality reactivated the city theaters, which had limited stages, in 2001. Stage and culture and arts centers such as Haller Youth Center, Culture and Art Palace, Atatürk Culture, Arts and Congress Center were opened by Eskişehir Metropolitan Municipality (Bozkurt, 2021: 200-201). Eskişehir Metropolitan Municipality has established children and youth drama courses for children to receive theater training. A Traditional Theater Unit was established in 2006 to continue the traditional Turkish theater concept, and courses and trainings were provided (Bizim Şehir, 2006: 13). The municipality also organized the International Eskişehir Children's and Youth Theaters Festival in 2006, which is regularly organized every year by the Eskişehir Municipality City Theater. Theater groups from different countries of the world were hosted by the municipality in Eskişehir. In the news dated May 17, 2011 and May 8, 2019 on the website of Eskişehir Metropolitan Municipality, it was stated that the *"6th International Eskişehir Children's and Youth Theaters Festival"* and the *"14th International Eskişehir Children's and Youth Theaters Festival"* were organized by the City Theaters and that the festival hosted theater groups from Italy, Germany, Spain, the Netherlands, Bulgaria, Czechia, Denmark, Croatia, Italy, the Netherlands, Romania, Russia, Russia, Germany, Austria, Brazil, Bulgaria, Germany, Bulgaria, Czechia, Denmark, Croatia, Italy, the Netherlands, Romania, Russia and different regions of Turkey. Eskişehir Metropolitan Municipality has regularly organized performances with artists from different countries of the world every year. It demonstrates that Eskişehir has created an image that attaches importance to culture and arts by other countries, supports Eskişehir's city diplomacy activities, and cultural diplomacy activities have been developed by introducing the culture of the city to other countries.

Eskişehir Metropolitan Municipality *Symphony Orchestra* organizes many local and foreign concerts in Eskişehir every year. It was renamed Eskişehir Metropolitan Municipality Symphony Orchestra in 2001 and has been organizing concerts with a staff of 60 people (EBB Symphony Orchestra About Us, n.d.). According to the news on the Eskişehir Metropolitan Municipality website, it was reported on December 3, 2015 that artists from Venezuela organized a concert in Eskişehir. On January 17, 2015, it was reported that Eskişehir Metropolitan Municipality hosted a violinist from Sweden as a guest soloist. It was stated that the Swedish Ambassador to Ankara attended the concert. The news article dated January 5, 2019 on the Municipality's website stated that the guest of the Metropolitan Municipality Symphony

Orchestra was accordionist Ladislav Horak. Eskişehir Metropolitan Municipality Symphony Orchestra has contributed to the development of city diplomacy by hosting artists from various countries in Eskişehir.

Eskişehir Metropolitan Municipality organized Opera and Ballet Days in 2011. The news published on the website of Eskişehir Metropolitan Municipality on March 9, 2011 reported that Eskişehir hosted the *"1st National Opera and Ballet Days"* for the first time. In the news dated May 4, 2019 on the website of the Municipality, it was stated that *"9th National Eskişehir Opera and Ballet Days"* were organized and world-famous opera and ballet pieces were introduced to the people of the city. Eskişehir Metropolitan Municipality has attached importance to organizing performances for the development of opera and ballet culture in Eskişehir." Thus, it is seen that city diplomacy activities are not only carried out against other countries and cities, but also promoted to the people of Eskişehir in the field of international culture and arts.

In the news article dated February 28, 2011 on the website of Eskişehir Metropolitan Municipality, it was stated that the Metropolitan Municipality organized *"French Days"* in Eskişehir in cooperation with the French Cultural Center. In the news article dated May 30, 2011 on Eskişehir Metropolitan Municipality's website, it was stated that in cooperation with Eskişehir Municipality and the Italian Embassy in Ankara, the gondola national team from Italy organized a demonstration race with Eskişehir gondoliers in Porsuk. According to the news examples given above, Eskişehir Municipality has organized international events to recognize the culture of various countries and establish good dialogues. It contributed to the formation of city diplomacy.

CONCLUSION

Public diplomacy and city diplomacy appear as studies that are frequently applied in country promotions. Countries carry out their activities through public diplomacy in order to promote themselves in international areas and to take part in international organizations and events. City Diplomacy is defined as the conduct of diplomacy activities by local governments. The conduct of city diplomacy is also linked to culture. It is known that city diplomacy is effective in transferring and promoting the cultures of countries to other countries, bringing the city to the level of developed countries, and improving urban living standards. As a result of the examination, Eskişehir Metropolitan Municipality has carried out important activities in the fields of public diplomacy and city diplomacy.

Eskişehir Metropolitan Municipality has carried out activities such as meetings with embassies and city administrators of various countries, events organized with sister cities, and support from international local governments. Through sister city agreements, Eskişehir Metropolitan Municipality provides cultural recognition, establishing an environment of trust and peace, ensuring investment in the city, and promoting culture, arts and tourism activities with the local governments of other countries. Sister cities create a dialog and build a relationship based on mutual compromise between cities. Examples of ways to create dialogue are international cooperation between sister municipalities, cultural and artistic events, projects supported by international organizations, visits and meetings with political leaders. Eskişehir Metropolitan Municipality has increased the international recognition of the city with its international events in theater, opera, ballet, symphony orchestra concerts, painting and sculpture. The Metropolitan Municipality has worked to create the image of a city that is a pioneer in the field of culture and arts and attaches importance to both art and artists. Eskişehir Metropolitan Municipality has not only brought together the dynamics of different cultures, people from different age groups, business lines, and educational backgrounds with its sister cities, but also created opportunities for different people to get to know each other, contributing to city diplomacy. Eskişehir Metropolitan Municipality organized concerts in the symphony orchestra of artists coming to the city from various countries to ensure the exchange of Turkish culture. Public diplomacy and city diplomacy activities have been developed by promoting Eskişehir and the country through culture and arts festivals such as the International Youth and Children's Theater Festival, International Opera and Ballet Days.

ACKNOWLEDGMENT

This chapter is derived from Y. Özçakıl's (2022) Master's Thesis, "City Diplomacy as a Type of Public Diplomacy: The Case of Eskişehir Metropolitan Municipality," published in Ankara Hacı Bayram Veli University.

REFERENCES

Bozkurt, M. (2021). *A Lifetime That Is the Success Story of Yılmaz Büyükerşen*. Dorlion Publications.

CIEE. (n.d.). *Mission*. https://www.ciee.org/about/what-we-do/ourmission

Erzen, M. (2012). *Public Diplomacy*. Deep Publications.

Eskişehir Metropolitan Municipality. (2015a, April 9). *Foreign Students in Eskişehir Met.* https://www.eskisehir.bel.tr/icerik_dvm.php?icerik_id=1077&cat_icerik=1menu_id=4

Eskişehir Metropolitan Municipality. (2011a, March 25). *USA Students in Eskişehir.* https://www.eskisehir.bel.tr/icerik_dvm.php?icerik_id=169&cat_icerik=1&menu_id4

Eskişehir Metropolitan Municipality. (2019a, May 28). *Visit to Croatia*. https://www.eskisehir.bel.tr/icerik_dvm.php?icerik_id=4832&cat_icerik=1n&menu_id=4

Eskişehir Metropolitan Municipality. (2019b, May 14). *Visit to Greece*. https://www.eskisehir.bel.tr/icerik_dvm.php?icerik_id=4851&cat_icerik=1&menu_id24

Eskişehir Metropolitan Municipality. (2015b, March 8). *From Sister City Frankfurt Cooperation to Eskişehir.* https://www.eskisehir.bel.tr/icerik_dvm.php?icerik_id=1075&cat_icrik=1&menu_id24

Eskişehir Metropolitan Municipality. (2015c, March 20). *Frankfurt Children with Pictures They Told Us about Eskişehir.* https://www.eskisehir.bel.tr/icerik_dvm.php?icerik_id=1102&cat_ierik=1&menu_id24

Eskişehir Metropolitan Municipality. (2019c, August 18). *Eskişehir Visuals Decorated the, Frankfurt underground.* https://www.eskisehir.bel.tr/icerik_dvm.php?icerik_id=4988&cat_icerik=1&menu_id=24

Eskişehir Metropolitan Municipality. (2015d, May 23). *At the Turkish Korean Friendship Concert World Premiere Was Held*. https://www.eskisehir.bel.tr/icerik_dvm.php?icerik_id=1177&cat_icrik=1menu_id=24

Eskişehir Metropolitan Municipality. (2011b, May 17). *Children's Theater Festival Great Start.* https://www.eskisehir.bel.tr/icerik_dvm.php?icerik_id=196&cat_icerik=1&menu_id24

Eskişehir Metropolitan Municipality. (2019d, May 8). *14th Anniversary of the Children's Festival Record of the Year Participation.* https://www.eskisehir.bel.tr/icerik_dvm.php?icerik_id=4770&cat_icerik=1&menu_id=24

Eskişehir Metropolitan Municipality. (2015e, December 3). *Venezuelan Jazz Night in Eskişehir.* https://www.eskisehir.bel.tr/icerik_dvm.php?icerik_id=1524&cat_icerik=1&menu_id=4

Eskişehir Metropolitan Municipality. (2015f, January 17). *Swedish Wind at the Symphony Ambassador: I am Always Glad to Come to Eskişehir.* https://www.eskisehir.bel.tr/icerik_dvm.php?icerik_id=936&cat_icerik=1&menu_id24

Eskişehir Metropolitan Municipality. (2019e, January 5). *Music Banquet from the famous Akerdeon Artist.* https://www.eskisehir.bel.tr/icerik_dvm.php?icerik_id=4453&cat_icerik=1&menu_id=4

Eskişehir Metropolitan Municipality. (2011c, March 9). *Turkey's First Opera and Ballet Days in Eskişehir the City of Culture and Arts.* https://www.eskisehir.bel.tr/icerik_dvm.php?icerik_id=162&cat_icerik=1&menu_id24

Eskişehir Metropolitan Municipality. (2019f, May 4). *9.National Eskişehir Opera and Ballet Days Start.* https://www.eskisehir.bel.tr/icerik_dvm.php?icerik_id=4756&cat_icerik=1&menu_i4

Eskişehir Metropolitan Municipality. (2011d, February 28). *French Days in Eskişehir.* https://www.eskisehir.bel.tr/icerik_dvm.php?icerik_id=157&cat_icerik=1&menu_id24

Eskişehir Metropolitan Municipality. (2011e, May 30). *Italian Gondoliers in Eskişehir.* https://www.eskisehir.bel.tr/icerik_dvm.php?icerik_id=203&cat_icerik=1&menu_id24

Kurtuluş, F. (2020). *City Diplomacy; The Increasing Importance of Cities in International Politics and a Case Study of the Istanbul Metropolitan Municipality* [Master's Thesis]. Arel University.

Municipality, E. M. (2006). Article. *Bizim Şehir Newspaper*, (13), 13.

Municipality, E. M. (2007). Article. *Bizim Şehir Newspaper*, (15), 14–15.

Ozçakıl, Y. (2022). *Urban Diplomacy as a Type of Public Diplomacy The Case of Eskişehir Metropolitan Municipality* [Master's Thesis]. Ankara Hacı Bayram Veli University.

Ozkan, A., & Öztürk, T. (Eds.). (2012). *On the opportunities and constraints offered by Public Diplomacy: Public Diplomacy.* Tasam Publications.

Sancar, A. (2012). *Public Diplomacy and International Public Relations.* Beta Publications.

Sarı, Ç. (2019). *Political Life in Eskişehir (1946-1960)* [Master's Thesis]. Marmara University.

Sizoo, A., & Musch, A. (2008). *City Diplomacy.* https://www.uclg.org/sites/default/files/City_Diplomacy_research_book_English_01.pdf

The Metropolitan Municipality of Eskişehir. (n.d.). *Sister Cities.* https://www.eskisehir.bel.tr/kardes-sehirler

The Municipality of Esenler. (n.d.). *Global City Diplomacy Access*. http://www.sehirdusunce.com/atolye/30/kuresel-kent-diplomasis

University Research Laboratory. (2020). *Student Friendly University Cities*. https://www.uniar.net/_files/ugd/779fe1_1a79aa7ad5a64a2aa81f732d1ad092b0.pdf

Yalçın, E. (2021). *Encyclopedia of Public Administration*. Astana Publications.

KEY TERMS AND DEFINITIONS

City Diplomacy: City diplomacy refers to cities using institutions and processes to engage relations with other actors on an international stage, with the aim of representing themselves and their interests to one another. Especially today, city administrations and networks are increasingly active in the realm of transnationally relevant questions and issues ranging from the climate crisis to migration and the promotion of smart technology. As such, cities and city networks may seek to address and re-shape national and sub-national conflicts, support their peers in the achievement of sustainable development, and achieve certain levels of regional integration and solidarity among each other. Whereas diplomacy pursued by nation-states is often said to be disconnected from the citizenry, city diplomacy fundamentally rests on its proximity to the latter and seeks to leverage these ties "to build international strategies integrating both their values and interests."

Eskişehir Metropolitan Municipality: It is the public institution responsible for the execution of municipal affairs within the metropolitan borders of Eskişehir. Eskişehir became Metropolitan in 1993.

Municipalism: Local governments established in settlements with a population of more than 5 thousand are defined as municipalities. They are organizations with legal personality, in which managers elected by the votes of the people of the town serve in order to solve the problems of the town and provide some services. Municipalism is the political system of home rule at the local level, such as of a city or town, thus a municipality with its own governing authority as an administrative division of a sovereign state. Municipalism is more than simple support for municipalities in that it supports the primacy of municipalities as a means of enacting political change locally, and by extension grassroots movements to enact political change at higher levels of government. It is an approach to implementing social change which focuses on using the municipality as the vehicle for implementing change. Although, as an approach, it has been adopted by such diverse political groupings as Catholics, Protestants, liberals, Marxists, and anarchists, it emerged in Europe as something which developed in the socialist parties. In 1881 the Federation of the Socialist Workers of France (a predecessor of the modern French Socialist Party) won control of Commentry. In subsequent municipal elections, socialist candidates and parties increased the number of municipalities they controlled to 70 in 1892, and then over 100 in 1896. Meanwhile, in Italy, changes in electoral laws enabled the Italian Socialist Party to gain its first municipality, Imola, under the leadership of Andrea Costa.

Political Communication: It is defined as the transmission of messages with political content to the source through communication studies.It deals with the production, dissemination, procession and effects of information, both through mass media and interpersonally, within a political context. This includes the study of the media, the analysis of speeches by politicians, those that are trying to influence the political process, and the formal and informal conversations among members of the public, among other aspects.

The media acts as a bridge between government and public. Political communication can be defined as the connection concerning politics and citizens and the interaction modes that connect these groups to each other. Whether the relationship is formed by the modes of persuasion, Pathos, Ethos or Logos.

Public Diplomacy: Public diplomacy, deals with the influence of public attitudes on the formation and execution of foreign policies. It encompasses dimensions of international relations beyond traditional diplomacy; the cultivation by governments of public opinion in other countries; the interaction of private groups and interests in one country with another; the reporting of foreign affairs and its impact on policy; communication between those whose job is communication, as diplomats and foreign correspondents; and the process of intercultural communications.

Public Relations: Public relations (PR) are the practice of managing and disseminating information from an individual or an organization (such as a business, government agency, or a nonprofit organization) to the public in order to influence their perception. Public relations and publicity differ in that PR is controlled internally, whereas publicity is not controlled and contributed by external parties. Public relations may include an organization or individual gaining exposure to their audiences using topics of public interest and news items that do not require direct payment. The exposure mostly is media-based. This differentiates it from advertising as a form of marketing communications. Public relations aims to create or obtain coverage for clients for free, also known as earned media, rather than paying for marketing or advertising also known as paid media. But in the early 21st century, advertising is also a part of broader PR activities. Public relations specialists establish and maintain relationships with an organization's target audience, the media, relevant trade media, and other opinion leaders. Common responsibilities include designing communications campaigns, writing press releases and other content for news, working with the press, arranging interviews for company spokespeople, writing speeches for company leaders, acting as an organization's spokesperson, preparing clients for press conferences, media interviews and speeches, writing website and social media content, managing company reputation (crisis management), managing internal communications, and marketing activities like brand awareness and event management. Success in the field of public relations requires a deep understanding of the interests and concerns of each of the company's many stakeholders. The public relations professional must know how to effectively address those concerns using the most powerful tool of the public relations trade, which is publicity.

Compilation of References

AB'den Türkiye'ye bir yıl süre. (2021). https://www.milliyet.com.tr/dunya/ab-den-turkiye-ye-bir-yil-sure-2441174

Abbasov, A. (2007). *Digital Diplomacy: Embedding Information and Communication Technologies in the Department of Foreign Affairs and Trade*. Australian National University.

Abdurahmanli & Bagis. (2021). Definition of Diplomacy and Types of Diplomacy Available in the International Conjuncture. *Anadolu Academy Journal of Social Sciences*, 141-160.

Abdurahmanlı, E., & Bagis, E. (2021). Definition of Diplomacy and Types of Diplomacy Available in the International Conjuncture. *Anadolu Academy Journal of Social Sciences*, *3*(1), 140–160.

Acar, D. Ş. (2006). Küreselleşen dünyada diploması. *Journal of Selçuk University Social Sciences Vocational School*, *9*(1-2), 417–440.

Adesina, O. S. (2017). Foreign policy in an era of digital diplomacy. *Cogent Social Sciences*, *3*(1), 113. doi:10.1080/23311886.2017.1297175

Adhikari, D. (2016). The Role of Media in Shaping Foreign Policy Discourse in Nepal. In P. Singh (Ed.), *The Role of Media in Promoting Regional Understanding in South Asia* (pp. 209–218). Pentagon Press.

Agile, B. S. (2014). *Humanitarian Aid in International Public Relations: Public Diplomacy Dimension*. Institute of Strategic Thinking.

Akçadağ, E. (2010). *Dünya'da ve Türkiye'de Kamu Diplomasisi*. https://www.kamudiplomasisi.org/makaleler

Akçadağ, E. (2022). *Dűnya'da Ve Tűrkiye'de Kamu Diplomasisi*. Retrieved from Kamu Diplomasisi Web Sitesi: http://www.kamudiplomasisi.org/pdf/emineakcadag.pdf

Akdoğan, I. (2014). *Dijital politik fanteziler*. İletişim Publishing.

Akgün, B. (2009). Türk Dış Politikası ve Uluslararası Örgütler. *Akademik Orta Doğu, 3*(2).

Akgür, Z. G. (1997). *Migration from Rural Areas to Urban Areas and Imbalances between Regions in Turkey*. T.C. Ministry of Culture Publications, Prime Ministry Press Office.

Aktaş, A. (2021). *Tika's Studies in Kyrgyzstan as a Humanitarian Diplomacy Tool in the Context of Public Relations* [doctoral dissertation]. Kyrgyz-Turkish Manas University Institute of Social Sciences, Department of Communication Sciences.

Alankuş, S., & Yanardağoğlu, E. (2016). Vacillation in Turkey's popular global TV exports: Toward a more complex understanding of distrubution. *International Journal of Communication*, *10*(17), 3615–3631.

Al-Ghazzi, O., & Kraidy, M. (2013). Neo-Ottoman cool 2: Turkish nation branding and Arabic-Language transnational broadcasting. *International Journal of Communication*, *7*, 2341–2360.

Anaz, N. (2014). The geography of reception: Why do Egytptians watch Turkish soap operas. *Arab World Geographer*, *17*(3), 255–274.

Anaz, N., & Ozcan, C. C. (2016). Geography of Turkish soap operas: Tourism, soft power, and alternative narratives. In I. Egresi (Ed.), *Alternative Tourism inTurkey: Role, Potential Development and Sustainability* (pp. 247–259). Springer. doi:10.1007/978-3-319-47537-0_15

Anderson, M. S. (1993). *The Rise of Modern Diplomacy*. Longman Press.

Apuke, O. D., & Tunca, E. A. (2018). Social media and crisis management: A review and analysis of existing studies. *EUL Journal of Social Sciences*, *9*(2), 199–215.

Archetti, C. (2010). Media impact on diplomatic practice: An evolutionary model of change. *American Political Science Association (APSA) Annual Convention.*

Arıkan, H. (2006). Turkey and the EU: An Awkward Candidate for EU Membership. Ashgate.

Arısoy, C. (2016). Turkish series: Products of popular culture and tools for inclusive globalization. *Online Journal of Communication and Media Technologies*, *6*(1), 129–142. doi:10.29333/ojcmt/2543

Armstrong, M. (2009). Social Media as Public Diplomacy. *Perspectives*, *1*(2).

Artunç, R. T. (2021). Ad Hoc Diplomasi (Ad Hoc Diplomacy). In M. Güneş (Ed.), *Diplomasi Kavramları Sözlüğü* (pp. 22–24). SDE Publications.

Aslan, P., & Göksu, O. (2016). Digital Diplomacy, Global Perception and Turkey. *14th International Symposium Communication in the Millennium*, 573-590.

Avrupa Birliği ve Dış İlişkiler Genel Müdürlüğü. (n.d.). *IPA*. https://www.ipa.gov.tr/IPA_1070

Avrupa Komisyonu. (2016). *AB Genişleme Politikasına İlişkin 2016 Bildirimi*. Brüksel.

Ayata, B. (2014). Turkish foreign policy in a changing Arab World: Rise and fall of a regional actor? *journal of European Integration*, *37*(1), 95–112. doi:10.1080/07036337.2014.975991

Aydemir, E. (2005). Uluslararası krizlerde kriz iletişimi ve uygulaması. *Sosyal Ekonomik Araştırmalar Dergisi*, *5*(10), 204–231.

Aydin, A. (2022). *The Effect of Public Diplomacy Practices in Digital Environment on Perceptual Processes: The Example of Digital Natives* [Doctoral Thesis]. Marmara University Institute of Social Sciences.

Aydoğan, B., & Aydın, H. (2011). Güç Kavramı, Kamu Diplomasisi ve Güvenlik. *Ekopolitik*, *11*(2), 13.

Aytürk, İ., & Esen, B. (2022). *Post-Post Kemalizm / Türkiye çalışmalarında yeni arayışlar*. İletişim.

Aziz, A. (2010). Sosyal Bilimlerde Araştırma Yöntemleri ve Teknikleri (5. ed.). İstanbul: Nobel.

Aziz, A. (2011). *Siyasal İletişim*. Nobel Yayınları.

Baç, M.M. (2001). *Türkiye ve Avrupa Birliği; Soğuk Savaş sonrası İlişkiler*. İstanbul: Alfa yayınları.

Baç, M. M. (2005). Turkey's Political Reforms and the Impact of the European Union. *South European Society & Politics*, *10*(1), 17–31. doi:10.1080/13608740500037916

Baker, C. (2006). *Zorunlu Eğitime Hayır* (A. G. Sönmezoğlu, Trans.). Ayrıntı Publishing.

Baker, L. M. (2006, Summer). Observation: A Complex Research Method. *Library Trends, 55*(1), 171–189. doi:10.1353/lib.2006.0045

Baldwin, D. A. (1997). The concept of security. *Review of International Studies, 23*(1), 5–26. doi:10.1017/S0260210597000053 PMID:10164688

Balzacq, T. (2005). The Three Faces of Securitization: Political Agency, Audience and Context. *European Journal of International Relations, 11*(2), 171–201. doi:10.1177/1354066105052960

Başak, C. (2011). *Refugees, Asylum Seekers and Illegal Migrants.* Republic of Turkey Ministry of Interior Publication.

Baştan, Y., & Karagül, S. (2021). Diplomasinin dönüşümü ve dijital diplomasi. *TroyAcademy International Journal of Social Sciences, 6*(3), 777–803.

Bauman, Z. (1999). *Sosyolojik Düşünmek* (A. Yılmaz, Trans.). Ayrıntı Publishing.

Baykasoğlu, A., Dereli, T., Sönmez, A. İ., & Yağcı, E. (2004). İmaj Yönetimi. *Journal of the Social Sciences, 1*(1), 3–18.

Baylis, J., & Smith, S. (Eds.). (2006). *The globalization of world politics.* Oxford University Press.

BBC Türkçe. (2021). Retrieved from https://www.bbc.com/turkce/haberler-turkiye-59223909#:~:text=Netflix'te%206%20b%C3%B6l%C3%BCm%20olarak,kendi%20ifadeleriyle%20%22g%C3%B6r%C3%BCn%C3%BCr%22%20oldu

Becker, G. S. (1983). A Theory of Competition Among Pressure Groups for Political Influence. *The Quarterly Journal of Economics, 98*(3), 371–400. doi:10.2307/1886017

Bektaş, A. (1996). *Public opinion, communication and democracy.* Bağlam Publishing.

Bektaş, A. (2002). *Political propaganda.* Bağlam Publishing.

Bennett, W. L. (2000). *Politik İlüzyon ve Medya* (S. Say, Trans.). Nehir Publishing.

Berg, M. (2017). Turkish drama serials as a Tool for soft power. *Participation Journal of Audience and Perception Studies, 14*(2), 32–52.

Berg, M. (2020). Turkish drama serials and Arab audiences: Why Turkish serials are succesfull in the Arab World. In Y. Kaptan & E. Algan (Eds.), *Television in Turkey* (pp. 223–244). Palgrave Macmillan. doi:10.1007/978-3-030-46051-8_12

Berridge, G. R., & James, A. (2003). *A Dictionary of Diplomacy.* Palgrave Macmillan. doi:10.1057/9780230501348

Bilgin, P., & Elis, B. (2008). Hard Power, Soft Power: Toward a More Realistic Power Analysis. *Insight Turkey, 10*(2), 5–20.

Bjola, C., & Holmes, M. (Eds.). (2015). *Digital diplomacy theory and practice.* Routledge. doi:10.4324/9781315730844

Bjola, C., & Manor, I. (2022). The rise of hybrid diplomacy: From digital adaptation to digital adoption. *International Affairs, 98*(2), 471–491. doi:10.1093/ia/iiac005

Boin, A. (2009). The new world of crises and crisis management: Implications for policymaking and research. *The Review of Policy Research, 26*(4), 367–377. doi:10.1111/j.1541-1338.2009.00389.x

Boin, A., Hart, P., Stern, E., & Sundelius, B. (2005). *The politics of crisis management: public leadership under pressure.* Cambridge University Press. doi:10.1017/CBO9780511490880

Bostancı, M. (2012). *Kamu Diplomasisinde Medyanın Rolü ve Önemi - Stratejik Bir İletişim Aracı Olarak Kamu Diplomasisi.* Anahtar Books.

Bostancı, M. (2012). *Stratejik Bir İletişim Aracı Olarak Kamu Diplomasisi - Kamu Diplomasisinde Medyanın Rolü ve Önemi*. Anahtar Kitaplar.

Bozkurt, M. (2021). *A Lifetime That Is the Success Story of Yılmaz Büyükerşen*. Dorlion Publications.

Broadhurst, A. I., & Ledgerwood, G. (1998). Environmental Diplomacy of States, Corporations and Non-Governmental Organizations: The Worldwide Web of Influence. *International Relations, 14*(2), 1–19. doi:10.1177/004711789801400201

Brown, J. A. C. (2000). Beyin Yıkama. İstanbul: Boğaziçi Yayınları.

Bruce, S., & Yearley, S. (2006). *The Sage Dictionary of Sociology*. Sage Publications. doi:10.4135/9781446279137

Buccianti, A. (2010). Dubbed Turkish soap operas conquering the Arab World: Social liberation or cultural alienation? *Arab Media & Society, 3*, 1–7.

Buck, R. C. (1993). *International crisis and conflict*. Martin's Press.

Budak, M. M. (2022). Kamu diplomasisi ve dijital iletişim. *Erciyes İletişim Dergisi, 9*(1), 317–335. doi:10.17680/erciyesiletisim.997103

Bull, H. (1997). *The Anarchical Society: A Study of Order in World Politics*. Macmillan.

Bulut, Y., & Bimay, M. (2020). In Y. B. Akin (Ed.), *The Problem of Migration And Refugees With Local, National And Global Dimensions* (pp. 9–33). Çizgi Publishing House.

Buzan, B. (1991). New patterns of global security in the twenty-first century. *International Affairs, 67*(3), 439–451. doi:10.2307/2621945

Buzan, B., Weaver, O., & De Wilde, J. (1998). *Security: a framework analysis*. Lynne Rienner Publishers.

Caglar, A. (2019). *Power: Hard Power, Soft Power and Smart Power*. http://www.alicaglar.net: Retrieved from http://www.alicaglar.net.tr/StaticFiles/file/guc-sert-yumusak-ve-akilli-guc.pdf

Çakır, M. (2014). Küresel Şirketlerin Yeni MedyaOdaklı Tüketim ve Tüketici Tasarımları. In S. Çakır (Ed.), *Medya ve Tasarım* (pp. 163–196). Urzeni.

Çalışır, G. (2014). *Siyaset ve İletişim Bağlamında Kitle İletişim Araçları Üzerine Bir Değerlendirme* (M. Tosun & N. Yılmaz, Eds.). Değişim Publishing.

Carelli, P. (2015). Pan-Arabism through television: Arab TV series between national identities and transnational media. *Communicazioni Sociali, 2*, 218–229.

Carney, J. (2018). Resur(e)recting as spectacular hero: Diriliş Ertuğrul, necropolitics, and popular culture in Turkey. *Review of Middle East Studies, 52*(1), 93–114. doi:10.1017/rms.2018.6

Cassidy, J. (2018). *Digital diplomatic crisis communication: reconceptualising diplomatic signalling in an age of real time governance*. Working Paper No 3. Oxford Digital Diplomacy Research Group. Retrieved June 15, 2022, from https://www.qeh.ox.ac.uk/sites/www.odid.ox.ac.uk/files/DigDiploROxWP3.pdf

Castells, M. (2008). *Enformasyon Çağı: Ekonomi, Toplum ve Kültür: Ağ Toplumunun Yükselişi*. İstanbul: Publications of Bilgi University.

Cerami, C. (2021). Rethinking Turkey's soft power in the Arab World: Islam, secularism and democracy. *Journal of Levantine Studies, 3*(2), 129–150.

Cercel, M., & Saftescu, R. (2018). Digital diplomacy-perspectives and impact traditional diplomatic practices-case study: Digitization impact on Romanian and Belgian national diplomatic systems. *International Journal of Social Sciences and Education Research, 1*(2), 318–328. doi:10.24289/ijsser.106416

Cevher, E. (2015). Kamu üniversiteleri web sayfalarının kullanılabilirliğinin içerik analizi ile incelenmesi. *Gaziantep University Journal of Social Sciences, 14*(2), 387-402.

Çevik, S. B. (2019). Turkish historical television series: Public broadcasting of Neo-Ottoman illusions. *Southeast European and Black Sea Studies, 19*(2), 227–242. doi:10.1080/14683857.2019.1622288

Ceyhan, A. İ. (2020). Dijitalleşen Kamu Diplomasisi Üzerine Kısa Bir Analiz. *International Journal of Economics Administrative and Social Sciences, 3*(2), 85–100.

Christin, A. (2018). Counting Clicks: Quantification and Variation in Web Journalism in the United States and France. *American Journal of Sociology, 123*(5), 1382–1415. Advance online publication. doi:10.1086/696137

CIEE. (n.d.). *Mission.* https://www.ciee.org/about/what-we-do/ourmission

Çıtak, E. (2019a). Değişen güvenlik anlayışında savaş ve barış. In E. Çıtak & S. Kiraz (Eds.), *Uluslararası İlişkiler Kuramlarında Savaş ve Barış* (pp. 39–62). Orion.

Çıtak, E. (2019b). Silahsız savaş sahası: Yeni savaş anlayışında istihbaratın yeri. *Güvenlik Bilimleri Dergisi, 8*(2), 191–213. doi:10.28956/gbd.646263

Clinton, D. (2016). Diplomacy and International Law. In C. M. Constantinou, P. Kerr, & P. Sharp (Eds.), The SAGE Handbook of Diplomacy (pp. 185-196). SAGE Publications. doi:10.4135/9781473957930.n16

Çomu, T., & Halaiqa, İ. (2014). Web İçeriklerinin Metin Temelli Çözümlenmesi. In M. Binark (Ed.), *Yeni Medya Çalışmalarında Araştırma Yöntem ve Teknikleri* (pp. 27–87). Ayrıntı Publications.

Connoly-Ahern, C., & Ma, L. (2015). Taking It to the Streets: The Evolving Use of VNRs as a Public Diplomacy Tool in the Digital Age. In G. J. Golan (Ed.), *International Public Relations and Public Diplomacy* (pp. 229–244). Peter Lang Publishing.

Conserva, H. (2009). *Propaganda: a question and answer approach.* AuthorHouse.

Coombs, W. T., & Holladay, S. J. (2008). Comparing apology to equivalent crisis response strategies: Clarifying apology's role and value in crisis communication. *Public Relations Review, 34*(3), 252–257. doi:10.1016/j.pubrev.2008.04.001

Cooper, R. (2004). Hard Power, Soft Power and the Goals of Diplomacy. In D. Held & M. Koenig-Archibugi (Eds.), *American Power in the 21st Century* (pp. 167–180). Polity Press.

Corbin, J., & Strauss, A. (1990). Grounded Theory Research: Procedures, Canons, and Evaluative Criteria. *Qualitative Sociology, 13*(1), 3–21. doi:10.1007/BF00988593

Costantinou, C. M. (1996). *On the Way to Diplomacy.* University of Minnesota Press.

Cowan, G., & Arsenault, A. (2008). Moving From Monologue to Dialogue to Collaboration: The Three Layers of Public Diplomacy. *The Annals of the American Academy of Political and Social Science, 616*(10), 6–10. doi:10.1177/0002716207312143

Cull, N. J. (2006), *Public diplomacy before gullion: the evolution of a phrase.* Retrieved July 26, 2022, from https://www.uscpublicdiplomacy.org/blog/public-diplomacy-gullion-evolution-phrase

Cull, N. (2009). *Public Diplomacy: Lessons From the Past.* Figueroa Press.

Cull, N. J. (2003). Public diplomacy. In N. J. Cull, D. H. Culbert, & D. Welch (Eds.), *Propaganda and mass persuasion: a historical encyclopedia. 1500 to the present* (p. 327). ABC-CLIO, Inc.

Cull, N. J. (2009). Public diplomacy before gullion: the evolution of a phrase. In N. Snow & P. M. Taylor (Eds.), *Routledge handbook of public diplomacy* (pp. 19–23). Routledge.

Cull, N. J. (2009). *Public Diplomacy: Lessons from the Past*. Figueroa Press.

De Gouveia, P. F., & Plumridge, H. (2005). *European Infopolitik: Developing EU Public Diplomacy Strategy*. The Foreign Policy Centre.

Demirkol, F. (2020). Operation Peace Spring in the Context of Public Diplomacy. Bartın University Faculty of Economics and Administrative Sciences Journal, 11(21).

Derneği, M. (2022). *Number of Syrians in Turkey August 2022*. https://multeciler.org.tr/turkiyedeki-suriyelisayisi/#:~:text=T%C3%BCrkiye'de%20kay%C4%B1t%20alt%C4%B1na%20al%C4%B1nm%C4%B1%C5%9F,652%20bin%20813%20ki%C5%9Fi%20oldu

Dijk, T. A. (1988). *New Analysis: Case Studies of International and National News in the Press*. Lawrence Erlbaum Associates Publishers.

Dinçer, M. K. (1998). *Kişisel İmaj*. Alfa Publishing.

diplomacy data. (2022). *History of Digital Diplomacy and Main Milestones*. Retrieved April 3, 2022, from http://diplomacydata.com/history-of-digital-diplomacy-and-main-milestones/

Dixit, K. (2010, February). *Nepal's media brave threats in 'interesting times'*. Retrieved from Committee to Protect Journalists: https://cpj.org/2010/02/nepals-media-brave-threats-in-interesting-times/

Doğan, E. (2012). Kamu Diplomasisinin Sunduğu Fırsatlar ve Kısıtları Üzerine. In A. Özkan & T. E. Öztürk (Eds.), *Kamu Diplomasisi Enstitüsü Serisi: 1* (pp. 13–30). TASAM Publications.

Dogan, M. (2013). *Digital Communication and New Media*. Anadolu University.

Domenach, J. (1995). *Politics and Propaganda*. Varlık Publishing.

Dönmez, E., & Kırık, A. M. (2019). Yeni Medya ile Değişen Televizyon Yayıncılığında İçerik Üretimi: Küresel ve Yerel Ölçekli Platformlar. In Ü. Üniversitesi (Ed.), 6. Uluslararası İletişim Günleri Dijital Dönüşüm Sempozyumu (pp. 182-206). Academic Press.

Efegil, E. (2018). *Türk Dış Politikası ve Kamu Diplomasisi*. Kamu Diplomasisi Enstitüsü. https://www.kamudiplomasisi.org/makaleler/makaleler/94-tuerk-di-poltkasi-ve-kamu-dplomass

Ekşi, M. (2014). *Public Diplomacy and Turkish Foreign Policy in the Ak Party Era*. Political Bookstore.

Ekşi, M. (2016). Türk Dış Politikasında Diplomasinin Yeni İletişimsel Boyutları ve Mekanizmaları: Dijital Diplomasi. In B. S. Cankurtaran (Ed.), *Uluslararası İlişkilere Disiplinlerarası Bir Yaklaşım: Uluslararası İletişim Perspektifi* (pp. 75–92). Röle Akademik Yayıncılık.

Emre-Çetin, K. B. (2014). The 'politicization' of Turkish television dramas. *International Journal of Communication, 8*, 2462–2483.

Eralp, A. (2009). The Role of Temporality and Interaction in the Turkey-EU Relationship. *New Perspectives on Turkey, 40*, 152. doi:10.1017/S0896634600005252

Erdoğan, İ. (2012). Pozitivis Metodoloji ve Ötesi (5. ed.). Ankara: Erk.

Erkazancı-Durmuş, H. (2016). The representation of Turkey through narrative framing-Saudi Arabian and Turkish Newspapers' coverage of the Arabic dubbed Turkish series noor. *Moment Dergi. Sinema ve Politika*, *3*(2), 483–507. doi:10.17572/mj2016.2.483507

Eskişehir Metropolitan Municipality. (2011a, March 25). *USA Students in Eskişehir.* https://www.eskisehir.bel.tr/icerik_dvm.php?icerik_id=169&cat_icerik=1&menu_id4

Eskişehir Metropolitan Municipality. (2011b, May 17). *Children's Theater Festival Great Start.* https://www.eskisehir.bel.tr/icerik_dvm.php?icerik_id=196&cat_icerik=1&menu_id24

Eskişehir Metropolitan Municipality. (2011c, March 9). *Turkey's First Opera and Ballet Days in Eskişehir the City of Culture and Arts.* https://www.eskisehir.bel.tr/icerik_dvm.php?icerik_id=162&cat_icerik=1&menu_id24

Eskişehir Metropolitan Municipality. (2011d, February 28). *French Days in Eskişehir.* https://www.eskisehir.bel.tr/icerik_dvm.php?icerik_id=157&cat_icerik=1&menu_id24

Eskişehir Metropolitan Municipality. (2011e, May 30). *Italian Gondoliers in Eskişehir.* https://www.eskisehir.bel.tr/icerik_dvm.php?icerik_id=203&cat_icerik=1&menu_id24

Eskişehir Metropolitan Municipality. (2015a, April 9). *Foreign Students in Eskişehir Met.* https://www.eskisehir.bel.tr/icerik_dvm.php?icerik_id=1077&cat_icerik=1menu_id=4

Eskişehir Metropolitan Municipality. (2015b, March 8). *From Sister City Frankfurt Cooperation to Eskişehir.* https://www.eskisehir.bel.tr/icerik_dvm.php?icerik_id=1075&cat_icrik=1&menu_id24

Eskişehir Metropolitan Municipality. (2015c, March 20). *Frankfurt Children with Pictures They Told Us about Eskişehir.* https://www.eskisehir.bel.tr/icerik_dvm.php?icerik_id=1102&cat_ierik=1&menu_id24

Eskişehir Metropolitan Municipality. (2015d, May 23). *At the Turkish Korean Friendship Concert World Premiere Was Held.* https://www.eskisehir.bel.tr/icerik_dvm.php?icerik_id=1177&cat_icrik=1menu_id=24

Eskişehir Metropolitan Municipality. (2015e, December 3). *Venezuelan Jazz Night in Eskişehir.* https://www.eskisehir.bel.tr/icerik_dvm.php?icerik_id=1524&cat_icerik=1&menu_id=4

Eskişehir Metropolitan Municipality. (2015f, January 17). *Swedish Wind at the Symphony Ambassador: I am Always Glad to Come to Eskişehir.* https://www.eskisehir.bel.tr/icerik_dvm.php?icerik_id=936&cat_icerik=1&menu_id24

Eskişehir Metropolitan Municipality. (2019a, May 28). *Visit to Croatia.* https://www.eskisehir.bel.tr/icerik_dvm.php?icerik_id=4832&cat_icerik=1n&menu_id=4

Eskişehir Metropolitan Municipality. (2019b, May 14). *Visit to Greece.* https://www.eskisehir.bel.tr/icerik_dvm.php?icerik_id=4851&cat_icerik=1&menu_id24

Eskişehir Metropolitan Municipality. (2019c, August 18). *Eskişehir Visuals Decorated the, Frankfurt underground.* https://www.eskisehir.bel.tr/icerik_dvm.php?icerik_id=4988&cat_icerik=1&menu_id=24

Eskişehir Metropolitan Municipality. (2019d, May 8). *14th Anniversary of the Children's Festival Record of the Year Participation.* https://www.eskisehir.bel.tr/icerik_dvm.php?icerik_id=4770&cat_icerik=1&menu_id=24

Eskişehir Metropolitan Municipality. (2019e, January 5). *Music Banquet from the famous Akerdeon Artist.* https://www.eskisehir.bel.tr/icerik_dvm.php?icerik_id=4453&cat_icerik=1&menu_id=4

Eskişehir Metropolitan Municipality. (2019f, May 4). *9.National Eskişehir Opera and Ballet Days Start.* https://www.eskisehir.bel.tr/icerik_dvm.php?icerik_id=4756&cat_icerik=1&menu_i4

EtvNepal. (2020, May 15). एक्कासी लिपुलेक छिर्यो नेपाली सेना || नेपाली सेनापनि एक्सनमा उत्रियो *Lipulek Kalapani Nepal*. Retrieved October 29, 2021, from Etv Nepal: https://www.youtube.com/watch?v=-A5I2fFlBJY

European Commission. (1997). Agenda 2000: For a Stronger and Wider Union. *Bulletin of the European Union*, COM(97) 2000 final, Supplement 5/97.

European Commission. (2011). Commission Staff Working Document. Turkey 2011 progress report. SEC (2011) 1201 final.

European Commission. (2012). Commission Staff Working Document. Turkey 2012 progress report. SWD (2012) 336 final.

European Commission. (2013). Commission Staff Working Document. Turkey 2013 progress report. SWD (2013) 417 final.

European Commission. (2014). Commission Staff Working Document. Turkey 2014 progress report. SWD (2014) 307 final.

European Commission. (2015). Commission Staff Working Document. Turkey 2015 Report. SWD (2015) 216 final.

European Commission. (2016). Commission Staff Working Document. Turkey 2016 Report. SWD (2016) 316 final.

European Commission. (2018). Commission Staff Working Document. Turkey 2018 Report. SWD (2018) 153 final.

European Commission. (2019). Commission Staff Working Document. Turkey 2019 Report. SWD (2019) 220 final.

European Commission. (2020). Commission Staff Working Document. Turkey 2020 Report. SWD (2020) 355 final.

European Commission. (n.d.). Commission Opinion on Turkey's Request for Accession to the Community. *Bulletin of the European Communities*, SEC (89) 2290 final, Brussel, 20 December 1989, par. 13. http://aei.pitt.edu/4475/

European Council. (2016). *EU-Turkey Statement*. https://www.consilium.europa.eu/en/press/press-releases/2016/03/18/euturkey-statement/

Explained: The Border Dispute Between India and Nepal | The Quint. (2020, June 18). Retrieved November 2, 2021, from The Quint: https://www.youtube.com/watch?v=WjITzeOcEhY

Fairclough, N. (1995). *Critical discourse analysis: the critical study of language*. Longman. Retrieved from https://www.felsemiotica.com/descargas/Fairclough-Norman-Critical-Discourse-Analysis.-The-Critical-Study-of-Language.pdf

Fan, Y. (2008). Soft Power: Power of Attractıon or Confusion? *Place Branding and Public Diplomacy*, *4*(2), 7–9. doi:10.1057/pb.2008.4

Femic. (2021). Irena. In M. Güneş (Ed.), *Diplomasi Kavramları Sözlüğü* (pp. 117-120). Ankara: Stratejik Düşünce Enstitüsü Yayinlari.

Fichter, J. (1990). *Sociology Nedir?* Selcuk University Publication.

Fisher, A. (2009). Four Seasons in One Day. In Handbook of Public Diplomacy. Routledge.

Fisher, A. (2011). Looking at the man in the mirror: understanding of power and influence in public diplomacy. In A. Fisher & S. Lucas (Eds.), *Trials of engagement: the future of us public diplomacy* (p. 273). Martinus Nijhoff Publishers. doi:10.1163/ej.9789004179400.i-309.72

Fiske, J. (1999). Popüler Kültürü Anlamak. Ark Publishing.

Fitzpatrick, K. R. (2011). U.S. Public Diplomacy. In *A Post-9/11 World: From Messaging To Mutuality*. Figueroa Press.

Fraenkel, J. R., Wallen, N. E., & Hyun, H. H. (2012). How to Design and Evaluate Research in Education (8. ed.). The McGraw-Hill.

Friedman, T. L. (2005). *The World is Flat A Brief History of The Twenty-first Century*. Farrar, Straus and Giroux.

Gaikwad, K. B. (2017). Protagonist: A prime mover of the plot of a literary work. *An International Multidiciplinary Journal*, *2*(6), 1–8.

Gallarotti, G. (2011). Soft Power: What it is, it's importance, and the conditions for its effective use. *Journal of Political Power*, *4*(1), 25–47. doi:10.1080/2158379X.2011.557886

Ghannam, J. (2011). *Social media in the arab world: leading up to the uprisings of 2011*. Center for International Media Assistance. Retrieved June 15, 2022, from https://www.cima.ned.org/wp-content/uploads/2015/02/CIMA-Arab_Social_Media-Report-10-25-11.pdf

Ghazanfar, S., Zeeshan, M., Ullah, K., Shehnaz, S., & Hussain, M. (n. d.). Changes in family values due to information communication Technologies. *The Explorer Islamabad: Journal of Social Sciences*, *1*(10), 385–389.

Ghimire, B. (2020, June 13). *Constitution amendment bill to update Nepal map endorsed unanimously at the Lower House*. Retrieved November 9, 2021, from The Kathmandu Post: https://kathmandupost.com/national/2020/06/13/constitution-amendment-bill-to-update-nepal-map-endorsed-unanimously-at-the-lower-house

Giddens, A. (1985). *The Nation-State and Violence*. Polity Press.

Giddens, A. (2000). *Sosyoloji*. Ayraç Publishing.

GIGM. (2022a). *Göç Hakkında Genel Bilgi*. Retrieved July, 22, 2022, from https://www.goc.gov.tr/genel-bilgi56420

GIGM. (2022b). *Göç İdaresi ve İnsan Ticareti*. Retrieved July, 22, 2022, from https://www.goc.gov.tr/insan-ticareti-sss

GIGM. (2022c). *Geçici Korumamız Altındaki Suriyeliler*. Retrieved July, 22, 2022, from https://www.goc.gov.tr/gecici-korumamiz-altindaki-suriyeliler

Gilboa, E. (2000). Mass communication and diplomacy: A theoretical frame work. *Communication Theory*, *10*(3), 275–309. doi:10.1111/j.1468-2885.2000.tb00193.x

Gilboa, E. (2008). Searching for a Theory of Public Diplomacy. *The Annals of the American Academy of Political and Social Science*, *616*(1), 55–77. doi:10.1177/0002716207312142

Golan, G. J. (2014). An Integrated Approach to Public Diplomacy. In International Public Relations and Public Diplomacy (pp. 417-440). Peter Lang.

Gönlübol, M. (1993). *Uluslararası Politika: İlkeler, Kavramlar, Kuramlar*. Atilla Kitabevi.

Gönlübol, M. (1993). *Uluslararası Politika: İlkeler, Kavramlar, Kurumlar*. Attila Bookstore.

Goodman, M. B. (2006). The Role of Business in Public Diplomacy. *Journal of Business Strategy*. *27*(3).

Graham, T., Broersma, M., Hazelhoff, K., & van't Haar, G. (2013). Between broadcasting political messages and interacting with voters. *Information Communication and Society*, *16*(5), 692–716. doi:10.1080/1369118X.2013.785581

Gregory, B. (2011). American Public Diplomacy: Enduring Characteristics. Elusive Transformation. *The Hauge of Diplomacy*, *6*(3-4), 351–372. doi:10.1163/187119111X583941

Güllüoğlu, Ö. (2021). Bir Kitle İletişim Aracı Olarak Televizyonun Popüler Kültür Ürünlerini Benimsetme ve Yayma İşlevi Üzerine Bir Değerlendirme. *Global Media Journal*, *2*(4), 64–86.

Gültekin, Z. (2016). Irak'dan önce: Kurtlar Vadisi dizisi. *İletişim Kuram ve Araştırma Dergisi*, *22*(9), 9-36.

Günerbüyük, C. (2009). *Kurtlar Vadisi dizisinde politik söylem* [Unpublished Master Thesis]. Marmara University.

Gürdal, E. (2021). Dijital Kamu Diplomasisi mi Dijital Gözetim mi? *Mecmua Uluslararası Sosyal Bilimler Dergisi, 6*(11), 417–434.

Hackbarth, J. R. (2008). *Soft Power and Smart Power in Africa*. Strategic Insights.

Hall, S. (1999). "Kültür, Medya ve İdeolojik Etki" Medya, İktidar, İdeoloji (M. Küçük, Comp. and Trans.). Ark Publishing.

Hamilton, K., & Langhorne, R. (2011). *The Practice of Diplomacy: Its Evolution, Theory and Administration*. Taylor&Francis Group.

Hanson, F. (2012). *Revolution @State: The Spread of Ediplomacy*. Lowy Institute for International Policy.

Helsinki Zirvesi. (1999). https://www.mfa.gov.tr/helsinki-zirvesi-10-11-aralik-1999.tr.mfa

Hobolt, S. B., Van der Brug, W., De Vreese, C. H., Boomgaarden, H. G., & Hinrichsen, M. C. (2011). Religious Intolerance and Euroscepticism. *European Union Politics, 12*(3), 359–379. doi:10.1177/1465116511404620

Hobolt, S. B., & Wratil, C. (2015). Public opinion and the crisis: The dynamics of support for the euro. *Journal of European Public Policy, 22*(2), 238–256. doi:10.1080/13501763.2014.994022

Houben, M. (2005). *International crisis management: the approach of european states*. Routledge.

Huijgh, E. (2016). Public Diplomacy. In C. M. Constantinou, P. Kerr, & P. Sharp (Eds.), *The SAGE Handbook of Diplomacy* (pp. 437–450). SAGE Publications. doi:10.4135/9781473957930.n36

Huntington, S. P. (2004). *Asker ve Devlet Sivil Asker îlişkilerinin Kuram ve Siyasası* (K. U. Kızılaslan, Trans.). Salyangoz Yayınları.

India vs Nepal Border Dispute | Explained by Dhruv Rathee. (2020, May 23). Retrieved November 1, 2021, from Dhruv Rathee: https://www.youtube.com/watch?v=ssUvFPn8DzQ

Interfax. (2022, January 30). *Voyna Sanksi*. Retrieved from interfax.ru: https://www.interfax.ru/story/111

IOM. (2016). *Europe / Medıterranean Mıgratıon Response Internatıonal Organızatıon For Mıgratıon, Sıtuatıon Report*. Retrieved July, 22, 2022, from https://turkiye.iom.int/sites/g/files/tmzbdl1061/files/documents/20160829121909_3-2.pdf

IOM. (2018-2019). *MCOF: Göç Krizi Operasyonel Çerçevesi*. Retrieved July, 22, 2022, from https://turkiye.iom.int/sites/g/files/tmzbdl1061/files/documents/MCOF_TR.pdf

IOM. (2022a). *Members and Observers*. Retrieved July, 22, 2022, from https://www.iom.int/members-and-observers

IOM. (2022b). *Migration Management*. Retrieved July, 22, 2022, from https://www.iom.int/migration-management

IOM. (2022c). *İnsan Ticareti ile Mücadele*. Retrieved July, 22, 2022, from https://turkiye.iom.int/tr/node/108261

İskit, T. (2007). *Diplomasi, Tarihi, Teorisi, Kurumları ve Uygulaması*. İstanbul: Publications of Bilgi University.

Jabbour, J. (2015). An illusionary power of seduction? An assesment of Turkey's cultural power in the Arab World in light of its audio-visual presence in the region. *European Journal of Turkish Studies, 21*(2015).

Janks, H. (n.d.). *Critical Discourse Analysis as a Research Tool*. Retrieved November 10, 2021, from https://www.uv.es/gimenez/Recursos/criticaldiscourse.pdf

Jessica, C. E., Gienow-Hecht, J. C. E., & Donfried, M. C. (2013). The model of cultural diplomacy: power, distance, and the promise of civil society. In Searching for a cultural diplomacy (pp. 13-30). Berghahn Books.

Jupp, V. (2006). *The Sage Dictionary of Social Research.* Sage Publications.

Kaldor, M. (2012). *New&Old wars: organized violence in a global era.* Polity Press.

Kalın, İ. (2010). *Türk Dış Politikası ve Kamu Diplomasisi.* MÜSİAD.

Kalın, İ. (2011). *2000'li Yıllar: Türkiye'de Dış Politika.* Meydan Yayıncılık.

Kalın, I. (2011). Soft Power and Public Diplomacy in Turkey. *Perceptions Journal of International Affairs, 16*(3), 5–23.

Kalin, I. (2011, Autumn). Soft Power and Public Diplomacy in Turkey. *Perceptions, 16*(3), 5–23.

Kamu kurumları işlemleri sistemi. (n.d.). Retrieved June 18, 2022, from www.kakis.gov.tr

Karadağ, H. (2019). Kriz yönetimi ve uluslararası ilişkiler. *Güvenlik Yazıları Serisi*, 34. Retrieved June 15, 2022, from https://trguvenlikportali.com/wp-content/uploads/2019/11/KrizYonetimi_HalukKaradag_v.1.pdf

Karadağ, H. (2012). *Bir Dış Politika Tekniği Olarak Kamu Diplomasisi: Karar Verem Sürecine Etkisi.* Gazi Üniversitesi Sosyal Bilimler Enstitü, Uluslararası İlişkiler Anabilim Dalı, Doktora Tezi.

Karaduman, S., & Aciyan, E. (2019). Netflix'in İlk Türk Dizisi "hakan Muhafiz" Üzerine Bir Alımlama Analizi. *AKİL Akdeniz İletişim Dergisi*, (32), 669–687. doi:10.31123/akil.620457

Karagülle, A. E. (2015). *Kamu dipolomasisi aracı olarak dijital medya, dijital diplomasi.* Marmara Üniversitesi, Sosyal Bilimler Üniversitesi.

Karatzogianni, A., Nguyen, D., & Serafinelli, E. (Eds.). (2016). *The digital transformation of the public sphere: conflict, migration, crisis and culture in digital networks.* Palgrave Macmillan. doi:10.1057/978-1-137-50456-2

Kawulich, B. B. (2005). Participant Observation as a Data Collection Method. *Qualitative Social Research, 6*(2).

Kaygusuz, Ö. (2012). Democracy Anchored in the Presidential System: The 'Solution Process', Constitution Making and the Future of Europeanization in Turkey. *The Turkish Yearbook of International Relations*, (43), 159–196.

Kelley, J. R. (2009). Between "take-offs" and "crash landings"- situational aspects of public diplomacy. In N. Snow & P. M. Taylor (Eds.), *Handbook of public diplomacy* (pp. 72–86). Routledge.

Kemp, S. (2022). *Digital 2022: Another year of bumper growth.* Retrieved from https://wearesocial.com/uk/blog/2022/01/digital-2022-another-year-of-bumper-growth-2/

Kennedy, P. (2001). Büyük Güçlerin Yükseliş ve Çöküşleri (8. b.). İstanbul: Türkiye İş Bankası Cultural Publications.

Kennedy, P. (2001). *Büyük Güçlerin Yükseliş ve Çöküşleri* (B. Karanakçı, Trans.). Türkiye İş Bankası Yayınları.

Keohane, R. O. (2002). *Power and Governance in A Partially Globalized World.* Routledge.

KhabarNepal. (2019, November 21). भारतले *Kalapani Lipulek* नदयि जे पनि हुिन सक्छ भन्दै *Jasmine Ojha Interview with Sheshmani.* Retrieved October 29, 2021, from ABCE Khabar Nepal: https://www.youtube.com/watch?v=4OiImIYxnKg

Khan, M., & Ulrike, R. (2020). Transnationalization, exportation, and capitalization of Turkish television and its impact on the audience of the Egypt and Pakistan. *European Journal of Soil Science, 59*(2), 123–137.

Kietzmann, J. H., Hermkens, K., McCarthy, I. P., & Silvestre, B. S. (2011). Social media? Get serious! Understanding the functional building blocks of social media. *Business Horizons, 54*(3), 241–251. doi:10.1016/j.bushor.2011.01.005

Kılıçaslan, E. (2021). Bölgesel güç olma bağlamında siyasal pazarlama açısından kamu diplomasisi: Kurtlar Vadisi dizisi söylem analizi. *Meriç Uluslararası Sosyal ve Stratejik Araştırmalar Dergisi, 5*(14), 167–185.

Kocabıyık, H. (2019). Changing Understanding of Diplomacy. *Public Diplomacy and Turkey, Eurasian Studies, 55.*

Kocabıyık, H. (2019). Değişen Diplomasi Anlayışı, Kamu Diplomasisi ve Türkiye. *Avrasya Etüdleri, 55*(1), 163–196.

Köksoy, E. (2014). Kamu Diplomasisi ve Halkla İlişkiler İlişkisi: Kuramsal Bir Değerlendirme. Marmara İletişim Dergisi. *Sayı, 22*, 211–231.

Koyuncu, S. (2017). *Bir İletişim Pratiği Olarak Kamu Diplomasisi: T.C. Başbakanlık Basın Yayın ve Enformasyon Genel Müdürlüğü'nün Türk Kamu Diplomasisindeki Yeri* [Unpublished PhD Thesis]. Gazi University Institute of Social Sciences.

Kozinets, R. (2010). *Netnography: Doing Ethnographic Research Online.* Sage Publications.

Kraidy, M. M., & Al-Ghazzi, O. (2013). Neo-Ottoman cool: Turkish popular culture in the Arab public sphere. *Popular Communication, 11*(1), 17–29. doi:10.1080/15405702.2013.747940

Krause, K., & Williams, M. C. (1996). Broadening the agenda of security studies: Politics and methods. *Mershon International Studies Review, 40*(2), 229–254. doi:10.2307/222776

Kress, G. (2011). Multimodal discourse analysis. In J. P. Gee & M. Handford (Eds.), *The Routledge Handbook of Discourse Analysis* (pp. 35–50). Routledge.

Krut', V. (2022). Sanctions against Russia: Historical Background and Contemporaneity. *Topical Issues of Contemporary International Relations*, 95-99.

Kunczik, M. (1997). *Images Of Nations and International Public Relations.* Lawrence Earlbaum.

Kurtuluş, F. (2020). *City Diplomacy; The Increasing Importance of Cities in International Politics and a Case Study of the Istanbul Metropolitan Municipality* [Master's Thesis]. Arel University.

Kutlay, M. & Yılmaz, Ö. (2015). Mülteci Krizi ve Türkiye-AB İlişkilerinde Eksen Kayması Riski. *Uluslararası Stratejik Araştırmalar Kurumu, 29.*

L'Etang, J. (2009). Public Relations and Diplomacy in a Globalized World: An Issue of Public Communication. *The American Behavioral Scientist, 53*(4), 607–626. doi:10.1177/0002764209347633

Lacan, J. (1975). Le sinthome. *Seminar, 23*. https://www.lacanonline.com/wp-content/uploads/2014/11/Seminar-XXIII-The-Sinthome-Jacques-Lacan-Thurston-translation.pdf

Lakomy, M. (2014). *Tweety na szczycie. Polityka responsywna. In Studia Medioznawcze Media.* Wydział Dziennikarstwa i Nauk Politycznych Instytut Dziennikarstwa Uniwersytetu Warszawskiego.

Laswell, H. D. (1973). *Propaganda technique in world war.* The MIT Press.

Lavrov, S. (2022, April 14). *Minister of Foreign Affairs of the Russian Federation S.V. Lavrov's "International Relations in the Context of the Digitization of Public Life" speech at the plenary session "Digital International Relations 2022" of the International Scientific and Practical Conference.* Retrieved from Russian Embassy: https://www.rus.rusemb.org.uk/fnapr/6175

Leira, H. (2016). A Conceptual History of Diplomacy. C. M. Constantinou. In P. Kerr & P. Sharp (Eds.), *The SAGE Handbook of Diplomacy* (pp. 28–38). SAGE Publications.

Lenczowskı, J. (2008). Cultural diplomacy, political influence, and integrated strategy. In Strategic Influence: Public Diplomacy, Counterpropaganda and Political Warfare (pp. 3-30). The Institute of World Politics Press.

Leonard, M., Stead, C., & Smewing, C. (2002). Public Diplomacy. London: The Foreign Policy Center.

Leonard, M. (2002). *Public Diplomacy*. Center for Foreign Policy.

Leonard, M., & Small, A. (2003). *Norwegian Public Diplomacy*. The Foreign Center.

Lipulekh Border Dispute Case. (2019, November 9). Retrieved November 4, 2021, from Routine of Nepal Banda: https://www.facebook.com/officialroutineofnepalbanda/posts/3191843110848460

Lister, M., Dovey, J., Giddings, S., Grant, I., & Kelly, K. (2009). New Media: A critical introduction (2. ed.). Taylor & Francis Group.

Lister, M., Dovey, J., Giddings, S., Grant, L., & Kelly, K. (2009). *New Media: A Critical Introduction*. Routledge.

Lüfkens, M. (2022). *Twiplomacy*. Retrieved February 27, 2022 from https://twiplomacy.com/blog/twiplomacy-study-2012/

Lukes, S. (1974). *Power: A Radical View*. MacMillan Press. doi:10.1007/978-1-349-02248-9

Machin, D., & Mayr, A. (2012). How to do critical discourse analysis: A multimodal introduction. *Sage (Atlanta, Ga.)*.

Makarichev, V. (2022, March 9). *Istorii Sanksiy Antirossiyskih*. Retrieved from Morskiye Vesti Rossiya: http://www.morvesti.ru/analitika/1691/94407/

Malone, G. D. (1985). Managing public diplomacy. *The Washington Quarterly*, *8*(3), 199–213. doi:10.1080/01636608509450301

Manheim, J. (1990). *Strategic public diplomacy: The evolution of influence*. Oxford University Press.

Manheim, J. (2002). Talking Points for Meeting with Staff of Senate Foreign Relations Committee. *The Washington Quarterly*, 75.

Manor, I. (2021). When diplomats go MAD: How the crisis framing of ministries of foreign affairs results in mutually assured delegitimization. *Journal of Public Diplomacy*, *1*(2), 75–116.

Manor, I., & Bjola, C. (2021). Public diplomacy in the age of "post-reality. In P. Surowiec & I. Manor (Eds.), *Public diplomacy and the politics of uncertainty* (pp. 111–143). Palgrave Macmillan. doi:10.1007/978-3-030-54552-9_5

Manovich, L. (2018). *The Language of New Media*. Ad Marginem Press.

Mark, L. (2002). *Public Diplomacy*. Foreign Policy Center.

Mark, S. (2009). A Greater Role For Cultural Diplomacy. Discussion Papers in Diplomacy, Netherlands Institute of International Relations 'Clingendael', 1.

Mark, S. (2009). A greater role for cultural diplomacy. In Discusion Papers in Diplomacy (pp. 1-44). Netherlands Institute of International Relations 'Clingendael'.

Marra, F. J. (1998). Crisis communication plans: Poor predictors of excellent crisis public relations. *Public Relations Review*, *24*(4), 461–474. doi:10.1016/S0363-8111(99)80111-8

Mazıcı, E. T. (2020). Covid-19 Pandemi Sürecinde Dijital Diplomasi: T.C. Dışişleri Bakanlığı Üzerine Bir Araştırma. *Turkish Studies*, *15*(4), 1087–1104.

medyafaresi. (2021). Retrieved from https://www.medyafaresi.com/haber/squid-game-diger-kore-yapimlarina-da-ilgiyi-artirdi/975357

Melissen, J. (2005). The New Public Diplomacy: Between Theory and Practice. In J. Melissen (Ed.), *Studies in Diplomacy and International Relations* (pp. 3–27). Palgrave Macmillan.

Melissen, J. (2005). The New Public Diplomacy: Between Theory and Practice. In J. Melissen (Ed.), *The New Public Diplomacy* (pp. 3–27). Palgrave Macmillan. doi:10.1057/9780230554931_1

Melissen, J. (2005). *The new public diplomacy: soft power in ınternational relations*. Palgrave Macmillan. doi:10.1057/9780230554931

Mertoglu, S. (2021). *The Genealogy of Views from Paganism to Neo-Paganism: The Rise of Eye Cult in the Age of Social Media*. Ataturk University Press.

MFA. (2022). *Türkiye Cumhuriyeti Dışişleri Bakanlığı Türkiye'nin İnsan Ticaretiyle Mücadelesi*. Retrieved July, 22, 2022, from http:// www. mfa. gov. tr/ turkiye_nin- insan- ticaretiyle- mucadelesi-. tr.mfa

Mikos, L. (2016). Digital Media Platforms and the Use of TV Content: Binge Watching and Video-on-Demand in Germany. *Media and Communication*, *4*(3), 154–161. doi:10.17645/mac.v4i3.542

MoFA. (2020, May 9). *Press Release*. Retrieved November 10, 2021, from Ministry of Foreign Affairs: https://mofa.gov.np/press-release-regarding-lipu-lekh/

Mohapatra, A. K. (2008). Democratization in the Arab world. *International Studies*, *45*(4), 271–294. doi:10.1177/002088170904500401

Municipality, E. M. (2006). Article. *Bizim Şehir Newspaper*, (13), 13.

Nepal radio stations bombard border villages with anti-India songs. (2020, June 21). Retrieved October 29, 2021, from The Times of India: https://www.facebook.com/watch/?v=3055343814532794

Nepal's Kalapani border dispute with India: What is the crux of the issue. A detailed analysis. (2020, July 10). Retrieved October 29, 2021, from Bisbo: https://www.youtube.com/watch?v=ldYtV8pc9kE

Netflix. (2022). Retrieved Nisan 20, 2022, from https://help.netflix.com/tr/node/412

Newman, E. (2004). The 'new wars' debate: A historical perspective is needed. *Security Dialogue*, *35*(2), 173–189. doi:10.1177/0967010604044975

Nicolson, H. (1939). *Diplomacy*. Oxford University Press.

Norris, S. (2004). Multimodal discourse analysis: A comceptual framework. In P. LeVine & R. Scollon (Eds.), *Discourse and Technology: Multimodal Discourse Analysis* (pp. 101–115). Georgetown University.

NTV. (2022). Retrieved from https://www.ntv.com.tr/teknoloji/netflixin-abone-sayisi-dustu-hisseleri-cakildi,ruqaZq6qXk2OgbI4KlhDwg

Nye, J. (2005). *Yumuşak Güç, Çev. Reyhan İnan Aydın*. Elips Kitap.

Nye, J. (2020). Soft power: The evolution of a concept. *Journal of Political Power*, *14*(1), 196–208. doi:10.1080/2158379X.2021.1879572

Nye, J. S. (1990). Soft power. *Foreign Policy*, *80*(80), 153–171. doi:10.2307/1148580

Nye, J. S. (2002). *The Paradox of American Power*. Oxford University Press.

Nye, J. S. (2004). *Soft Power*. PublicAffairs.

Nye, J. S. (2005). *Yumuşak Güç: Dünya Siyasetinde Başarının Yolu*. Elips Publishing.

Nye, J. S. Jr. (2004). Soft Power and American Foreign Policy. *Political Science Quarterly, 119*(2), 255–270. doi:10.2307/20202345

Nye, J. S. Jr. (2008). Public Diplomacy and Soft Power. *The Annals of the American Academy of Political and Social Science, 616*(1), 94–109. doi:10.1177/0002716207311699

O'Halloran, K. L. (2008). Systemic functional-multimodal discourse analysis (SF-MDA): Constructing ideational meaning using language and visual imagery. *Visual Communication, 7*(4), 443–475. doi:10.1177/1470357208096210

O'Halloran, K. L. (2011). Multimodal discourse analysis. In K. Hyland & B. Paltridge (Eds.), *Companion to Discourse* (pp. 120–137). Continuum.

O'Halloran, K. L. (2013). Multimodal analysis and digital technology. In E. Montagna (Ed.), *Readings in Intersemiosis and Multimedia* (pp. 35–53). IBIS Editions.

Official website of the Ministry of Culture, Information, Sports and Youth Policy of the Kyrgyz Republic. (n.d.). Retrieved June 27, 2022, from https://minculture.gov.kg/ru/

Official website of the Ministry of Youth and Sports of Turkey. (n.d.). Retrieved June 27, 2022, from https://gsb.gov.tr/anasayfa.html

OIM. 2022. *Migration Law Database*. Retrieved July, 22, 2022, from https://imldb.iom.int/_layouts/15/IML.Portal/AppPages/Home.aspx

Orhan, O. (2014). *The Situation of Syrian Refugees in the Countries Neighboring Syria: Findings, Conclusions and Recommendations*. ORSAM Publication.

Orhan, O., & Gündoğar, S. Ş. (2015). *The Effects of Syrian Refugees on Turkey*. ORSAM Publication.

Ovalı, A. Ş. (2020). Türkiye-ABD İlişkilerinde Twitter Diplomasisi. *Uluslararası İlişkiler, 17*(65), 23–45.

Ozçakıl, Y. (2022). *Urban Diplomacy as a Type of Public Diplomacy The Case of Eskişehir Metropolitan Municipality* [Master's Thesis]. Ankara Hacı Bayram Veli University.

Özcüre, G. (2014). *Avrupa Birliği'nin İstihdam ve Sosyal Politikası*. Derin Yayınları.

Ozer, O. (2015). Critical discourse analysis in the case of Teun Adrian van Dijk. In B. Yıldırım (Ed.), *Methods in Communication Studies* (pp. 197–287). Literaturk.

Özkan, A. (2015). 21. Yüzyılın Stratejik Vizyonu Kamu Diplomasisi ve Türkiye'nin Kamu Diplomasisi İmkânları. Stratejik Rapor, TASAM.

Özkan, A. (2015). *21. Yüzyılın Stratejik Vizyonu Kamu Diplomasisi ve Türkiye'nin Kamu Diplomasisi İmkânları, Rapor no:70*. Tasam Yayınları.

Ozkan, A., & Öztürk, T. (Eds.). (2012). *On the opportunities and constraints offered by Public Diplomacy: Public Diplomacy*. Tasam Publications.

Özlü, Ö. (2019). *Kamu diplomasisi oluşturulmasında dijital diplomasinin etkisi: Türkiye'de bulunan büyükelçiliklerin Twitter kullanımı*. Maltepe University, Institute of Social Sciences.

Öztürk, T. (2009). *Dış Politikadaki Etkin Unsur: Kamu Diplomasisi ve Türkiye'nin Kamu Diplomasisi Etkinliği*. Academic Press.

Özyakışır, D. (2013). *Migration (Theory and Regional Practice)*. Nobel Publications.

Pamment, J. (2013). *New public diplomacy in the 21st century*. Routledge.

Pamment, J. (2016). *British public diplomacy and soft power: diplomatic influence and the digital revolution*. Palgrave. doi:10.1007/978-3-319-43240-3

Panjeta, L. (2014). The changing soaps and telenovela genre: Turkish series impact. *Epiphany Journal of Transdisciplinary*, *7*(1), 137–168. doi:10.21533/epiphany.v7i1.89

Panteleev, E. (2013). Foreign Service: Modern Modes of Interaction with the Media. *Law and Administration. XXI century*, 94-104.

Papacharissi, Z. (2015). *Affective Publics: Sentiment, Technology, and Politics*. Oxford University Press.

Parmar, I. (2007). Responding to anti-americanism: the politics of public diplomacy. In B. O'Connor & M. Griffiths (Eds.), *Anti-Americanism: in the 21st century* (pp. 239–263). Greenwood World Publishing.

Patton, M. Q. (1988). Qualitative Evacuation Methods (9. ed.). Sage Publications.

Paul, C. (2011). *Strategic communication: origins, concepts, and current debates*. Praeger.

Payne, Sevin, & Bruya. (2011). Public Diplomacy in the Digital Age. *Comunicação Publica*, 45-70.

Pothou, E. (2020). Why so successful? An audience research on the Turkish TV series in Greece. *VIEW Journal of European Television History and Culture*, *9*(17), 62–78. doi:10.18146/view.211

Potter, E. H. (2002). Canada and the New Public Diplomacy. Discussion Papers in Diplomacy, Netherlands Institute of International Relations. doi:10.2307/40203812

Pratkanis, A. (2009). Public Diplomacy in International Confilcs. In *PM Nancy Snow, Routledge Handbook of Public Diplomacy* (pp. 111–154). Routledge.

Qadri, S. N. (2019). *Framing terrorism and migration in the USA: the role of media in securitization processes*. University of Glasgow.

Qualter, T. H. (1980). Propaganda theory and development of propaganda. *Journal of Ankara University Faculty of Political Sciences*, *35*(1), 255–307.

Radhakrishnan, R. (2019, AUG 19). *Syrian refugee children get education in Turkey*. TRT World. Retrieved from https://www.trtworld.com/turkey/syrian-refugee-children-get-education-in-turkey-19676

Rashica, V. (2018). The benefits and risks of digital diplomacy. *SEEU Review*, *13*(1), 75–89.

Reform Action Group Meetings. (n.d.). https://www.ab.gov.tr/49767_en.html

Richardson, J. L. (1994). *Crisis diplomacy: the great powers since the mid-nineteenth century*. Cambridge University Press. doi:10.1017/CBO9780511559112

Riggins, J. (1998). *A Strategic Assessment of Public Diplomacy*. USAF.

Riordan, S. (2007). Dialogue-based Public Diplomacy. A New Foreign Policy Paradigm? In The New Public Diplomacy Soft Power in International Relations. Palgrave Macmillan.

Roberts, W. R. (2007). What Is Public Diplomacy? Past Practices, Present Conduct, Possible Future. *Mediterranean Quarterly, 18*(4).

Robins, K. (1999). *İmaj* (N. Türkoğlu, Trans.). Ayrıntı Publishing.

Rose, A. K. (2007). The foreign service and foreign trade: Embassies as export promotion. *World Economy*, *30*(1), 22–38. doi:10.1111/j.1467-9701.2007.00870.x

Rowe, D. (1996). *Popüler Kültürler Rock ve Sporda Haz Politikası* (M. Küçük, Trans.). Ayrıntı Publishing.

Rugh, W. A. (2014). *Front Line Public Diplomacy: How Us Embassies Communicate with Foreign Publics*. Palgrave MacMillan. doi:10.1057/9781137444158

Russian Ministry of Foreign Affairs . (2022, April 6). Retrieved from www.mid.ru: https://www.mid.ru/

Sağlık Bakanlığı, T. C. (2017). *Suriyeli Sığınmacılar İçin 'SIHHAT' Projesi*. Retrieved July, 22, 2022, from https://sggm.saglik.gov.tr/TR,25460/suriyeli-siginmacilar-icin-sihhat-projesi.html

Samaan, J. L. (2013). The rise and fall of the 'Turkish Model' in the Arab World. *Turkish Policiy Quarterly*, *2013*(Fall), 61–69.

Sancar, S. A. (2014). *Public Diplomacy and International Public Relations*. Republic of Turkey Ministry of Foreign Affairs. Retrieved June 6, 2022, from https://www.mfa.gov.tr/site_media/html/disisleri-tanitim.pdf

Sancar, A. (2012). *Public Diplomacy and International Public Relations*. Beta Publications.

Sancar, G. A. (2012). *Kamu Diplomasisi ve Uluslararası Halkla İlişkiler*. Beta Yayınları.

Sancar, G. A. (2012). *Public diplomacy and International Public Relations*. Beta Publications.

Sancar, G. A. (2017). Turizm Diplomasisi Kapsaminda Yer Markalama: Turkey Home Kampanya Analizi. *Selçuk İletişim Dergisi*, *9*(4), 89–108.

Sander, O. (2008). *The rise and fall of phoenix: an essay on the history of ottoman diplomacy*. İmge Publishing.

Sarı, Ç. (2019). *Political Life in Eskişehir (1946-1960)* [Master's Thesis]. Marmara University.

Schneider, C. P. (2007). Culture Communicates: US Diplomacy That Works. In The New Public Diplomacy: Soft Power in International Relations. Palgrave Macmillan.

Seib, P. (2011). Preface. In Essays on Faith Diplomacy. Figuroa Press.

Seib, P. (2012). *Real-Time Diplomacy, Politics and Power in the Social Media Era*. Palgrave Macmillan.

Şenel, B. (2012). Savaş İle Barış Arasında Bir Kriz Yönetim Stratejisi Olarak Zorlayıcı Diplomasi ve Türk Dış Politikasındaki Örnekleri. *Security Ecosystem and Multileteral Cost*, 157-190.

Sevin, E. (2017). Digital diplomacy as crisis communication: Turkish digital outreach after July 15. *Mexican Journal of Foreign Policy*, *113*, 185–207.

Shakya, M. (2020). The politics of border and nation in Nepal in the time of pandemic. *Dialectical Anthropology*, *44*(3), 223–231. doi:10.100710624-020-09599-x PMID:32836686

Shirky, C., & Gladwell, M. (2011). From innovation to revolution: do social media make protests possible? *Foreign Affairs*. Retrieved June 15, 2022, from https://www.foreignaffairs.com/articles/2011-01-19/innovation-revolution

Signitzer, B., & Wamser, C. (2006). Public Diplomacy: A Specific Governmental Public Relations Function. In *Public Relations Theory II* (pp. 435-465). Lawrence Erlbaum.

Signitzer, B., & Coombs, T. (1992). Public Relations and Public Diplomacy: Conceptual Covergences. *Public Relations Review*, *18*(2), 137–147. doi:10.1016/0363-8111(92)90005-J

Sizoo, A., & Musch, A. (2008). *City Diplomacy.* https://www.uclg.org/sites/default/files/City_Diplomacy_research_book_English_01.pdf

Smith-Windsor, B. A. (2000). Hard Power, Soft Power reconsidered. *Canadian Military Journal, 1*(3), 51–56.

Snow, N. (2010). *Propaganda. inc.: selling america's culture to the world.* Seven Stories Press.

Snyder, G., & Diesing, P. (1977). *Conflict among nations: bargaining, decision-making and system structure in international crises.* Princeton University Press.

Steinberg, J. B. (2008). Real Leaders do Soft Power: Learning Lessons of Iraq. *The Washington Quarterly, 31*(2), 155–164. doi:10.1162/wash.2008.31.2.155

Stelzner, M. A. (2009). *Social media marketing industry report.* Retrieved online February 26, 2010 from http://www.socialmediasummit09.com/

Suleiman, K. A. (2012). *The international crisis and the international system: a study on the interplay between the management of international strategic crises and the structure of the international system.* Arab Center for Research & Policy Studies (Research Paper). Retrieved June 15, 2022, from https://www.jstor.org/stable/resrep12667?seq=1

Surowiec, P., & Manor, I. (Eds.). (2021). *Public diplomacy and the politics of uncertainty.* Palgrave. doi:10.1007/978-3-030-54552-9

Syrians living in Turkey to become citizens, Erdogan says. (2016, July 3). *TRT World.* Retrieved from https://www.trtworld.com/mea/syrians-living-in-turkey-to-become-citizens-136720

Szondi, G. (2008). *Public Diplomacy and Nation Branding: Conceptual Similarities and Diffirences.* Netherlands Institute of International Relations Clingendael.

Szondi, G. (2009). Central and Eastern European Public Diplomacy. In N. S. Taylor (Ed.), *Routledge Handbook of Public Diplomacy* (pp. 292–314). Routledge.

T24. (2018, March 14). *Wall Street Journal: Suudi Arabistan'da Türk dizileri yasağının arkasında Selman var.* https://t24.com.tr/haber/wall-street-journal-suudi-arabistanda-turk-dizileri-yasaginin-arkasinda-selman-var,580819

Takvim. (2021, November 22). *Taliban'dan yeni yasak! Türk dizileri de etkilenecek. Kadınların oynadığı yapımların gösterilmesi yasaklandı.* https://www.takvim.com.tr/dunya/2021/11/22/son-dakika-talibandan-yeni-yasak-turk-dizileri-de-etkilenecek-kadinlarin-oynadigi-yapimlarin-gosterilmesi-yasaklandi

Taşpınar, Ö. (2008, October 7). *Turkey's Middle East policies: Between Neo-Ottomanism and Kemalism.* Carnegie Endowment for International Peace. https://carnegieendowment.org/2008/10/07/turkey-s-middle-east-policies-between-neo-ottomanism-and-kemalism-pub-22209

Tench, R., & Yeomans, L. (2006). Exploring Public Relations. Prentice Hall.

Terzi, Ö. (2019). The EU-Turkey Customs Union. Shortcomings and Prospects for Modernization. In *The Proliferation of Privileged Partnerships between the European Union and its Neighbours.* Routledge.

Thapa, G. S. (2020, May 13). *Nepal confronts India in Lipulekh border dispute.* Retrieved November 3, 2021, from Asia Times: https://asiatimes.com/2020/05/nepal-confronts-india-in-lipulekh-border-dispute/

The EU Facility for Refugees in Turkey. (n.d.). https://ec.europa.eu/neighbourhood-enlargement/enlargement-policy/negotiations-status/turkey/eu-facility-refugees-turkey_en

The Hindustan Mirror. (2020, May 17). Retrieved October 29, 2021, from Nepal Kalapani News | KalaPani Lipulekh | Kalapani Nepal news | Nepal Kalapani Border: https://www.youtube.com/watch?v=BmSe6jmtJAo

The Metropolitan Municipality of Eskişehir. (n.d.). *Sister Cities*. https://www.eskisehir.bel.tr/kardes-sehirler

The Municipality of Esenler. (n.d.). *Global City Diplomacy Access*. http://www.sehirdusunce.com/atolye/30/kuresel-kent-diplomasis

The Presidency of the Republic of Turkey. (n.d.). *Turkey is the Country that Provides the Most Humanitarian Aid in the World Compared to its National Income*. Retrieved June 6, 2022, from https://www.tccb.gov.tr/haberler/410/102167/-turkiye-mill-gelire-oranla-dunyada-en-more-humanitarian-aid-the-country

The Truth behind Events in Ukraine and Donbass. (2022). Retrieved from https://www.mid.ru/: https://russische-botschaft.ru/wp-content/uploads/2022/03/The-Truth-Behind-Events-in-Ukraine and-Donbass.pdf

Tiedeman, A. (2004, May 4). *US Public Diplomacy in the Middle East*. Seminar on Geography, Foreign Policy and the World Order.

Tie, Y. C., Birks, M., & Francis, K. (2019). Grounded theory research: A design framework for novice researchers. *SAGE Open Medicine*, *7*, 1–8. PMID:30637106

TİKA. (2022). *TİKA*. Retrieved March 13, 2022, from https://www.tika.gov.tr/tr

Timofeyev, A. (2022, March 3). *History of Restrictions: Why Have There Always been Sanctions against Russia?* Retrieved from Gazeta.ru: https://www.gazeta.ru/social/2022/03/03/1596663.shtml

Tolan, B. (1975). *Introduction to sociology*. Kitle Publishing.

Tören, D. (2021). *Diplomasi ve Tarih Boyunca Geçirdiği Evrim*. Retrieved February, 16, from tuicakademi.org/diplomasi-ve-tarih-boyunca-gecirdigi-evrim/

Tsifrovaya Diplomatiya: Vizovy i perspectivy . (2018, February 28). Retrieved from 2035.media: http://2035.media/2018/02/28/digital-diplomacy/

Tuch, H. N. (1990). Communicating with the world: U.S. public diplomacy overseas. New York: St. Martin's Press.

Tuch, H. N. (1990). *Communicating with the world: U.S. public diplomacy overseas*. St. Martin's. doi:10.1007/978-1-349-60512-5

Tuncer, H. (2009). *Old and New Diplomacy*. Ümit Publishing. Retrieved June 6, 2022, from https://sozluk.gov.tr/

Tuncer, H. (1995). *Eski Ve Yeni Diplomasi*. Ümit Yayıncılık.

Tuncer, H. (2009). *Diplomasinin Evrimi*. Kaynak Yay.

Tunch, H. N. (1990). *Communicating With the World: US Public Diplomacy Overseas*. St. Martin's Press.

Türk İşbirliği ve Koordinasyon Ajansı Başkanlığı (TİKA) Tarihçe. (n.d.). https://www.tika.gov.tr/tr/sayfa/tarihce-222

Türk, C. N. N. (2012, August 23). *Mısır'dan Türk dizilerine yasak!* https://www.cnnturk.com/2013/dunya/08/20/misirdan.turk.dizilerine.yasak/720165.0/index.html

Turkey Development Assistance. (2020). Retrieved June 6, 2022, from https://www.tika.gov.tr/upload/sayfa/Pictures/Turkiye%20Kalk%C4%B1nma%20Yard%C4%B1mlar%C4%B1%202020_tr.pdf

Turkey-EU High Level Economic Dialogue Joint Press Communique. (n.d.). https://www.avrupa.info.tr/en/pr/turkey-eu-high-level-economic-dialogue-joint-press-communique-9286

Türkkahraman, D. D. M. (2011). Günümüzün Büyüsü İmaj Ve Gerçek Hayat. *Istanbul Journal of Sociological Studies, 0*(30), 1–14.

Türksat. (2009). Kamu kurumları internet siteleri standartları ve önerileri rehberi. *Sürüm, 1*(1).

UNHCR. (2022). *What is a Refugee?* The UN Refugee Agency. Retrieved from https://www.unhcr.org/what-is-a-refugee.html

University Research Laboratory. (2020). *Student Friendly University Cities.* https://www.uniar.net/_files/ugd/779fe1_1a79aa7ad5a64a2aa81f732d1ad092b0.pdf

Uysal, N., & Schroeder, J. (2019). Turkey's Twitter public diplomacy: Towards a "new" cult of personality. *Public Relations Review, 45*(5), 1–9.

van Dijk, T. (2011). Discourse and ideology. In T. Van Dijk (Ed.), *Discourse Studies. A Multidisciplinary Introduction* (pp. 379–407). SAGE. doi:10.4135/9781446289068.n18

Varna Zirvesi Sonuçlarini Olumlu Olarak Değerlendiriyoruz. (n.d.). https://www.ikv.org.tr/ikv.asp?id=3140

Varnalı, K. (2012). *Dijital Kabilelerin İzinde: Sosyal Medyada Netnografik Araştırmalar.* MediaCat Publications.

Vasquez, J. A. (2009). *The war puzzle revisited.* Cambridge University Press. doi:10.1017/CBO9780511627224

Vergeer, M., & Hermans, L. (2013). Campaigning on Twitter: Microblogging And Online Social Networking As Campaign Tools in The 2010 General Elections in The Netherlands. *Journal of Computer-Mediated Communication, 18*(4), 399–419. doi:10.1111/jcc4.12023

Verrakia, B. (2017). Digital diplomacy and ıts effect on ınternational relations. *SIT Graduate Institute/SIT Study Abroad SIT Digital Collections.*

Visa Liberalisation Dialogue. (n.d.). https://www.avrupa.info.tr/en/visa-liberalisation-dialogue-6896

Voronina, D. (2019). The Development of Russian Digital Diplomacy at the Current Stage. *Journal of "International Communication",* 1-11.

Waever, O. (2007). Securitization and Desecuritization. In B. Buzan & L. Hansen (Eds.), *International Security: Widening Security* (Vol. 3, pp. 66–99). SAGE Publications.

Wagle, A. (2020, May 25). *The Kathmandu Post.* Retrieved October 30, 2021, from Return to the dialogue table: https://kathmandupost.com/columns/2020/05/25/return-to-the-dialogue-table

Wagner, C., (2005). From Hard Power to Soft Power? *Heidelberg Papers in South Asian and Comparative Politics, 26.*

Waller, J. M. (2007). *The public diplomacy reader.* Institute of World Politics Press.

Walt, S. (1991). Renaissance of security studies. *International Studies Quarterly, 35*(2), 211–239. doi:10.2307/2600471

Waters, R. D., & Jamal, J. Y. (2011). Tweet, tweet, tweet: A content analysis of nonprofit organizations' Twitter updates. *Public Relations Review, 37*(3), 321–324. doi:10.1016/j.pubrev.2011.03.002

Waters, R. D., & Williams, J. M. (2011). Squawking, tweeting, cooing, and hooting: Analyzing the communication patterns of government agencies on Twitter. *Journal of Public Affairs, 11*(4), 353–363. doi:10.1002/pa.385

Watson, A. (1982). *Diplomacy: The Dialogue Between States.* Routledge.

Watson, A. (1984). *Diplomacy: The Dialogue between States*. Methuen.

Webrazzi. (2021). Retrieved from https://webrazzi.com/2021/03/29/netflix-2021-de-40-yeni-anime-yayinlayacagini-acikladi/

Wescott, N. (2008). *Digital Diplomacy: The Impact of the Internet on International Relations*. Oxford Internet Institute.

Westcott, N. (2008). Digital diplomacy: The ımpact of the ınternet on ınternational relations. Oxford Internet Institute, Research Report.

Westcott, N. (2008). Digital Diplomacy: The Impact of the Internet on International Relations. Oxford Internet Institute.

White, B. (2005). Diplomacy. In J. Baylis & S. Smith (Eds.), *The Globalization of World Politics: An Introduction to International Relations* (pp. 387–403). Oxford University Press.

Williams, M. C. (2003). Words, Images, Enemies: Securitization and International Politics. *International Studies Quarterly*, *47*(4), 511–531. doi:10.1046/j.0020-8833.2003.00277.x

Williams, P. (1976). *Crisis management: confrontation and diplomacy in the nuclear age*. John Wiley.

Williams, P. D. (Ed.). (2008). *Security studies: An ıntroduction*. Routledge. doi:10.4324/9780203926604

Wilson, E. J. III. (2008a). Hard Power, Soft Power, Smart Power. *The Annals of the American Academy of Political and Social Science*, *616*(1), 110–125. doi:10.1177/0002716207312618

Yağmurlu A. (2019). Digital Diplomacy: Internet Applications of European Union Member States and Turkish Ministry of Foreign Affairs Within the Framework of Public Diplomacy. *e-Gifder, 7*(2).

Yağmurlu, A. (2019). Dijital Diplomasi: Kamu Diplomasisi Çerçevesinden Avrupa Birliği Üye Ülkeleri Ve Türkiye Dişişleri Bakanliklari İnternet Uygulamalari. *Gümüşhane Üniversitesi İletişim Fakültesi Elektronik Dergisi*, *7*(2), 1267–1295.

Yalçın, E. (2021). *Encyclopedia of Public Administration*. Astana Publications.

Yalkın, C. (2018). A brand culture approach to managing nation-brands. *European Management Review*, *15*(1), 137–149. doi:10.1111/emre.12129

Yanardağoğlu, E. & Karam, I. N. (2013). The fever that hit Arab satellite television audience perceptions of Turkish TV series. *Identities, 19*, 561-579.

Yavuz, M. H. (1998). Turkish identity and foreign policy in flux: The rise of Neo-Ottomanism. *Journal for Critical Studies of The Middle East.*, *7*(12), 19–41. doi:10.1080/10669929808720119

Yavuz, M. H. (2020). *Nostalgia fot the empire: The politics of Neo-Ottomanism*. Oxford University. doi:10.1093/oso/9780197512289.001.0001

Yeni Şafak. (2018, March 7). *Türk dizilerinin yasaklanmasının ardındaki kirli oyun*. https://www.yenisafak.com/hayat/turk-dizilerinin-yasaklanmasinin-ardindaki-kirli-oyun-3166022

Yepsen, E. A. (2012). Practicing Successful Twitter Public Diplomacy: A Model And Case Study Of U.S. Efforts. In *Venezuela*. Figueroa Press.

Yeşil, B. (2015). Transnationalization of Turkish dramas: Exploring the convergence of local and global market imperatives. *Global Media and Communication*, *11*(1), 43–60. doi:10.1177/1742766515573274

Yiğit, A. (2013). *Turkish drama in the Middle East: Secularism and cultural influence*. IEMED Mediterranean Yearbook 2013. https://www.iemed.org/publication/turkish-drama-in-the-middle-east-secularism-and-cultural-influence/

Yıldırım, A., & Şimşek, H. (2013). Sosyal Bilimlerde Nitel Araştırma Yöntemleri (9. ed.). Ankara: Seçkin Yay.

Yıldırım, A., & Şimşek, H. (2011). *Qualitative Research Methods in Social Sciences*. Seçkin Publishing.

Yıldırım, A., & Şimşek, H. (2013). *Sosyal Bilimlerde Nitel Araştırma Yöntemleri*. Seçkin Publications.

Yılmaz, G. (2016). From Europeanization to de-Europeanization: The Europeanization Process of Turkey in 1999–2014. *Journal of Contemporary European Studies*, *24*(1), 86–100. doi:10.1080/14782804.2015.1038226

Yücel, G. (2016). Dijital Diplomasi. TRT Akademi Dijital Medya Sayısı, 1(2), 748-760.

Yücel, G. (2016). Dijital diplomasi. *TRT Akademi Issue: Digital Media*, *7*(1), 748–760.

Yücel, G. (2016). Dijital Diplomasi. *TRT Akademi*, *1*(2), 747–760.

Yukaruç, U. (2017). *A constructivist approach to popular culture and foreign policy: The case of Turkey and Valley of Wolves: Ambush* [Unpublished Doctorate Thesis]. University of East Aglia.

Zaharna, R. S. (2010). *Battles to Bridges*. Palgrave Macmillan. doi:10.1057/9780230277922

Zee News. (2020, May 20). Retrieved October 29, 2021, from DNA:नए नक़्शे से Nepal आखरि साबति क्या करना चाहता है? DNA Sudhir Chaudhary |Sudhir Chaudhary On Nepal: https://www.youtube.com/watch?v=FYUA70vDjBY

Zhang, J. (2011). China's Faith Diplomacy: Inıtıatives and Vulnerabilities. In Essays on Faith Diplomacy. Figuroa Press.

Zhang, J., & Fahmy, S. (2015). Live Tweeting at Work: TheUse of Social Media in Public Diplomacy. In G. J. Golan (Ed.), *International Public Relations And Public Diplomacy* (pp. 315–332). Peter Lang Publishing.

Zhang, J., & Swartz, B. C. (2009). Public diplomacy to promote global public goods (GPG): Conceptual expansion, ethical grounds, and rhetoric. *Public Relations Review*, *35*(4), 382–387. doi:10.1016/j.pubrev.2009.08.001

Zinovieva, E. (2013). Digital Diplomacy, International Security and Opportunities for Russia. *Index Bezopasnosti*, 213-228.

About the Contributors

Türker Elitaş was born in Erzurum Turkey. He completed his primary, secondary and high school education in Erzurum. He started his high school education at Atatürk University Faculty of Communication Department of Radio, Television, and Cinema and graduated in 2005. In 2014 he completed his master's degree Radio, Television and Cinema Atatürk University Institute of Social Sciences. In 2017 he completed his doctorate's degree in Radio, Television, and Cinema in Marmara University Institute of Social Sciences with his thesis titled " New communication Technologies in Distance Education License Period: Ataturk University Distance Education Center ". He is still working in Communication faculty, Hatay Mustafa Kemal University in Turkey, as an associate professor.

* * *

Ömer Alanka was born in Erzurum, Türkiye. He completed his primary, secondary and high school education in Erzurum. He started his high school education at Ataturk University Faculty of Communication Department of Journalism and graduated in 2005. In 2008 he completed his master's degree in Journalism in Ataturk University Institute of Social Sciences. In 2012 he completed his doctoral degree in Journalism in Agean University Institute of Social Sciences. He is still working in Hatay Mustafa Kemal University as associate professor.

Niyazi Ayhan completed his primary and high school education in Turkey. He completed his university education at Kyrgyzstan-Turkey Manas University, Faculty of Communication, Department of Journalism in 2008. He completed his master's degree in Kyrgyzstan-Turkey Manas University, in the department of communication sciences, in 2010 with the thesis titled Workplaces's Names Which Are Reflected In The Streets: Analytical And Ideology Analysis Toward Bishkek Transportation Main Arter. He completed his Ph.D. in 2017 with his thesis titled Construction Of The Hegemony And Ideology In The Sembolic Structures (Case Of Bishkek Monuments). He received the title of Assistant Professor in 2018 and Associate Professor in 2021. He works in fields such as the Soviet period, post-Soviet period ideology, hegemony, political communication, and communication sociology. He works as a lecturer in the Department of Journalism at the Faculty of Communication at the Kyrgyzstan-Turkey Manas University. He conducts undergraduate, graduate, and Ph.D. such as Scientific Research Methods, Modern Political Ideologies, Discourse and Ideology, Public Opinion, and Media.

Tolkun Bekturgan Kyzy graduated from the English Language and Literature Department of Kyrgyz-Turkish Manas University in Bishkek, Kyrgyzstan. She worked afterwards in the private sector.

In 2018, she enrolled in a master's degree in the Department of English Language and Literature, and later decided to study communication. Currently, she is doctoral candidate in Communication studies, and she is also involved in different translation projects and conducting research on a UNESCO project "Assessment of Media Development in Kyrgyzstan".

Kadir Bendaş was born in Ceyhan, Adana, Turkey. He completed his primary, secondary and high school education in Seyhan, Adana. He started his university education at Erciyes University Faculty of Communication Department of Journalism and graduated in 2013. In 2016 he completed her master's degree in Journalism in Ataturk University Institute of Social Sciences with his thesis titled "Semiotics of The Cities of Republic: The Effect of Atatürk Houses to Turkish Collective Memory". In 2022 he completed her doctora's degree in Journalism in Ataturk University Institute of Social Sciences with his thesis titled "Development Discourse in The Period of The Democrat Party and Zafer Newspaper". He is still working in Sivas Cumhuriyet University as Research Assistant.

Atilla Cakar was born in Adapazarı, Sakarya. He completed his primary, secondary and high school education in Adapazarı. He started his university education at Abant İzzet Baysal University School of Physical Education and Sports and graduated in 2007. In 2013, he completed his master's degree in Bishkek Social Sciences University, Department of Business Administration. He is still working as an instructor at the Faculty of Sport Sciences, at Kyrgyz-Turkish Manas University.

Ülhak Çimen was born in Erzurum, Turkey. He completed his primary, secondary and high school education in Erzurum. Having graduated from Atatürk University, Faculty of Communication, Department of Radio, Television and Cinema, Çimen is still an Associate Professor at the same institution. He works as Ülhak Çimen is married and has two children.

Fatih Degirmenci was born in Erzurum, Turkey. He completed his primary and secondary school education in Erzurum. He graduated Istanbul University Faculty of Political Sciences. He completed master's and doctorate at Ankara University Institute of Social Sciences. He is still working as an assistant professor at Atatürk University, Faculty of Communication. Academic interests: Political science, communication studies, political communication.

Banu Erdoğan Çakar was born in Kayseri, Turkey. She completed his primary, secondary and high school education in Kayseri. She graduated from the Bishkek Humanities University Department of Russian Language and Literature Teaching in 2010. She received her master's degree in Communication Sciences from Kyrgyz-Turkish Manas University Institute of Social Sciences in 2015. She completed her doctora's degree Communication Sciences in Kyrgyz-Turkish Manas University Institute of Social Sciences with her thesis titled "Khrushchev Period And Cultural Identity Aspects In Soviet Cinema". She is working at Kyrgyz-Turkish Manas University as a research assistant.

Savas Keskin was born in 1990 in Diyarbakır/ Turkey. He has Bachelor's Degree in the Department of Public Relations and Advertising in the Faculty of Communication in Fırat State University/Elazığ-Turkey. He has Master Degree in the Department of Communication Sciences in the Institute of Social Sciences in Fırat State University Elazığ/Turkey. He has Doctoral degree in the Department of Radio,

Television and Cinema in the Institute of Social Sciences in Istanbul University/Istanbul-Turkey. He is lecturer in the Health Services Vocational School in Bayburt University.

Serpil Kır Elitaş was born in Alasehir, Manisa, Turkey. She completed his primary, secondary and high school education in Alaşehir. She started his high school education at Selçuk University Faculty of Communication Department of Public Relations and Publicity and graduated in 2011. In 2014 she completed her master's degree in Public Relations and Publicity in Selcuk University Institute of Social Sciences with her thesis titled "Test Drives in the Context of Experiential Marketing". In 2018 she completed her doctoral degree in Public Relations and Publicity in Selcuk University Institute of Social Sciences with her thesis titled "Investigation of Factors Affecting Online Shopping Tendency in the Context of Sensory Activation Technology Acceptance Model". She is still working in Hatay Mustafa Kemal University as associate professor.

Sami Kiraz was born in Ankara, Turkey. He received his BS in 2009 and MS degrees in 2012 from Ege University and his PhD in 2018 from Gazi University in International Relations. He teaches various courses in the field of International Relations, especially in the fields of International Relations Theories, Conflict Resolution, International Politics, International Law and Turkish Foreign Policy. In addition to two books and many book chapters, Kiraz has articles and papers published in various national and international academic journals in English and Turkish. His research interests include Turkish Foreign Policy, International Relations Theory, International Security, Foreign Policy Analysis, Conflict Resolutions, Transnational Crimes, International Peacekeeping Operations, War and Peace Studies, 20th Century Political History. He is still working in Hitit University as associate professor.

Selver Mertoğlu was born in 1989 in Kastamonu. In 2009, he started his university education at Atatürk University, Faculty of Communication, Department of Journalism. In 2011, she worked as a reporter at İhlas News Agency as an intern. After graduating from Atatürk University in 2014, he started his master's degree with thesis at Atatürk University Social Sciences Institute Journalism Department in January 2015. She completed her master's degree in 2016 with her thesis titled The Role of Social Media in Reproducing Ethical Violations and Hate Speech: The Case of the Murder of Özgecan Aslan. He started his doctoral studies in 2017. He completed his doctorate in 2021 with the thesis title "The Genealogy of the Gaze: The Rise of the Eye Cult in the Age of Social Media".

Yasemin Özçakıl was born in Odunpazar, Eskişehir. He completed his primary, secondary and high school education in Eskişehir. He started his university education at Gazi University School of journalism in 2018. In 2022, he completed his master's degree in Ankara hacı bayram Veli University, Department of public relations and publicity.

Mehmet Ferhat Sönmez was born in Elazığ, Türkiye. She completed his primary, secondary and high school education in Elazığ. She started his high school education at Gazi University Faculty of Communication Department of Journalism and graduated in 2005. In 2012 he completed his master's degree in Communication Sciences in Fırat University Institute of Social Sciences with his thesis titled "Local Press - The Relatıonshıp Between Polıtıcal Neutralıty And News: 12 June 2011 General Electıon Case Study". In 2018 she completed his doctoral degree in Radio Television and Cinema in İstanbul University Institute of Social Sciences with his thesis titled "Comperetıve Analysıs Of Socıal Medıa In

The Constructıon Of Socıal Identıtıes From The Example Of Unıversıty Students In Dıfferent Regıons". He is still working in Fırat University as assistant professor. He is still working on identity, social media and identities, new media, and new communication technologies.

Elifnur Terzioğlu was born in Erzurum, Turkey. She graduated from Atılım University, Department of International Relations in 2010. After completing her master's degree in public relations and publicity in 2017, she completed her doctorate in the same department in 2022 with her thesis titled "Public Relations Activities of the European Union towards Republic of Turkey in the context of the Public Diplomacy: EU Information Centres Network". She worked at Erzurum Chamber of Commerce and Industry as a EUIC Coordinator for 8 years between the years 2011 and 2019. During her services at the Chamber of Commerce and Industry, she provided consultancy and capacity building to SMEs, business associations, and NGOs. She has worked on similar projects in Turkey. Elifnur has been working for COSME and HORIZONE Project at ATA Teknokent as a project expert. ORCID İD: 0000-0002-3467-1537.

Sudeep Uprety is a Kathmandu based researcher specializing in security and development communications research. Sudeep has a Masters in Conflict, Peace and Development Studies from Tribhuvan University, Nepal and has carried out several studies related to media research on disaster response, crisis communications, health, among others. He is also Contributing Author for Research to Action, one of the premier global web portals for development communications and research.

Index

I

M

N

O

P

R

S

T

U

V

W

www.ingramcontent.com/pod-product-compliance
Lightning Source LLC
LaVergne TN
LVHW080527300926
849162LV00007B/1553